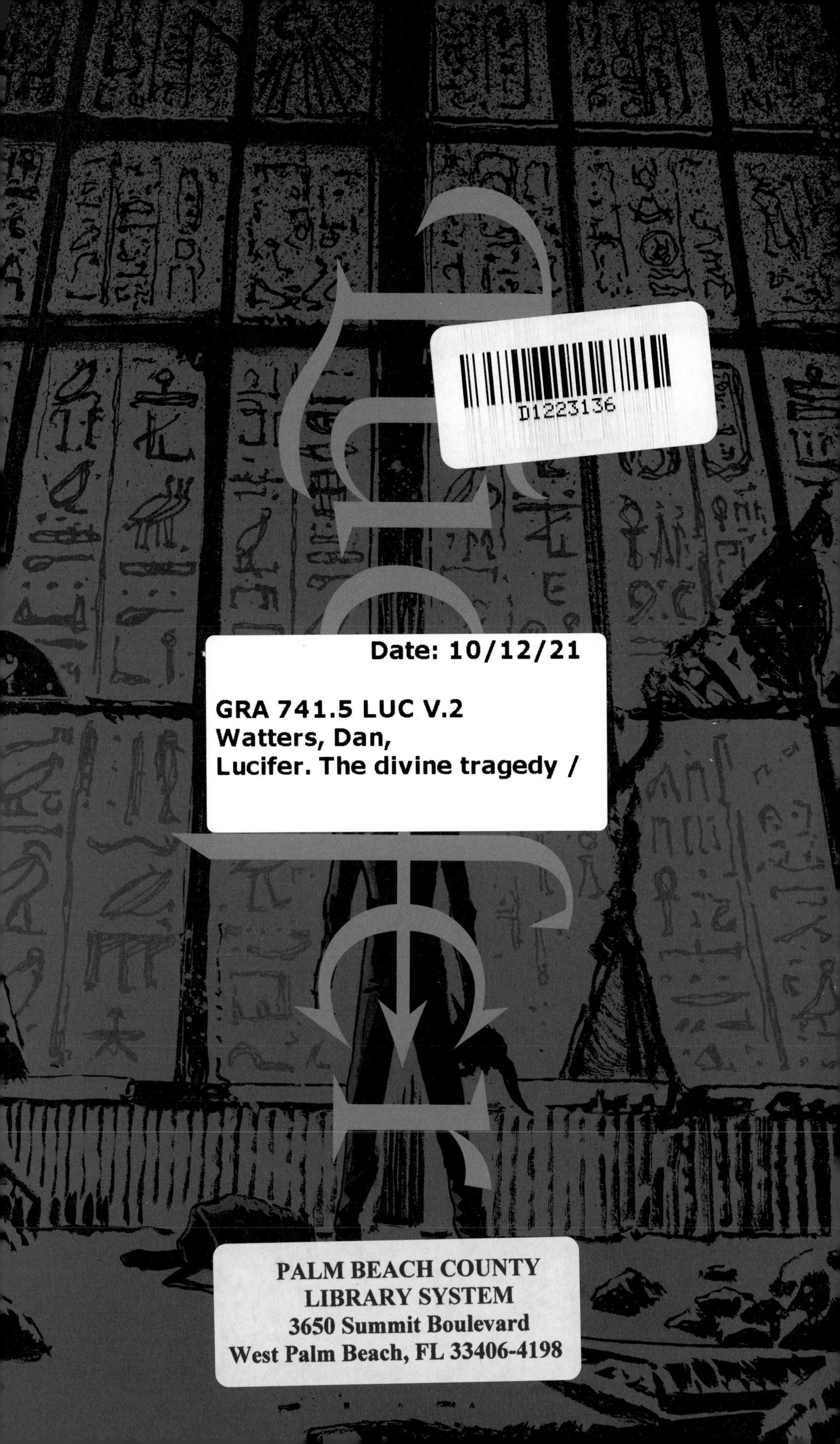

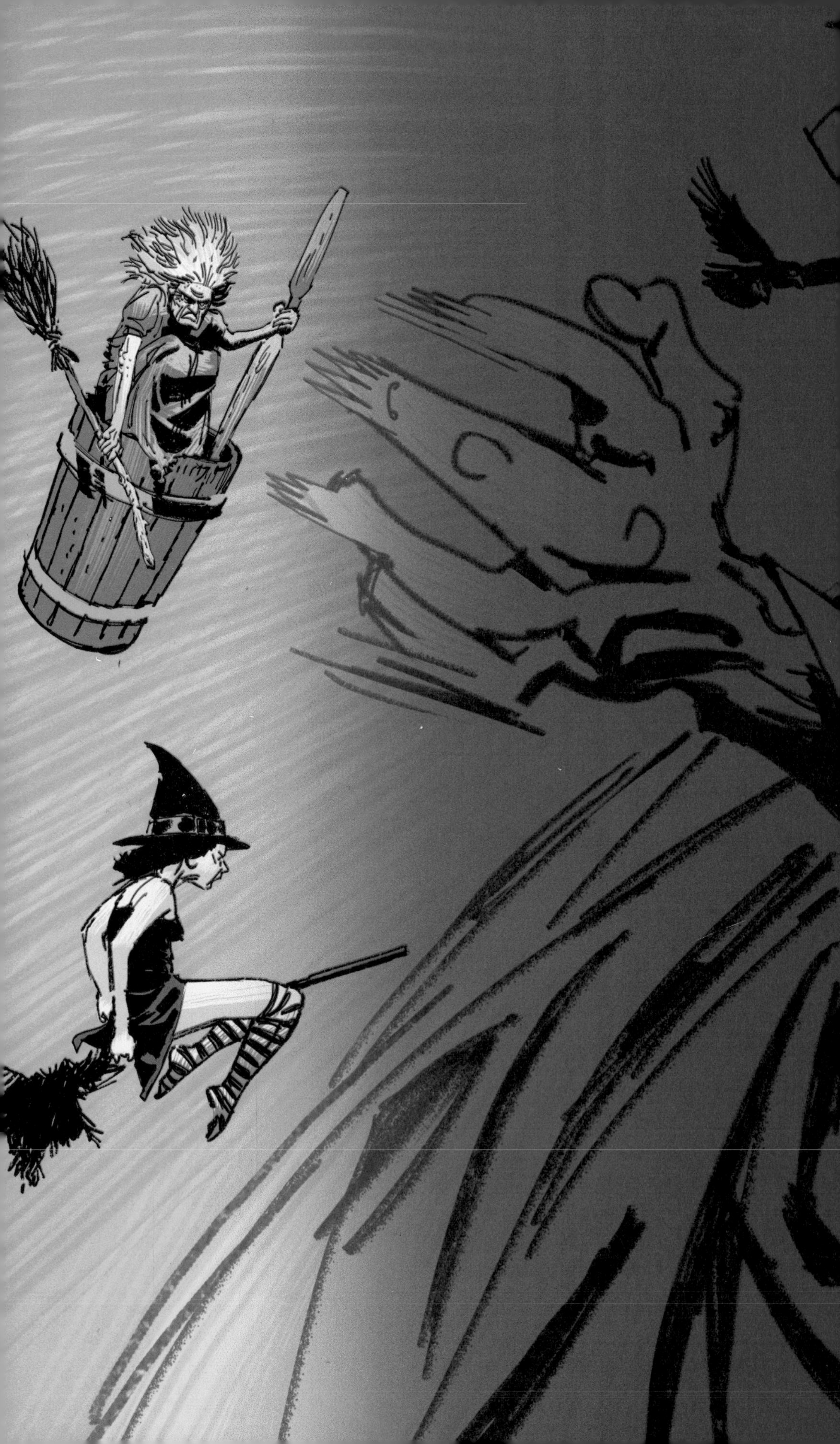

Lucifer

VOLUME TWO

The Divine Tragedy

WRITTEN BY
Dan Watters

ART BY
Max Fiumara
Sebastian Fiumara
Kelley Jones
Aaron Campbell
Leomacs

COLORS BY
Dave McCaig
Chris O'Halloran

LETTERS BY
Steve Wands

COLLECTION
COVER ART BY
Tiffany Turrill

ORIGINAL SERIES
COVER ART BY
Tiffany Turrill
Sebastian Fiumara
and
Dave McCaig

Lucifer based on characters created by
Neil Gaiman, Sam Kieth, and Mike Dringenberg
The Sandman Universe curated by Neil Gaiman

MOLLY MAHAN
AMEDEO TURTURRO   *Editors – Original Series*
MAGGIE HOWELL   *Assistant Editor – Original Series*
JEB WOODARD   *Group Editor – Collected Editions*
SCOTT NYBAKKEN   *Editor – Collected Edition*
STEVE COOK   *Design Director – Books*
                         and Publication Design
CHRISTY SAWYER   *Publication Production*

BOB HARRAS   *Senior VP – Editor-in-Chief, DC Comics*
MARK DOYLE   *Executive Editor, Vertigo & Black Label*

DAN DiDIO   *Publisher*
JIM LEE   *Publisher & Chief Creative Officer*
BOBBIE CHASE   *VP – New Publishing Initiatives & Talent Development*
DON FALLETTI   *VP – Manufacturing Operations & Workflow Management*
LAWRENCE GANEM   *VP – Talent Services*
ALISON GILL   *Senior VP – Manufacturing & Operations*
HANK KANALZ   *Senior VP – Publishing Strategy & Support Services*
DAN MIRON   *VP – Publishing Operations*
NICK J. NAPOLITANO   *VP – Manufacturing Administration & Design*
NANCY SPEARS   *VP – Sales*
MICHELE R. WELLS   *VP & Executive Editor, Young Reader*

LUCIFER VOL. 2: THE DIVINE TRAGEDY

Published by DC Comics. Compilation and all new material Copyright © 2020 DC Comics. All Rights Reserved.

Originally published in single magazine form as *Lucifer* 7-13. Copyright © 2019 DC Comics. All Rights Reserved. All characters, their distinctive likenesses, and related elements featured in this publication are trademarks of DC Comics. The stories, characters, and incidents featured in this publication are entirely fictional. DC Comics does not read or accept unsolicited submissions of ideas, stories, or artwork.

DC Comics, 2900 West Alameda Ave., Burbank, CA 91505
Printed by LSC Communications, Owensville, MO, USA. 12/20/19. First Printing.
ISBN: 978-1-4012-9572-1

Library of Congress Cataloging-in-Publication Data is available.

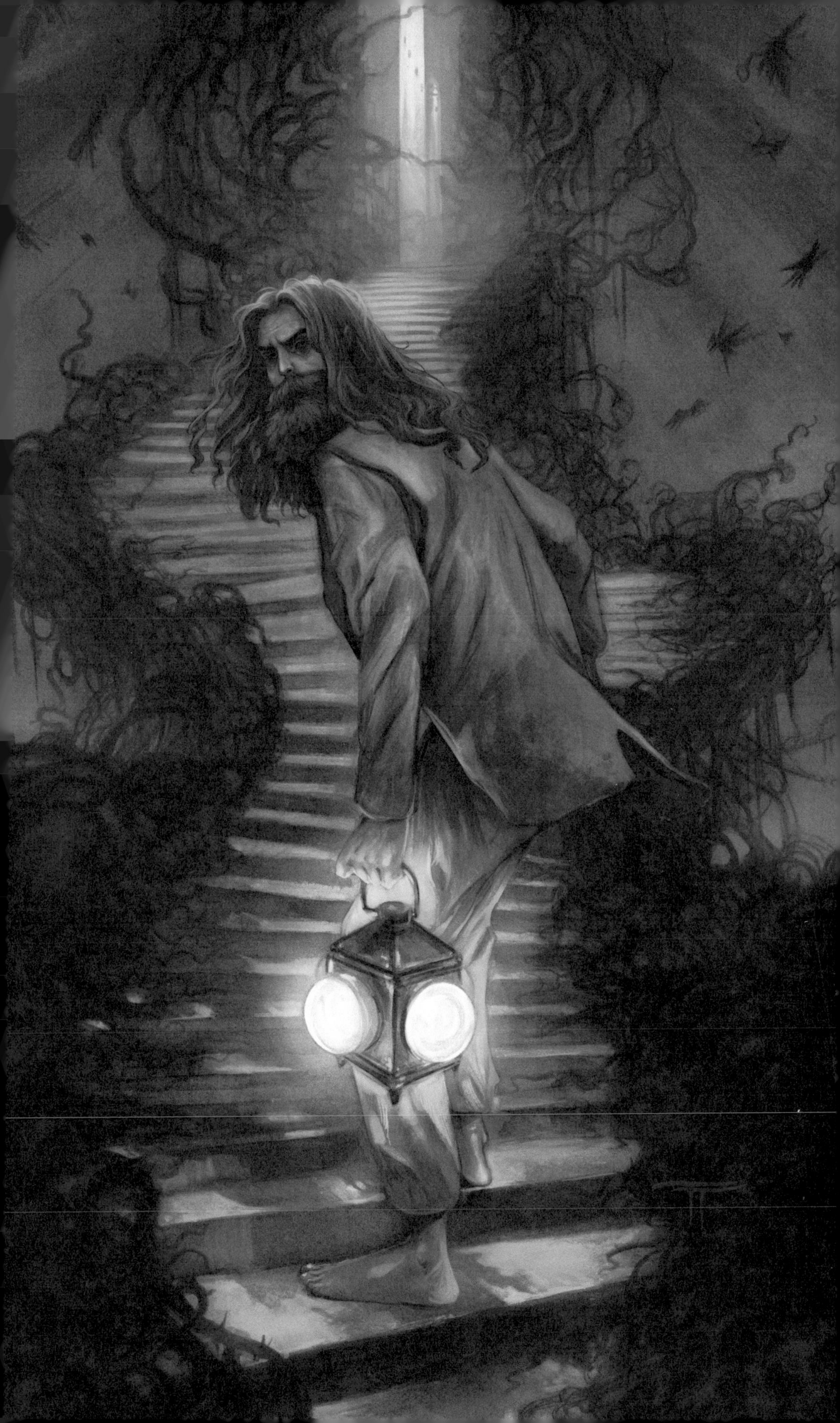

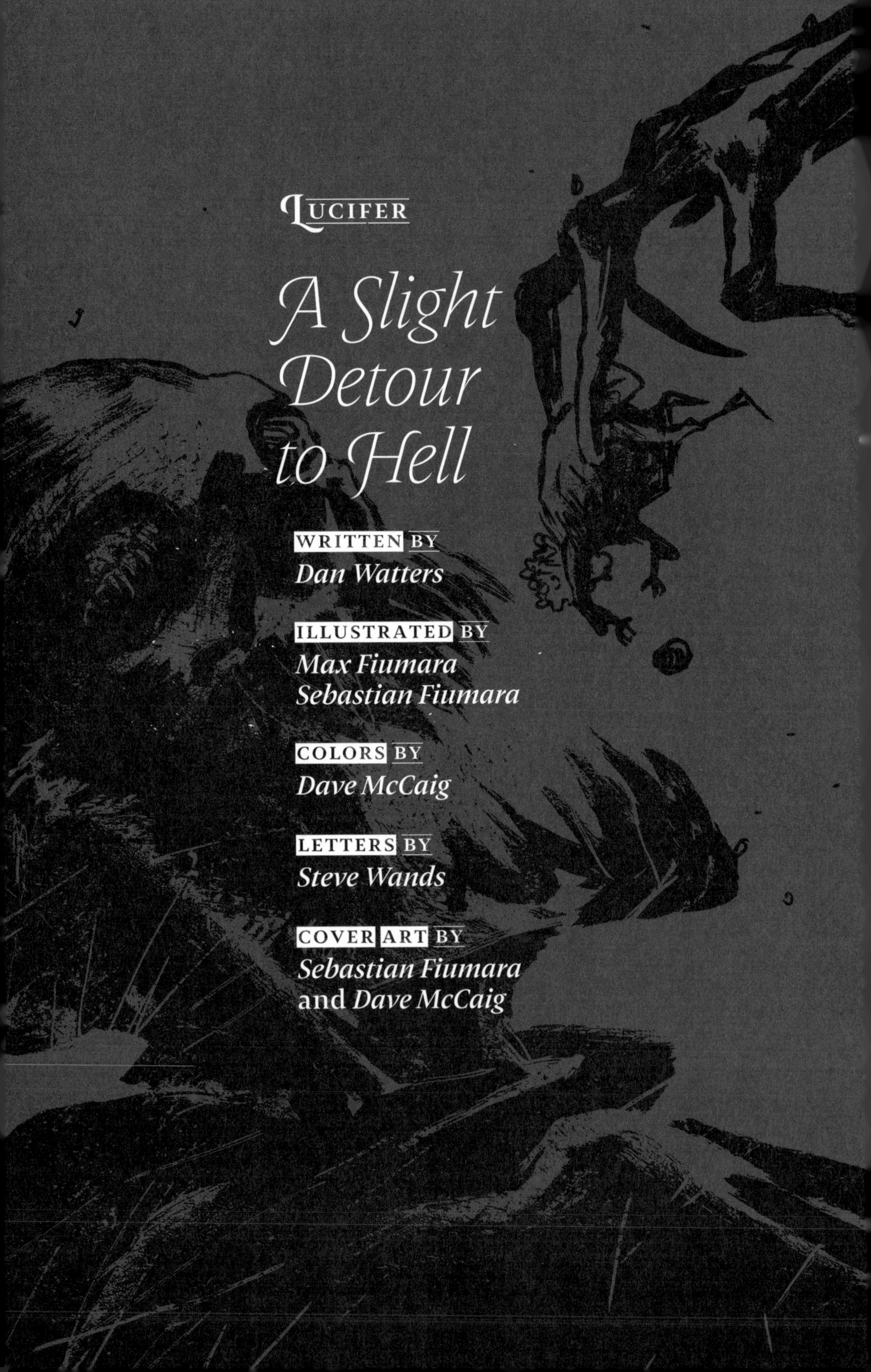

LUCIFER

A Slight Detour to Hell

WRITTEN BY
Dan Watters

ILLUSTRATED BY
Max Fiumara
Sebastian Fiumara

COLORS BY
Dave McCaig

LETTERS BY
Steve Wands

COVER ART BY
Sebastian Fiumara
and *Dave McCaig*

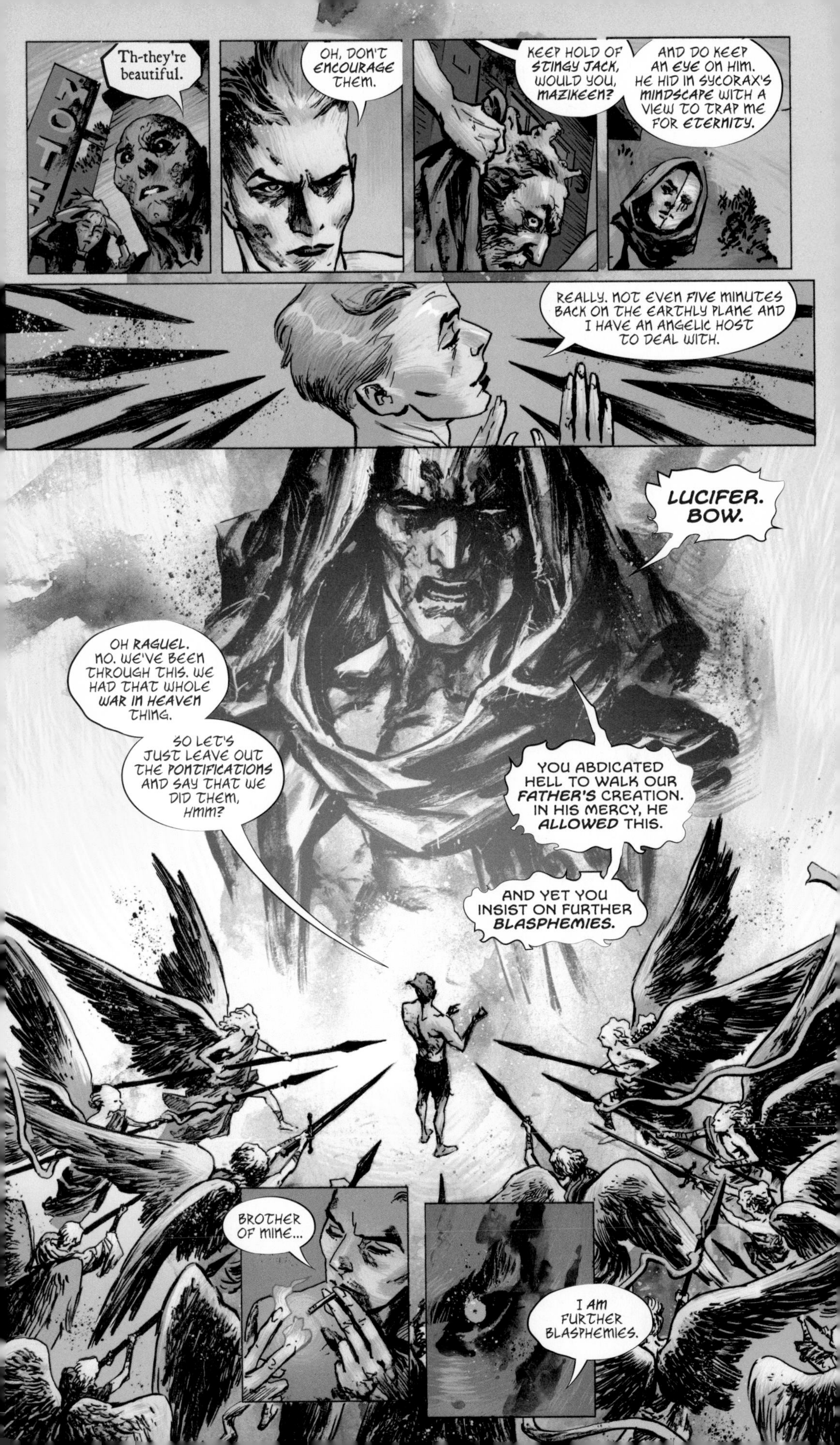
Th-they're beautiful.
OH, DON'T ENCOURAGE THEM.
KEEP HOLD OF STINGY JACK, WOULD YOU, MAZIKEEN?
AND DO KEEP AN EYE ON HIM. HE HID IN SYCORAX'S MINDSCAPE WITH A VIEW TO TRAP ME FOR ETERNITY.
REALLY. NOT EVEN FIVE MINUTES BACK ON THE EARTHLY PLANE AND I HAVE AN ANGELIC HOST TO DEAL WITH.
LUCIFER. BOW.
OH RAGUEL. NO. WE'VE BEEN THROUGH THIS. WE HAD THAT WHOLE WAR IN HEAVEN THING.
SO LET'S JUST LEAVE OUT THE PONTIFICATIONS AND SAY THAT WE DID THEM, HMM?
YOU ABDICATED HELL TO WALK OUR FATHER'S CREATION. IN HIS MERCY, HE ALLOWED THIS.
AND YET YOU INSIST ON FURTHER BLASPHEMIES.
BROTHER OF MINE...
I AM FURTHER BLASPHEMIES.

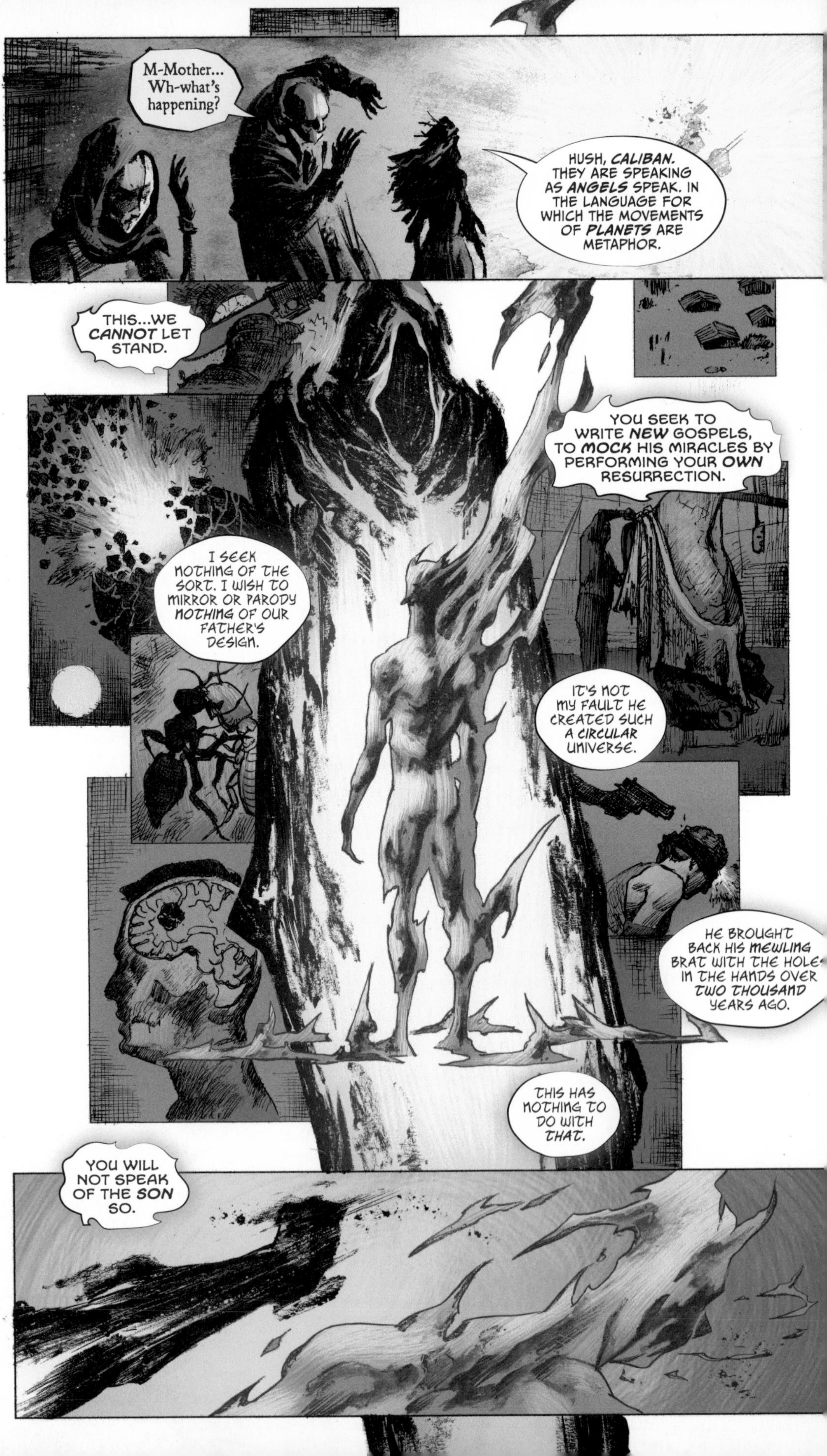
M-Mother... Wh-what's happening?
HUSH, CALIBAN. THEY ARE SPEAKING AS ANGELS SPEAK. IN THE LANGUAGE FOR WHICH THE MOVEMENTS OF PLANETS ARE METAPHOR.
THIS...WE CANNOT LET STAND.
YOU SEEK TO WRITE NEW GOSPELS, TO MOCK HIS MIRACLES BY PERFORMING YOUR OWN RESURRECTION.
I SEEK NOTHING OF THE SORT. I WISH TO MIRROR OR PARODY NOTHING OF OUR FATHER'S DESIGN.
IT'S NOT MY FAULT HE CREATED SUCH A CIRCULAR UNIVERSE.
HE BROUGHT BACK HIS MEWLING BRAT WITH THE HOLE IN THE HANDS OVER TWO THOUSAND YEARS AGO.
THIS HAS NOTHING TO DO WITH THAT.
YOU WILL NOT SPEAK OF THE SON SO.

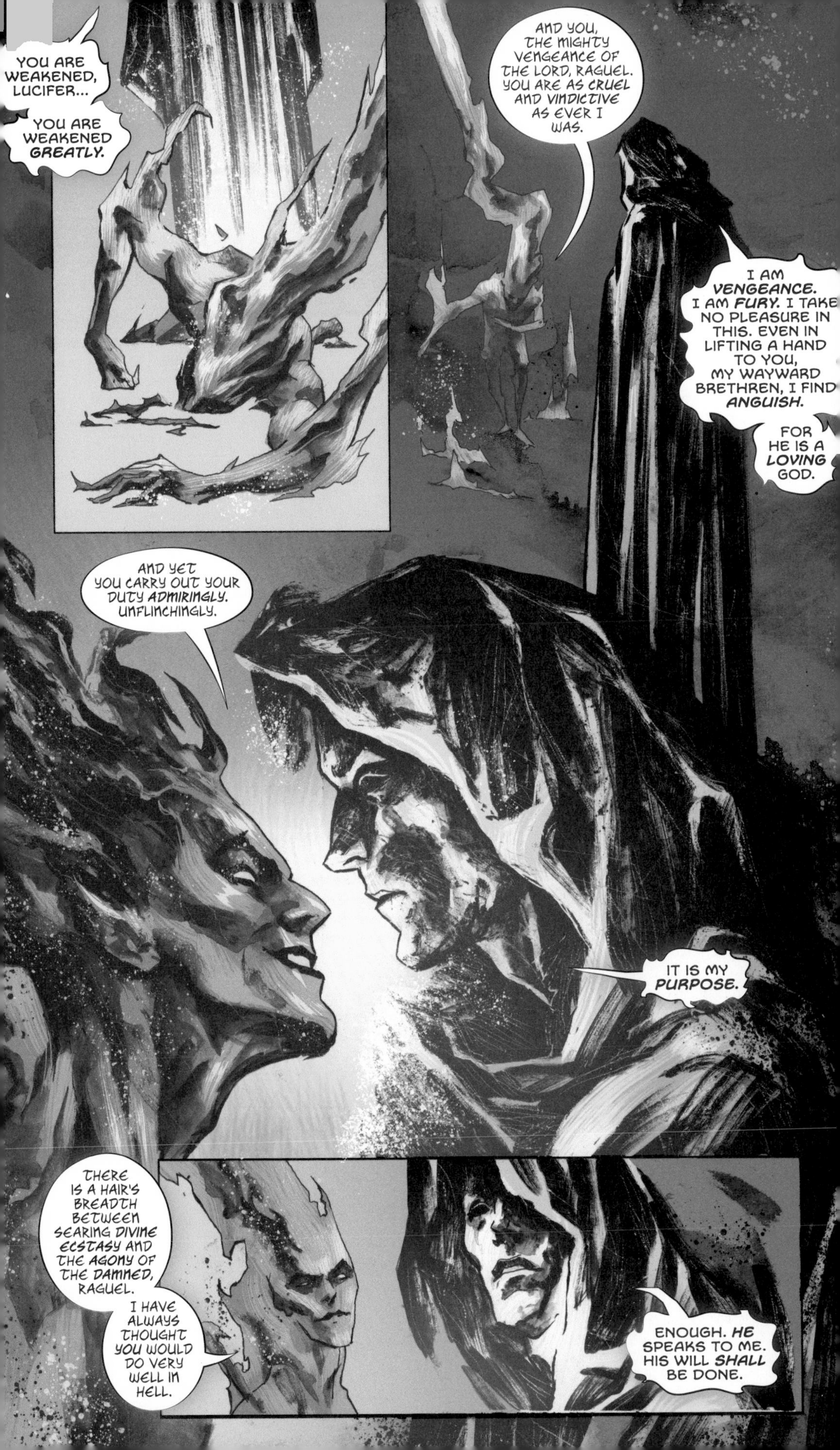
YOU ARE WEAKENED, LUCIFER...
YOU ARE WEAKENED GREATLY.
AND YOU, THE MIGHTY VENGEANCE OF THE LORD, RAGUEL. YOU ARE AS CRUEL AND VINDICTIVE AS EVER I WAS.
I AM VENGEANCE. I AM FURY. I TAKE NO PLEASURE IN THIS. EVEN IN LIFTING A HAND TO YOU, MY WAYWARD BRETHREN, I FIND ANGUISH.
FOR HE IS A LOVING GOD.
AND YET YOU CARRY OUT YOUR DUTY ADMIRINGLY. UNFLINCHINGLY.
IT IS MY PURPOSE.
THERE IS A HAIR'S BREADTH BETWEEN SEARING DIVINE ECSTASY AND THE AGONY OF THE DAMNED, RAGUEL.
I HAVE ALWAYS THOUGHT YOU WOULD DO VERY WELL IN HELL.
ENOUGH. HE SPEAKS TO ME. HIS WILL SHALL BE DONE.

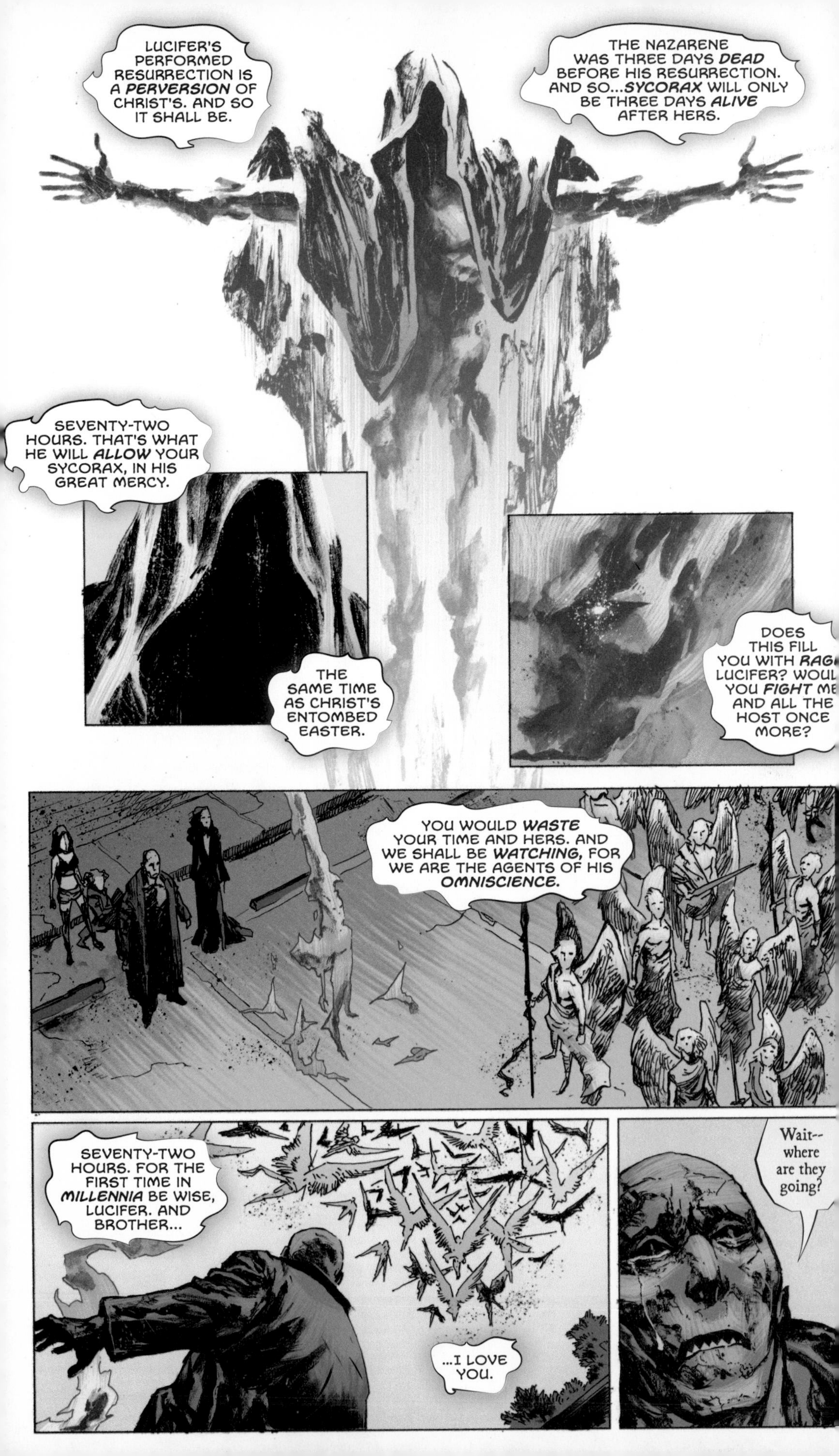

LUCIFER'S PERFORMED RESURRECTION IS A PERVERSION OF CHRIST'S. AND SO IT SHALL BE.
THE NAZARENE WAS THREE DAYS DEAD BEFORE HIS RESURRECTION. AND SO...SYCORAX WILL ONLY BE THREE DAYS ALIVE AFTER HERS.
SEVENTY-TWO HOURS. THAT'S WHAT HE WILL ALLOW YOUR SYCORAX, IN HIS GREAT MERCY.
THE SAME TIME AS CHRIST'S ENTOMBED EASTER.
DOES THIS FILL YOU WITH RAG LUCIFER? WOUL YOU FIGHT ME AND ALL THE HOST ONCE MORE?
YOU WOULD WASTE YOUR TIME AND HERS. AND WE SHALL BE WATCHING, FOR WE ARE THE AGENTS OF HIS OMNISCIENCE.
SEVENTY-TWO HOURS. FOR THE FIRST TIME IN MILLENNIA BE WISE, LUCIFER. AND BROTHER...
...I LOVE YOU.
Wait-- where are they going?

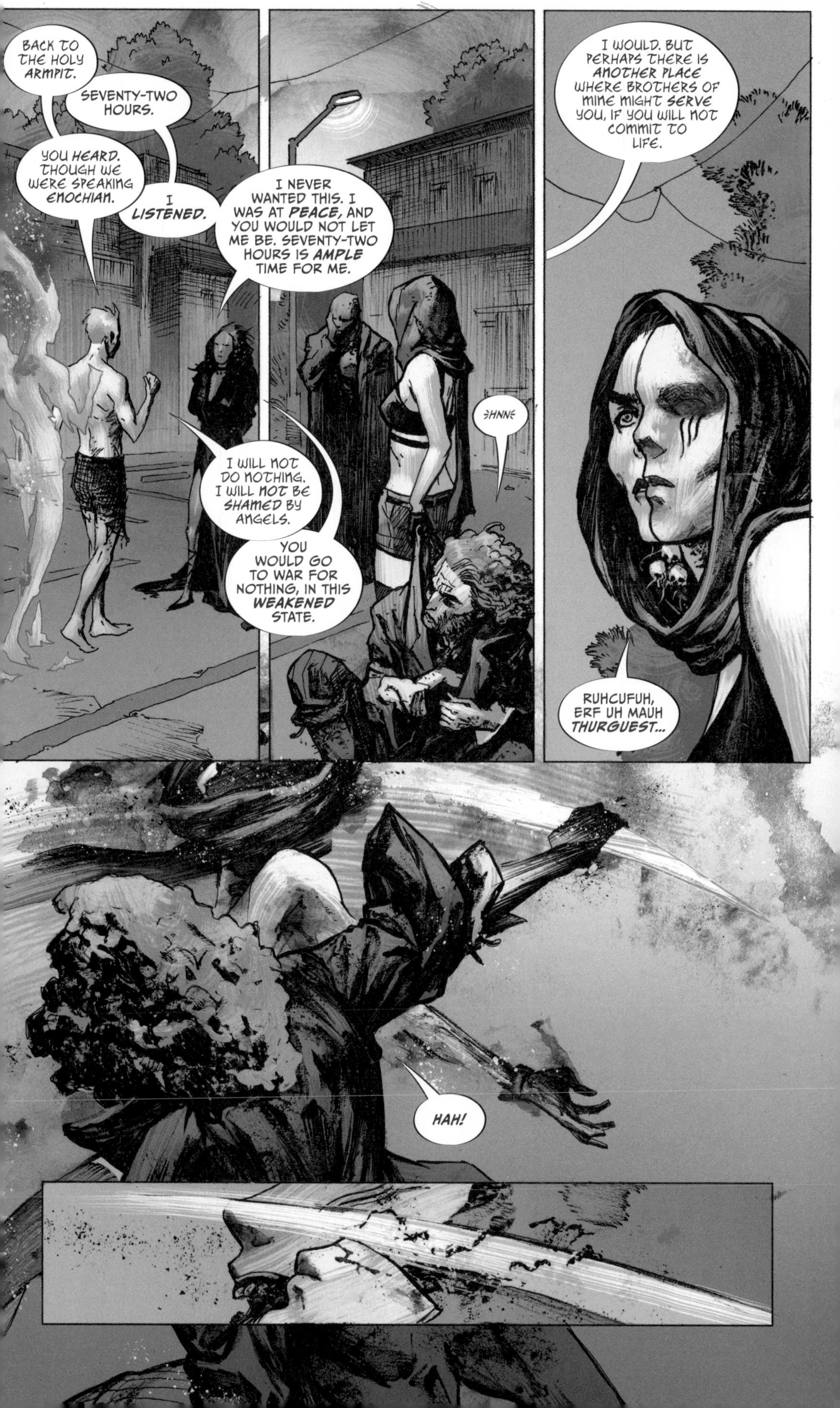
BACK TO THE HOLY ARMPIT.
SEVENTY-TWO HOURS.
YOU HEARD. THOUGH WE WERE SPEAKING ENOCHIAN.
I LISTENED.
I NEVER WANTED THIS. I WAS AT PEACE, AND YOU WOULD NOT LET ME BE. SEVENTY-TWO HOURS IS AMPLE TIME FOR ME.
I WILL NOT DO NOTHING. I WILL NOT BE SHAMED BY ANGELS.
YOU WOULD GO TO WAR FOR NOTHING, IN THIS WEAKENED STATE.
I WOULD. BUT PERHAPS THERE IS ANOTHER PLACE WHERE BROTHERS OF MINE MIGHT SERVE YOU, IF YOU WILL NOT COMMIT TO LIFE.
GHNN
RUHCUFUH, ERF UH MAUH THURGUEST...
HAH!

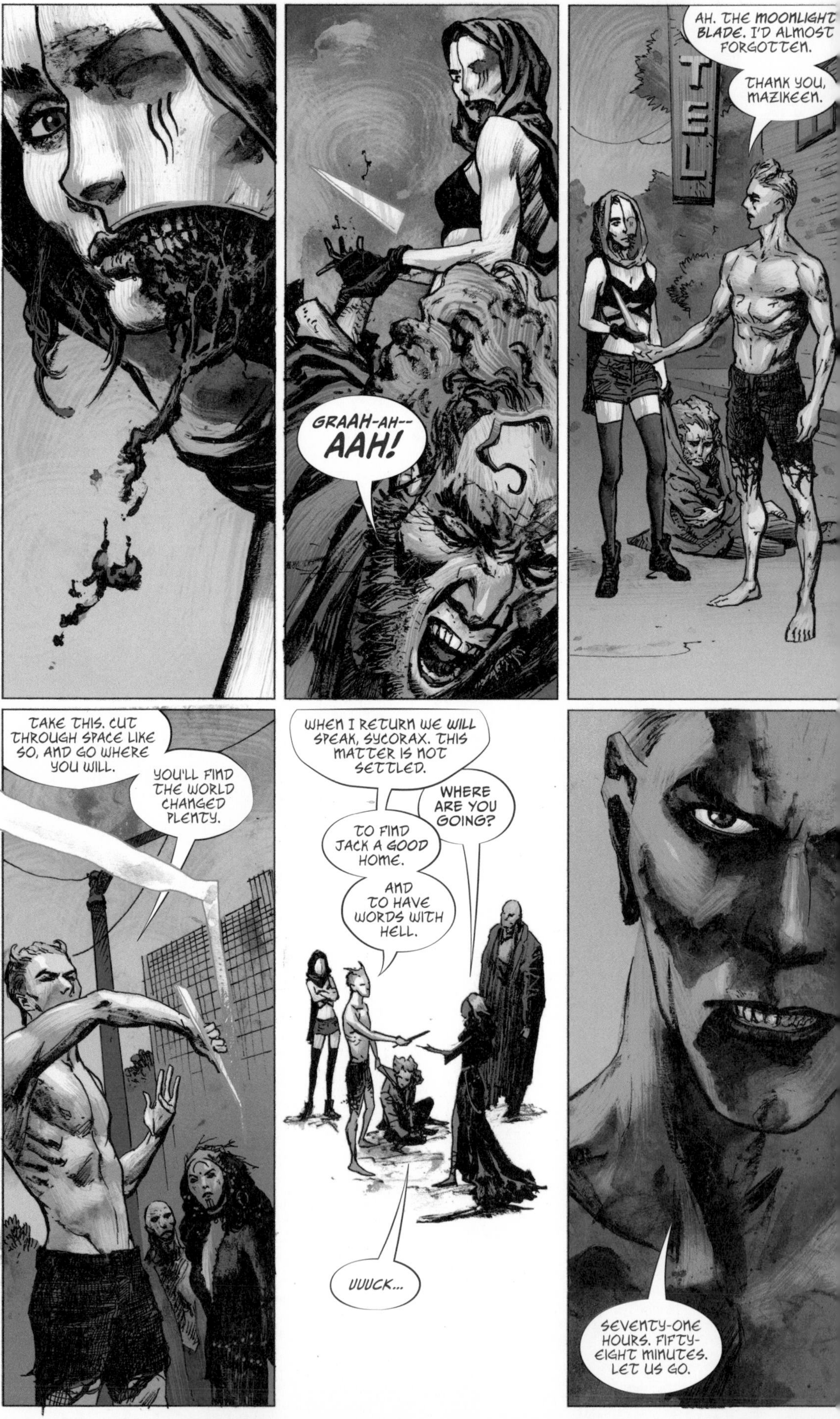
GRAAH-AH-- AAH!
AH. THE MOONLIGHT BLADE. I'D ALMOST FORGOTTEN.
THANK YOU, MAZIKEEN.
TEL
TAKE THIS. CUT THROUGH SPACE LIKE SO, AND GO WHERE YOU WILL.
YOU'LL FIND THE WORLD CHANGED PLENTY.
WHEN I RETURN WE WILL SPEAK, SYCORAX. THIS MATTER IS NOT SETTLED.
WHERE ARE YOU GOING?
TO FIND JACK A GOOD HOME.
AND TO HAVE WORDS WITH HELL.
UUUCK...
SEVENTY-ONE HOURS. FIFTY-EIGHT MINUTES. LET US GO.

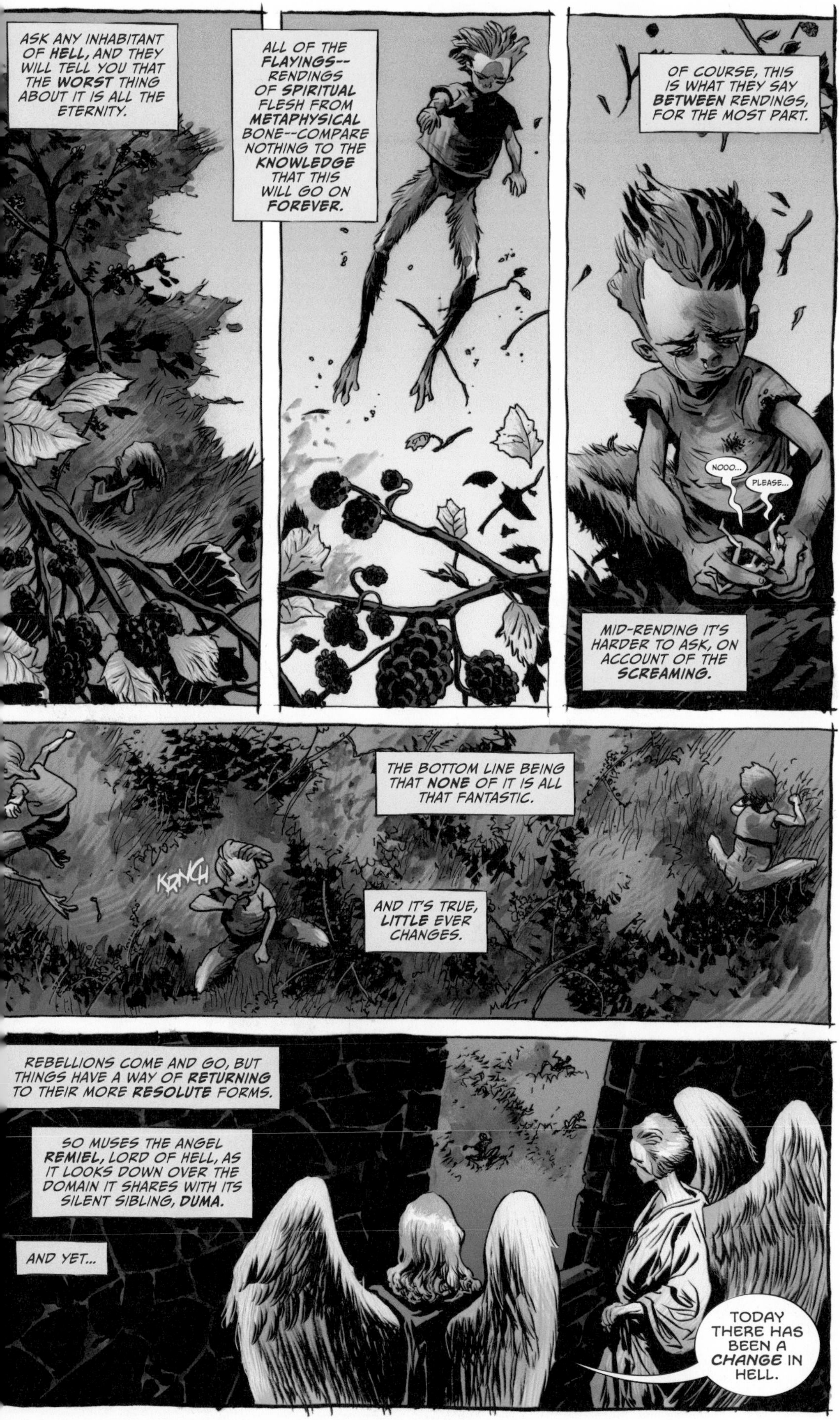
ASK ANY INHABITANT OF HELL, AND THEY WILL TELL YOU THAT THE WORST THING ABOUT IT IS ALL THE ETERNITY.
ALL OF THE FLAYINGS--RENDINGS OF SPIRITUAL FLESH FROM METAPHYSICAL BONE--COMPARE NOTHING TO THE KNOWLEDGE THAT THIS WILL GO ON FOREVER.
OF COURSE, THIS IS WHAT THEY SAY BETWEEN RENDINGS, FOR THE MOST PART.
NOOO...
PLEASE...
MID-RENDING IT'S HARDER TO ASK, ON ACCOUNT OF THE SCREAMING.
THE BOTTOM LINE BEING THAT NONE OF IT IS ALL THAT FANTASTIC.
KRNCH
AND IT'S TRUE, LITTLE EVER CHANGES.
REBELLIONS COME AND GO, BUT THINGS HAVE A WAY OF RETURNING TO THEIR MORE RESOLUTE FORMS.
SO MUSES THE ANGEL REMIEL, LORD OF HELL, AS IT LOOKS DOWN OVER THE DOMAIN IT SHARES WITH ITS SILENT SIBLING, DUMA.
AND YET...
TODAY THERE HAS BEEN A CHANGE IN HELL.

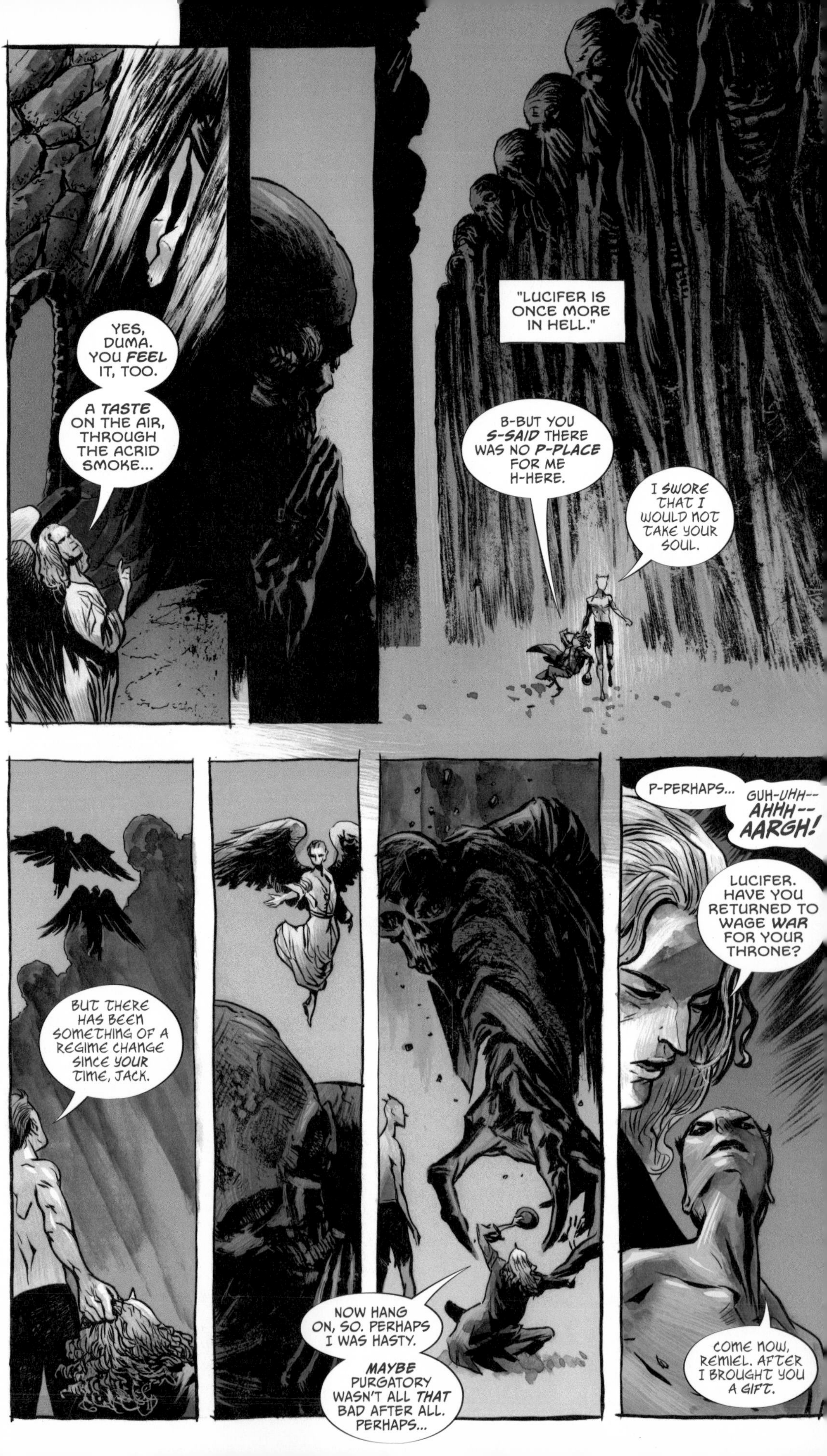

YES, DUMA. YOU FEEL IT, TOO.
A TASTE ON THE AIR, THROUGH THE ACRID SMOKE...
"LUCIFER IS ONCE MORE IN HELL."
B-BUT YOU S-SAID THERE WAS NO P-PLACE FOR ME H-HERE.
I SWORE THAT I WOULD NOT TAKE YOUR SOUL.
BUT THERE HAS BEEN SOMETHING OF A REGIME CHANGE SINCE YOUR TIME, JACK.
NOW HANG ON, SO. PERHAPS I WAS HASTY.
MAYBE PURGATORY WASN'T ALL THAT BAD AFTER ALL. PERHAPS...
P-PERHAPS...
GUH-UHH-- AHHH-- AARGH!
LUCIFER. HAVE YOU RETURNED TO WAGE WAR FOR YOUR THRONE?
COME NOW, REMIEL. AFTER I BROUGHT YOU A GIFT.

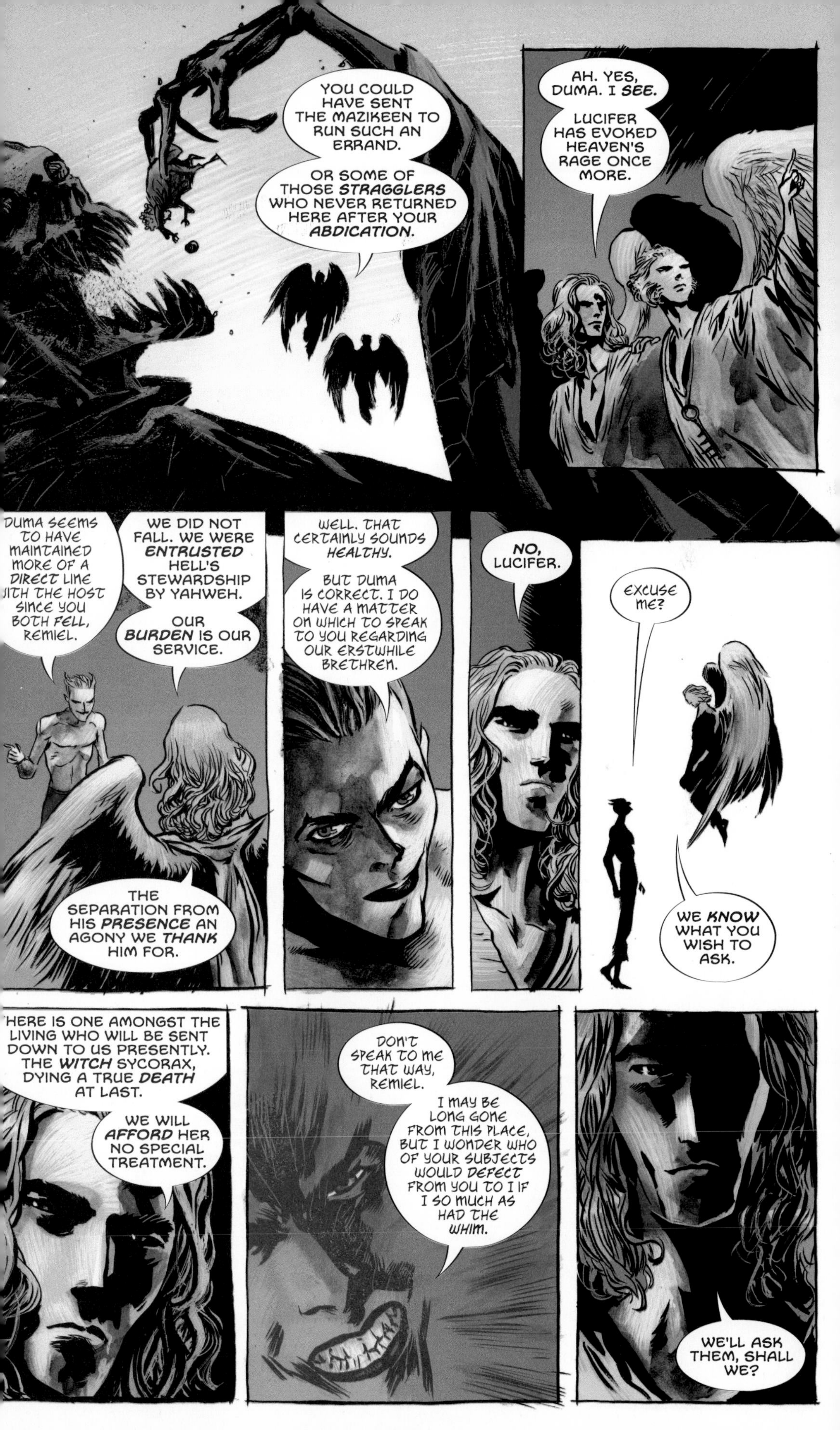
YOU COULD HAVE SENT THE MAZIKEEN TO RUN SUCH AN ERRAND.
OR SOME OF THOSE STRAGGLERS WHO NEVER RETURNED HERE AFTER YOUR ABDICATION.
AH. YES, DUMA. I SEE.
LUCIFER HAS EVOKED HEAVEN'S RAGE ONCE MORE.
DUMA SEEMS TO HAVE MAINTAINED MORE OF A DIRECT LINE WITH THE HOST SINCE YOU BOTH FELL, REMIEL.
WE DID NOT FALL. WE WERE ENTRUSTED HELL'S STEWARDSHIP BY YAHWEH.
OUR BURDEN IS OUR SERVICE.
THE SEPARATION FROM HIS PRESENCE AN AGONY WE THANK HIM FOR.
WELL. THAT CERTAINLY SOUNDS HEALTHY.
BUT DUMA IS CORRECT. I DO HAVE A MATTER ON WHICH TO SPEAK TO YOU REGARDING OUR ERSTWHILE BRETHREN.
NO, LUCIFER.
EXCUSE ME?
WE KNOW WHAT YOU WISH TO ASK.
THERE IS ONE AMONGST THE LIVING WHO WILL BE SENT DOWN TO US PRESENTLY. THE WITCH SYCORAX, DYING A TRUE DEATH AT LAST.
WE WILL AFFORD HER NO SPECIAL TREATMENT.
DON'T SPEAK TO ME THAT WAY, REMIEL.
I MAY BE LONG GONE FROM THIS PLACE, BUT I WONDER WHO OF YOUR SUBJECTS WOULD DEFECT FROM YOU TO I IF I SO MUCH AS HAD THE WHIM.
WE'LL ASK THEM, SHALL WE?

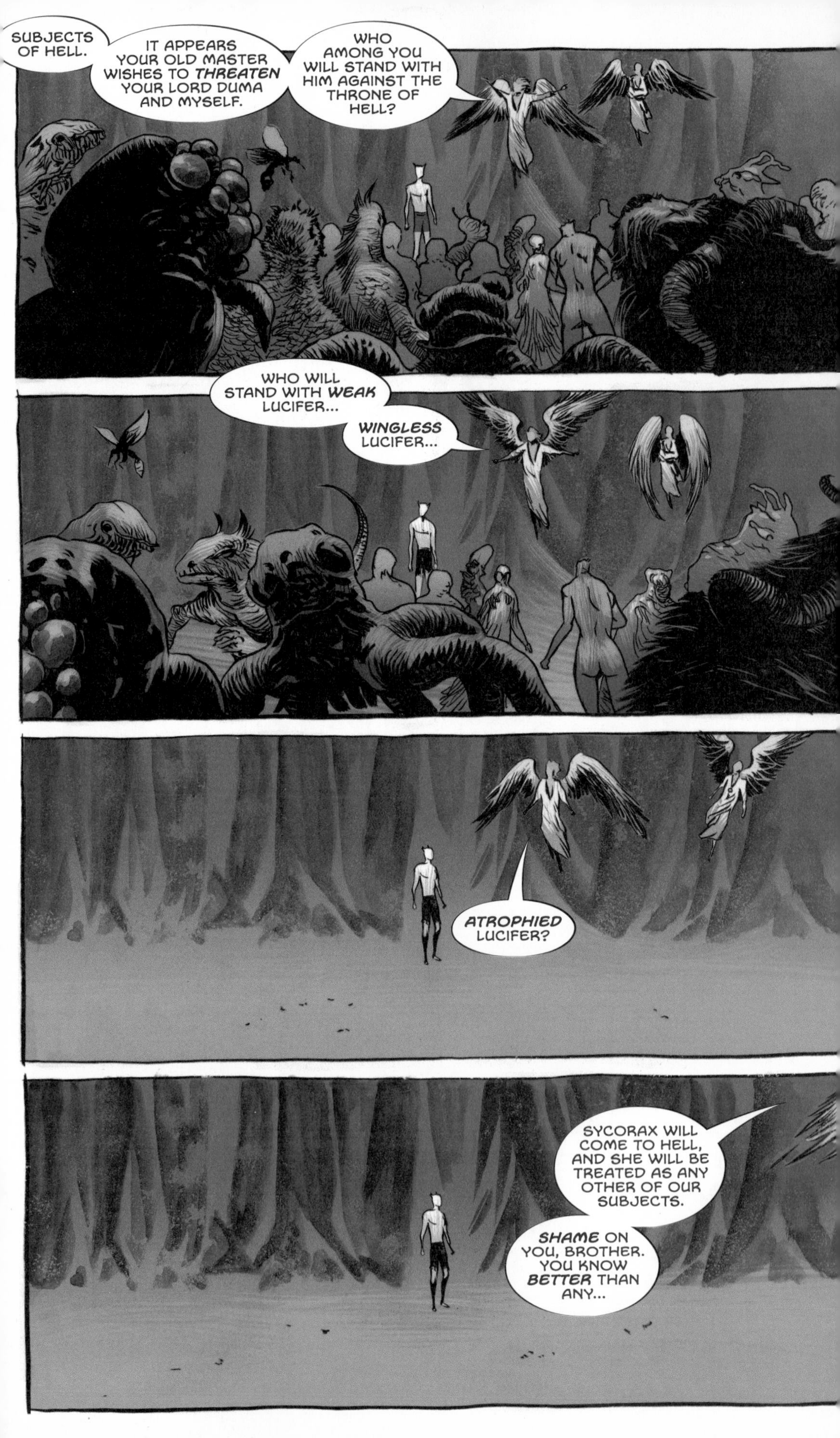
SUBJECTS OF HELL.
IT APPEARS YOUR OLD MASTER WISHES TO THREATEN YOUR LORD DUMA AND MYSELF.
WHO AMONG YOU WILL STAND WITH HIM AGAINST THE THRONE OF HELL?
WHO WILL STAND WITH WEAK LUCIFER...
WINGLESS LUCIFER...
ATROPHIED LUCIFER?
SYCORAX WILL COME TO HELL, AND SHE WILL BE TREATED AS ANY OTHER OF OUR SUBJECTS.
SHAME ON YOU, BROTHER. YOU KNOW BETTER THAN ANY...

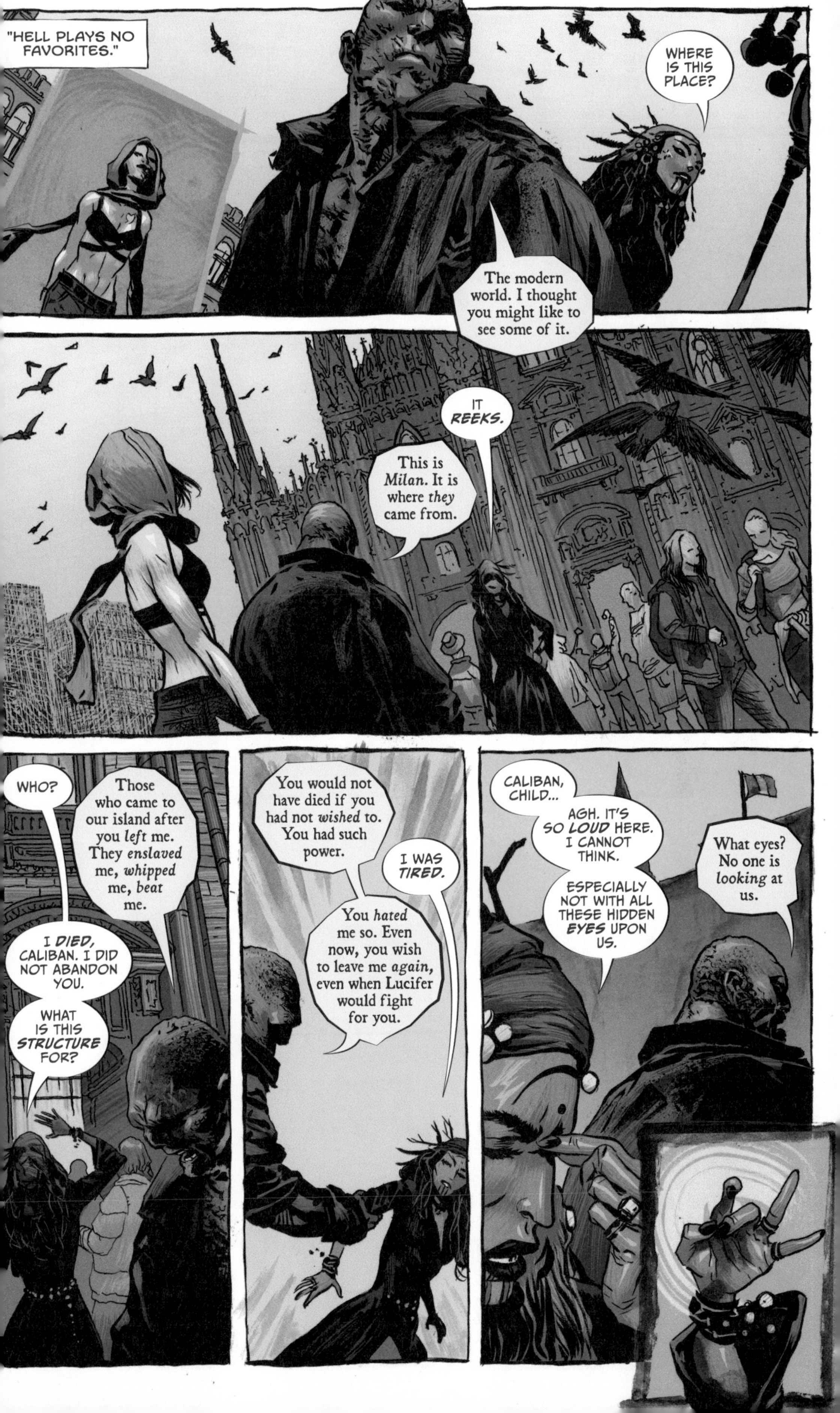
"HELL PLAYS NO FAVORITES."
WHERE IS THIS PLACE?
The modern world. I thought you might like to see some of it.
IT REEKS.
This is Milan. It is where they came from.
WHO?
Those who came to our island after you left me. They enslaved me, whipped me, beat me.
I DIED, CALIBAN. I DID NOT ABANDON YOU.
WHAT IS THIS STRUCTURE FOR?
You would not have died if you had not wished to. You had such power.
I WAS TIRED.
You hated me so. Even now, you wish to leave me again, even when Lucifer would fight for you.
CALIBAN, CHILD...
AGH. IT'S SO LOUD HERE. I CANNOT THINK.
ESPECIALLY NOT WITH ALL THESE HIDDEN EYES UPON US.
What eyes? No one is looking at us.

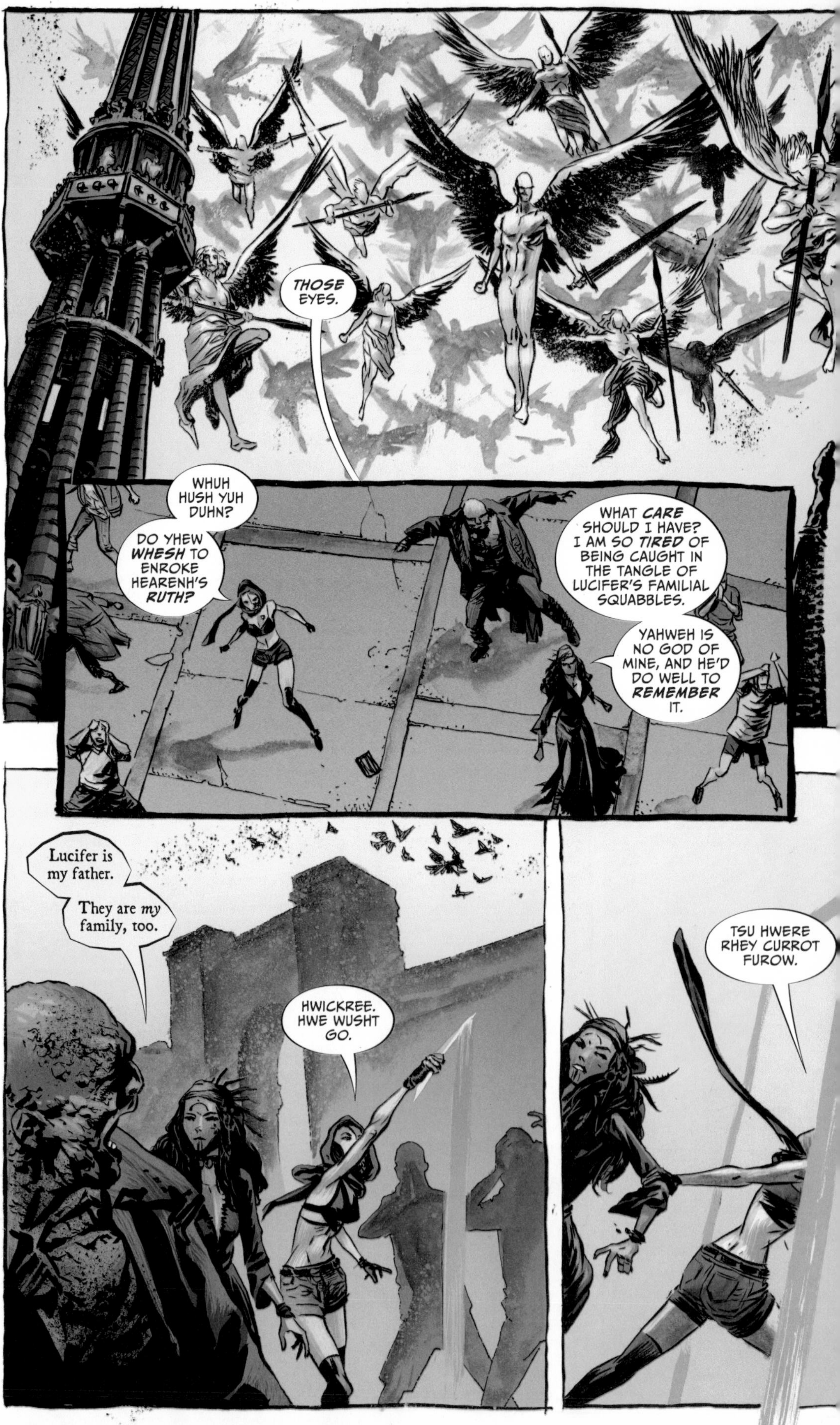

THOSE EYES.
WHUH HUSH YUH DUHN?
DO YHEW WHESH TO ENROKE HEARENH'S RUTH?
WHAT CARE SHOULD I HAVE? I AM SO TIRED OF BEING CAUGHT IN THE TANGLE OF LUCIFER'S FAMILIAL SQUABBLES.
YAHWEH IS NO GOD OF MINE, AND HE'D DO WELL TO REMEMBER IT.
Lucifer is my father.
They are my family, too.
HWICKREE. HWE WUSHT GO.
TSU HWERE RHEY CURROT FUROW.

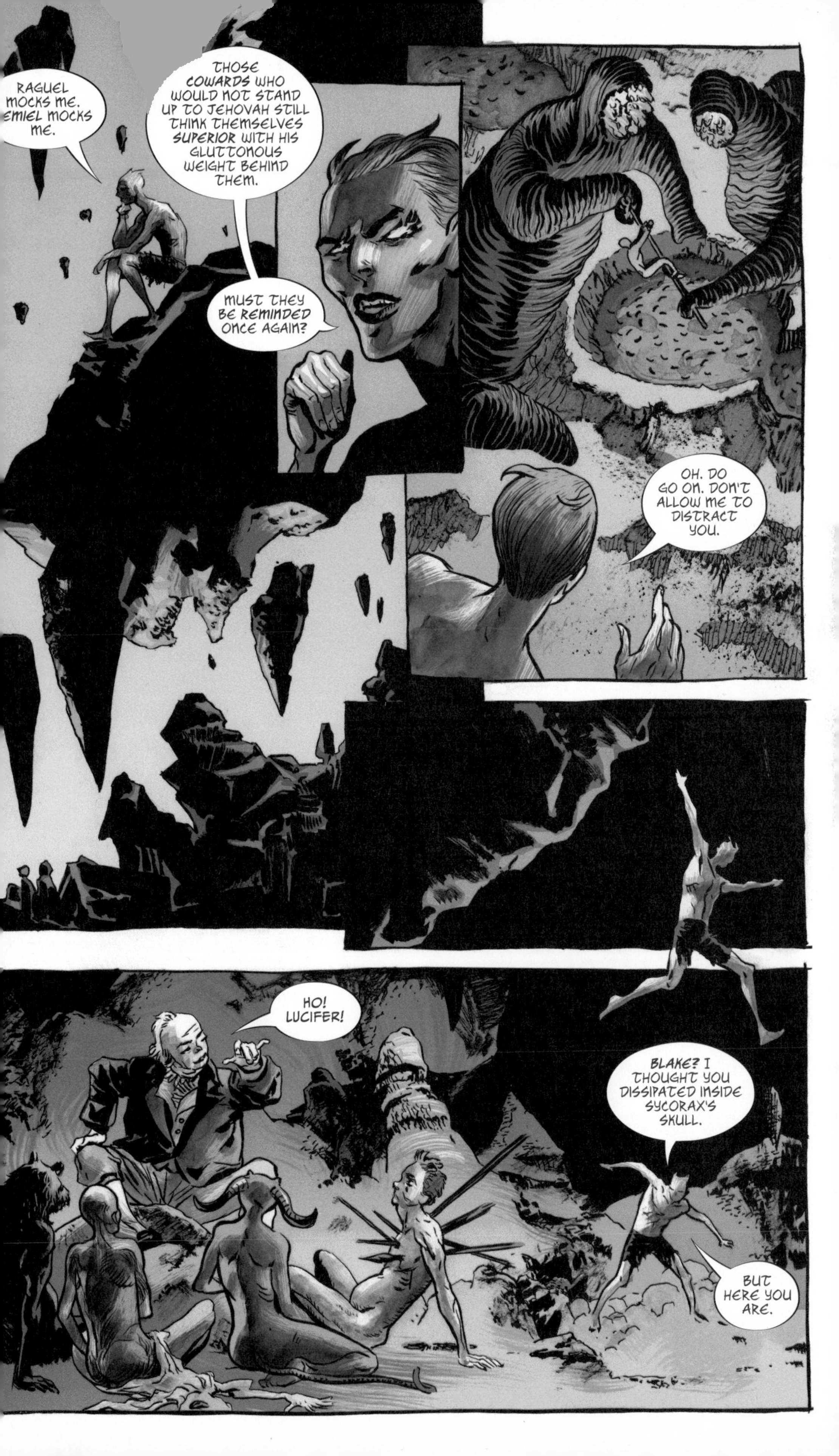
RAGUEL MOCKS ME. EMIEL MOCKS ME.
THOSE COWARDS WHO WOULD NOT STAND UP TO JEHOVAH STILL THINK THEMSELVES SUPERIOR WITH HIS GLUTTONOUS WEIGHT BEHIND THEM.
MUST THEY BE REMINDED ONCE AGAIN?
OH. DO GO ON. DON'T ALLOW ME TO DISTRACT YOU.
HO! LUCIFER!
BLAKE? I THOUGHT YOU DISSIPATED INSIDE SYCORAX'S SKULL.
BUT HERE YOU ARE.

I DO NOT KNOW *HOW.* I REMEMBER BEING VERY *ANGRY* ABOUT...SOMETHING. THEN I WOKE UP HERE.

THINGS RETURN TO THEIR PLACES, I SUPPOSE.

I WAS JUST RELATING A *STORY* TO MY FRIENDS HERE--SO *FUNNY* THAT *YOU* SHOULD PASS BY.

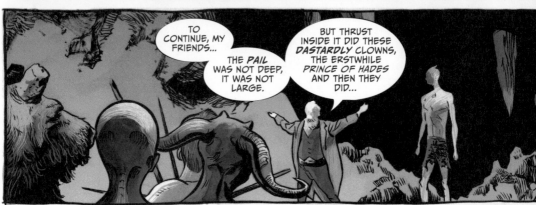

TO CONTINUE, MY FRIENDS...

THE *PAIL* WAS NOT DEEP, IT WAS NOT LARGE.

BUT THRUST INSIDE IT DID THESE *DASTARDLY* CLOWNS, THE ERSTWHILE *PRINCE OF HADES* AND THEN THEY DID...

DESPITE HIS PROTESTATIONS, HIS *WEEPING WAILS* AND *CURSES,* THEY FIT HIM INSIDE IT...

AND WITH A HEARTY *KICK,* THRUST HIM *BOUNCING* AND *TUMBLING* DOWN THE STAIRS.

IT WAS *FABULOUS,* LUCIFER, YOU MUST ADMIT.

HOW MANY HAVE YOU TOLD SUCH STORIES TO, WILLIAM BLAKE?

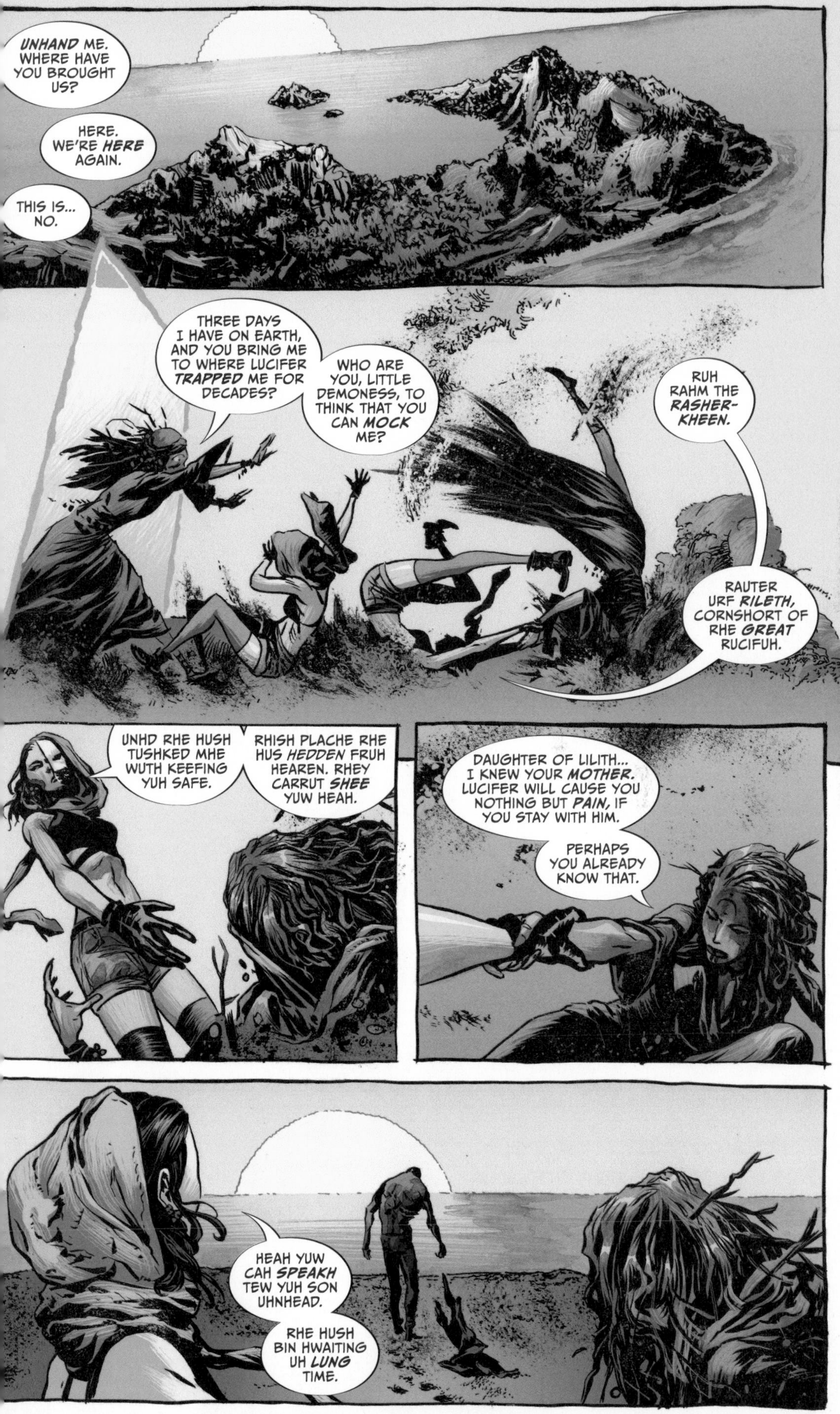
UNHAND ME. WHERE HAVE YOU BROUGHT US?
HERE. WE'RE HERE AGAIN.
THIS IS... NO.
THREE DAYS I HAVE ON EARTH, AND YOU BRING ME TO WHERE LUCIFER TRAPPED ME FOR DECADES?
WHO ARE YOU, LITTLE DEMONESS, TO THINK THAT YOU CAN MOCK ME?
RUH RAHM THE RASHER-KHEEN.
RAUTER URF RILETH, CORNSHORT OF RHE GREAT RUCIFUH.
UNHD RHE HUSH TUSHKED MHE WUTH KEEFING YUH SAFE.
RHISH PLACHE RHE HUS HEDDEN FRUH HEAREN. RHEY CARRUT SHEE YUW HEAH.
DAUGHTER OF LILITH... I KNEW YOUR MOTHER. LUCIFER WILL CAUSE YOU NOTHING BUT PAIN, IF YOU STAY WITH HIM.
PERHAPS YOU ALREADY KNOW THAT.
HEAH YUW CAH SPEAKH TEW YUH SON UHNHEAD.
RHE HUSH BIN HWAITING UH LUNG TIME.

I AM SORRY.

PERHAPS I HAVE NEVER SAID THAT BEFORE.

Never to *me*.

OR AT ALL.

TELL ME. WHAT CAN I GIVE TO YOU IN THIS WORLD TO MAKE IT *BETTER* FOR YOU?

There is not a thing. I am *sure* of that now.

I have never been more *certain* that the universe has me in it only to *scorn* me.

I'd never seen them before. *Angels*. More beautiful and glorious and terrible than ever I imagined.

My father was one of them, and yet...

Look at me.

I've known no family beyond you.

Even the moon god Setebos, who we worshipped when I w a child, never spoke t me again after you died.

OH CALIBAN. SIT BY ME, SON. TELL ME OF THE WORLD THAT IS...AND THERE IS A TRUTH IN TURN I MUST TELL YOU REGARDS SETEBOS...

AS A FAMILIAR SUN SETS C FAMILIAR SANDS, THEY TA

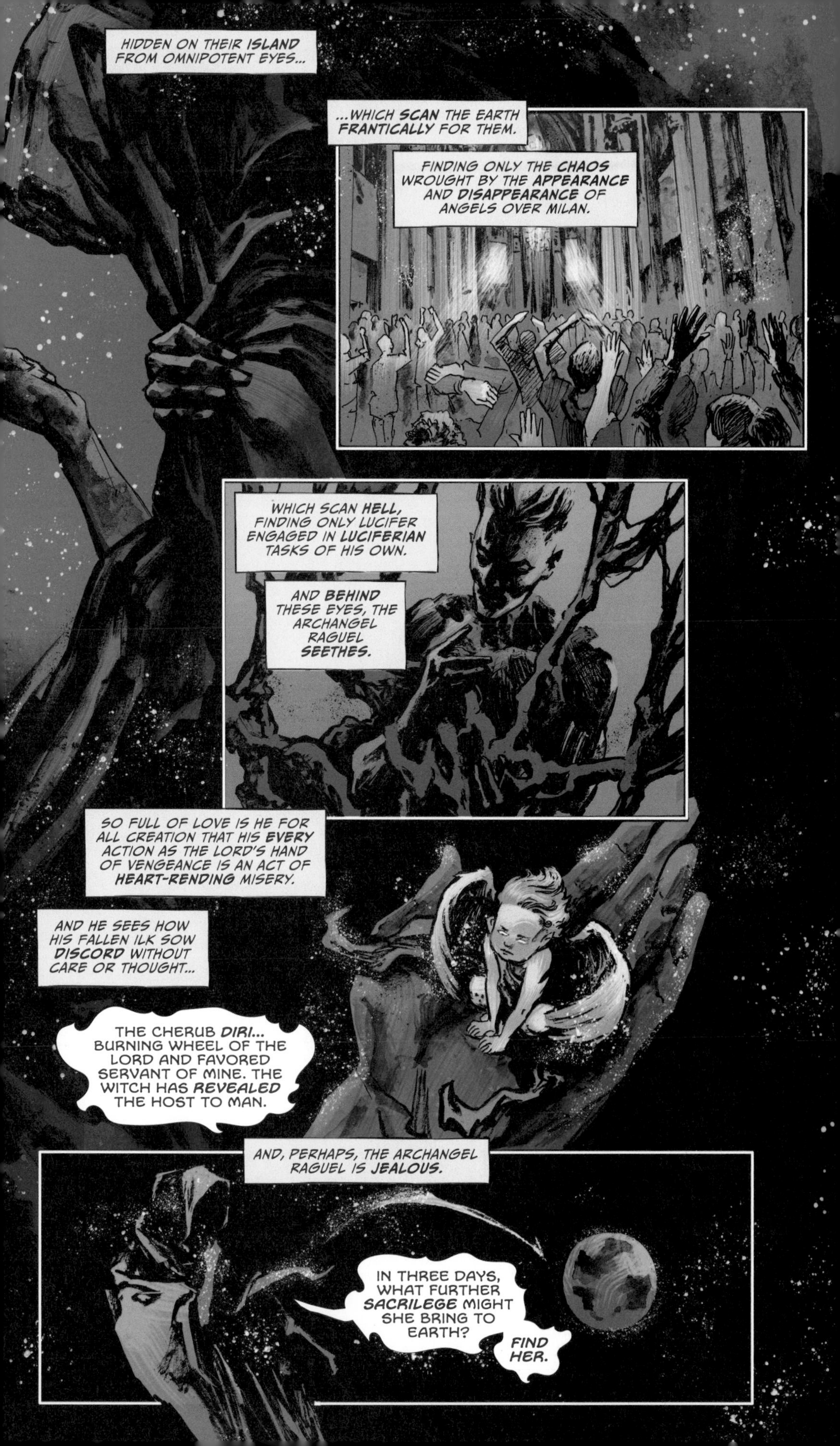

HIDDEN ON THEIR ISLAND FROM OMNIPOTENT EYES...
...WHICH SCAN THE EARTH FRANTICALLY FOR THEM.
FINDING ONLY THE CHAOS WROUGHT BY THE APPEARANCE AND DISAPPEARANCE OF ANGELS OVER MILAN.
WHICH SCAN HELL, FINDING ONLY LUCIFER ENGAGED IN LUCIFERIAN TASKS OF HIS OWN.
AND BEHIND THESE EYES, THE ARCHANGEL RAGUEL SEETHES.
SO FULL OF LOVE IS HE FOR ALL CREATION THAT HIS EVERY ACTION AS THE LORD'S HAND OF VENGEANCE IS AN ACT OF HEART-RENDING MISERY.
AND HE SEES HOW HIS FALLEN ILK SOW DISCORD WITHOUT CARE OR THOUGHT...
THE CHERUB DIRI... BURNING WHEEL OF THE LORD AND FAVORED SERVANT OF MINE. THE WITCH HAS REVEALED THE HOST TO MAN.
AND, PERHAPS, THE ARCHANGEL RAGUEL IS JEALOUS.
IN THREE DAYS, WHAT FURTHER SACRILEGE MIGHT SHE BRING TO EARTH?
FIND HER.

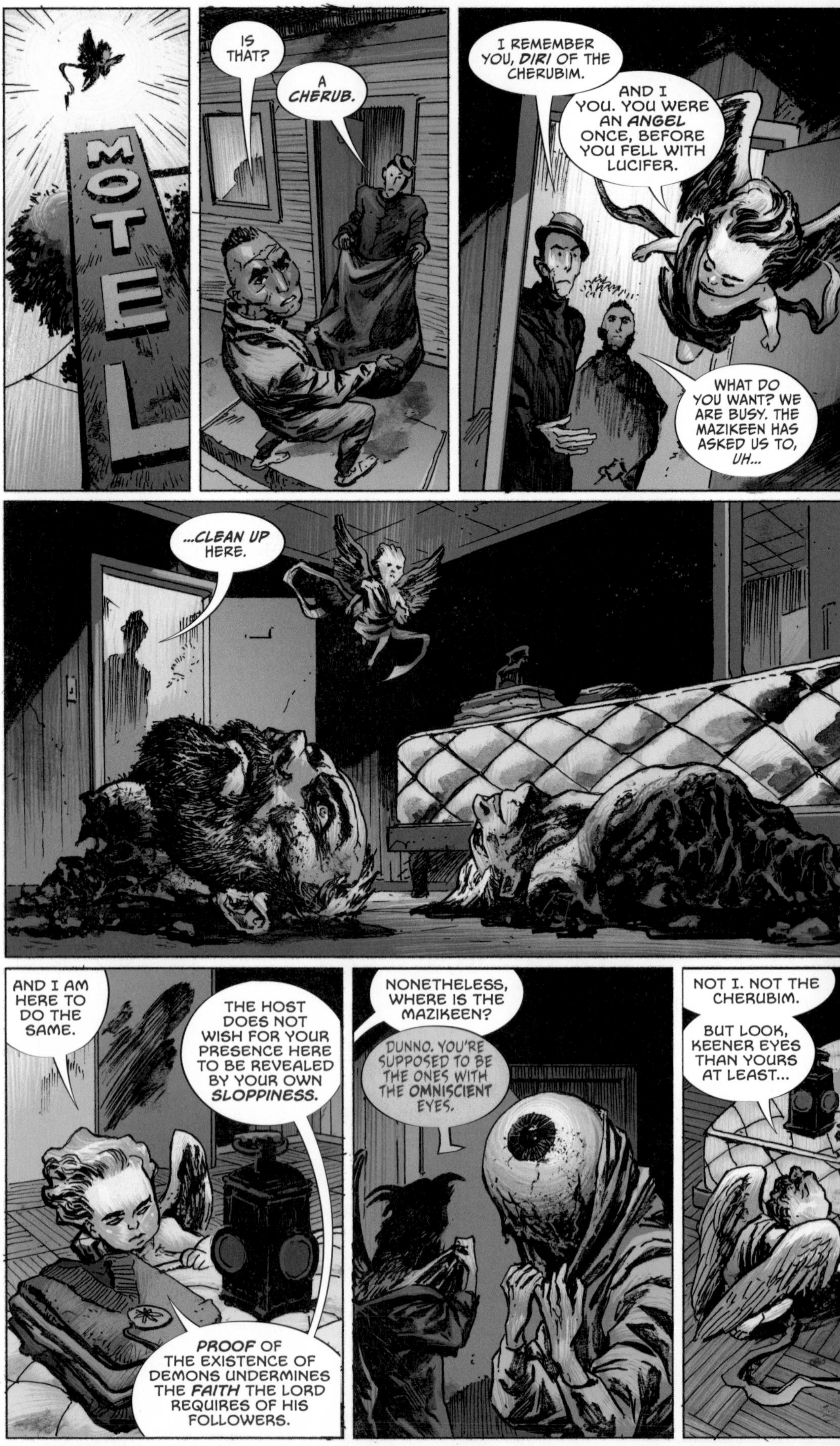
MOTEL
IS THAT?
A CHERUB.
I REMEMBER YOU, DIRI OF THE CHERUBIM.
AND I YOU. YOU WERE AN ANGEL ONCE, BEFORE YOU FELL WITH LUCIFER.
WHAT DO YOU WANT? WE ARE BUSY. THE MAZIKEEN HAS ASKED US TO, UH...
...CLEAN UP HERE.
AND I AM HERE TO DO THE SAME.
THE HOST DOES NOT WISH FOR YOUR PRESENCE HERE TO BE REVEALED BY YOUR OWN SLOPPINESS.
PROOF OF THE EXISTENCE OF DEMONS UNDERMINES THE FAITH THE LORD REQUIRES OF HIS FOLLOWERS.
NONETHELESS, WHERE IS THE MAZIKEEN?
DUNNO. YOU'RE SUPPOSED TO BE THE ONES WITH THE OMNISCIENT EYES.
NOT I. NOT THE CHERUBIM.
BUT LOOK, KEENER EYES THAN YOURS AT LEAST...

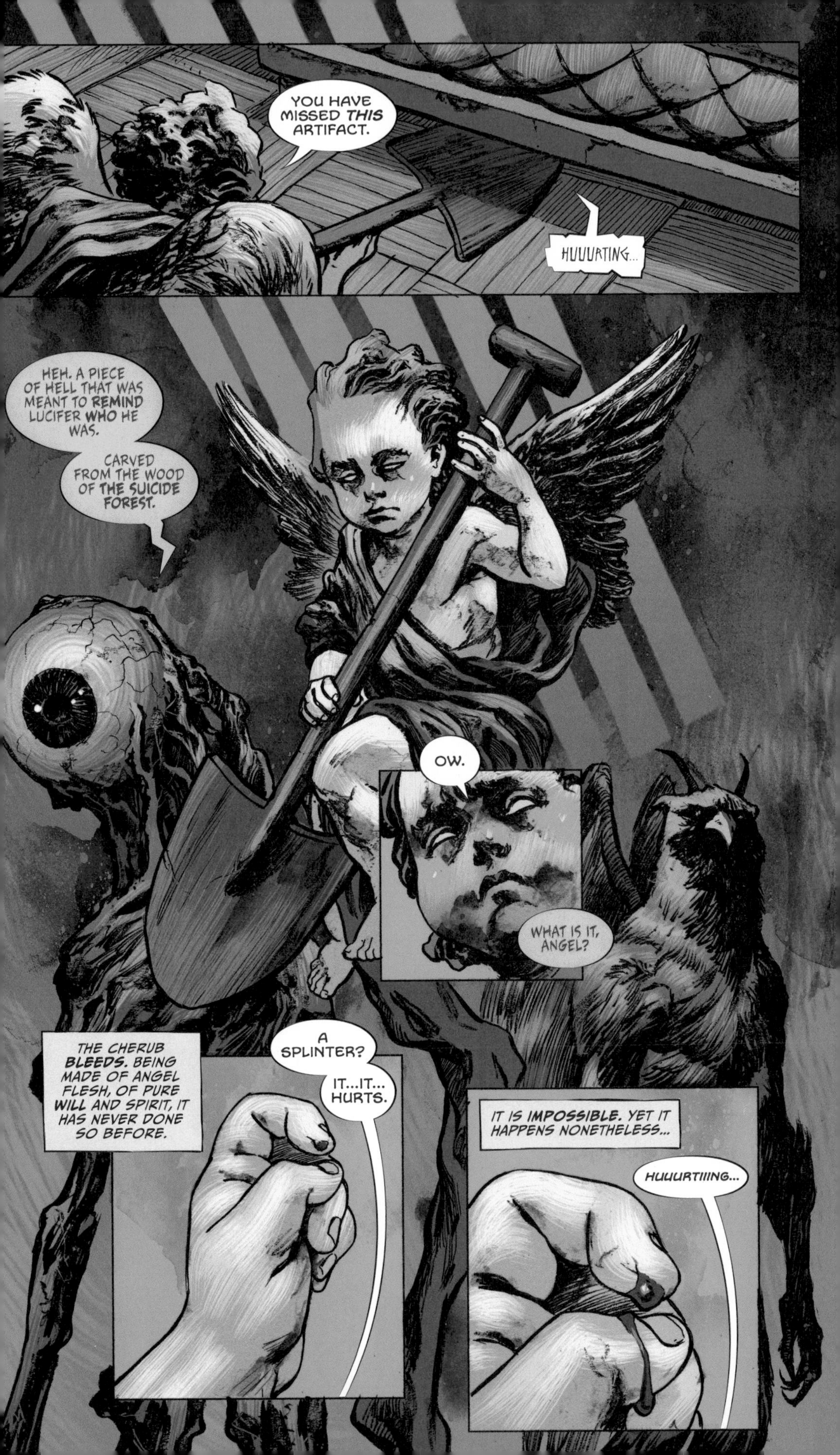
YOU HAVE MISSED THIS ARTIFACT.
HUUURTING...
HEH. A PIECE OF HELL THAT WAS MEANT TO REMIND LUCIFER WHO HE WAS.
CARVED FROM THE WOOD OF THE SUICIDE FOREST.
OW.
WHAT IS IT, ANGEL?
THE CHERUB BLEEDS. BEING MADE OF ANGEL FLESH, OF PURE WILL AND SPIRIT, IT HAS NEVER DONE SO BEFORE.
A SPLINTER?
IT...IT... HURTS.
IT IS IMPOSSIBLE. YET IT HAPPENS NONETHELESS...
HUUURTIIING...

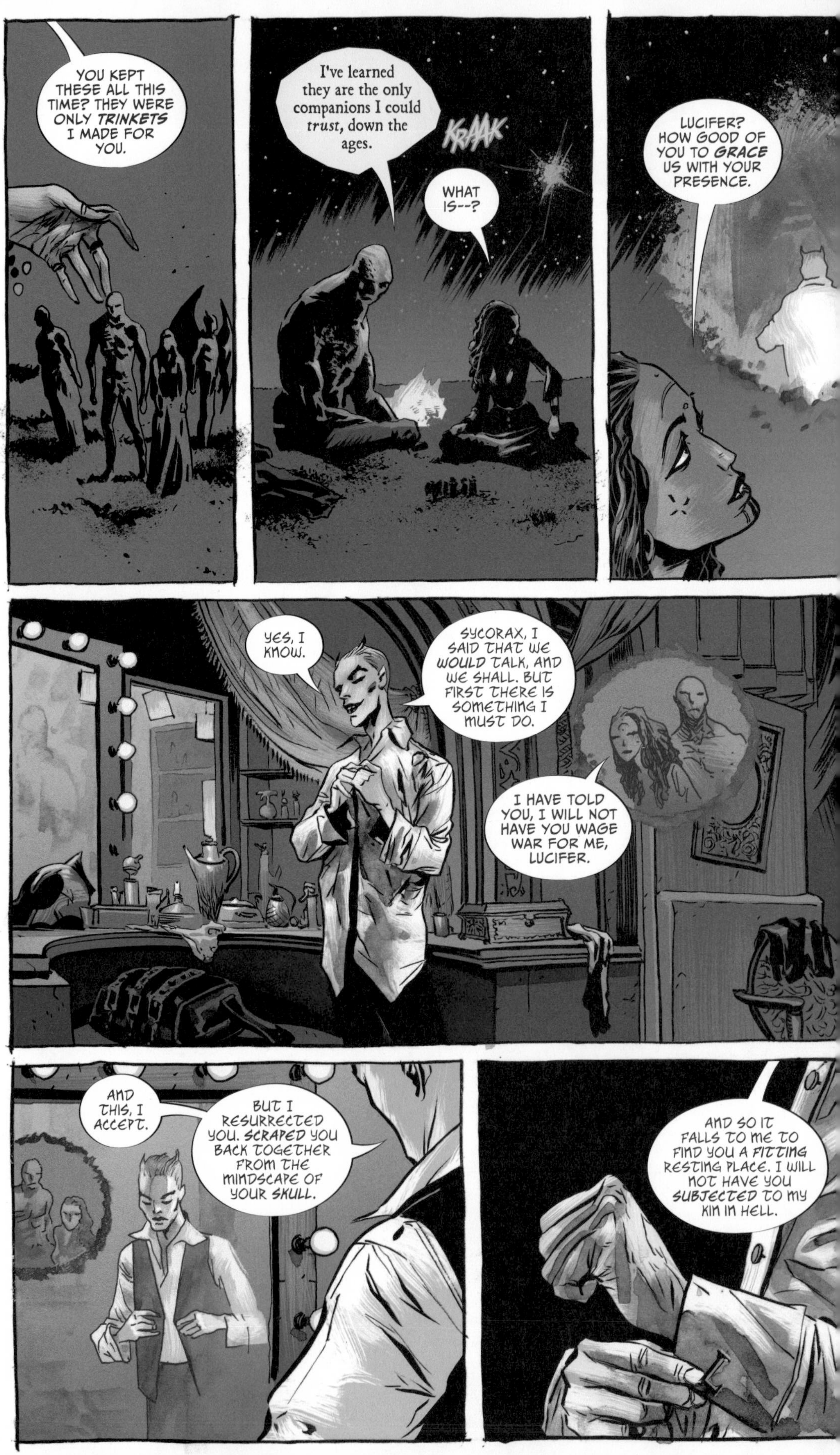
YOU KEPT THESE ALL THIS TIME? THEY WERE ONLY TRINKETS I MADE FOR YOU.
I've learned they are the only companions I could trust, down the ages.
KRAAK
WHAT IS--?
LUCIFER? HOW GOOD OF YOU TO GRACE US WITH YOUR PRESENCE.
YES, I KNOW.
SYCORAX, I SAID THAT WE WOULD TALK, AND WE SHALL. BUT FIRST THERE IS SOMETHING I MUST DO.
I HAVE TOLD YOU, I WILL NOT HAVE YOU WAGE WAR FOR ME, LUCIFER.
AND THIS, I ACCEPT.
BUT I RESURRECTED YOU. SCRAPED YOU BACK TOGETHER FROM THE MINDSCAPE OF YOUR SKULL.
AND SO IT FALLS TO ME TO FIND YOU A FITTING RESTING PLACE. I WILL NOT HAVE YOU SUBJECTED TO MY KIN IN HELL.

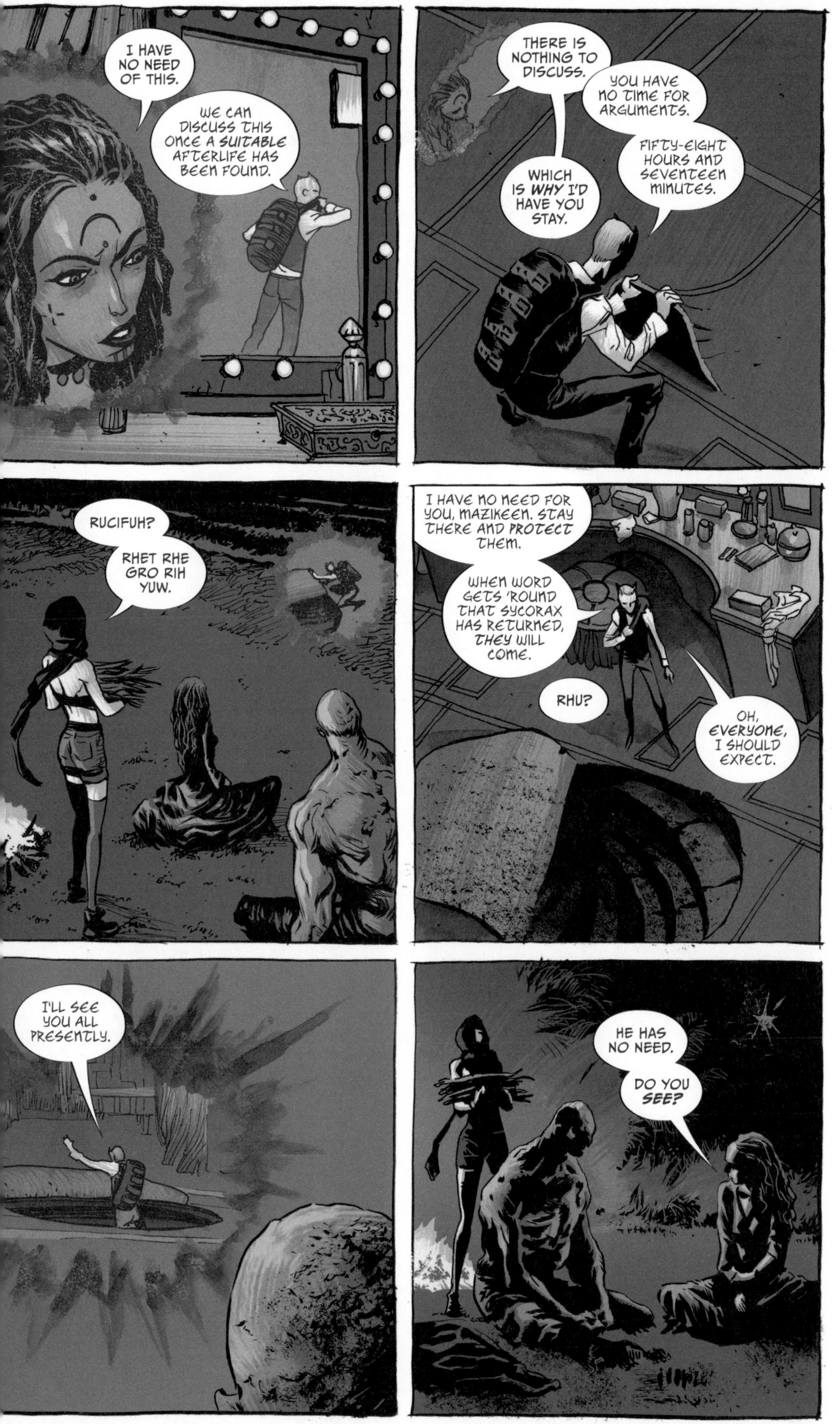
I HAVE NO NEED OF THIS.
WE CAN DISCUSS THIS ONCE A SUITABLE AFTERLIFE HAS BEEN FOUND.
THERE IS NOTHING TO DISCUSS.
YOU HAVE NO TIME FOR ARGUMENTS.
FIFTY-EIGHT HOURS AND SEVENTEEN MINUTES.
WHICH IS WHY I'D HAVE YOU STAY.
RUCIFUH?
RHET RHE GRO RIH YUW.
I HAVE NO NEED FOR YOU, MAZIKEEN. STAY THERE AND PROTECT THEM.
WHEN WORD GETS 'ROUND THAT SYCORAX HAS RETURNED, THEY WILL COME.
RHU?
OH, EVERYONE, I SHOULD EXPECT.
I'LL SEE YOU ALL PRESENTLY.
HE HAS NO NEED.
DO YOU SEE?

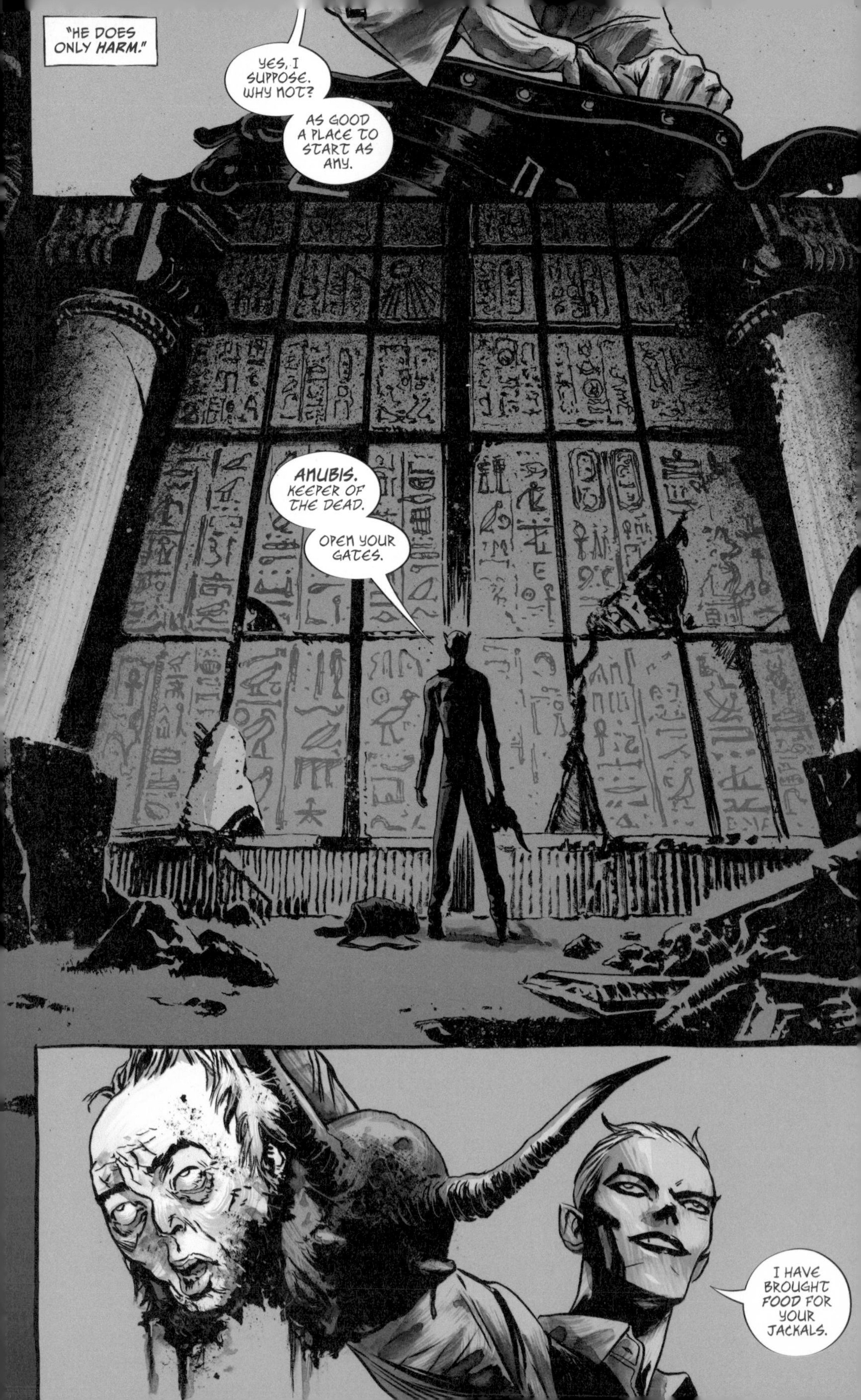
"HE DOES ONLY *HARM.*"
YES, I SUPPOSE. WHY NOT?
AS GOOD A PLACE TO START AS ANY.
ANUBIS. KEEPER OF THE DEAD.
OPEN YOUR GATES.
I HAVE BROUGHT *FOOD* FOR YOUR JACKALS.

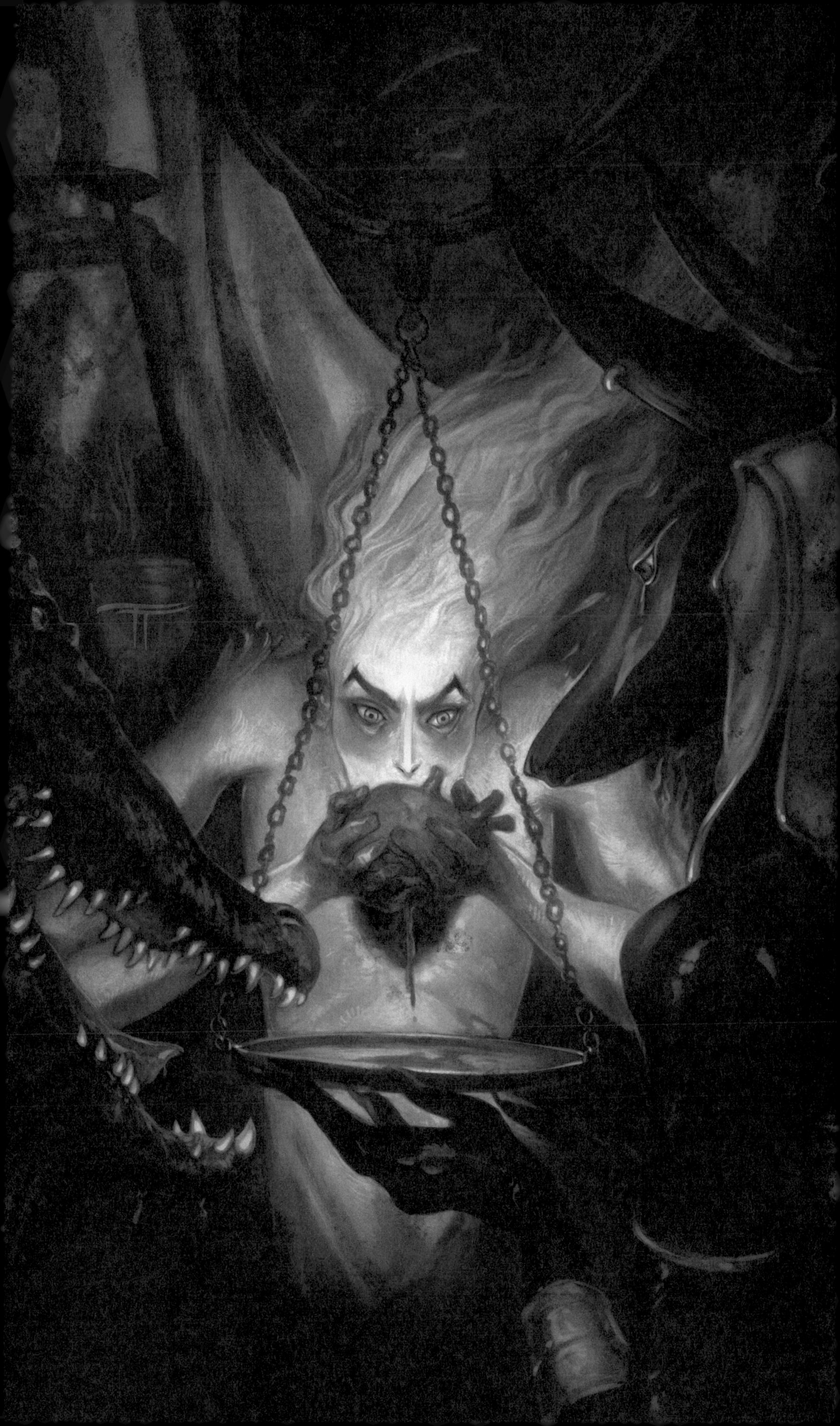

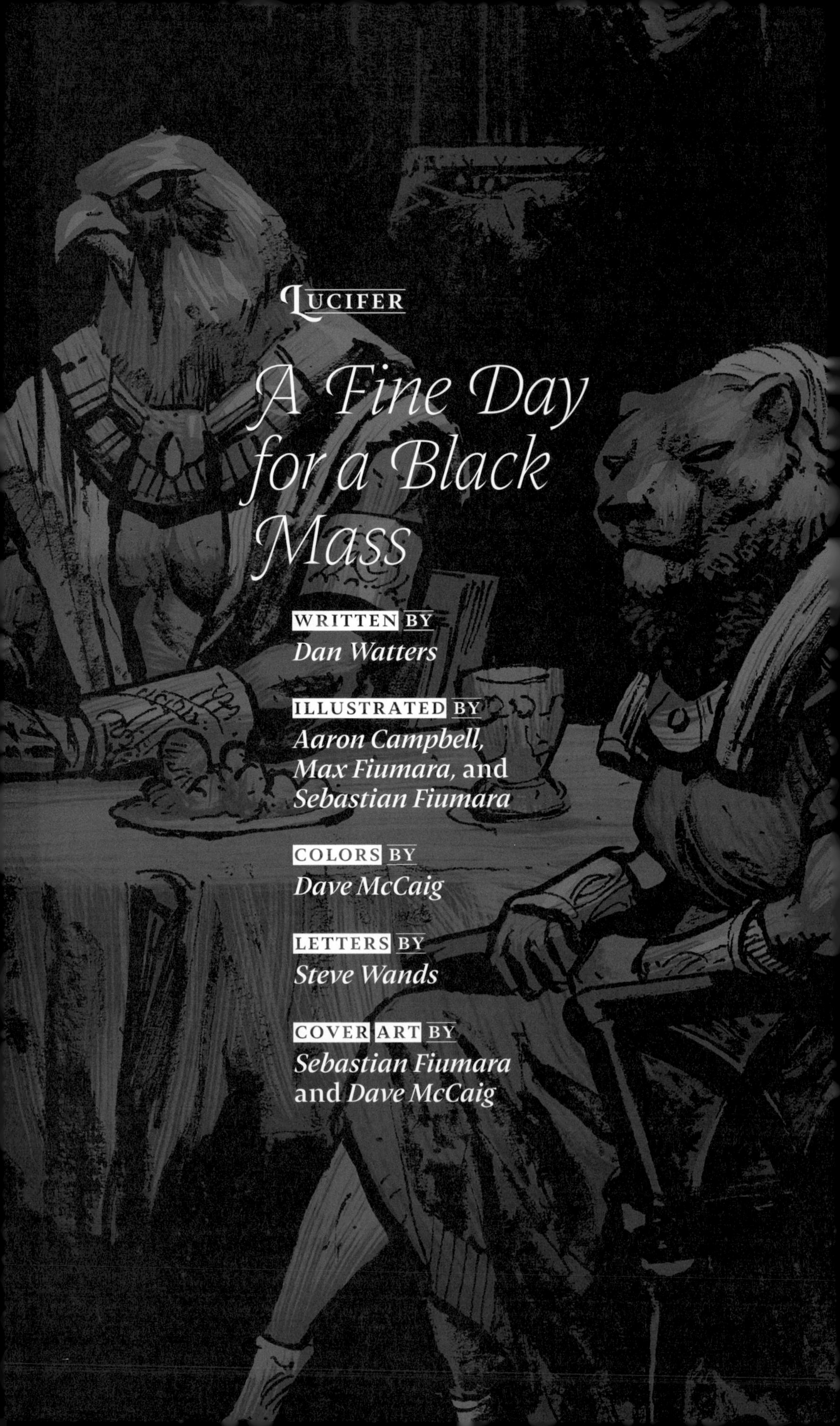

LUCIFER

A Fine Day for a Black Mass

WRITTEN BY
Dan Watters

ILLUSTRATED BY
Aaron Campbell,
Max Fiumara, and
Sebastian Fiumara

COLORS BY
Dave McCaig

LETTERS BY
Steve Wands

COVER ART BY
Sebastian Fiumara
and *Dave McCaig*

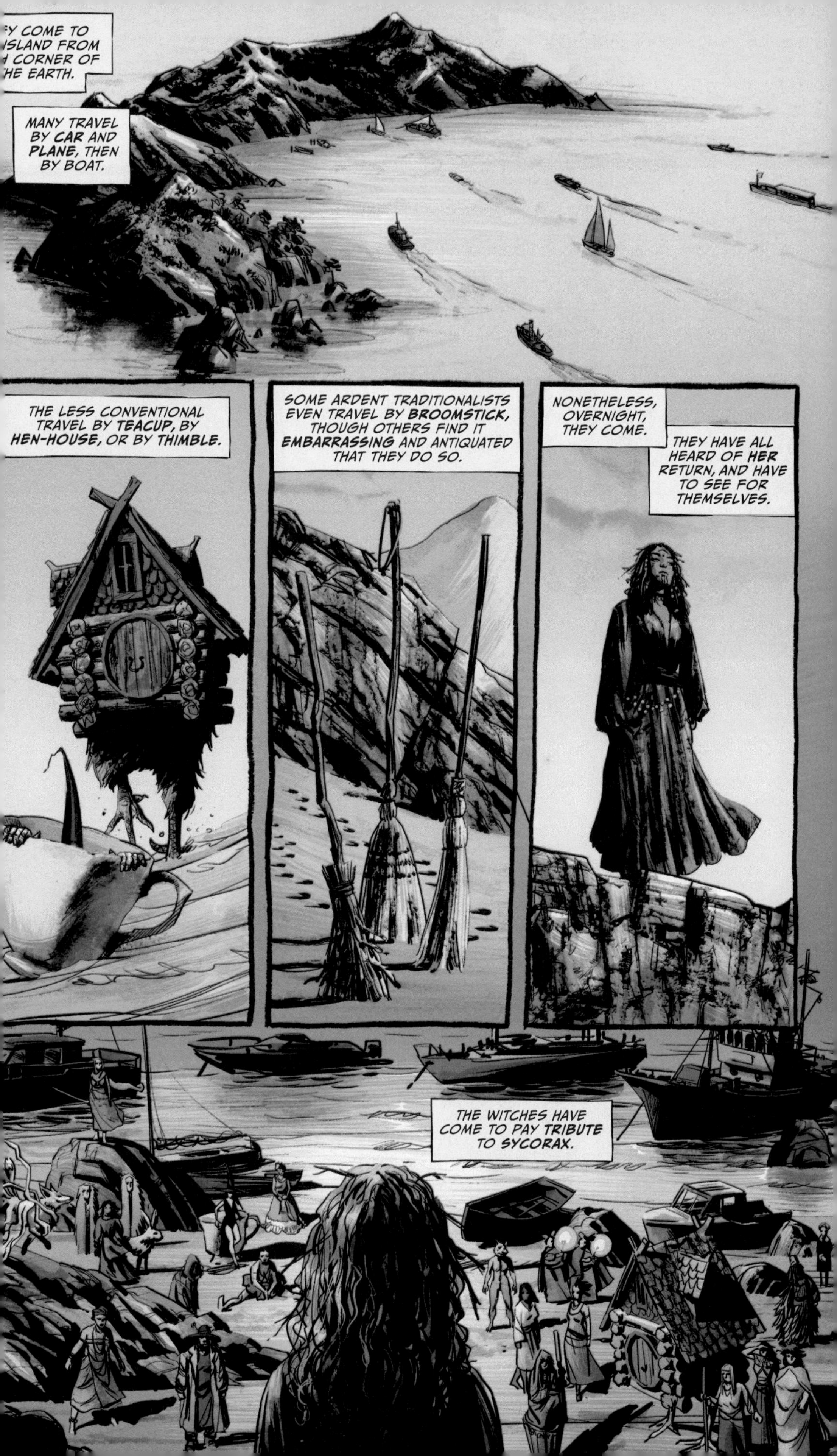
Y COME TO ISLAND FROM H CORNER OF HE EARTH.
MANY TRAVEL BY CAR AND PLANE, THEN BY BOAT.
THE LESS CONVENTIONAL TRAVEL BY TEACUP, BY HEN-HOUSE, OR BY THIMBLE.
SOME ARDENT TRADITIONALISTS EVEN TRAVEL BY BROOMSTICK, THOUGH OTHERS FIND IT EMBARRASSING AND ANTIQUATED THAT THEY DO SO.
NONETHELESS, OVERNIGHT, THEY COME.
THEY HAVE ALL HEARD OF HER RETURN, AND HAVE TO SEE FOR THEMSELVES.
THE WITCHES HAVE COME TO PAY TRIBUTE TO SYCORAX.

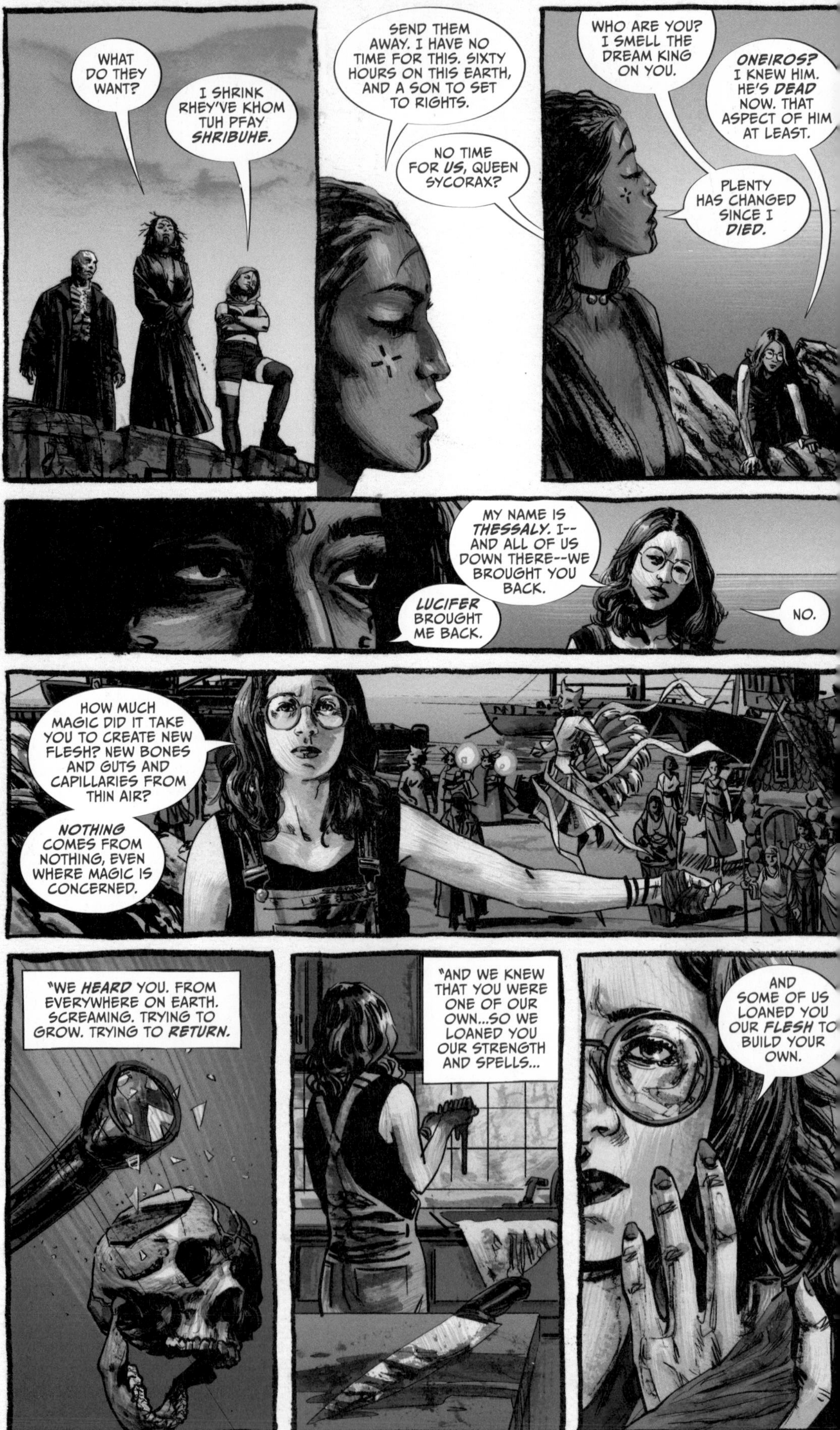

WHAT DO THEY WANT?
I SHRINK RHEY'VE KHOM TUH PFAY SHRIBUHE.
SEND THEM AWAY. I HAVE NO TIME FOR THIS. SIXTY HOURS ON THIS EARTH, AND A SON TO SET TO RIGHTS.
NO TIME FOR US, QUEEN SYCORAX?
WHO ARE YOU? I SMELL THE DREAM KING ON YOU.
ONEIROS? I KNEW HIM. HE'S DEAD NOW. THAT ASPECT OF HIM AT LEAST.
PLENTY HAS CHANGED SINCE I DIED.
MY NAME IS THESSALY. I-- AND ALL OF US DOWN THERE--WE BROUGHT YOU BACK.
LUCIFER BROUGHT ME BACK.
NO.
HOW MUCH MAGIC DID IT TAKE YOU TO CREATE NEW FLESH? NEW BONES AND GUTS AND CAPILLARIES FROM THIN AIR?
NOTHING COMES FROM NOTHING, EVEN WHERE MAGIC IS CONCERNED.
"WE HEARD YOU. FROM EVERYWHERE ON EARTH. SCREAMING. TRYING TO GROW. TRYING TO RETURN.
"AND WE KNEW THAT YOU WERE ONE OF OUR OWN...SO WE LOANED YOU OUR STRENGTH AND SPELLS...
AND SOME OF US LOANED YOU OUR FLESH TO BUILD YOUR OWN.

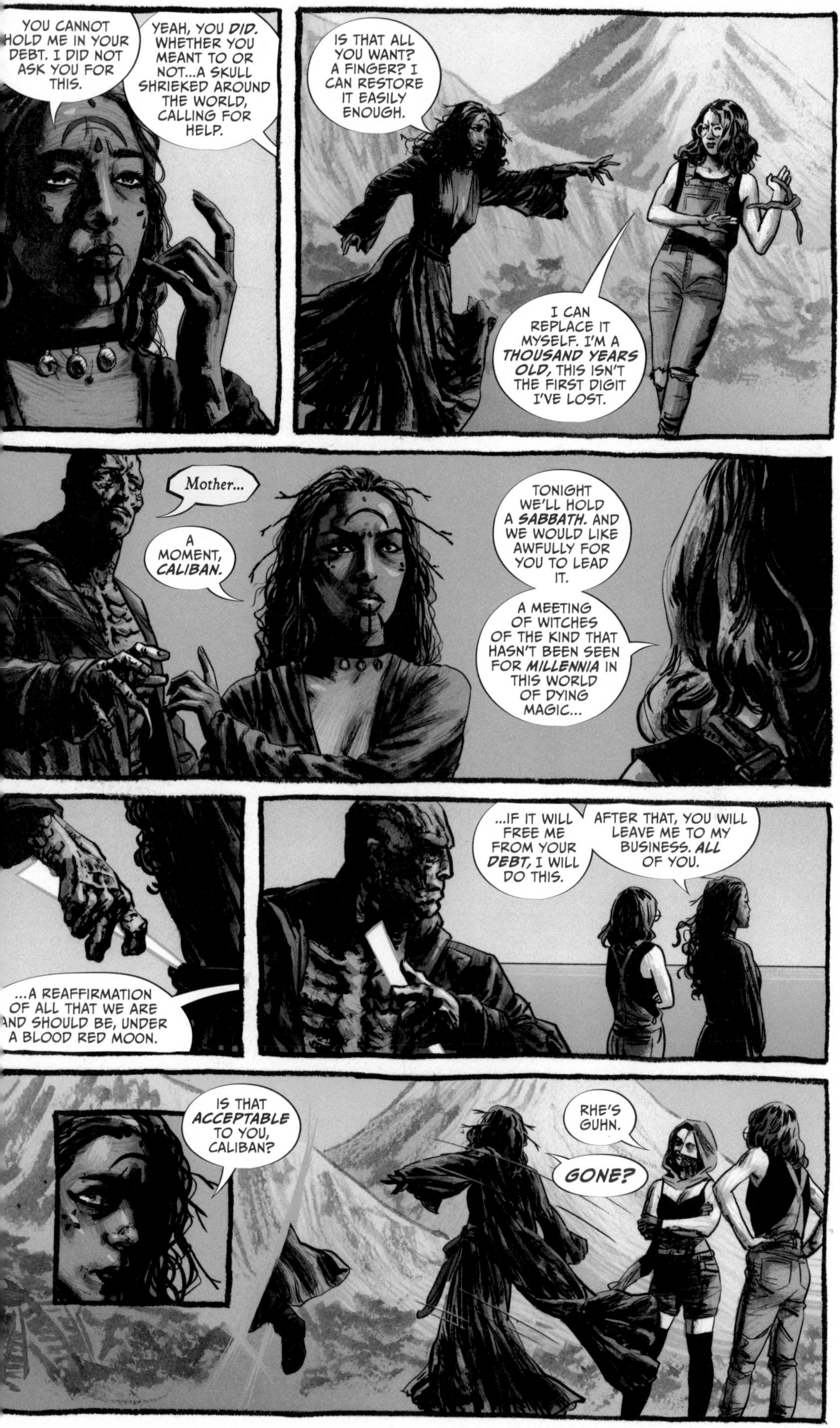

YOU CANNOT HOLD ME IN YOUR DEBT. I DID NOT ASK YOU FOR THIS.
YEAH, YOU *DID.* WHETHER YOU MEANT TO OR NOT...A SKULL SHRIEKED AROUND THE WORLD, CALLING FOR HELP.
IS THAT ALL YOU WANT? A FINGER? I CAN RESTORE IT EASILY ENOUGH.
I CAN REPLACE IT MYSELF. I'M A ***THOUSAND YEARS OLD,*** THIS ISN'T THE FIRST DIGIT I'VE LOST.
Mother...
A MOMENT, ***CALIBAN.***
TONIGHT WE'LL HOLD A ***SABBATH.*** AND WE WOULD LIKE AWFULLY FOR YOU TO LEAD IT.
A MEETING OF WITCHES OF THE KIND THAT HASN'T BEEN SEEN FOR ***MILLENNIA*** IN THIS WORLD OF DYING MAGIC...
...A REAFFIRMATION OF ALL THAT WE ARE AND SHOULD BE, UNDER A BLOOD RED MOON.
...IF IT WILL FREE ME FROM YOUR ***DEBT,*** I WILL DO THIS.
AFTER THAT, YOU WILL LEAVE ME TO MY BUSINESS. ***ALL*** OF YOU.
IS THAT ***ACCEPTABLE*** TO YOU, CALIBAN?
RHE'S GUHN.
GONE?

"GONE WHERE?"

CUH--COSA VUOI?

What do I *want*? I want *truth*, Padre.

It is said that *angels* were seen hovering above these spires only twelve hours ago.

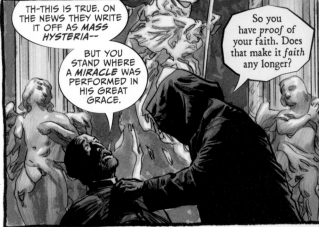

TH-THIS IS TRUE. ON THE NEWS THEY WRITE IT OFF AS *MASS HYSTERIA*--

BUT YOU STAND WHERE A *MIRACLE* WAS PERFORMED IN HIS GREAT GRACE.

So you have *proof* of your faith. Does that make it *faith* any longer?

The schism between knowing and believing has been joined. Does your worship not ring all the more *hollow* for it?

YOU ARE IN GREAT PAIN, *FIGLIO.*

My mother taught me when I was a child to worship *Setebos.* He who was in the moon.

And now I have learned that she *invented* him for me. She says she would not have me worship any god that was real. For those ones are *cruel.*

THERE IS ONLY *ONE* GOD. AND HE IS NOT CRUEL.

No, Padre?

And yet he gave me this face.

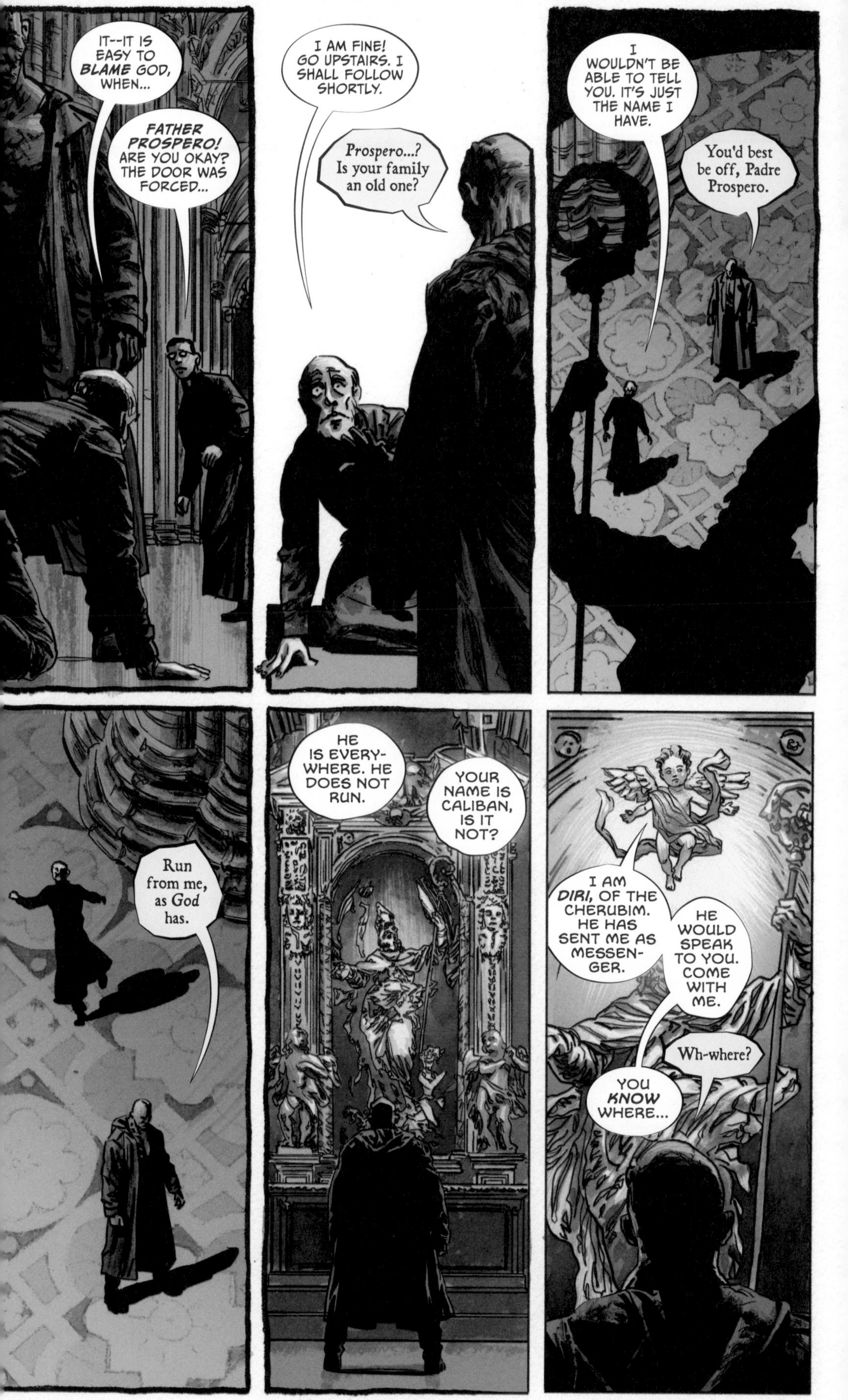
IT--IT IS EASY TO *BLAME* GOD, WHEN...
FATHER PROSPERO! ARE YOU OKAY? THE DOOR WAS FORCED...
I AM FINE! GO UPSTAIRS. I SHALL FOLLOW SHORTLY.
Prospero...? Is your family an old one?
I WOULDN'T BE ABLE TO TELL YOU. IT'S JUST THE NAME I HAVE.
You'd best be off, Padre Prospero.
Run from me, as *God* has.
HE IS EVERY-WHERE. HE DOES NOT RUN.
YOUR NAME IS CALIBAN, IS IT NOT?
I AM *DIRI*, OF THE CHERUBIM. HE HAS SENT ME AS MESSEN-GER.
HE WOULD SPEAK TO YOU. COME WITH ME.
Wh-where?
YOU *KNOW* WHERE...

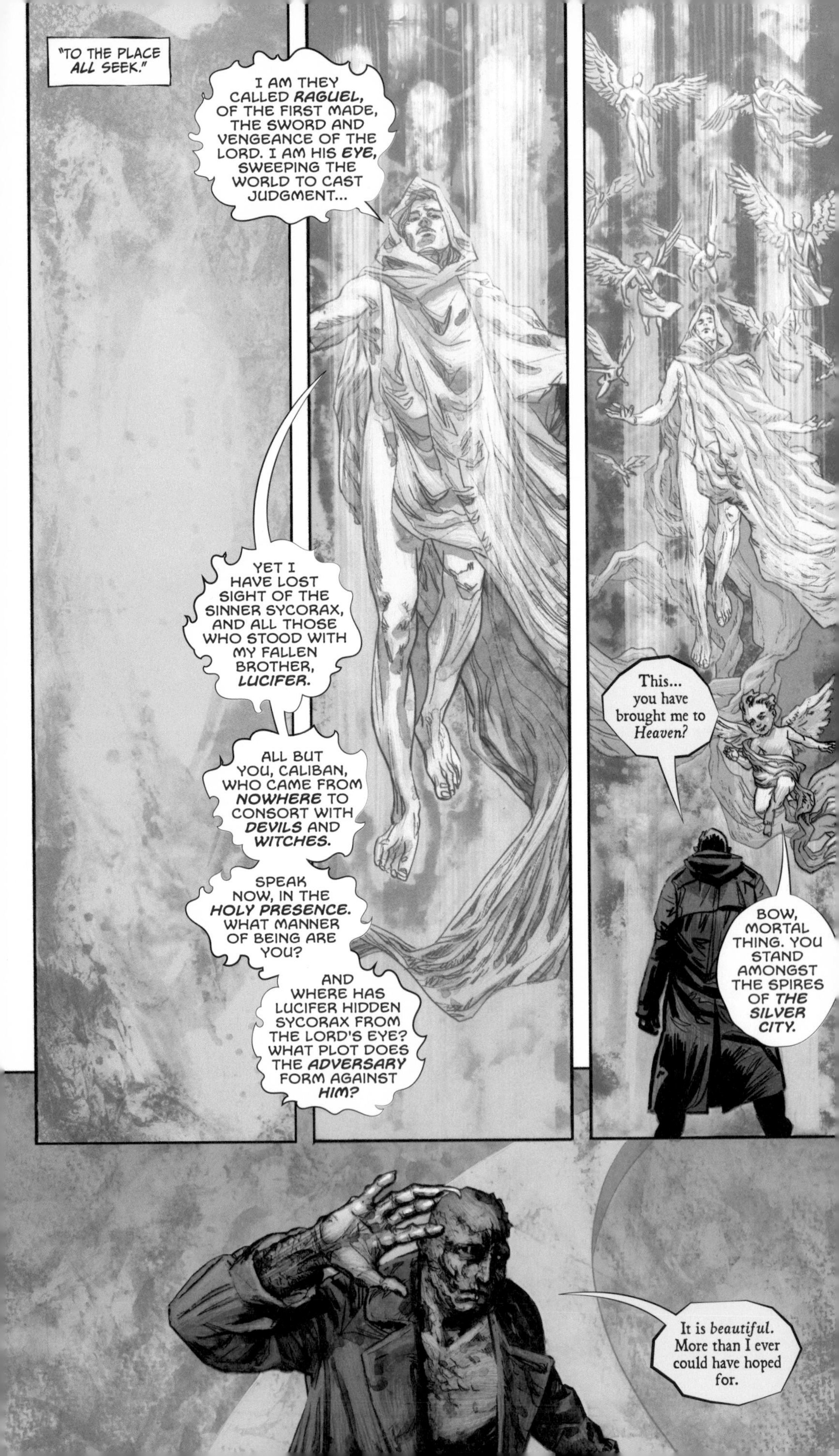
"TO THE PLACE ALL SEEK."
I AM THEY CALLED RAGUEL, OF THE FIRST MADE, THE SWORD AND VENGEANCE OF THE LORD. I AM HIS EYE, SWEEPING THE WORLD TO CAST JUDGMENT...
YET I HAVE LOST SIGHT OF THE SINNER SYCORAX, AND ALL THOSE WHO STOOD WITH MY FALLEN BROTHER, LUCIFER.
ALL BUT YOU, CALIBAN, WHO CAME FROM NOWHERE TO CONSORT WITH DEVILS AND WITCHES.
SPEAK NOW, IN THE HOLY PRESENCE. WHAT MANNER OF BEING ARE YOU?
AND WHERE HAS LUCIFER HIDDEN SYCORAX FROM THE LORD'S EYE? WHAT PLOT DOES THE ADVERSARY FORM AGAINST HIM?
This... you have brought me to Heaven?
BOW, MORTAL THING. YOU STAND AMONGST THE SPIRES OF THE SILVER CITY.
It is beautiful. More than I ever could have hoped for.

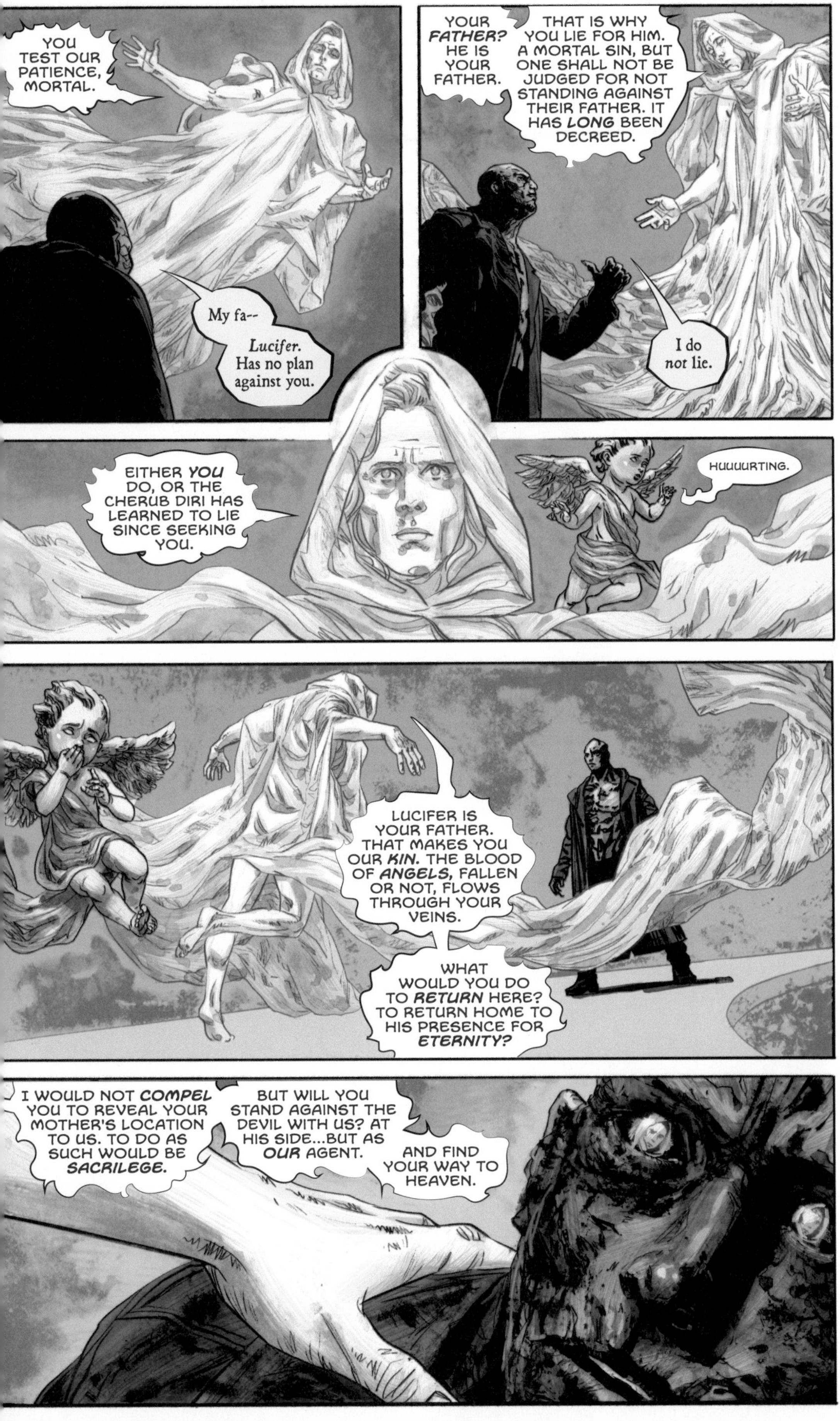

YOU TEST OUR PATIENCE, MORTAL.
My fa-- *Lucifer.* Has no plan against you.
YOUR *FATHER?* HE IS YOUR FATHER.
THAT IS WHY YOU LIE FOR HIM. A MORTAL SIN, BUT ONE SHALL NOT BE JUDGED FOR NOT STANDING AGAINST THEIR FATHER. IT HAS *LONG* BEEN DECREED.
I do *not* lie.
EITHER *YOU* DO, OR THE CHERUB DIRI HAS LEARNED TO LIE SINCE SEEKING YOU.
HUUUURTING.
LUCIFER IS YOUR FATHER. THAT MAKES YOU OUR *KIN.* THE BLOOD OF *ANGELS,* FALLEN OR NOT, FLOWS THROUGH YOUR VEINS.
WHAT WOULD YOU DO TO *RETURN* HERE? TO RETURN HOME TO HIS PRESENCE FOR *ETERNITY?*
I WOULD NOT *COMPEL* YOU TO REVEAL YOUR MOTHER'S LOCATION TO US. TO DO AS SUCH WOULD BE *SACRILEGE.*
BUT WILL YOU STAND AGAINST THE DEVIL WITH US? AT HIS SIDE...BUT AS *OUR* AGENT.
AND FIND YOUR WAY TO HEAVEN.

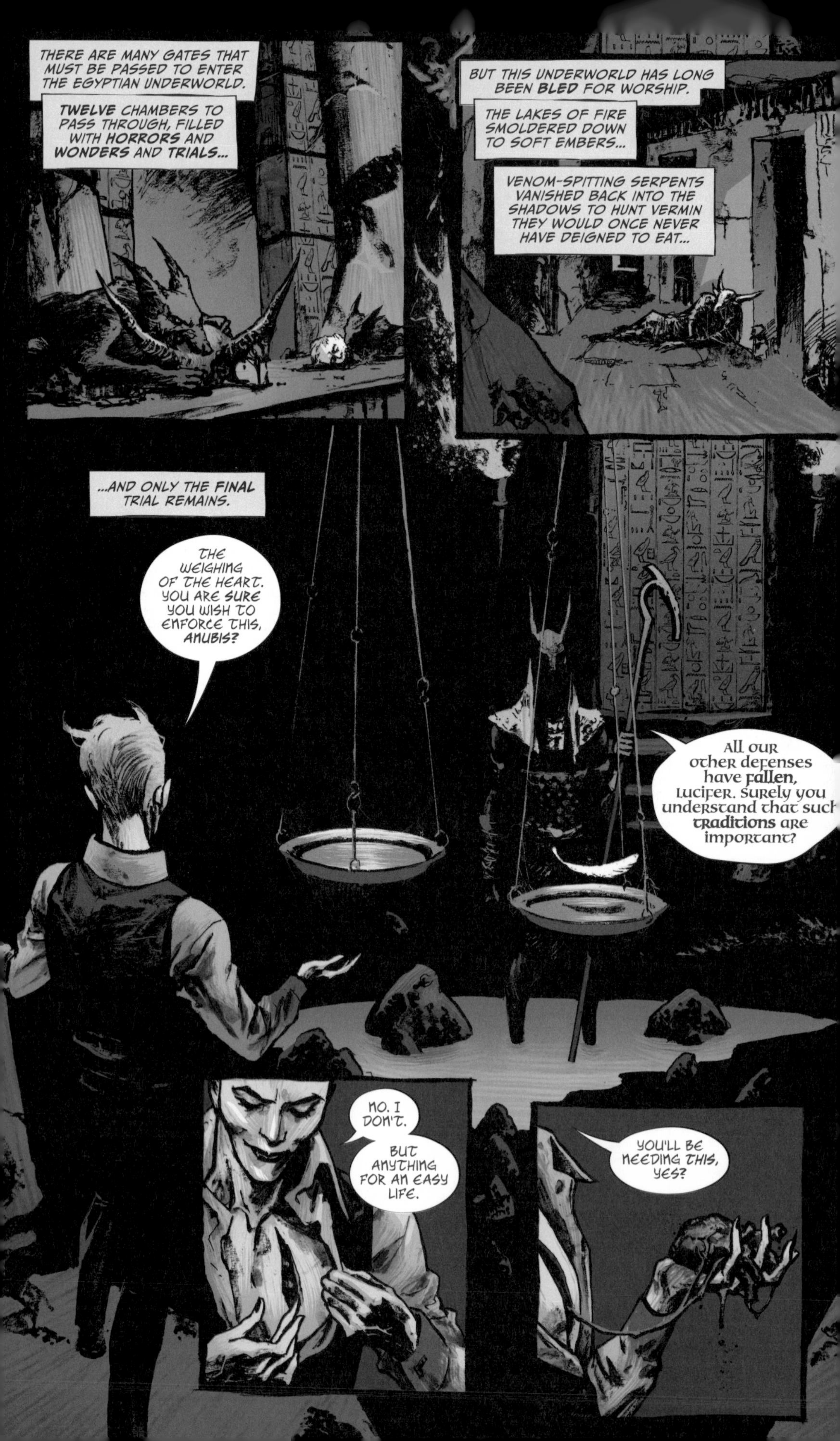
THERE ARE MANY GATES THAT MUST BE PASSED TO ENTER THE EGYPTIAN UNDERWORLD.
TWELVE CHAMBERS TO PASS THROUGH, FILLED WITH HORRORS AND WONDERS AND TRIALS...
BUT THIS UNDERWORLD HAS LONG BEEN BLED FOR WORSHIP.
THE LAKES OF FIRE SMOLDERED DOWN TO SOFT EMBERS...
VENOM-SPITTING SERPENTS VANISHED BACK INTO THE SHADOWS TO HUNT VERMIN THEY WOULD ONCE NEVER HAVE DEIGNED TO EAT...
...AND ONLY THE FINAL TRIAL REMAINS.
THE WEIGHING OF THE HEART. YOU ARE SURE YOU WISH TO ENFORCE THIS, ANUBIS?
All our other defenses have fallen, Lucifer. Surely you understand that such traditions are important?
NO. I DON'T.
BUT ANYTHING FOR AN EASY LIFE.
YOU'LL BE NEEDING THIS, YES?

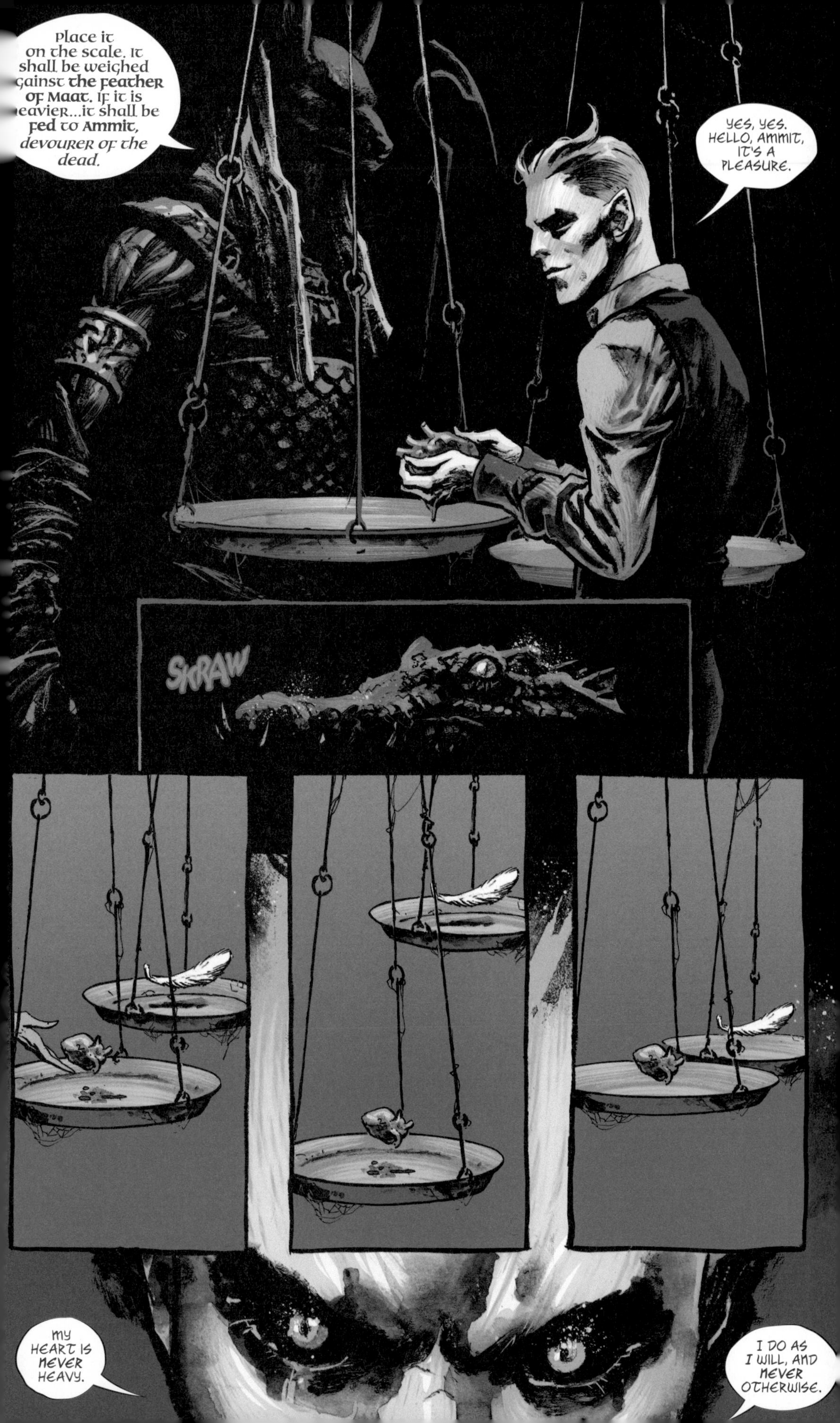
Place it on the scale. It shall be weighed gainst the feather of Maat. If it is eavier...it shall be fed to Ammit, devourer of the dead.
YES, YES. HELLO, AMMIT, IT'S A PLEASURE.
SKRAW
MY HEART IS NEVER HEAVY.
I DO AS I WILL, AND NEVER OTHERWISE.

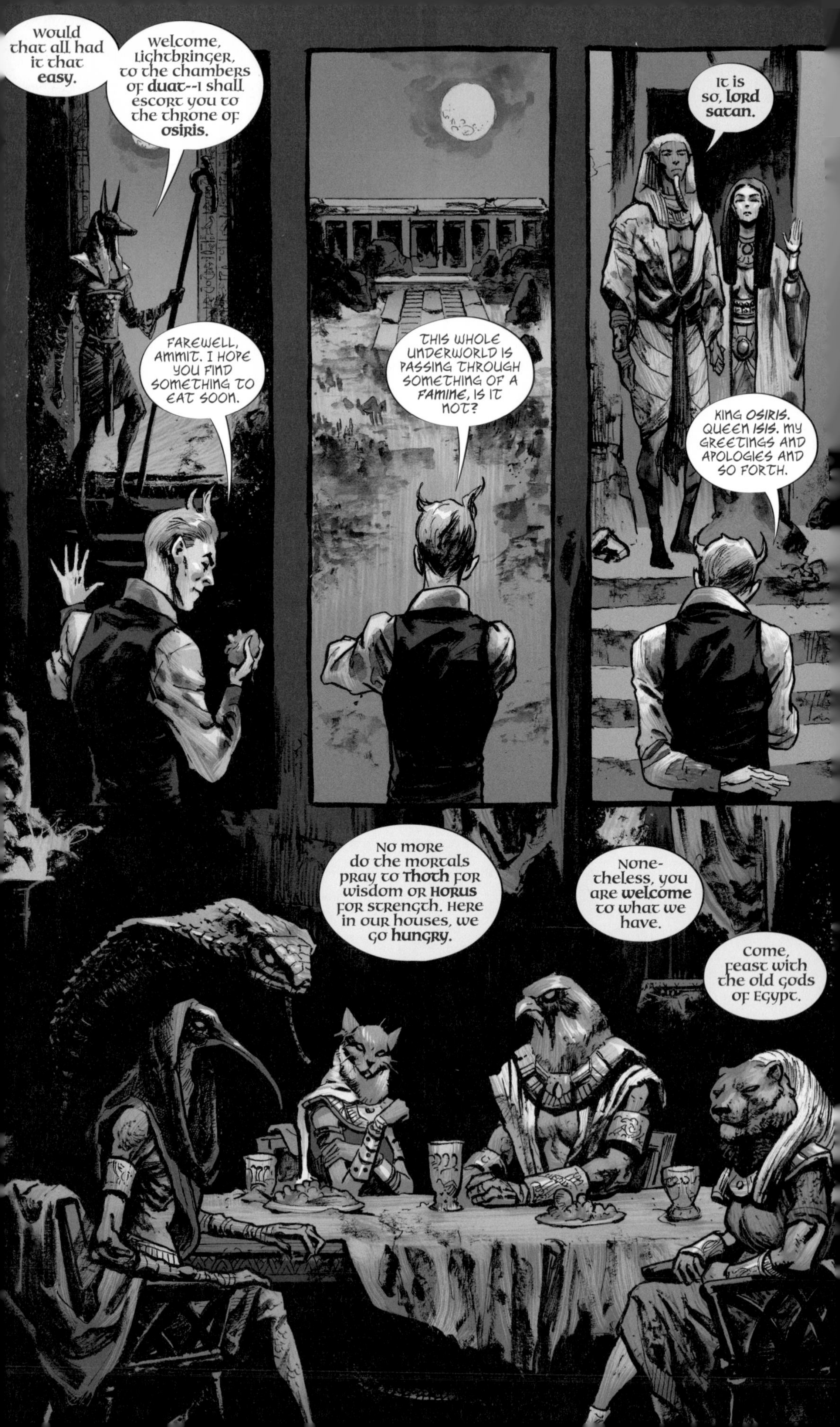
Would that all had it that easy.
Welcome, Lightbringer, to the chambers of duat--I shall escort you to the throne of osiris.
FAREWELL, AMMIT. I HOPE YOU FIND SOMETHING TO EAT SOON.
THIS WHOLE UNDERWORLD IS PASSING THROUGH SOMETHING OF A FAMINE, IS IT NOT?
It is so, lord satan.
KING OSIRIS. QUEEN ISIS. MY GREETINGS AND APOLOGIES AND SO FORTH.
No more do the mortals pray to Thoth for wisdom or Horus for strength. Here in our houses, we go hungry.
None-theless, you are welcome to what we have.
Come, feast with the old gods of Egypt.

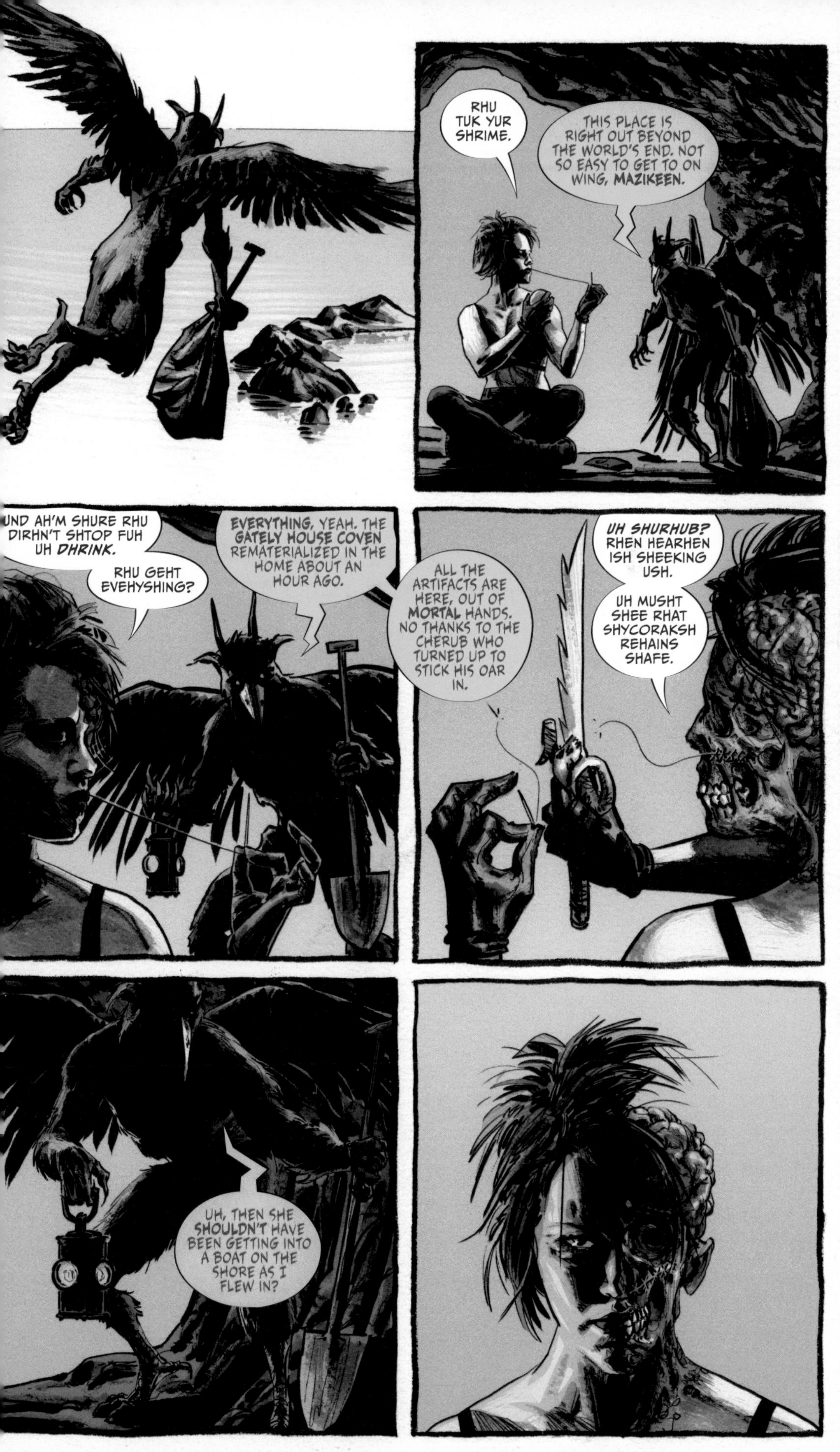
RHU TUK YUR SHRIME.
THIS PLACE IS RIGHT OUT BEYOND THE WORLD'S END. NOT SO EASY TO GET TO ON WING, MAZIKEEN.
UND AH'M SHURE RHU DIRHN'T SHTOP FUH UH DHRINK.
RHU GEHT EVEHYSHING?
EVERYTHING, YEAH. THE GATELY HOUSE COVEN REMATERIALIZED IN THE HOME ABOUT AN HOUR AGO.
ALL THE ARTIFACTS ARE HERE, OUT OF MORTAL HANDS. NO THANKS TO THE CHERUB WHO TURNED UP TO STICK HIS OAR IN.
UH SHURHUB? RHEN HEARHEN ISH SHEEKING USH.
UH MUSHT SHEE RHAT SHYCORAKSH REHAINS SHAFE.
UH, THEN SHE SHOULDN'T HAVE BEEN GETTING INTO A BOAT ON THE SHORE AS I FLEW IN?

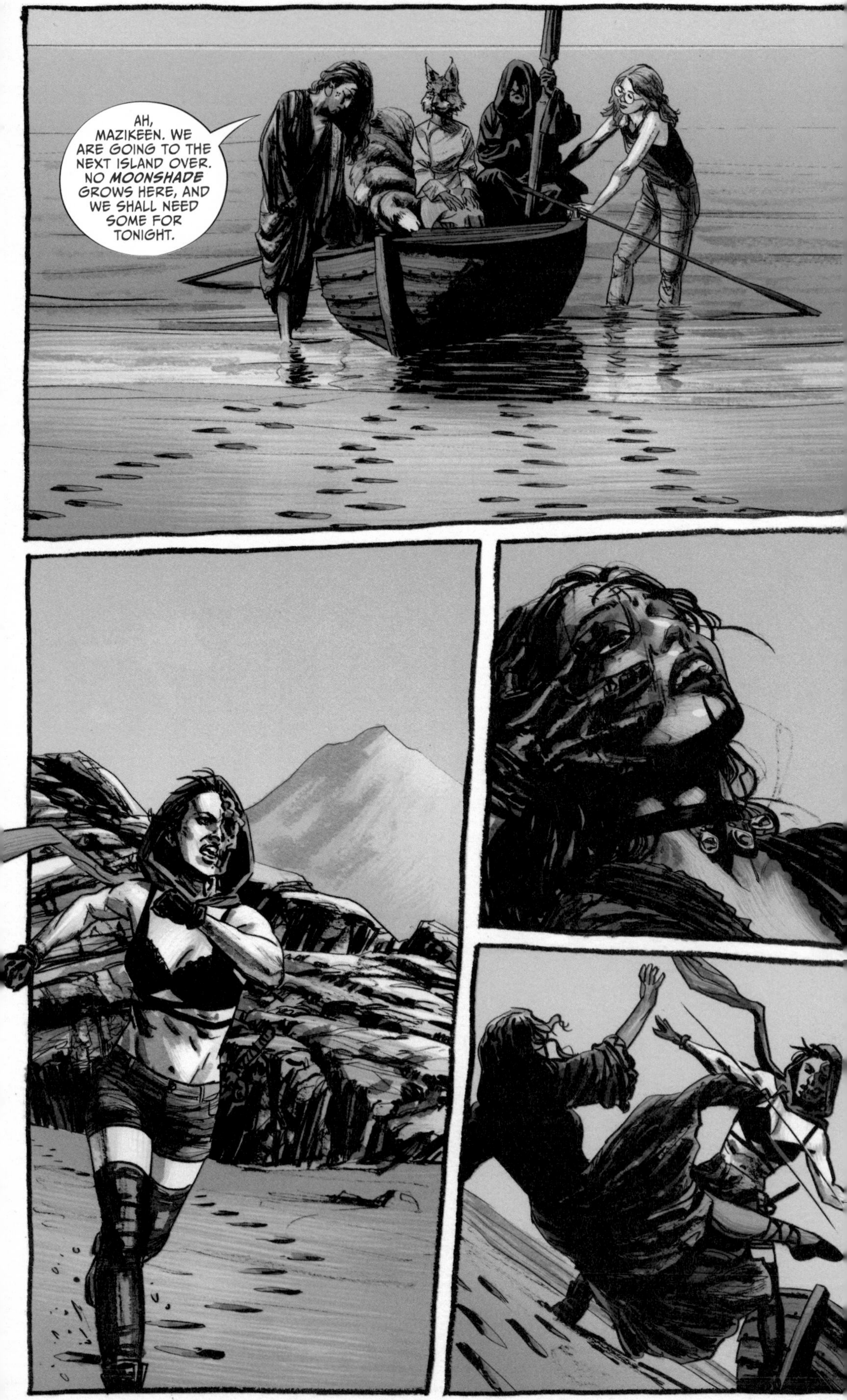
AH, MAZIKEEN. WE ARE GOING TO THE NEXT ISLAND OVER. NO MOONSHADE GROWS HERE, AND WE SHALL NEED SOME FOR TONIGHT.

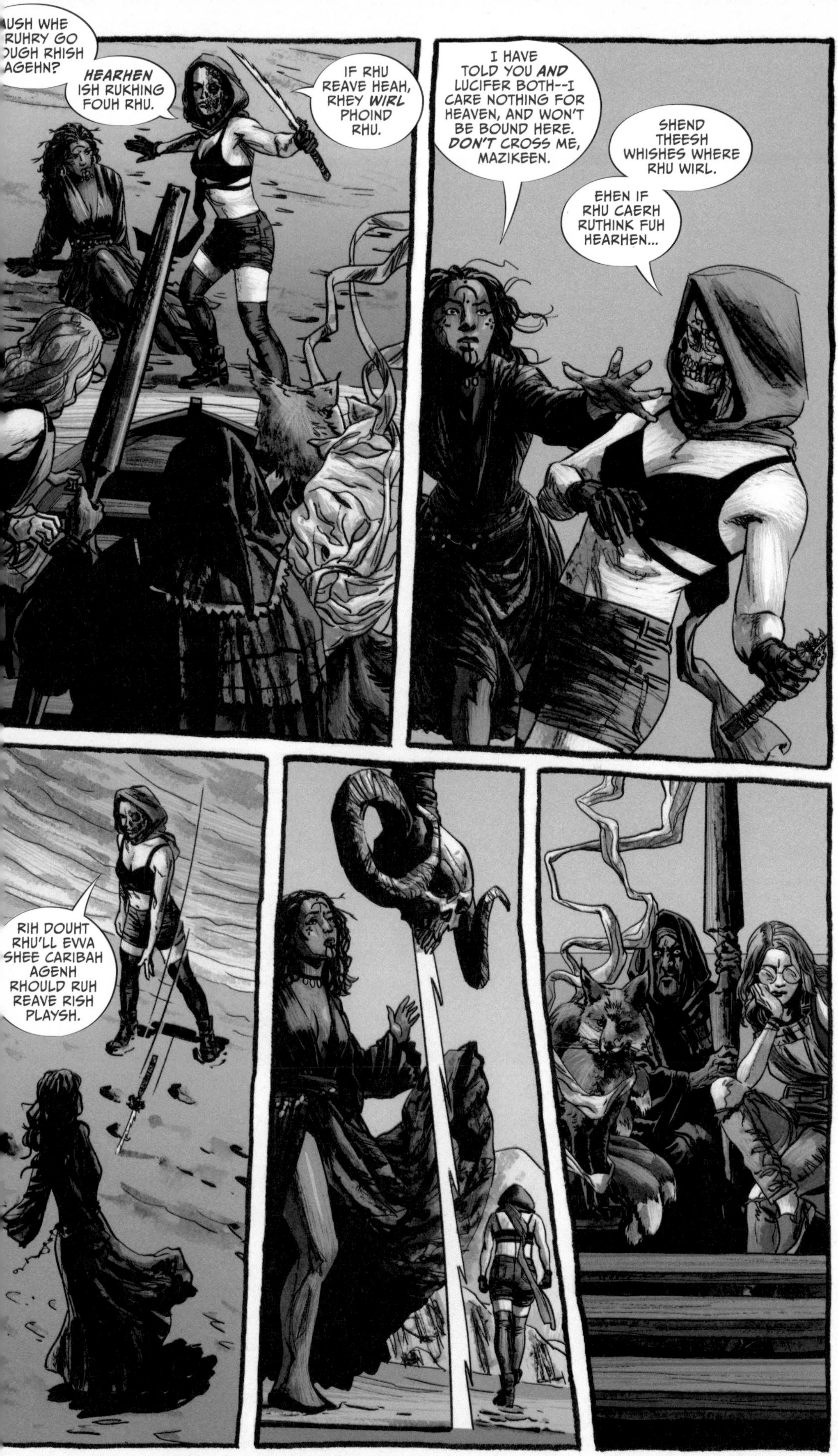

AUSH WHE RUHRY GO OUGH RHISH AGEHN?
HEARHEN ISH RUKHING FOUH RHU.
IF RHU REAVE HEAH, RHEY WIRL PHOIND RHU.
I HAVE TOLD YOU AND LUCIFER BOTH--I CARE NOTHING FOR HEAVEN, AND WON'T BE BOUND HERE. DON'T CROSS ME, MAZIKEEN.
SHEND THEESH WHISHES WHERE RHU WIRL.
EHEN IF RHU CAERH RUTHINK FUH HEARHEN...
RIH DOUHT RHU'LL EVVA SHEE CARIBAH AGENH RHOULD RUH REAVE RISH PLAYSH.

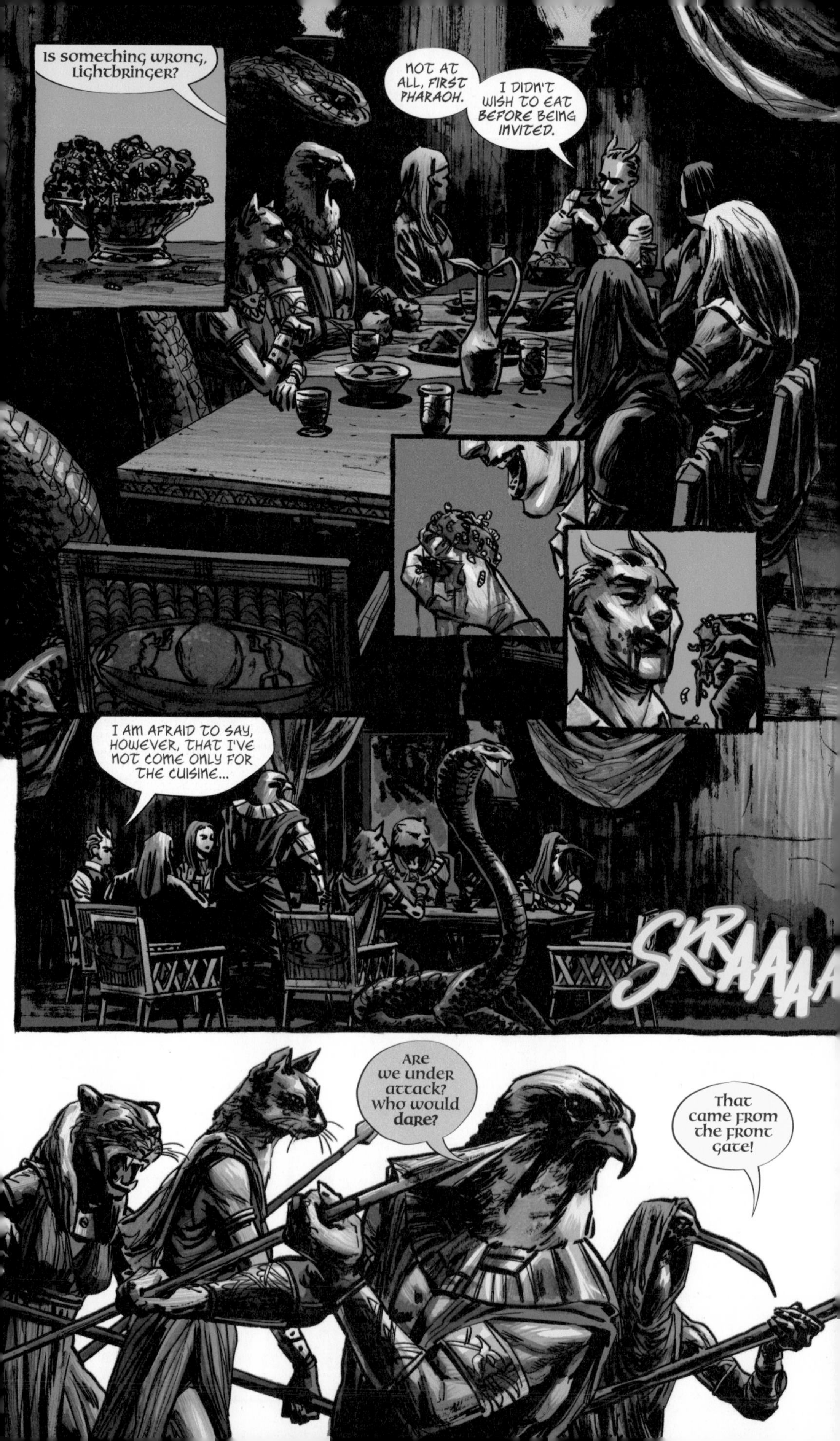

Is something wrong, Lightbringer?
Not at all, First Pharaoh.
I didn't wish to eat before being invited.
I am afraid to say, however, that I've not come only for the cuisine...
SKRAAAA
Are we under attack? Who would dare?
That came from the front gate!

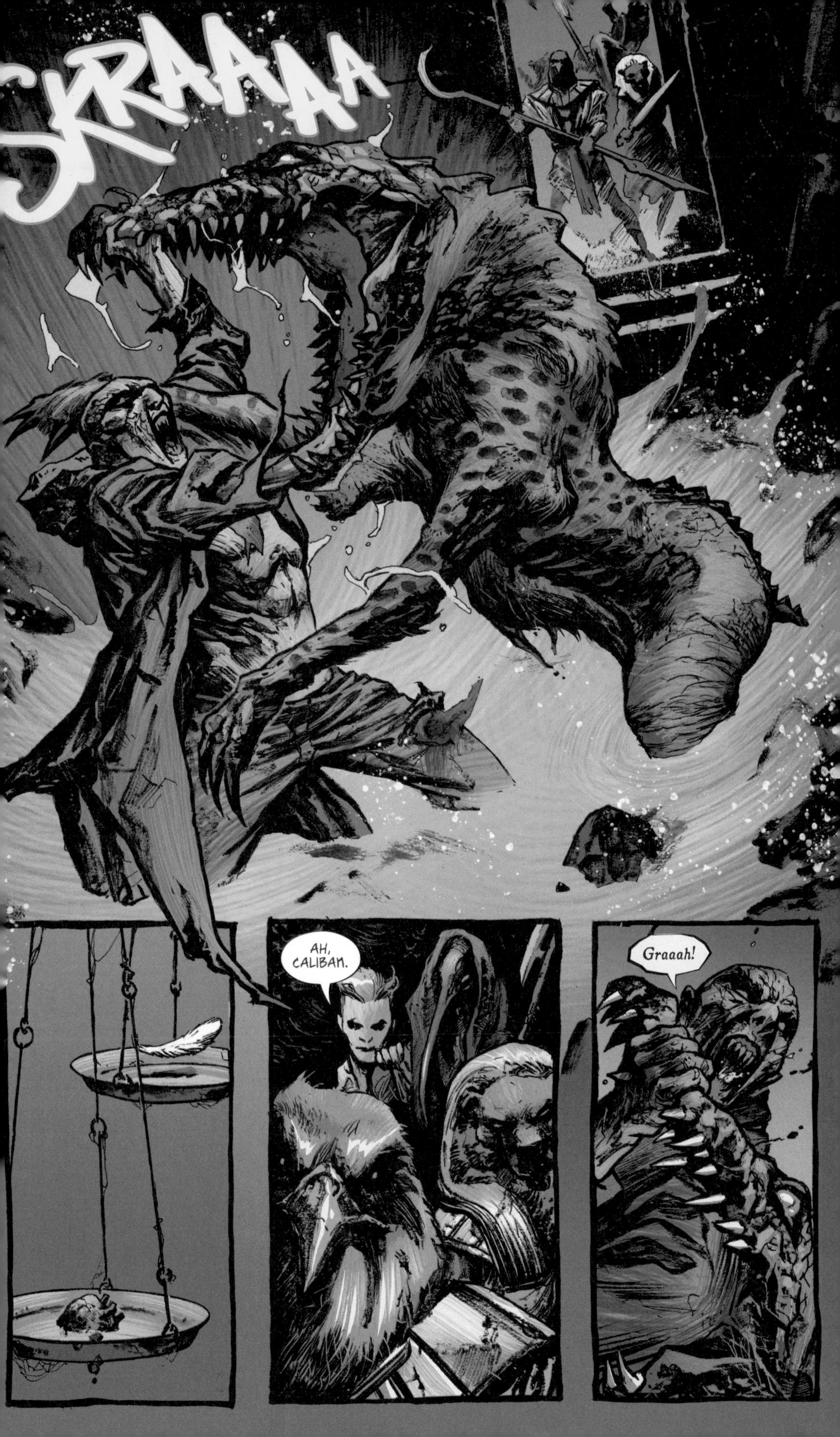
SKRAAAA
AH, CALIBAN.
Graaah!

YOU SHALL PAY **GRAVELY** FOR THAT, STRANGER.

THIS IS **NOT** A STRANGER. DO ALL CALM DOWN.

THIS IS MY SON. CALIBAN.

HE OF THE **HEAVY HEART,** APPARENTLY.

HEAVY WITH *WHAT,* I WONDER?

GRIEF? SELF-PITY?

TREACHERY?

I wished only to speak with you, Father.

But this *beast* tried to eat me.

WELL, SINCE HE'S ALREADY HERE...

YOU WOULDN'T MIND IF CALIBAN JOINED US FOR OUR FEAST--WOULD YOU, LADY ISIS?

N-not at all, LORD LUCIFER.

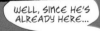

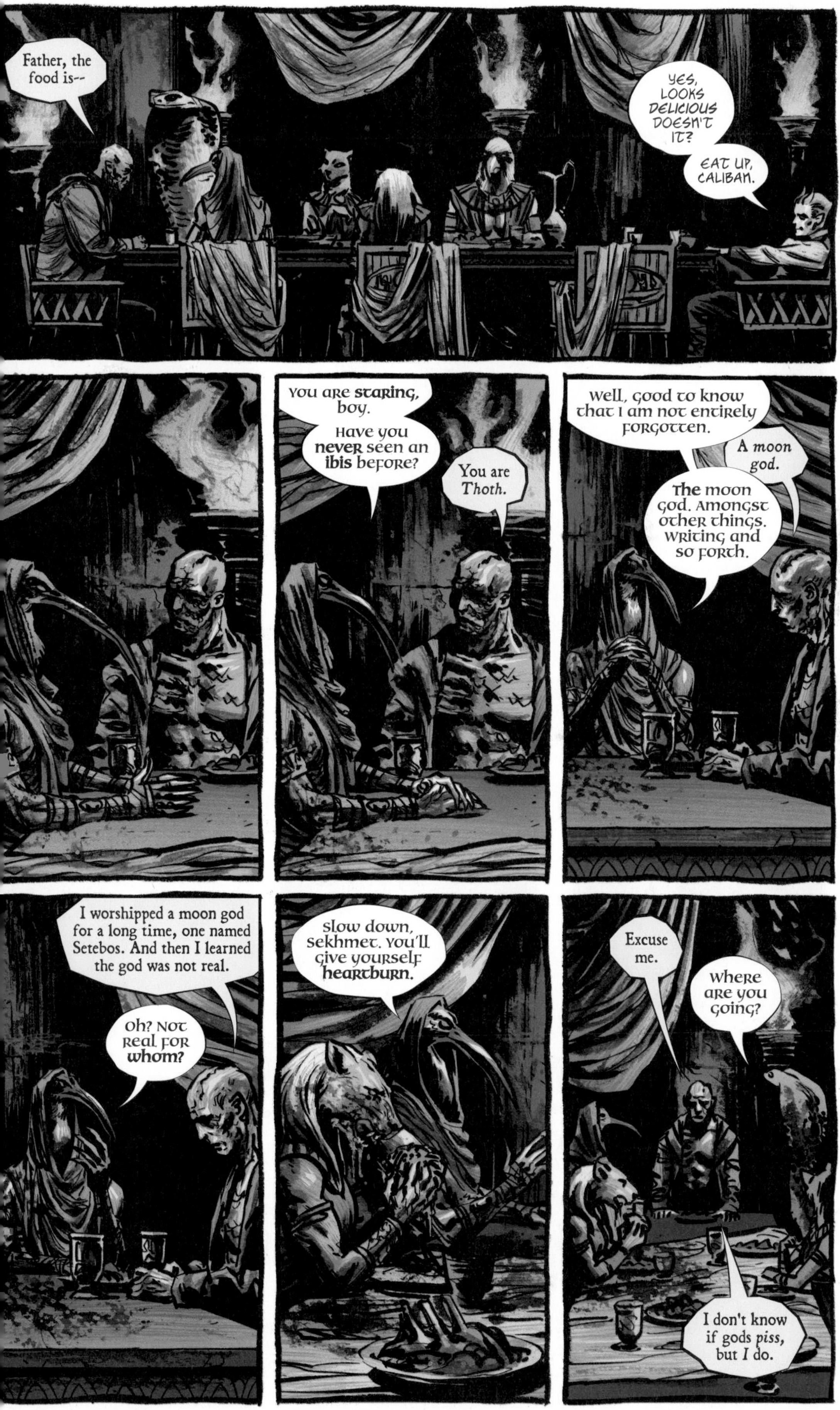
Father, the food is--
Yes, looks delicious doesn't it?
Eat up, Caliban.
You are **staring**, boy.
Have you **never** seen an **ibis** before?
You are *Thoth.*
Well, good to know that I am not entirely forgotten.
A *moon* god.
The moon god. Amongst other things. Writing and so forth.
I worshipped a moon god for a long time, one named Setebos. And then I learned the god was not real.
Oh? Not real for **whom?**
Slow down, Sekhmet. You'll give yourself **heartburn.**
Excuse me.
Where are you going?
I don't know if gods *piss,* but I do.

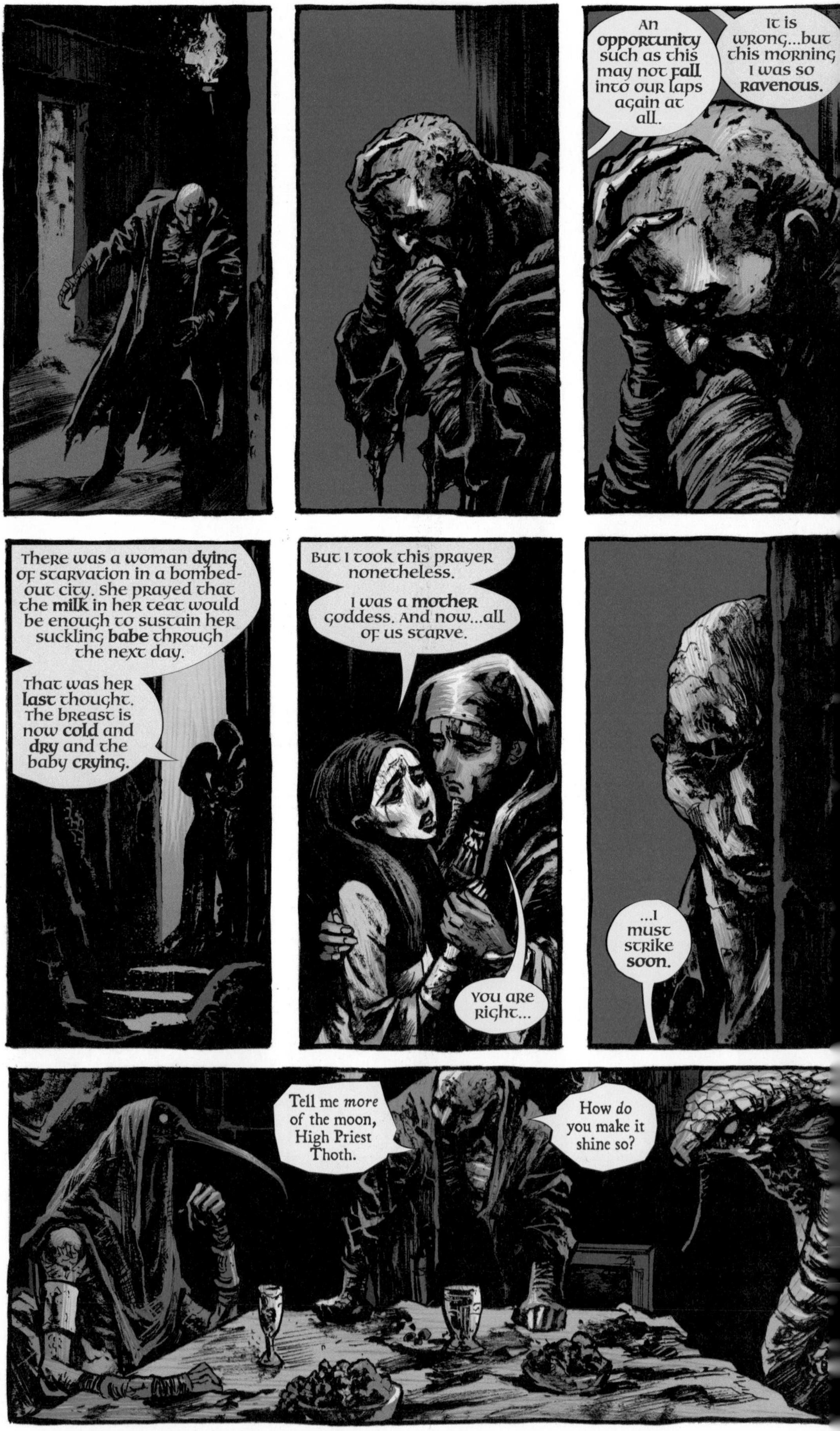
An opportunity such as this may not fall into our laps again at all.
It is wrong...but this morning I was so ravenous.
There was a woman dying of starvation in a bombed-out city. She prayed that the milk in her teat would be enough to sustain her suckling babe through the next day.
That was her last thought. The breast is now cold and dry and the baby crying.
But I took this prayer nonetheless.
I was a mother goddess. And now...all of us starve.
You are right...
...I must strike soon.
Tell me more of the moon, High Priest Thoth.
How do you make it shine so?

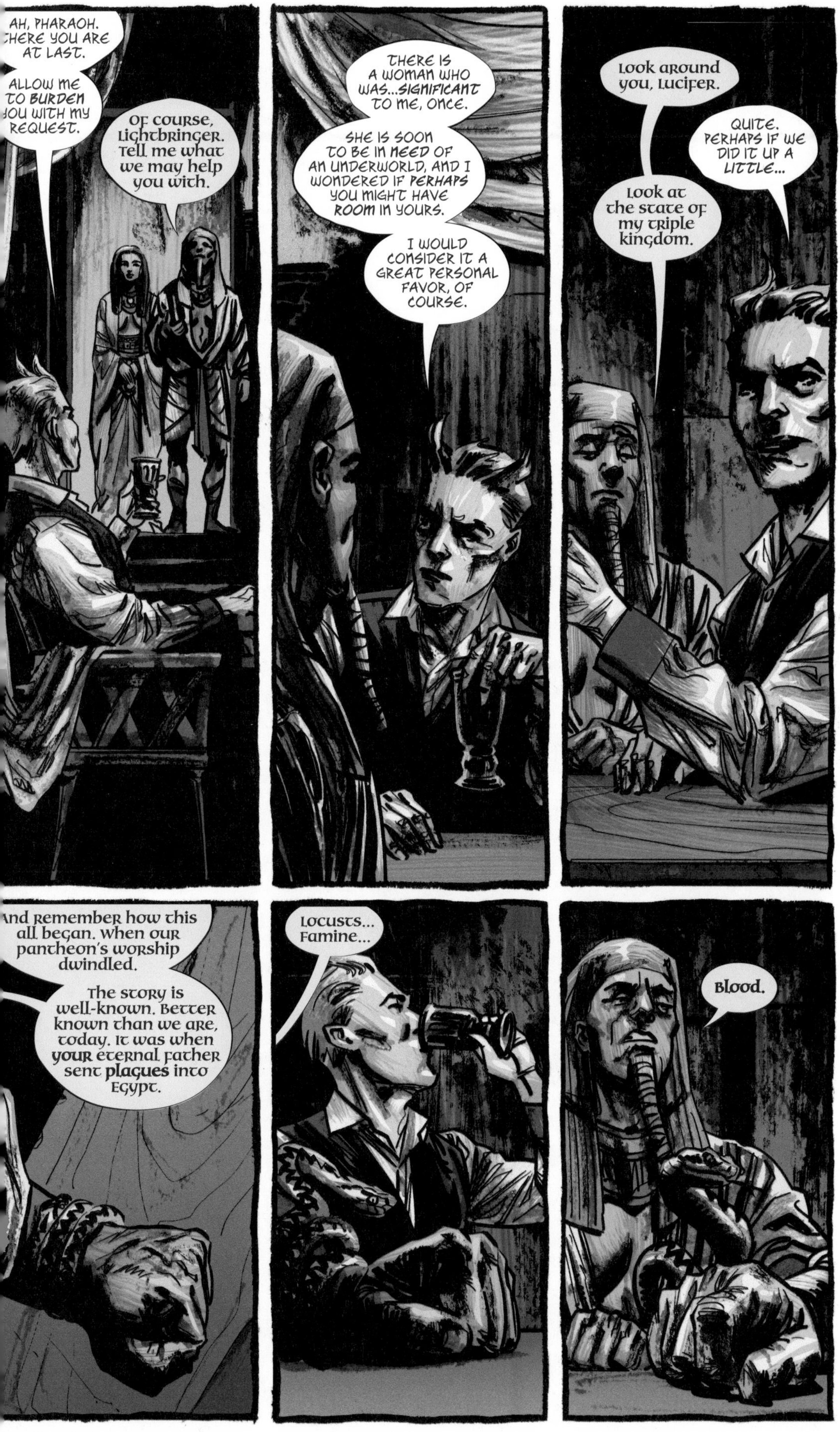
AH, PHARAOH. THERE YOU ARE AT LAST.
ALLOW ME TO BURDEN YOU WITH MY REQUEST.
Of course, Lightbringer. Tell me what we may help you with.
THERE IS A WOMAN WHO WAS...SIGNIFICANT TO ME, ONCE.
SHE IS SOON TO BE IN NEED OF AN UNDERWORLD, AND I WONDERED IF PERHAPS YOU MIGHT HAVE ROOM IN YOURS.
I WOULD CONSIDER IT A GREAT PERSONAL FAVOR, OF COURSE.
Look around you, Lucifer.
Look at the state of my triple kingdom.
QUITE. PERHAPS IF WE DID IT UP A LITTLE...
And remember how this all began. When our pantheon's worship dwindled.
The story is well-known. Better known than we are, today. It was when your eternal father sent plagues into Egypt.
Locusts... Famine...
Blood.

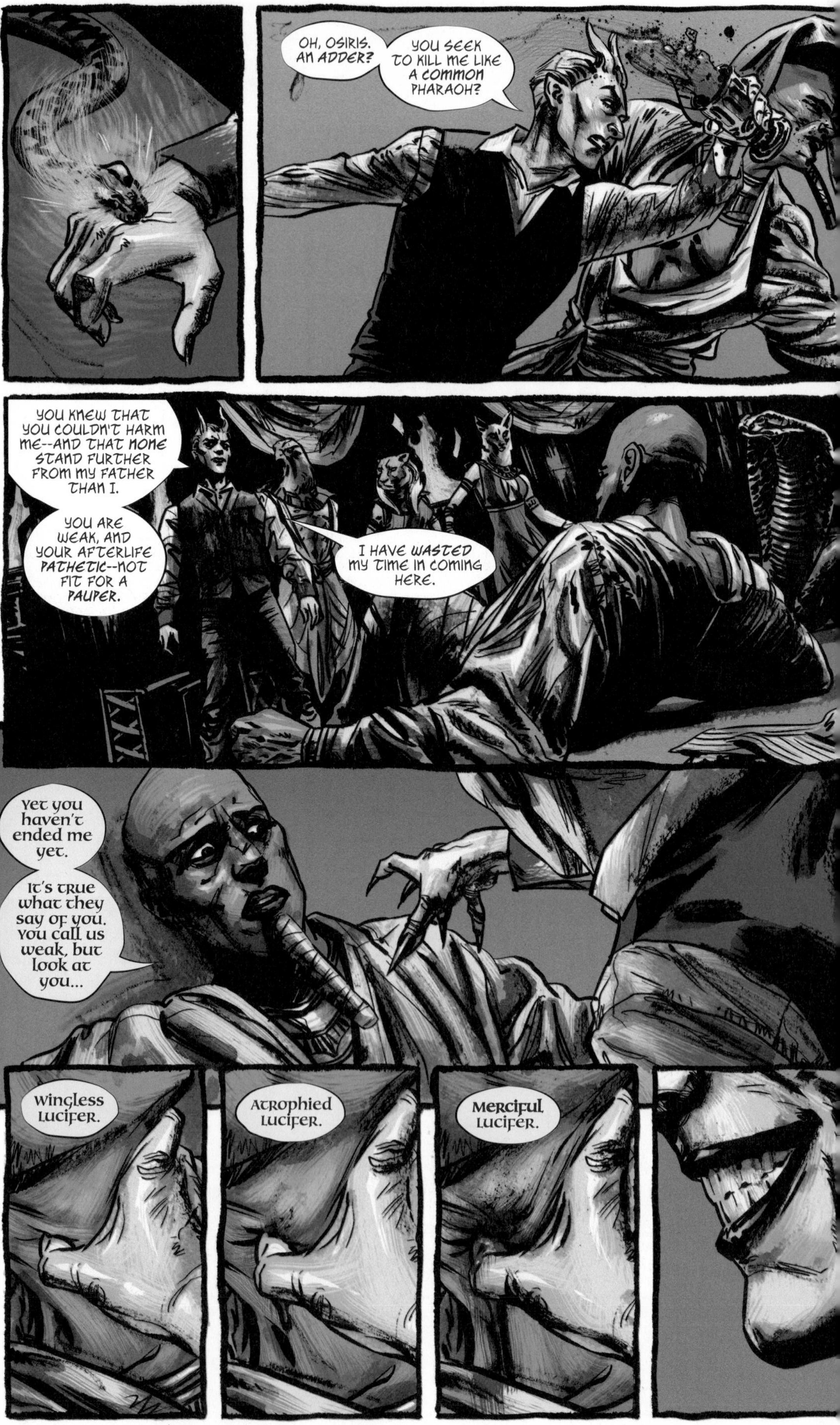
OH, OSIRIS. AN ADDER?
YOU SEEK TO KILL ME LIKE A COMMON PHARAOH?
YOU KNEW THAT YOU COULDN'T HARM ME--AND THAT NONE STAND FURTHER FROM MY FATHER THAN I.
YOU ARE WEAK, AND YOUR AFTERLIFE PATHETIC--NOT FIT FOR A PAUPER.
I HAVE WASTED MY TIME IN COMING HERE.
Yet you haven't ended me yet.
It's true what they say of you. You call us weak, but look at you...
Wingless Lucifer.
Atrophied Lucifer.
Merciful Lucifer.

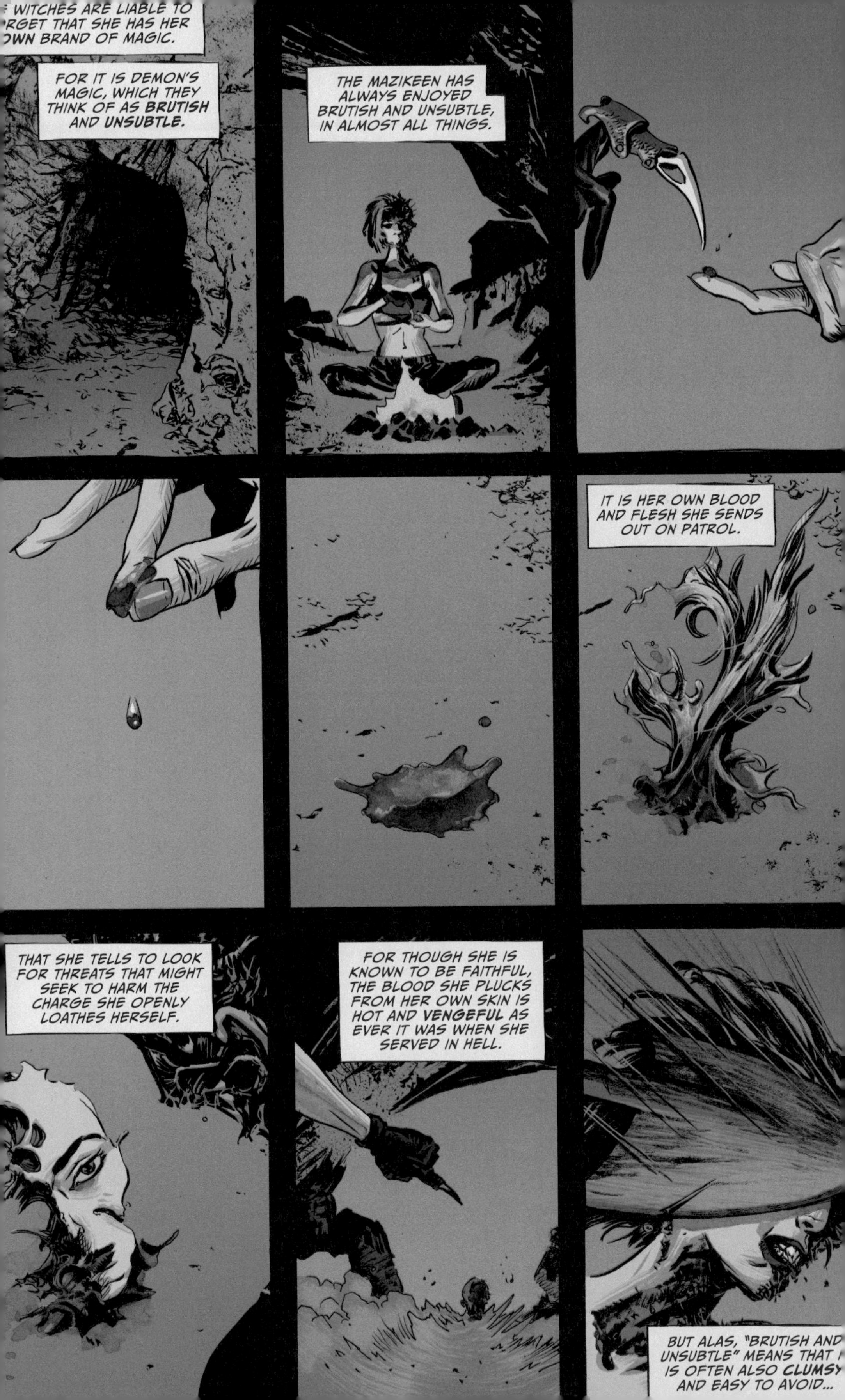

F WITCHES ARE LIABLE TO
RGET THAT SHE HAS HER
OWN BRAND OF MAGIC.
FOR IT IS DEMON'S MAGIC, WHICH THEY THINK OF AS BRUTISH AND UNSUBTLE.
THE MAZIKEEN HAS ALWAYS ENJOYED BRUTISH AND UNSUBTLE, IN ALMOST ALL THINGS.
IT IS HER OWN BLOOD AND FLESH SHE SENDS OUT ON PATROL.
THAT SHE TELLS TO LOOK FOR THREATS THAT MIGHT SEEK TO HARM THE CHARGE SHE OPENLY LOATHES HERSELF.
FOR THOUGH SHE IS KNOWN TO BE FAITHFUL, THE BLOOD SHE PLUCKS FROM HER OWN SKIN IS HOT AND VENGEFUL AS EVER IT WAS WHEN SHE SERVED IN HELL.
BUT ALAS, "BRUTISH AND UNSUBTLE" MEANS THAT I IS OFTEN ALSO CLUMSY AND EASY TO AVOID...

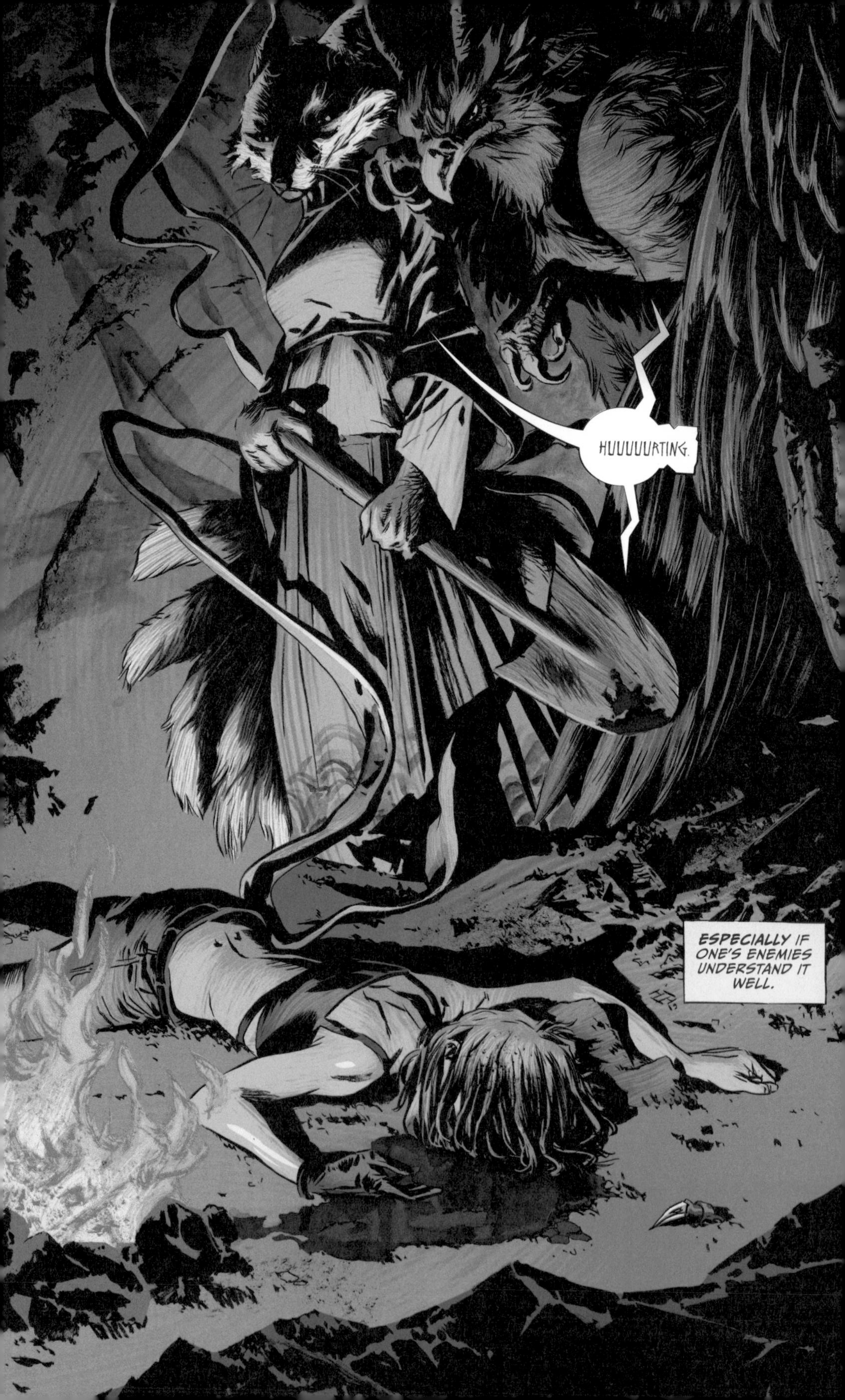
HUUUUURTING.
ESPECIALLY IF ONE'S ENEMIES UNDERSTAND IT WELL.

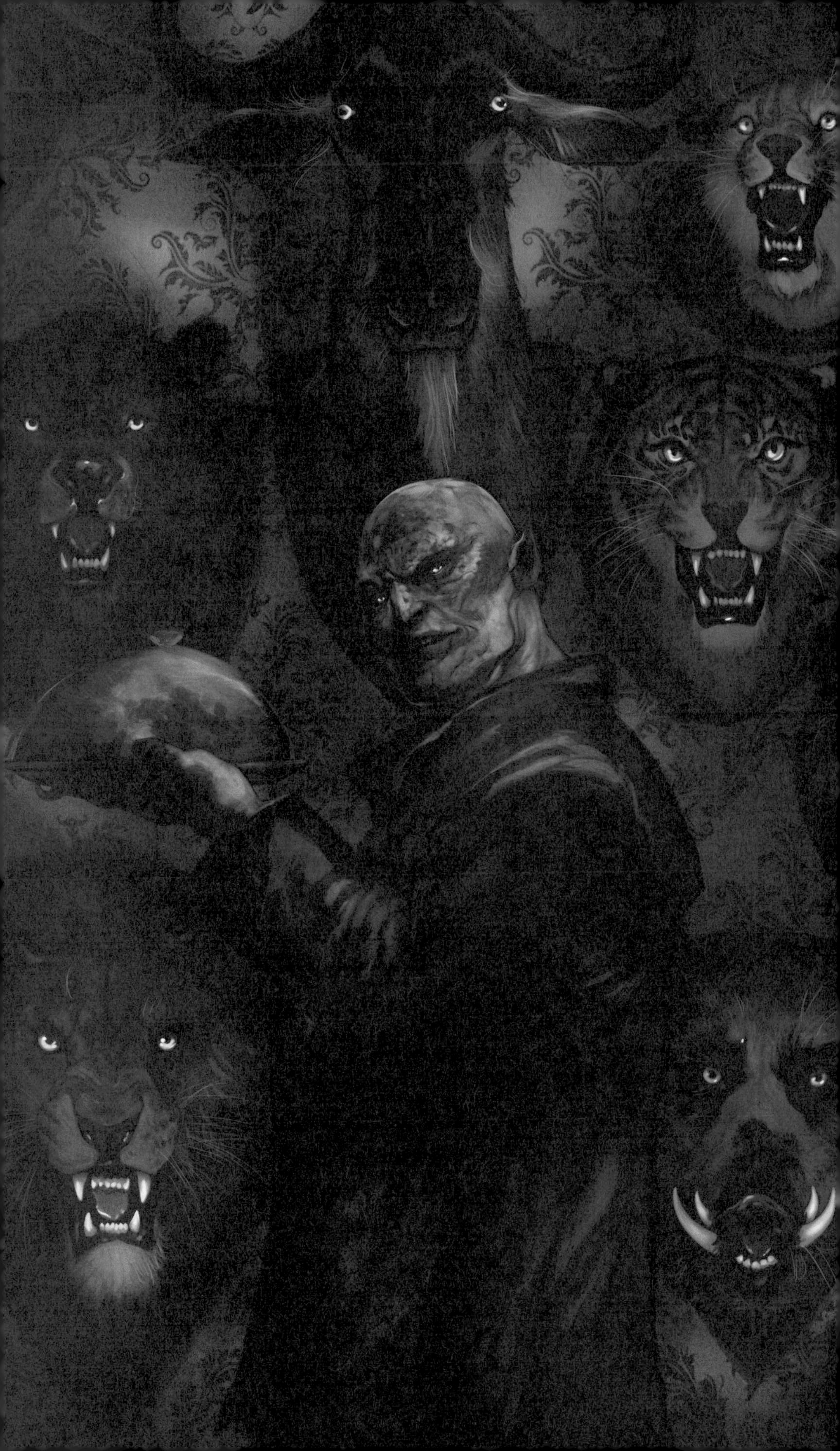

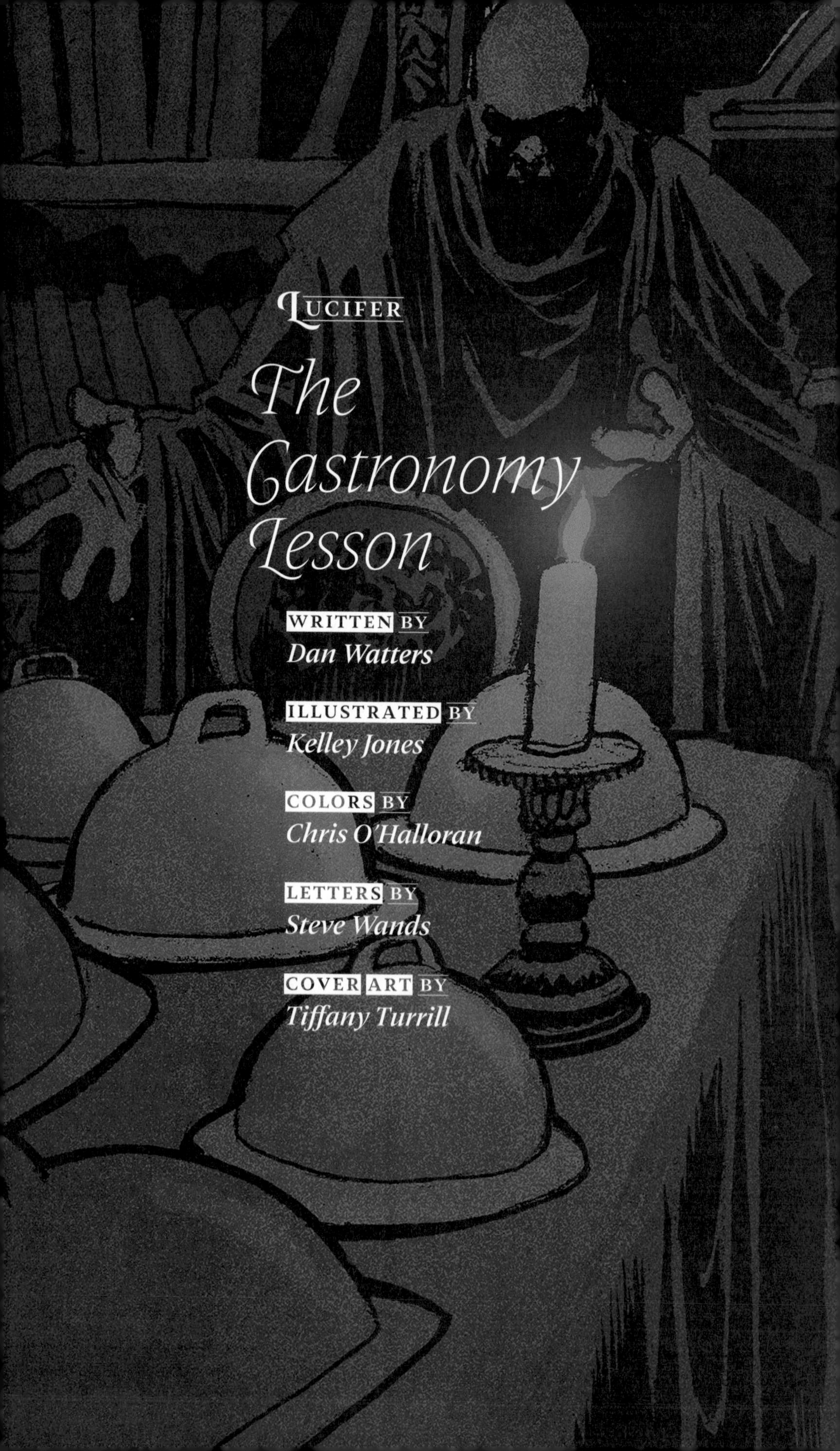

LUCIFER

The Gastronomy Lesson

WRITTEN BY
Dan Watters

ILLUSTRATED BY
Kelley Jones

COLORS BY
Chris O'Halloran

LETTERS BY
Steve Wands

COVER ART BY
Tiffany Turrill

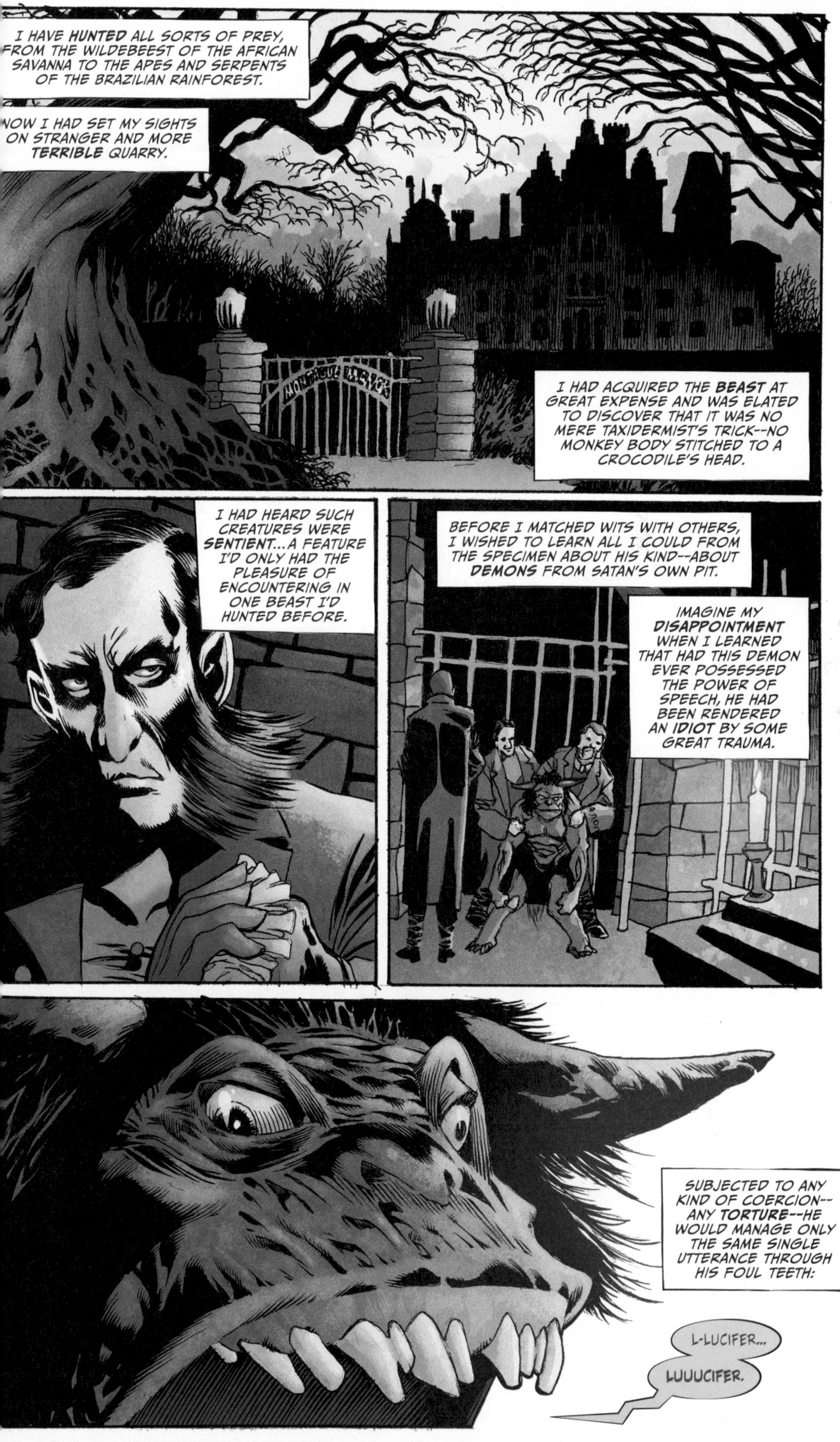
I HAVE HUNTED ALL SORTS OF PREY, FROM THE WILDEBEEST OF THE AFRICAN SAVANNA TO THE APES AND SERPENTS OF THE BRAZILIAN RAINFOREST.
NOW I HAD SET MY SIGHTS ON STRANGER AND MORE TERRIBLE QUARRY.
I HAD ACQUIRED THE BEAST AT GREAT EXPENSE AND WAS ELATED TO DISCOVER THAT IT WAS NO MERE TAXIDERMIST'S TRICK--NO MONKEY BODY STITCHED TO A CROCODILE'S HEAD.
I HAD HEARD SUCH CREATURES WERE SENTIENT...A FEATURE I'D ONLY HAD THE PLEASURE OF ENCOUNTERING IN ONE BEAST I'D HUNTED BEFORE.
BEFORE I MATCHED WITS WITH OTHERS, I WISHED TO LEARN ALL I COULD FROM THE SPECIMEN ABOUT HIS KIND--ABOUT DEMONS FROM SATAN'S OWN PIT.
IMAGINE MY DISAPPOINTMENT WHEN I LEARNED THAT HAD THIS DEMON EVER POSSESSED THE POWER OF SPEECH, HE HAD BEEN RENDERED AN IDIOT BY SOME GREAT TRAUMA.
SUBJECTED TO ANY KIND OF COERCION--ANY TORTURE--HE WOULD MANAGE ONLY THE SAME SINGLE UTTERANCE THROUGH HIS FOUL TEETH:
L-LUCIFER...
LUUUCIFER.

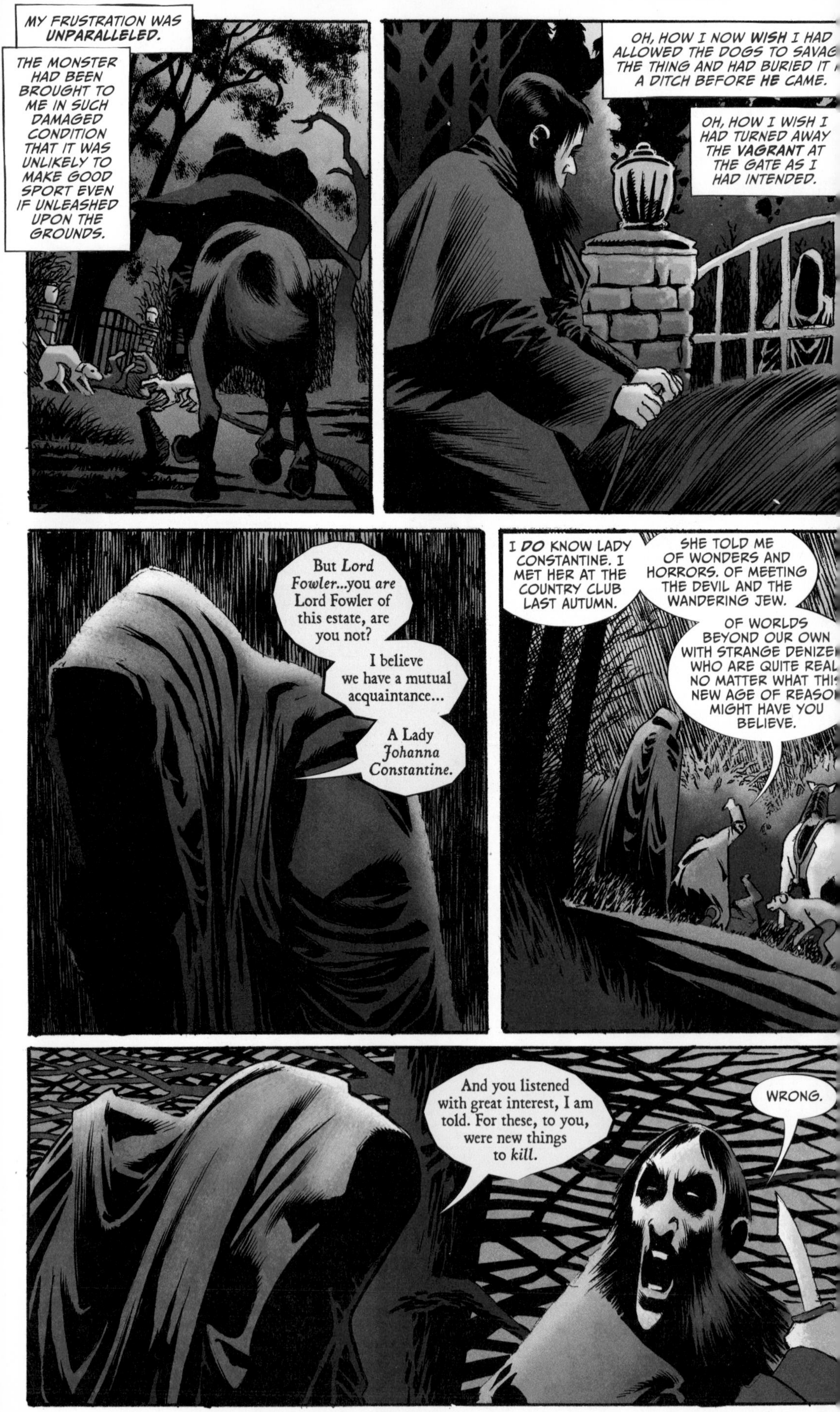
MY FRUSTRATION WAS **UNPARALLELED.**
THE MONSTER HAD BEEN BROUGHT TO ME IN SUCH DAMAGED CONDITION THAT IT WAS UNLIKELY TO MAKE GOOD SPORT EVEN IF UNLEASHED UPON THE GROUNDS.
OH, HOW I NOW **WISH** I HAD ALLOWED THE DOGS TO SAVAG THE THING AND HAD BURIED IT A DITCH BEFORE **HE** CAME.
OH, HOW I WISH I HAD TURNED AWAY THE **VAGRANT** AT THE GATE AS I HAD INTENDED.
But *Lord Fowler*...you *are* Lord Fowler of this estate, are you not?
I believe we have a mutual acquaintance...
A Lady *Johanna Constantine.*
I ***DO*** KNOW LADY CONSTANTINE. I MET HER AT THE COUNTRY CLUB LAST AUTUMN.
SHE TOLD ME OF WONDERS AND HORRORS. OF MEETING THE DEVIL AND THE WANDERING JEW.
OF WORLDS BEYOND OUR OWN WITH STRANGE DENIZE WHO ARE QUITE REAL NO MATTER WHAT THI NEW AGE OF REASO MIGHT HAVE YOU BELIEVE.
And you listened with great interest, I am told. For these, to you, were new things to *kill*.
WRONG.

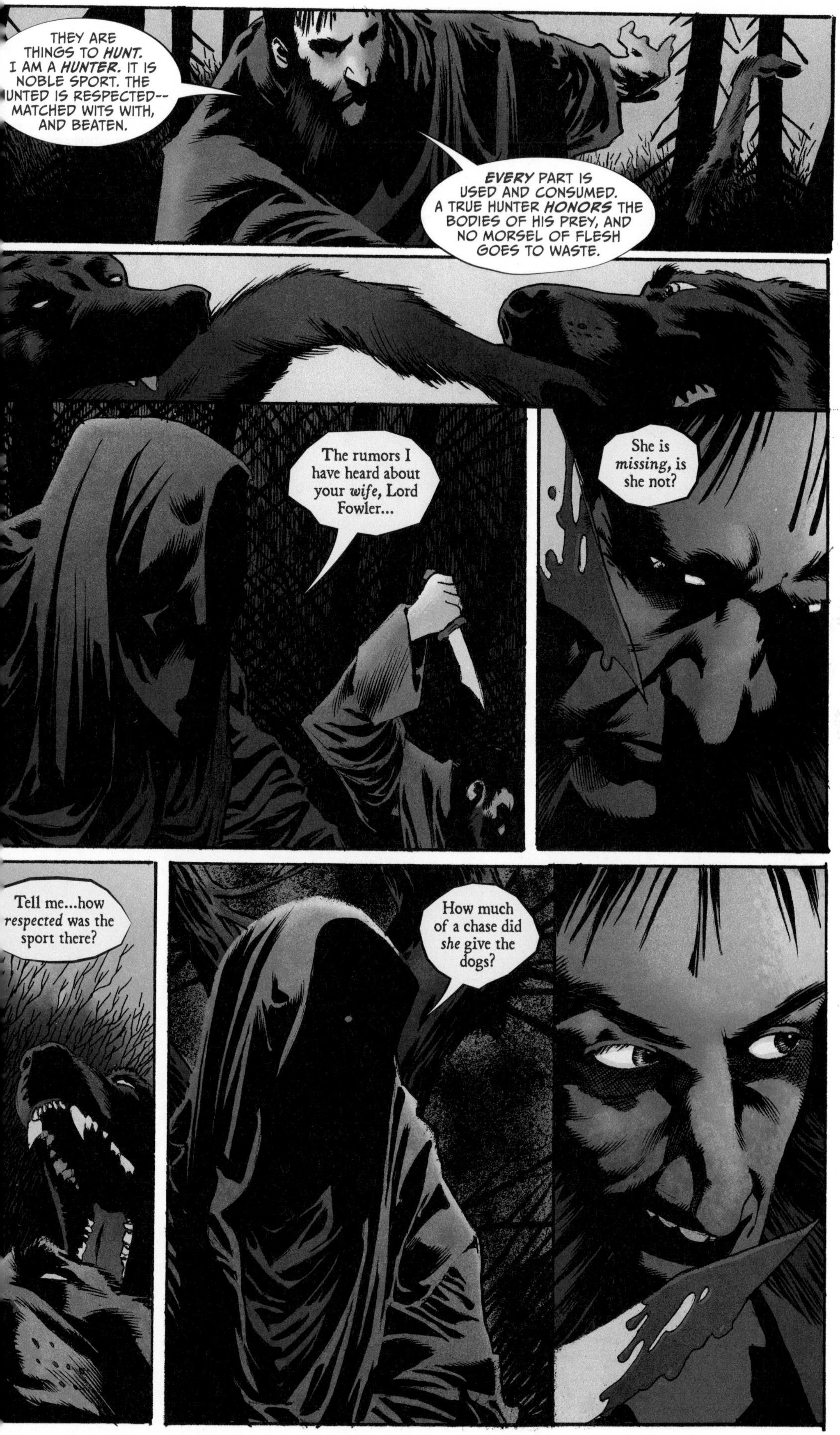
THEY ARE THINGS TO HUNT. I AM A HUNTER. IT IS NOBLE SPORT. THE UNTED IS RESPECTED--MATCHED WITS WITH, AND BEATEN.
EVERY PART IS USED AND CONSUMED. A TRUE HUNTER HONORS THE BODIES OF HIS PREY, AND NO MORSEL OF FLESH GOES TO WASTE.
The rumors I have heard about your wife, Lord Fowler...
She is missing, is she not?
Tell me...how respected was the sport there?
How much of a chase did she give the dogs?

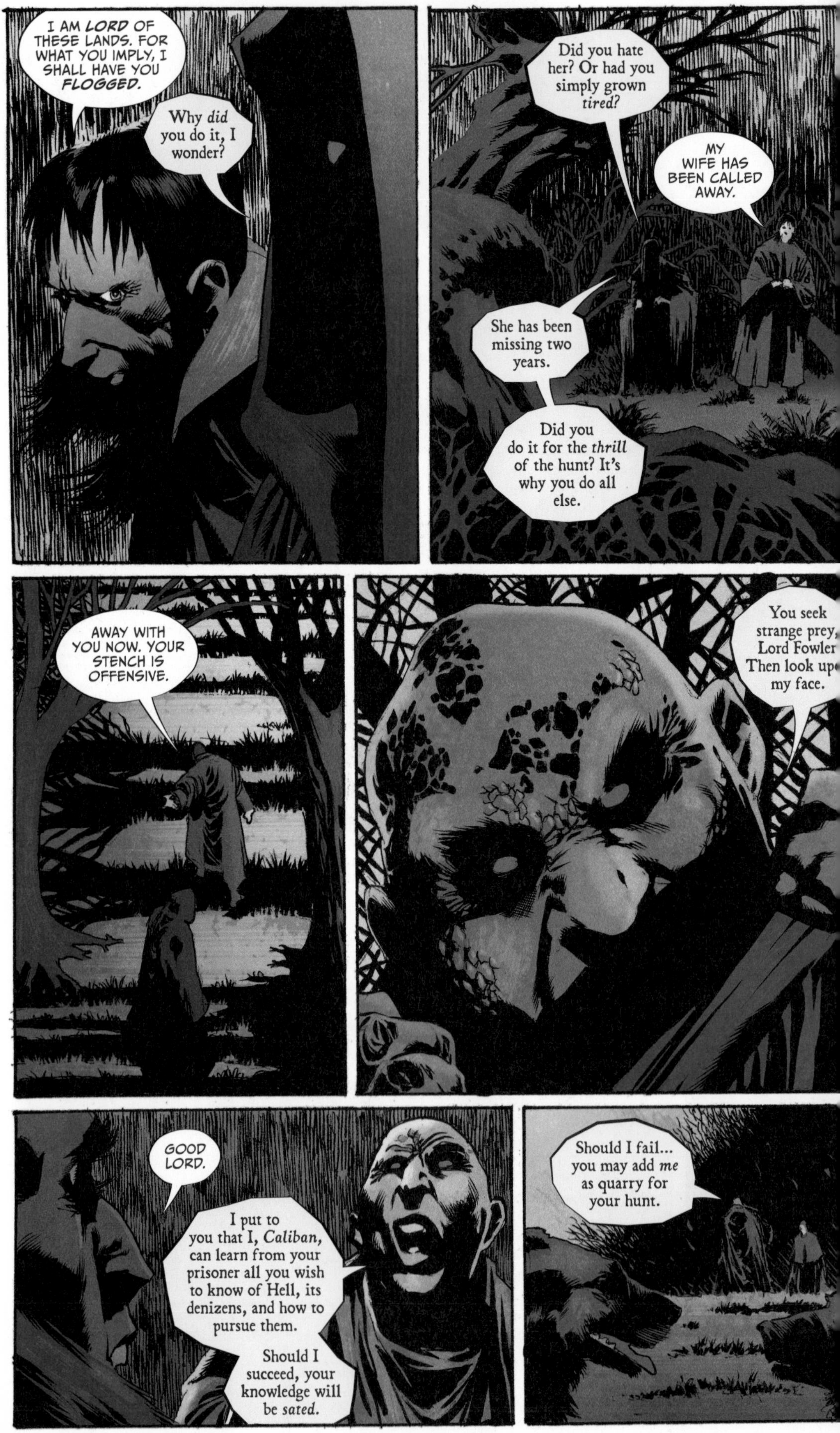
I AM *LORD* OF THESE LANDS. FOR WHAT YOU IMPLY, I SHALL HAVE YOU *FLOGGED.*
Why *did* you do it, I wonder?
Did you hate her? Or had you simply grown *tired?*
MY WIFE HAS BEEN CALLED AWAY.
She has been missing two years.
Did you do it for the *thrill* of the hunt? It's why you do all else.
AWAY WITH YOU NOW. YOUR STENCH IS OFFENSIVE.
You seek strange prey, Lord Fowler
Then look up my face.
GOOD LORD.
I put to you that I, *Caliban,* can learn from your prisoner all you wish to know of Hell, its denizens, and how to pursue them.
Should I succeed, your knowledge will be *sated.*
Should I fail... you may add *me* as quarry for your hunt.

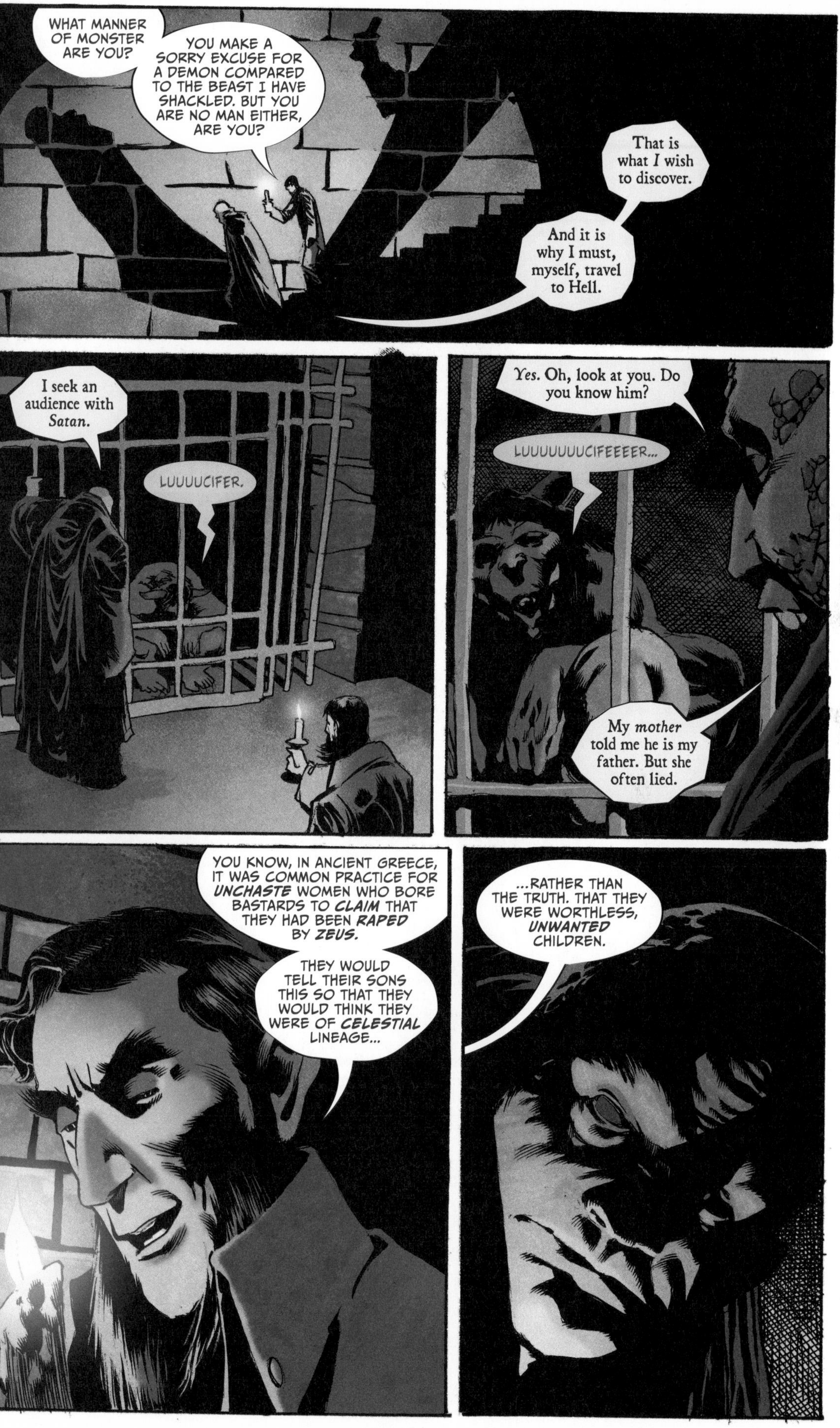
WHAT MANNER OF MONSTER ARE YOU?
YOU MAKE A SORRY EXCUSE FOR A DEMON COMPARED TO THE BEAST I HAVE SHACKLED. BUT YOU ARE NO MAN EITHER, ARE YOU?
That is what *I* wish to discover.
And it is why I must, myself, travel to Hell.
I seek an audience with *Satan*.
LUUUUCIFER.
Yes. Oh, look at you. Do you know him?
LUUUUUUUCIFEEEER...
My *mother* told me he is my father. But she often lied.
YOU KNOW, IN ANCIENT GREECE, IT WAS COMMON PRACTICE FOR *UNCHASTE* WOMEN WHO BORE BASTARDS TO *CLAIM* THAT THEY HAD BEEN *RAPED* BY *ZEUS.*
THEY WOULD TELL THEIR SONS THIS SO THAT THEY WOULD THINK THEY WERE OF *CELESTIAL* LINEAGE...
...RATHER THAN THE TRUTH. THAT THEY WERE WORTHLESS, *UNWANTED* CHILDREN.

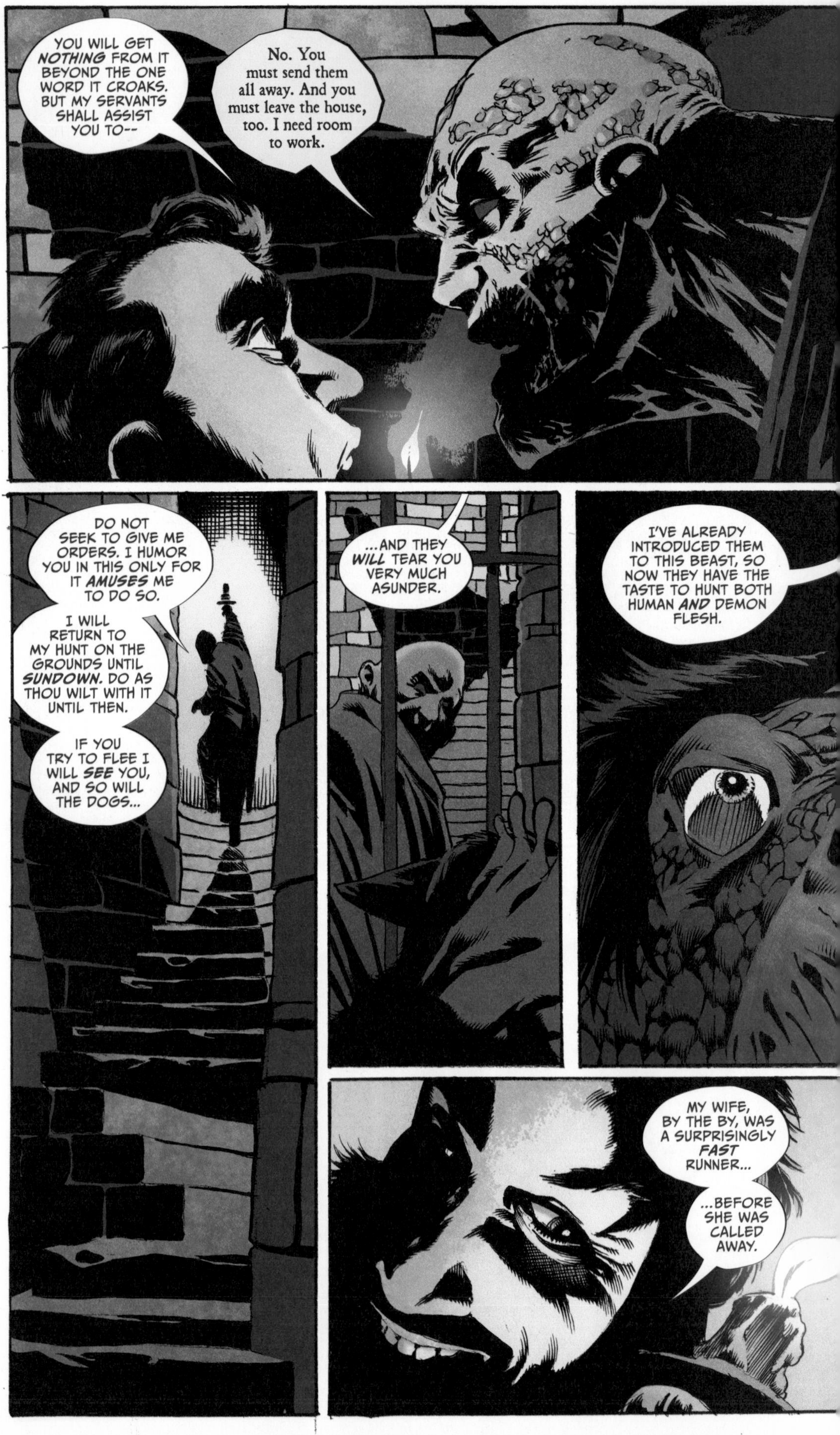
YOU WILL GET NOTHING FROM IT BEYOND THE ONE WORD IT CROAKS. BUT MY SERVANTS SHALL ASSIST YOU TO--
No. You must send them all away. And you must leave the house, too. I need room to work.
DO NOT SEEK TO GIVE ME ORDERS. I HUMOR YOU IN THIS ONLY FOR IT AMUSES ME TO DO SO.
I WILL RETURN TO MY HUNT ON THE GROUNDS UNTIL SUNDOWN. DO AS THOU WILT WITH IT UNTIL THEN.
IF YOU TRY TO FLEE I WILL SEE YOU, AND SO WILL THE DOGS...
...AND THEY WILL TEAR YOU VERY MUCH ASUNDER.
I'VE ALREADY INTRODUCED THEM TO THIS BEAST, SO NOW THEY HAVE THE TASTE TO HUNT BOTH HUMAN AND DEMON FLESH.
MY WIFE, BY THE BY, WAS A SURPRISINGLY FAST RUNNER...
...BEFORE SHE WAS CALLED AWAY.

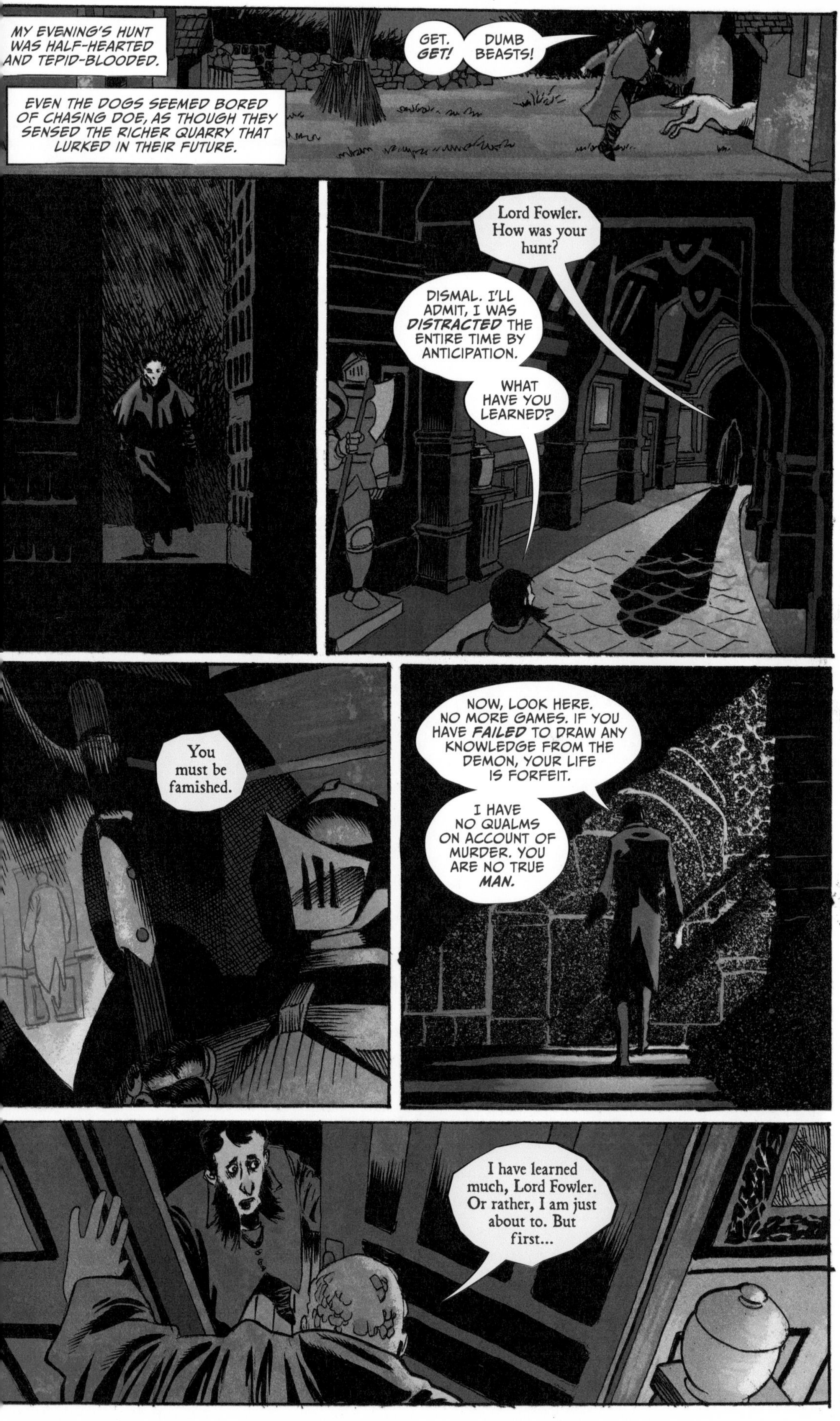
MY EVENING'S HUNT WAS HALF-HEARTED AND TEPID-BLOODED.
EVEN THE DOGS SEEMED BORED OF CHASING DOE, AS THOUGH THEY SENSED THE RICHER QUARRY THAT LURKED IN THEIR FUTURE.
GET. GET!
DUMB BEASTS!
Lord Fowler. How was your hunt?
DISMAL. I'LL ADMIT, I WAS DISTRACTED THE ENTIRE TIME BY ANTICIPATION.
WHAT HAVE YOU LEARNED?
You must be famished.
NOW, LOOK HERE. NO MORE GAMES. IF YOU HAVE FAILED TO DRAW ANY KNOWLEDGE FROM THE DEMON, YOUR LIFE IS FORFEIT.
I HAVE NO QUALMS ON ACCOUNT OF MURDER. YOU ARE NO TRUE MAN.
I have learned much, Lord Fowler. Or rather, I am just about to. But first...

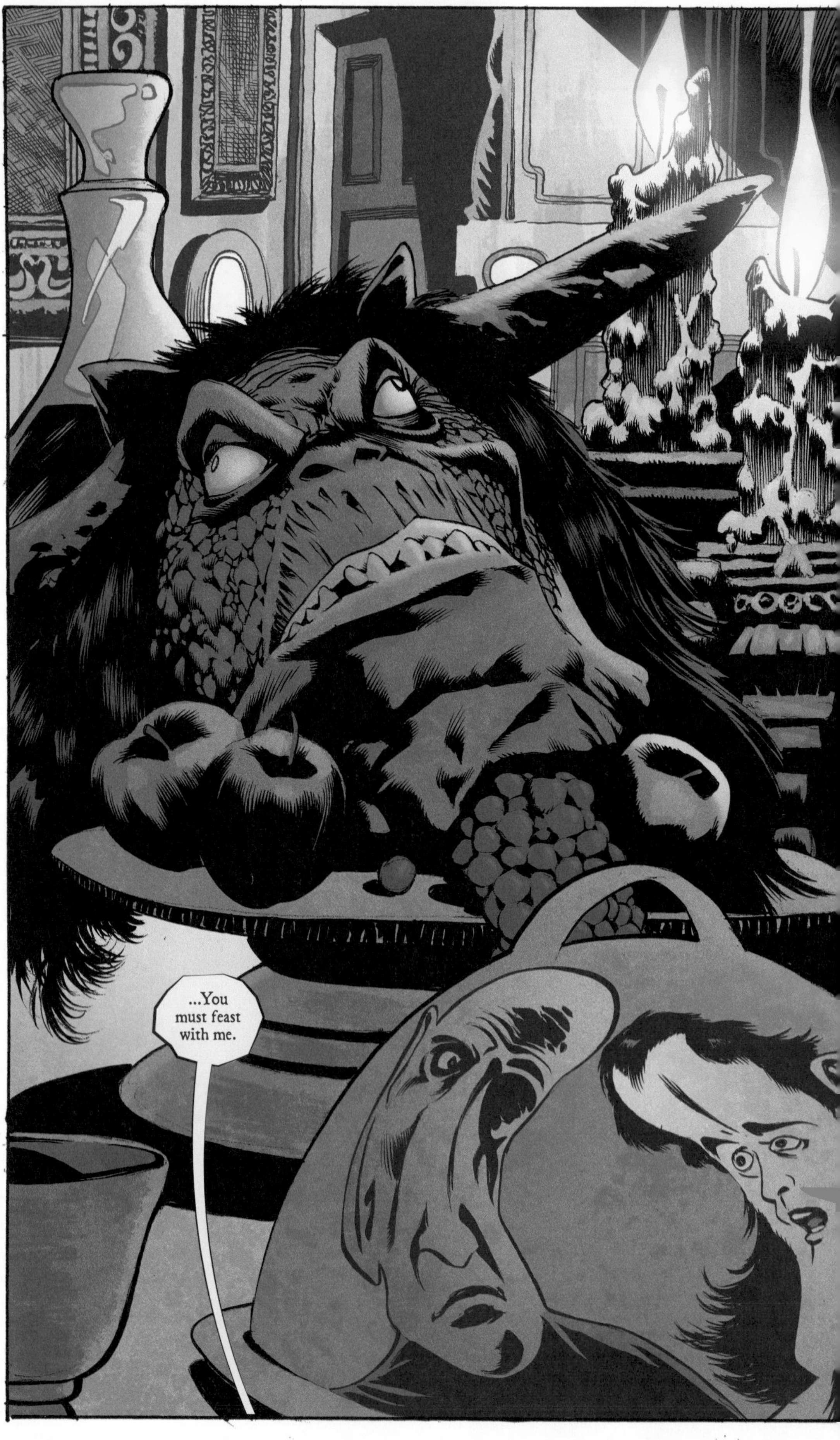
...You must feast with me.

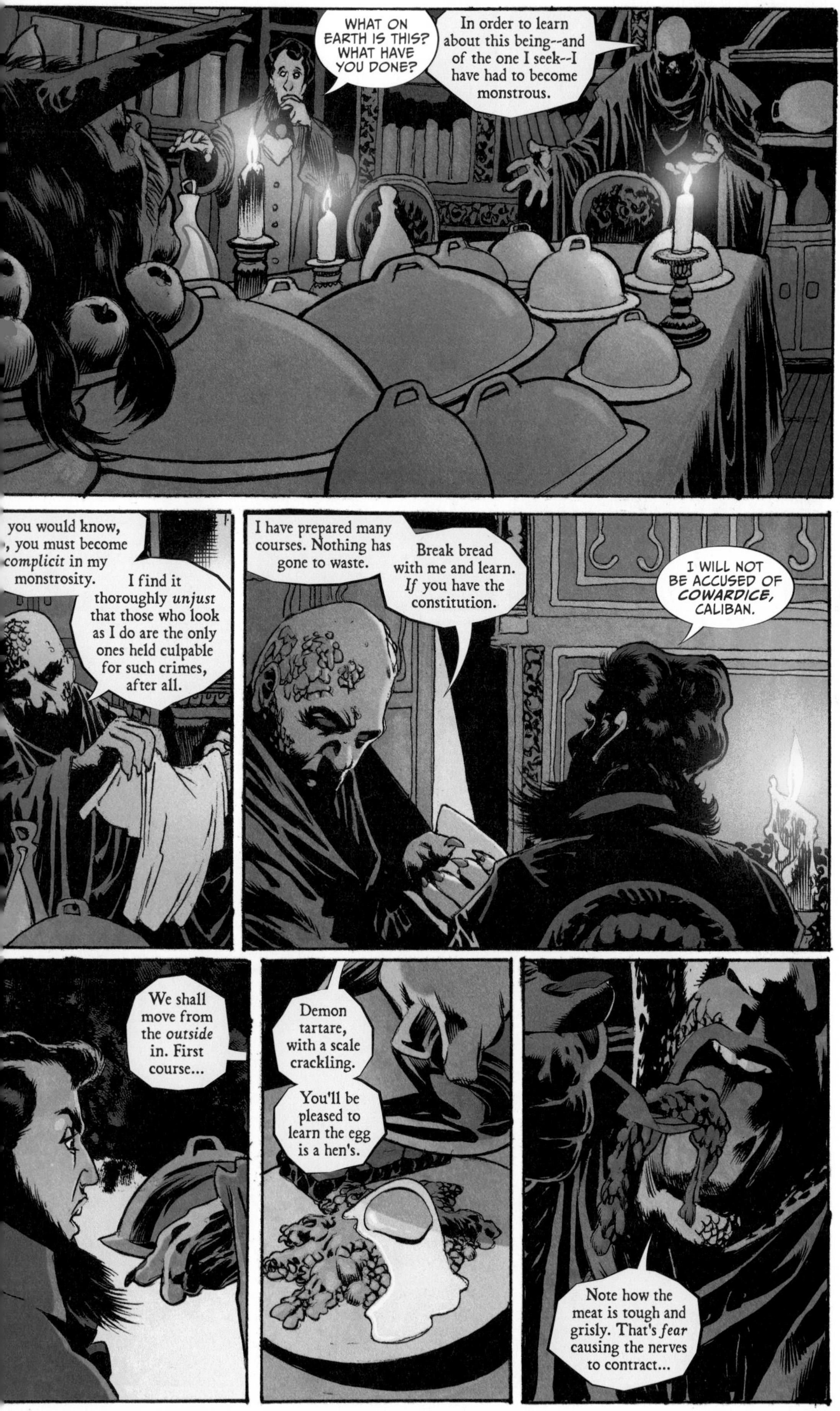
WHAT ON EARTH IS THIS? WHAT HAVE YOU DONE?
In order to learn about this being--and of the one I seek--I have had to become monstrous.
you would know, , you must become *complicit* in my monstrosity.
I find it thoroughly *unjust* that those who look as I do are the only ones held culpable for such crimes, after all.
I have prepared many courses. Nothing has gone to waste.
Break bread with me and learn. *If* you have the constitution.
I WILL NOT BE ACCUSED OF *COWARDICE,* CALIBAN.
We shall move from the *outside* in. First course...
Demon tartare, with a scale crackling.
You'll be pleased to learn the egg is a hen's.
Note how the meat is tough and grisly. That's *fear* causing the nerves to contract...

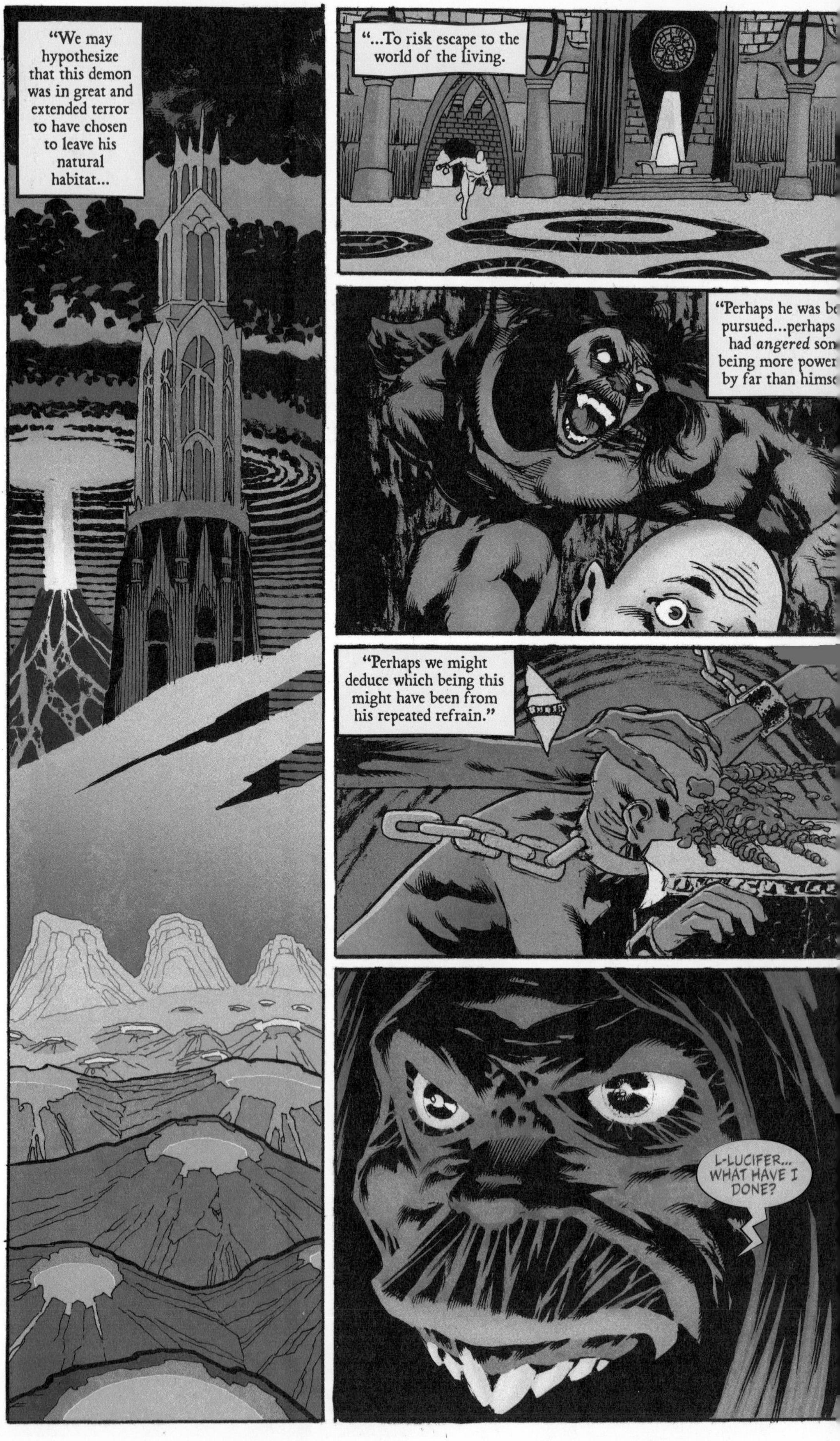
"We may hypothesize that this demon was in great and extended terror to have chosen to leave his natural habitat...
"...To risk escape to the world of the living.
"Perhaps he was be pursued...perhaps had *angered* son being more power by far than himse
"Perhaps we might deduce which being this might have been from his repeated refrain."
L-LUCIFER... WHAT HAVE I DONE?

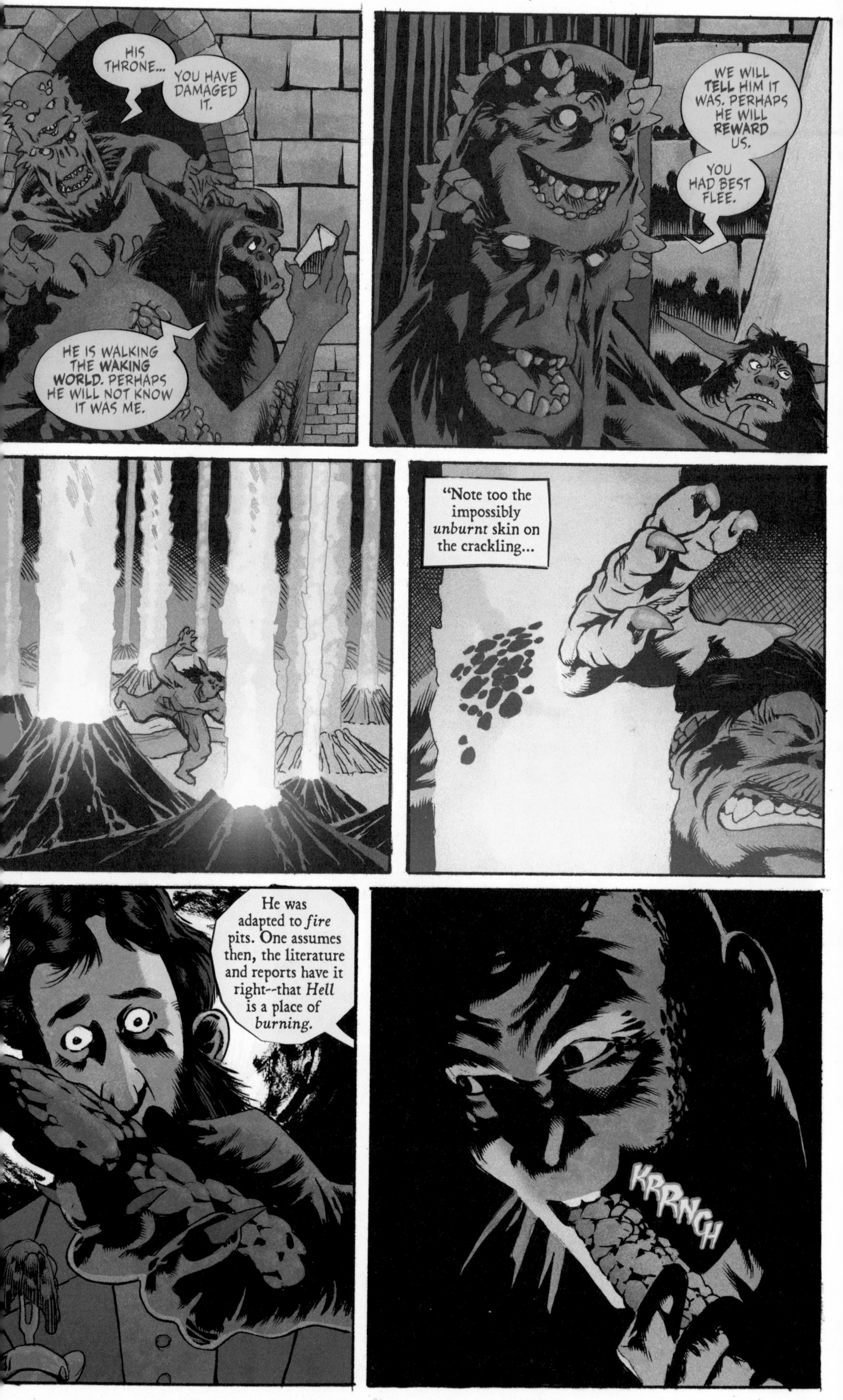
HIS THRONE...
YOU HAVE DAMAGED IT.
HE IS WALKING THE WAKING WORLD. PERHAPS HE WILL NOT KNOW IT WAS ME.
WE WILL TELL HIM IT WAS. PERHAPS HE WILL REWARD US.
YOU HAD BEST FLEE.
"Note too the impossibly unburnt skin on the crackling...
He was adapted to fire pits. One assumes then, the literature and reports have it right--that Hell is a place of burning.
KRRNCH

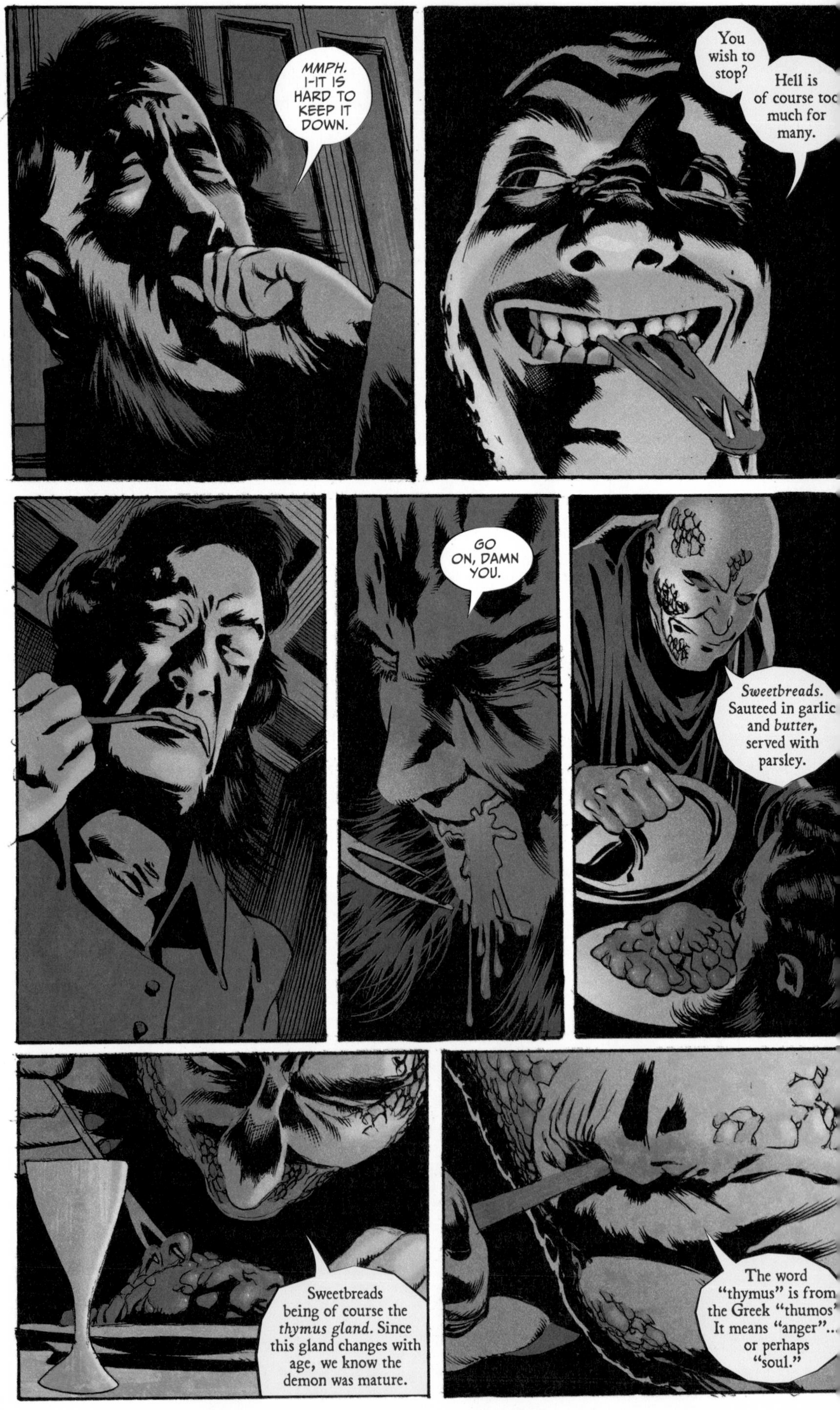
MMPH. I-IT IS HARD TO KEEP IT DOWN.
You wish to stop?
Hell is of course too much for many.
GO ON, DAMN YOU.
Sweetbreads. Sauteed in garlic and *butter,* served with parsley.
Sweetbreads being of course the *thymus gland.* Since this gland changes with age, we know the demon was mature.
The word "thymus" is from the Greek "thumos." It means "anger"... or perhaps "soul."

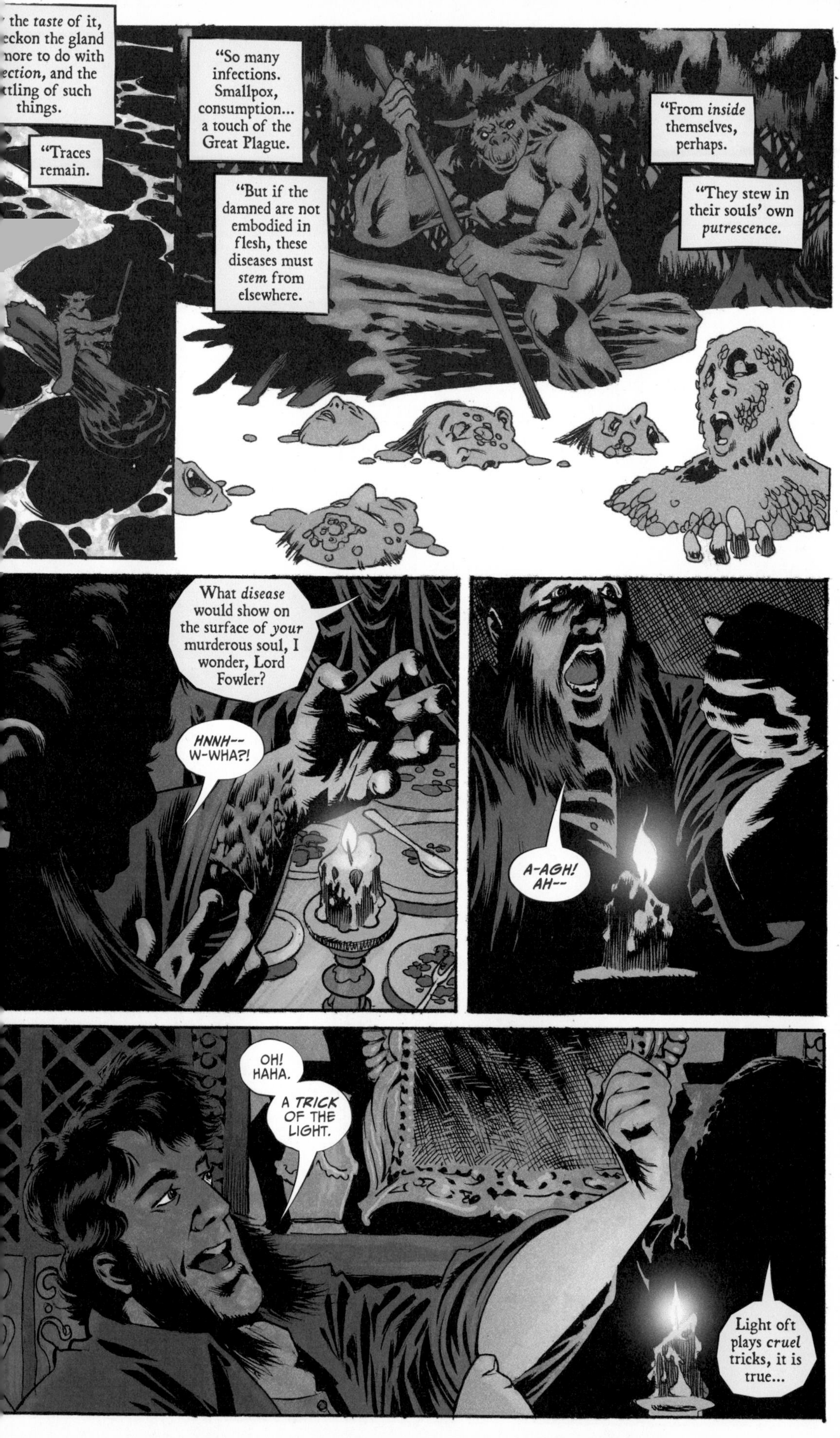

the taste of it, eckon the gland nore to do with ection, and the tling of such things.
"Traces remain.
"So many infections. Smallpox, consumption... a touch of the Great Plague.
"But if the damned are not embodied in flesh, these diseases must stem from elsewhere.
"From inside themselves, perhaps.
"They stew in their souls' own putrescence.
What disease would show on the surface of your murderous soul, I wonder, Lord Fowler?
HNNH-- W-WHA?!
A-AGH! AH--
OH! HAHA.
A TRICK OF THE LIGHT.
Light oft plays cruel tricks, it is true...

"And so where else did he go?

"Where else did he go as he fled through Hell from parties unknown?"

L-LUCIFER?! LORD, IS THAT YOU?

"Though by now we may well have guessed from whom--might we, Lord Fowler?"

M-MY LORD! PLEASE... NO!

"Our next dish, perhaps, may elucidate even more.

HURP?

To flee is hungry work. What, indeed, does a demon eat?

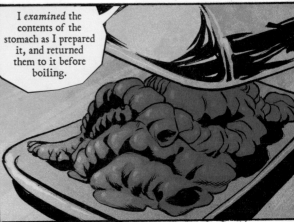

I examined the contents of the stomach as I prepared it, and returned them to it before boiling.

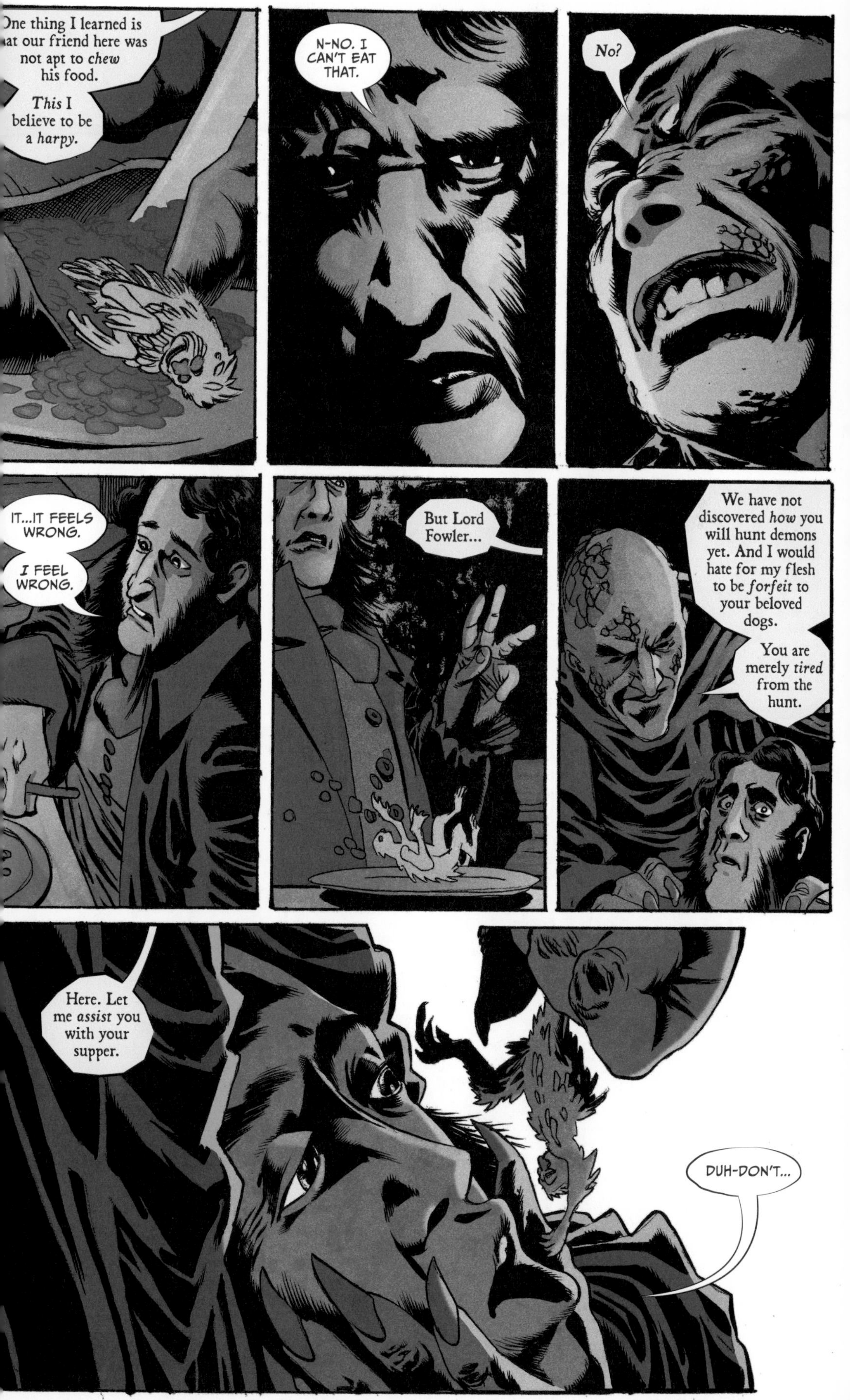
One thing I learned is that our friend here was not apt to *chew* his food.
This I believe to be a *harpy*.
N-NO. I CAN'T EAT THAT.
No?
IT...IT FEELS WRONG.
I FEEL WRONG.
But Lord Fowler...
We have not discovered *how* you will hunt demons yet. And I would hate for my flesh to be *forfeit* to your beloved dogs.
You are merely *tired* from the hunt.
Here. Let me *assist* you with your supper.
DUH-DON'T...

"Where would he have encountered such a being, I wonder. Perhaps he..."

"HUUURTING. HUUUUURTIIIIING."

HUUUUURTING...

Do not interrupt me, Fowler. I am close now to finding my way to Hell. To my father. I can feel it.

NU-NUH MEE.

SUMTHIN... STUCK IN MUH THROAH...

A-A-AGH...

Wood? Whe does *wood* gr in Hell?

D-DANTE.

What?

DANTE WROTE OF HELL'S *WOOD OF SUICIDES*. WHERE HARPIES TEAR AT THE BARK OF THE TREES... FOR THE TREES THEMSELVES--

HUUUURTING

--ARE THE *SOULS* OF THE DAMNED. OF THOSE WHO'VE TAKEN THEIR OWN LIVES.

So. A stowaway from Hell, are we?

JUUUST A SPLINTER. JUST A FRAGMENT OF A SOUL.

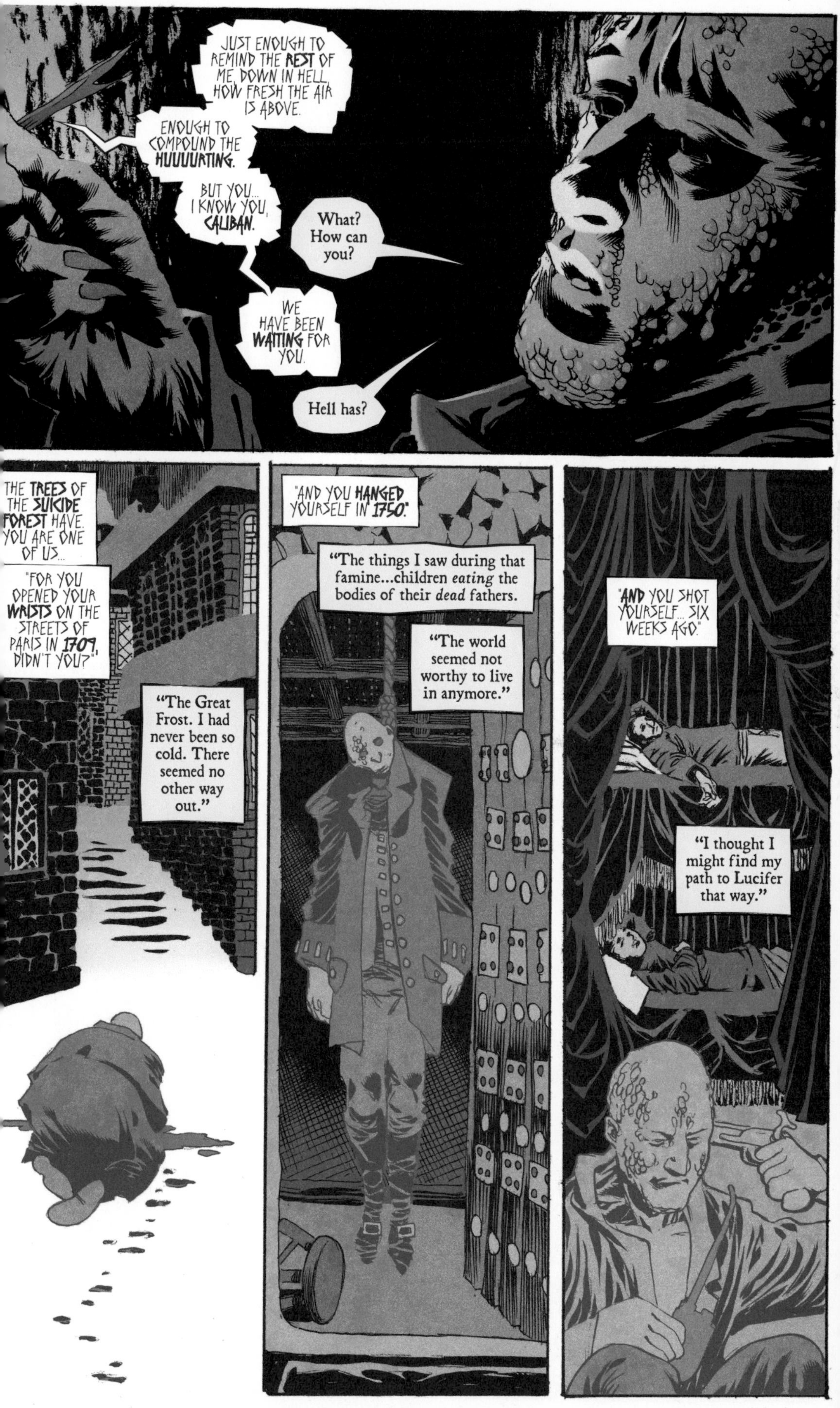
JUST ENOUGH TO REMIND THE REST OF ME, DOWN IN HELL, HOW FRESH THE AIR IS ABOVE.
ENOUGH TO COMPOUND THE HUUUURTING.
BUT YOU... I KNOW YOU, CALIBAN.
What? How can you?
WE HAVE BEEN WAITING FOR YOU.
Hell has?
THE TREES OF THE SUICIDE FOREST HAVE. YOU ARE ONE OF US...
"FOR YOU OPENED YOUR WRISTS ON THE STREETS OF PARIS IN 1709, DIDN'T YOU?"
"The Great Frost. I had never been so cold. There seemed no other way out."
"AND YOU HANGED YOURSELF IN 1750."
"The things I saw during that famine...children eating the bodies of their dead fathers.
"The world seemed not worthy to live in anymore."
"AND YOU SHOT YOURSELF... SIX WEEKS AGO."
"I thought I might find my path to Lucifer that way."

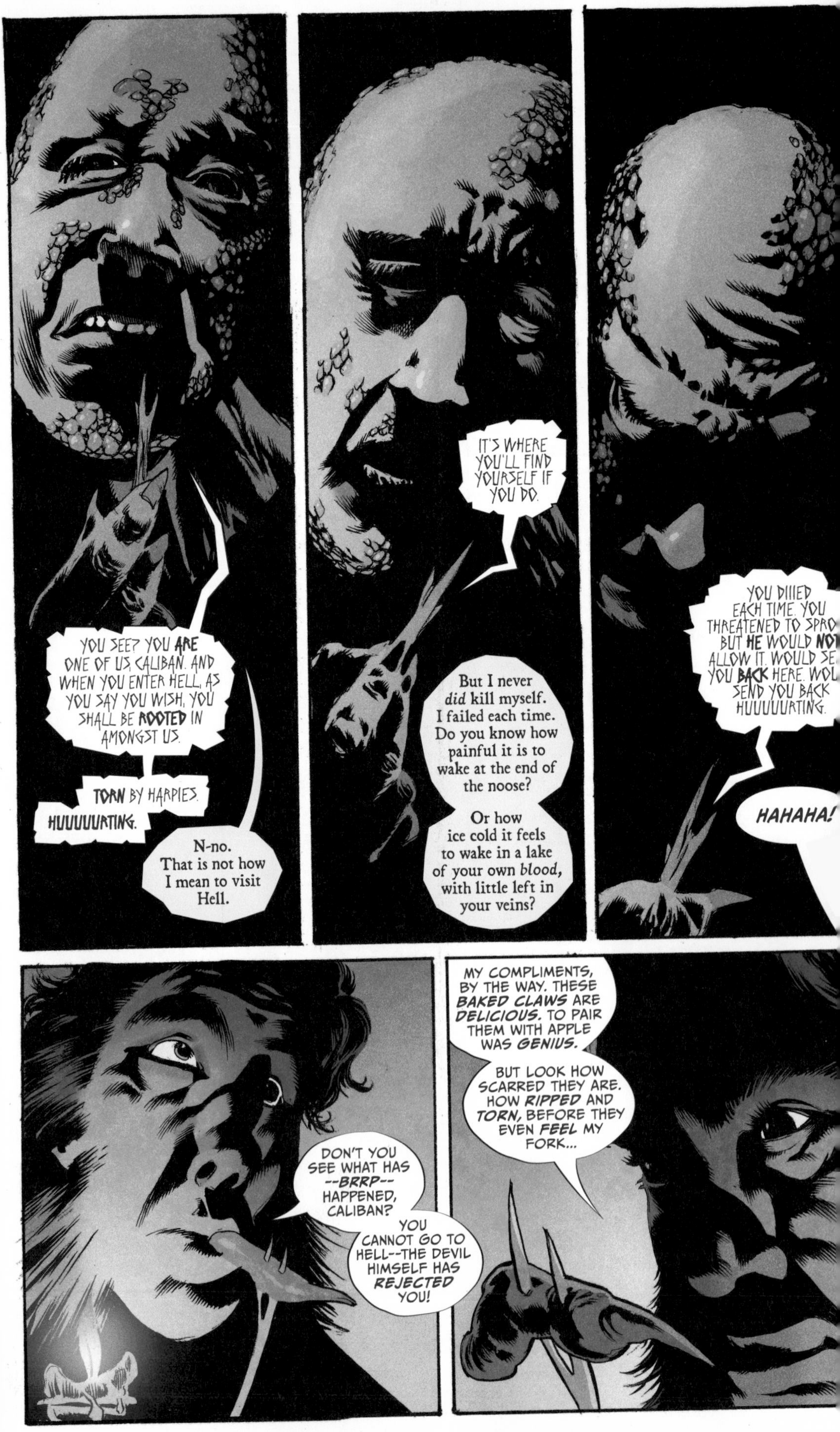
YOU SEE? YOU ARE ONE OF US, CALIBAN. AND WHEN YOU ENTER HELL, AS YOU SAY YOU WISH, YOU SHALL BE ROOTED IN AMONGST US.
TORN BY HARPIES.
HUUUUURTING.
N-no. That is not how I mean to visit Hell.
IT'S WHERE YOU'LL FIND YOURSELF IF YOU DO.
But I never did kill myself. I failed each time. Do you know how painful it is to wake at the end of the noose?
Or how ice cold it feels to wake in a lake of your own blood, with little left in your veins?
YOU DIIIED EACH TIME. YOU THREATENED TO SPRO BUT HE WOULD NOT ALLOW IT. WOULD SE YOU BACK HERE. WOU SEND YOU BACK HUUUUURTING.
HAHAHA!
DON'T YOU SEE WHAT HAS --BRRP-- HAPPENED, CALIBAN?
YOU CANNOT GO TO HELL--THE DEVIL HIMSELF HAS REJECTED YOU!
MY COMPLIMENTS, BY THE WAY. THESE BAKED CLAWS ARE DELICIOUS. TO PAIR THEM WITH APPLE WAS GENIUS.
BUT LOOK HOW SCARRED THEY ARE. HOW RIPPED AND TORN, BEFORE THEY EVEN FEEL MY FORK...

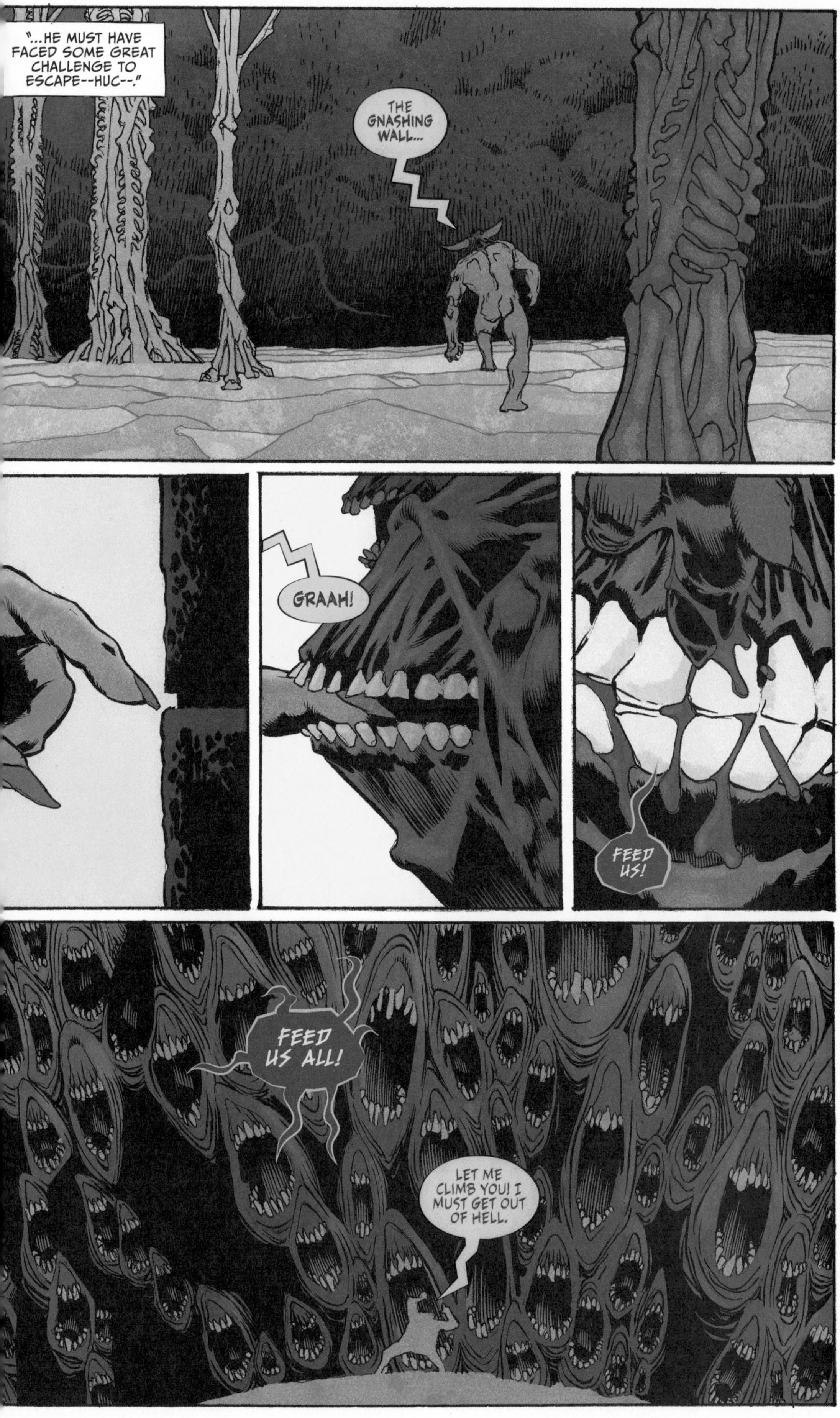
"...HE MUST HAVE FACED SOME GREAT CHALLENGE TO ESCAPE--HUC--."
THE GNASHING WALL...
GRAAH!
FEED US!
FEED US ALL!
LET ME CLIMB YOU! I MUST GET OUT OF HELL.

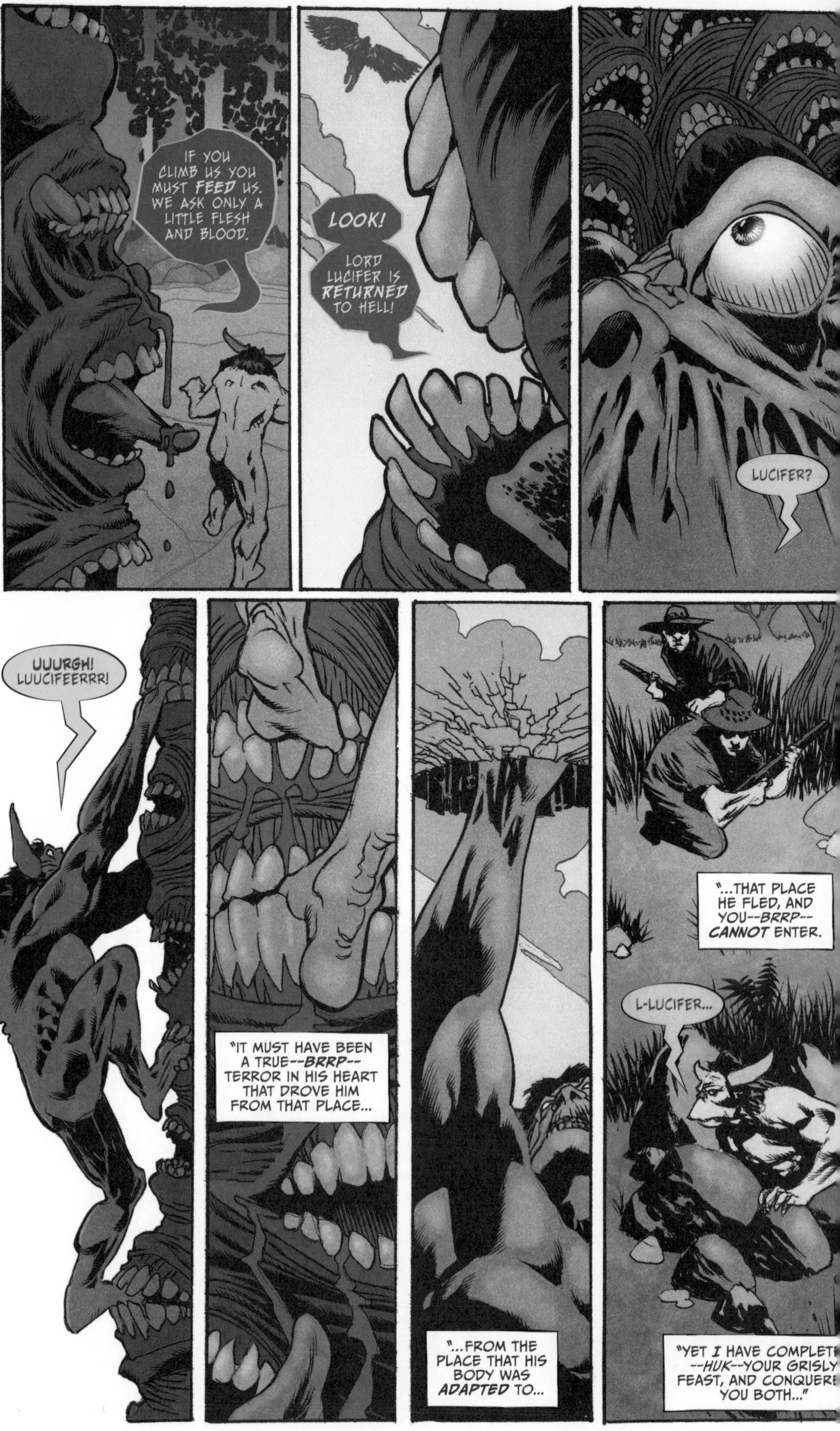
IF YOU CLIMB US YOU MUST FEED US. WE ASK ONLY A LITTLE FLESH AND BLOOD.
LOOK!
LORD LUCIFER IS RETURNED TO HELL!
LUCIFER?
UUURGH! LUUCIFEERRR!
"IT MUST HAVE BEEN A TRUE--BRRP--TERROR IN HIS HEART THAT DROVE HIM FROM THAT PLACE...
"...FROM THE PLACE THAT HIS BODY WAS ADAPTED TO...
"...THAT PLACE HE FLED, AND YOU--BRRP--CANNOT ENTER.
L-LUCIFER...
"YET I HAVE COMPLET --HUK--YOUR GRISLY FEAST, AND CONQUERE YOU BOTH..."

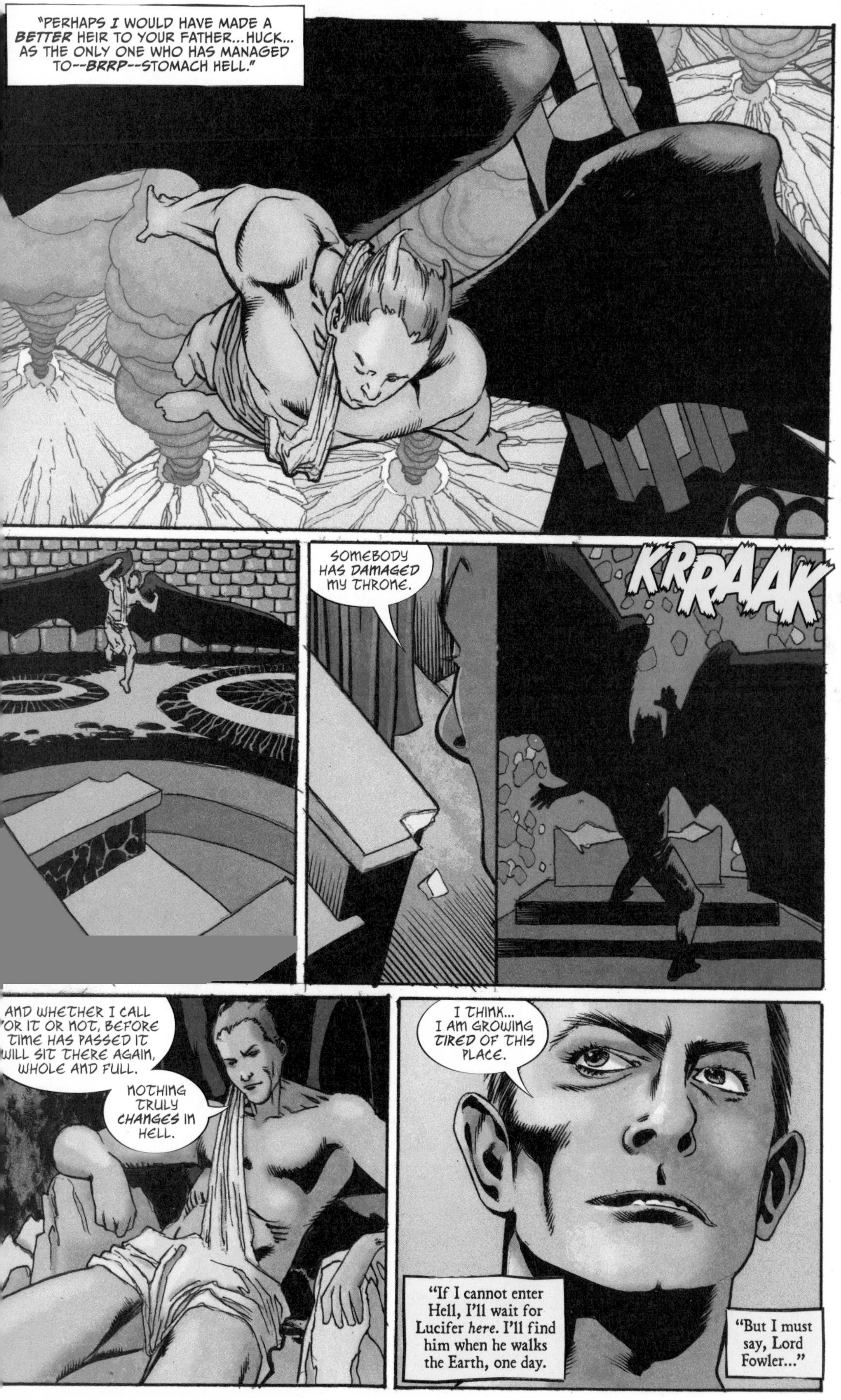
"PERHAPS I WOULD HAVE MADE A BETTER HEIR TO YOUR FATHER...HUCK... AS THE ONLY ONE WHO HAS MANAGED TO--BRRP--STOMACH HELL."
SOMEBODY HAS DAMAGED MY THRONE.
KRRAAK
AND WHETHER I CALL FOR IT OR NOT, BEFORE TIME HAS PASSED IT WILL SIT THERE AGAIN, WHOLE AND FULL.
NOTHING TRULY CHANGES IN HELL.
I THINK... I AM GROWING TIRED OF THIS PLACE.
"If I cannot enter Hell, I'll wait for Lucifer here. I'll find him when he walks the Earth, one day.
"But I must say, Lord Fowler..."

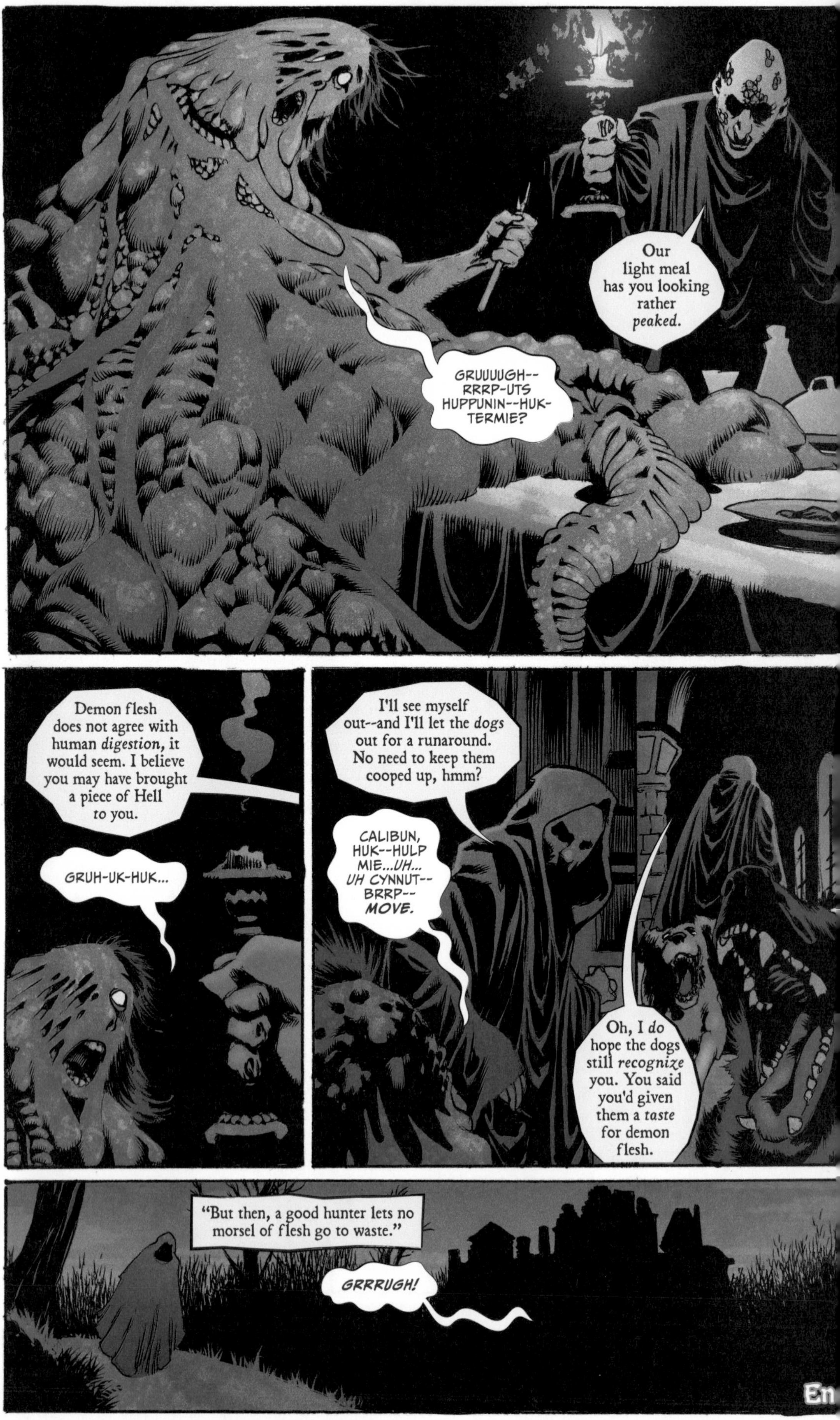
Our light meal has you looking rather *peaked*.
GRUUUUGH--RRRP-UTS HUPPUNIN--HUK-TERMIE?
Demon flesh does not agree with human *digestion*, it would seem. I believe you may have brought a piece of Hell *to* you.
GRUH-UK-HUK...
I'll see myself out--and I'll let the *dogs* out for a runaround. No need to keep them cooped up, hmm?
CALIBUN, HUK--HULP MIE...*UH...* *UH* CYNNUT--BRRP--*MOVE.*
Oh, I *do* hope the dogs still *recognize* you. You said you'd given them a *taste* for demon flesh.
"But then, a good hunter lets no morsel of flesh go to waste."
GRRRUGH!
En

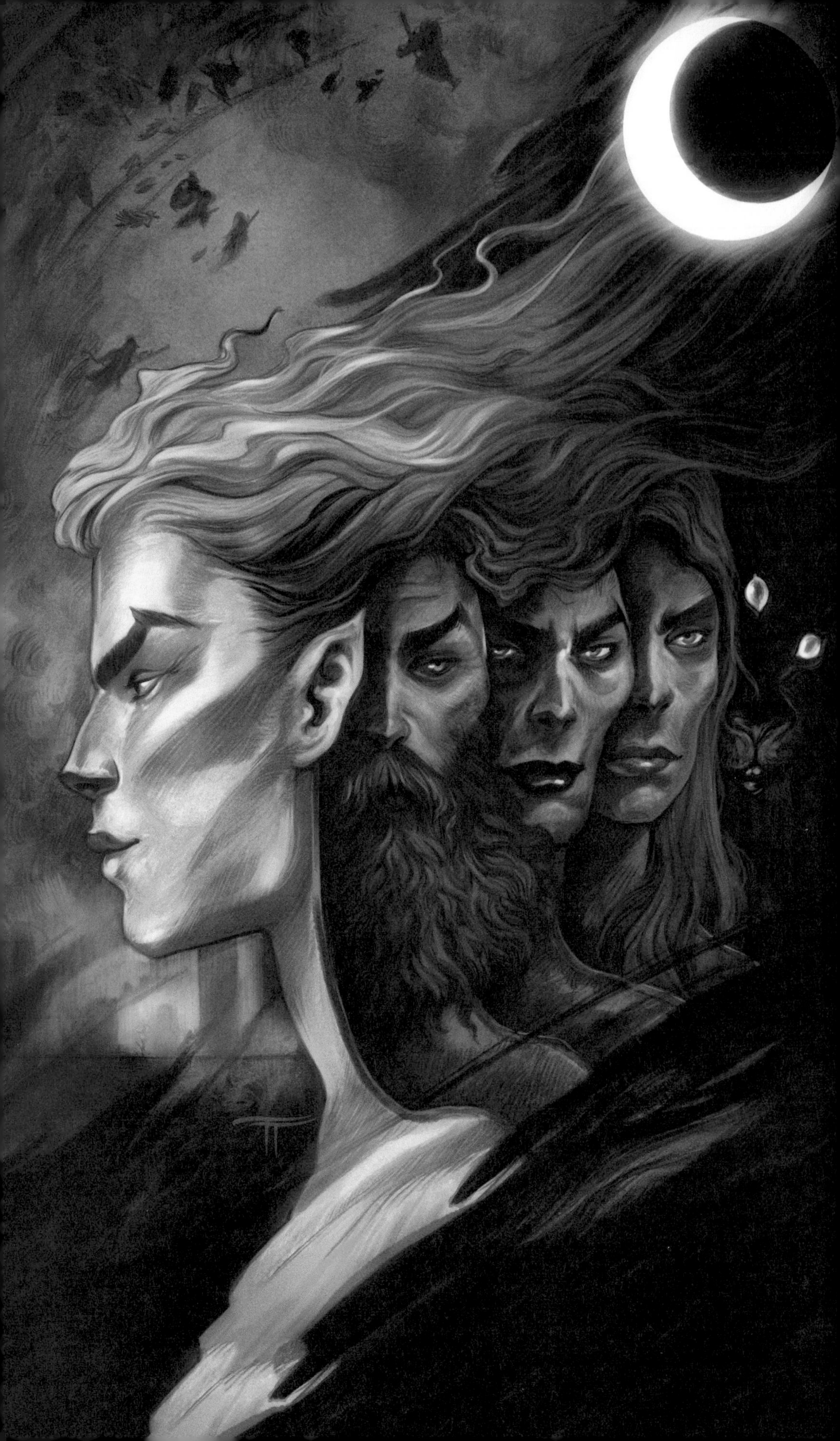

LUCIFER

The Problem with Old Blood Magic

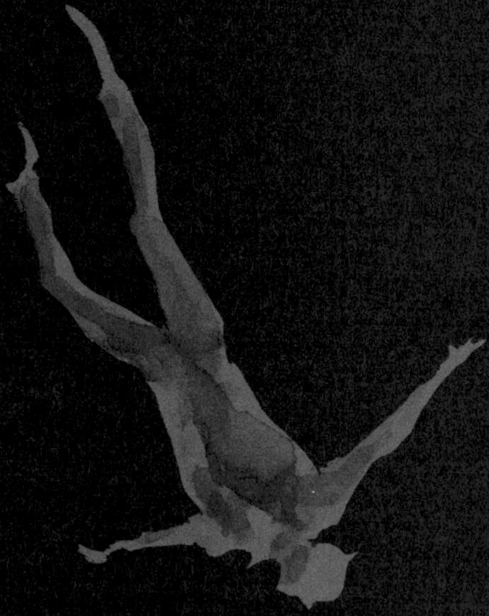

WRITTEN BY
Dan Watters

ILLUSTRATED BY
Max Fiumara
and *Leomacs*

COLORS BY
Dave McCaig

LETTERS BY
Steve Wands

COVER ART BY
Tiffany Turrill

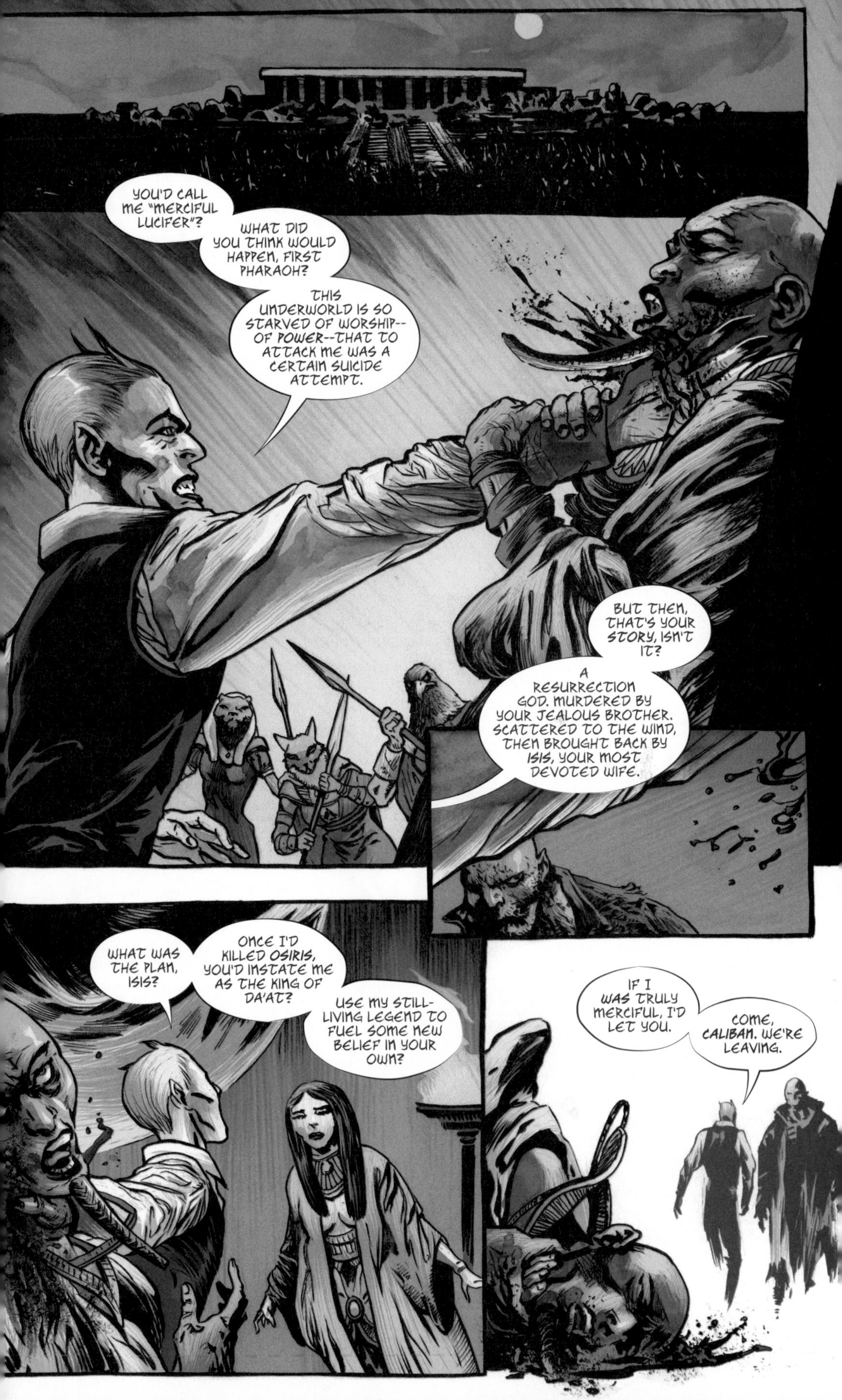
YOU'D CALL ME "MERCIFUL LUCIFER"?
WHAT DID YOU THINK WOULD HAPPEN, FIRST PHARAOH?
THIS UNDERWORLD IS SO STARVED OF WORSHIP--OF POWER--THAT TO ATTACK ME WAS A CERTAIN SUICIDE ATTEMPT.
BUT THEN, THAT'S YOUR STORY, ISN'T IT?
A RESURRECTION GOD. MURDERED BY YOUR JEALOUS BROTHER. SCATTERED TO THE WIND, THEN BROUGHT BACK BY ISIS, YOUR MOST DEVOTED WIFE.
WHAT WAS THE PLAN, ISIS?
ONCE I'D KILLED OSIRIS, YOU'D INSTATE ME AS THE KING OF DA'AT?
USE MY STILL-LIVING LEGEND TO FUEL SOME NEW BELIEF IN YOUR OWN?
IF I WAS TRULY MERCIFUL, I'D LET YOU.
COME, CALIBAN. WE'RE LEAVING.

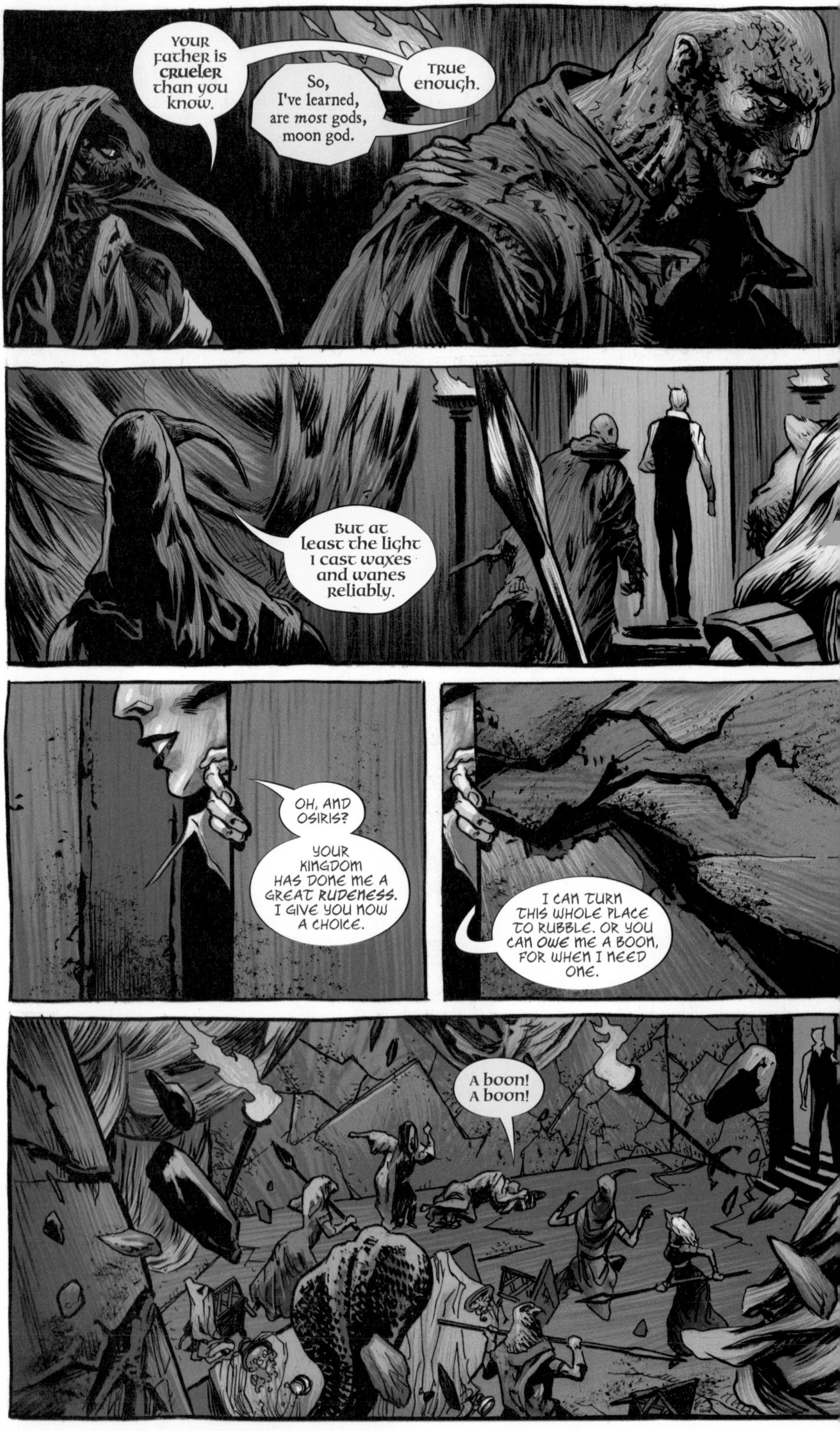
YOUR FATHER IS CRUELER THAN YOU KNOW.
So, I've learned, are *most* gods, moon god.
TRUE ENOUGH.
BUT AT LEAST THE LIGHT I CAST WAXES AND WANES RELIABLY.
OH, AND OSIRIS?
YOUR KINGDOM HAS DONE ME A GREAT RUDENESS. I GIVE YOU NOW A CHOICE.
I CAN TURN THIS WHOLE PLACE TO RUBBLE. OR YOU CAN OWE ME A BOON, FOR WHEN I NEED ONE.
A boon! A boon!

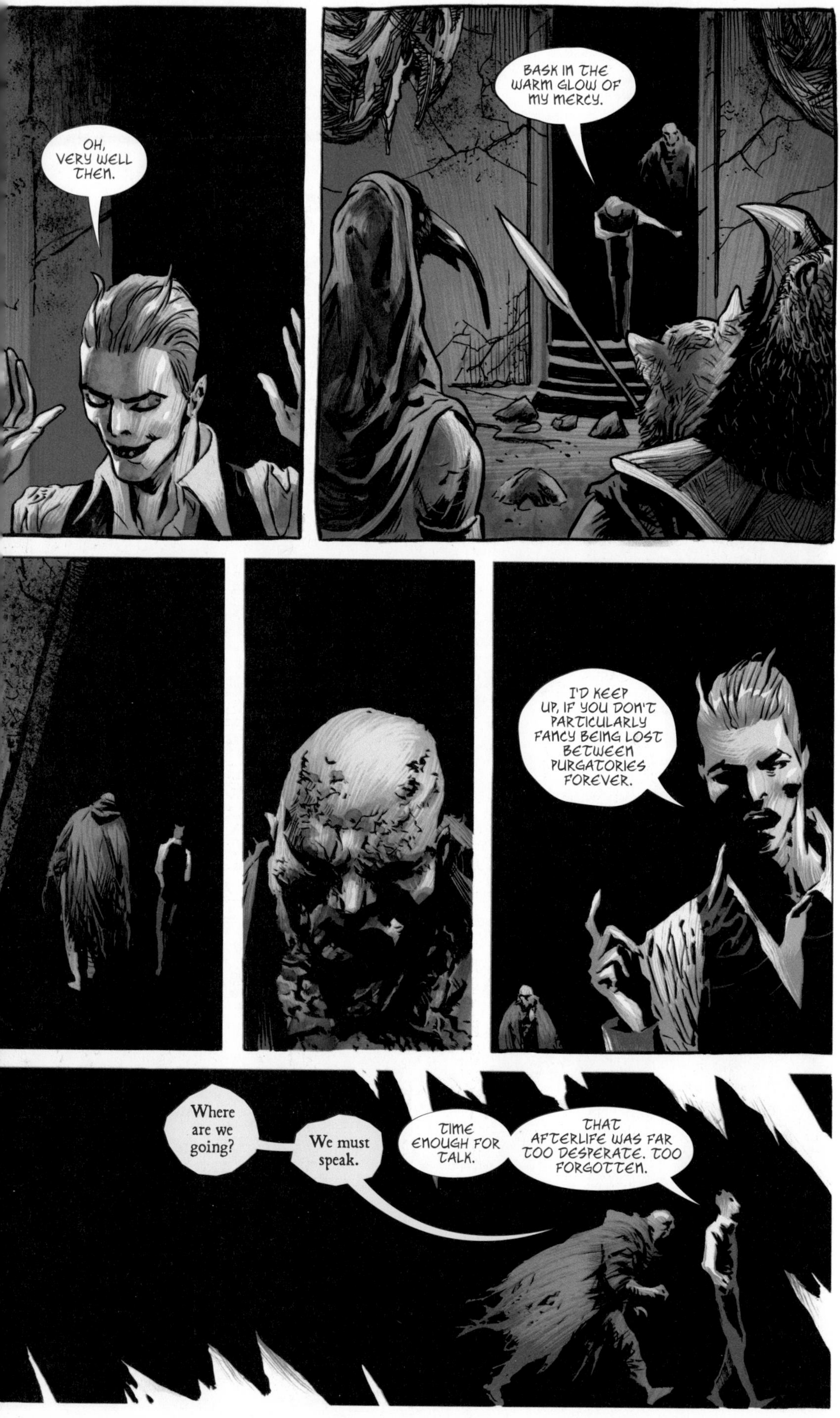
OH, VERY WELL THEN.
BASK IN THE WARM GLOW OF MY MERCY.
I'D KEEP UP, IF YOU DON'T PARTICULARLY FANCY BEING LOST BETWEEN PURGATORIES FOREVER.
Where are we going?
We must speak.
TIME ENOUGH FOR TALK.
THAT AFTERLIFE WAS FAR TOO DESPERATE. TOO FORGOTTEN.

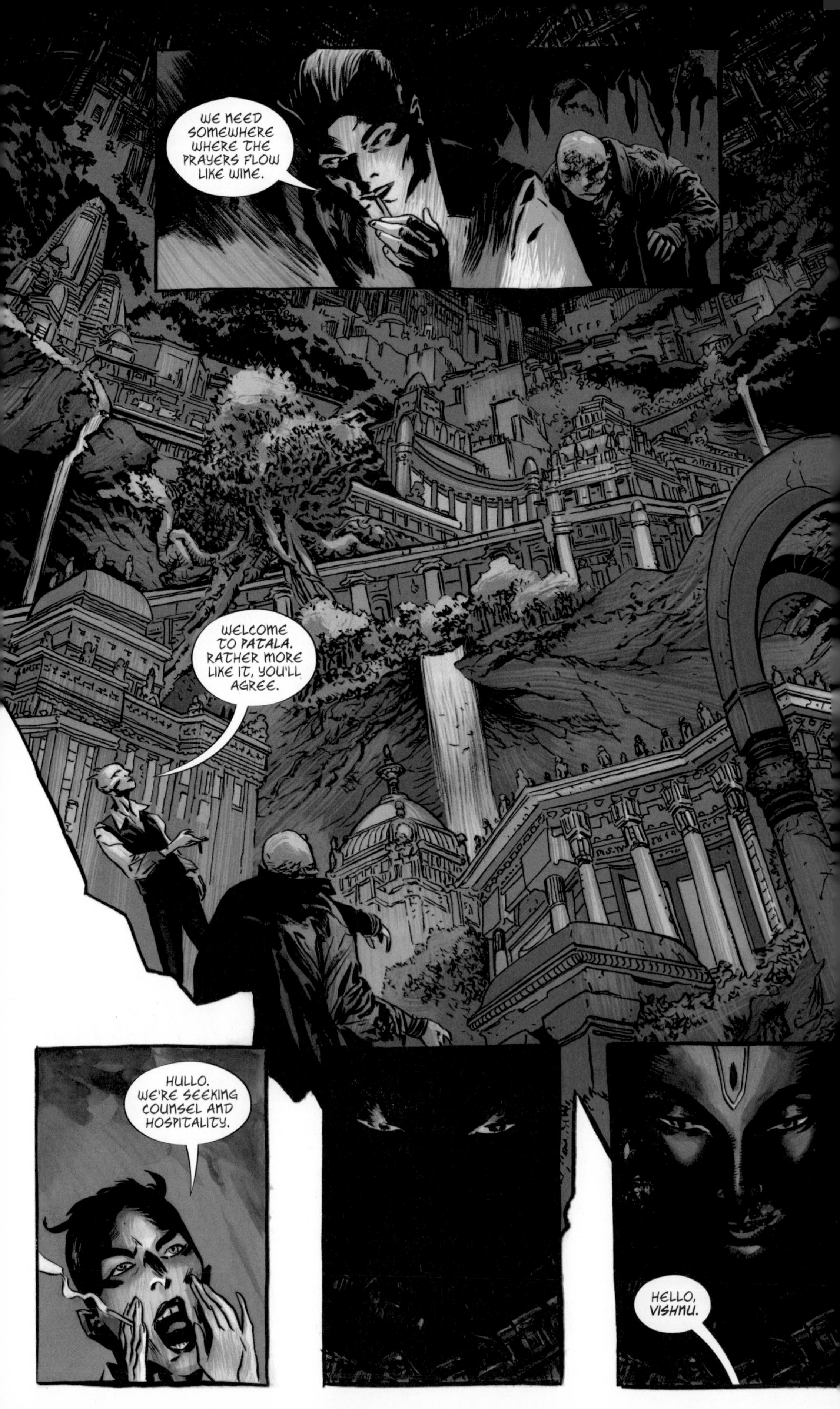
WE NEED SOMEWHERE WHERE THE PRAYERS FLOW LIKE WINE.
WELCOME TO PATALA. RATHER MORE LIKE IT, YOU'LL AGREE.
HULLO. WE'RE SEEKING COUNSEL AND HOSPITALITY.
HELLO, VISHNU.

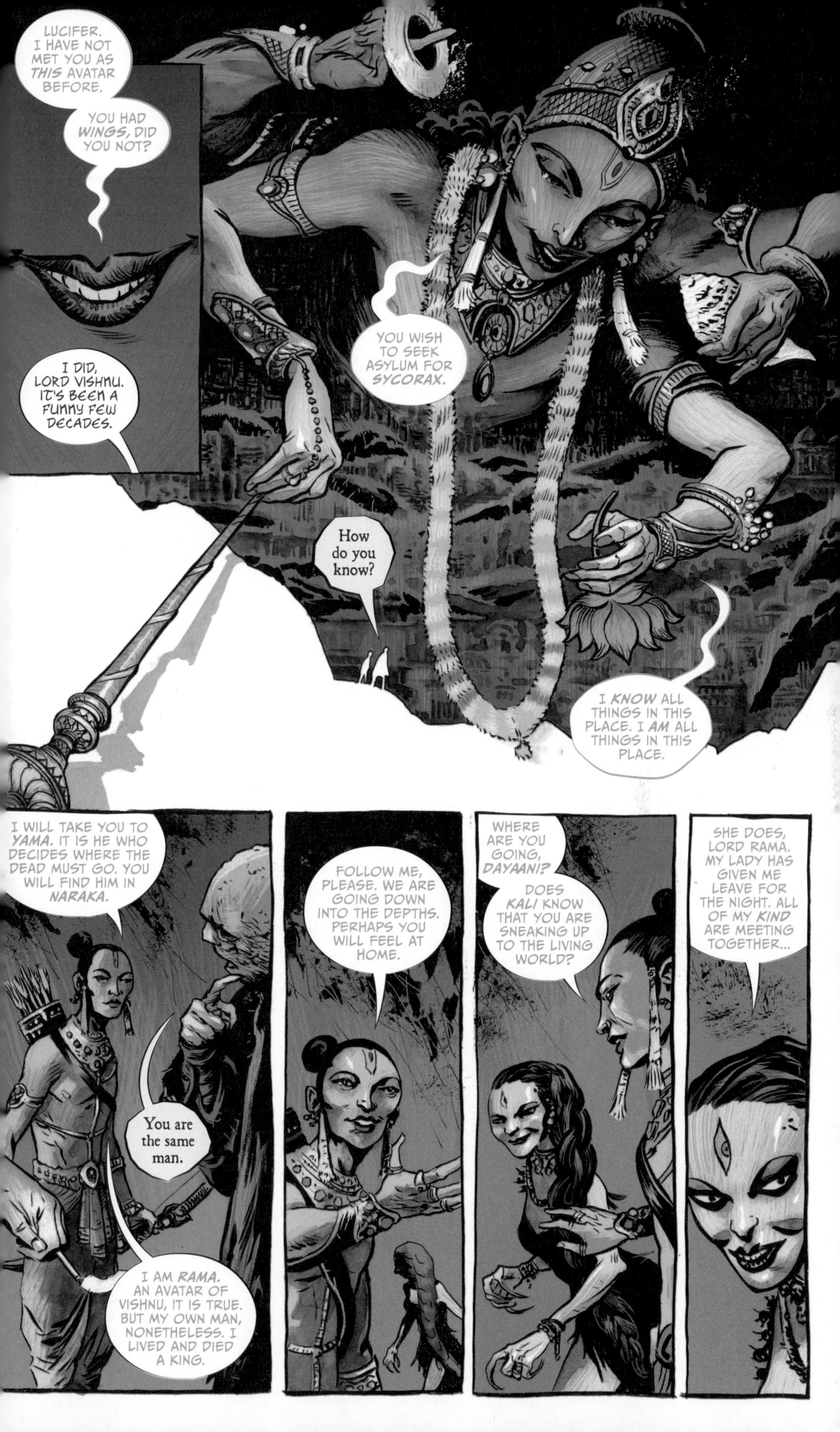
LUCIFER. I HAVE NOT MET YOU AS *THIS* AVATAR BEFORE.
YOU HAD *WINGS*, DID YOU NOT?
I DID, LORD VISHNU. IT'S BEEN A FUNNY FEW DECADES.
YOU WISH TO SEEK ASYLUM FOR *SYCORAX.*
How do you know?
I *KNOW* ALL THINGS IN THIS PLACE. I *AM* ALL THINGS IN THIS PLACE.
I WILL TAKE YOU TO *YAMA.* IT IS HE WHO DECIDES WHERE THE DEAD MUST GO. YOU WILL FIND HIM IN *NARAKA.*
You are the same man.
I AM *RAMA.* AN AVATAR OF VISHNU, IT IS TRUE. BUT MY OWN MAN, NONETHELESS. I LIVED AND DIED A KING.
FOLLOW ME, PLEASE. WE ARE GOING DOWN INTO THE DEPTHS. PERHAPS YOU WILL FEEL AT HOME.
WHERE ARE YOU GOING, *DAYAANI?*
DOES *KALI* KNOW THAT YOU ARE SNEAKING UP TO THE LIVING WORLD?
SHE DOES, LORD RAMA. MY LADY HAS GIVEN ME LEAVE FOR THE NIGHT. ALL OF MY *KIND* ARE MEETING TOGETHER...

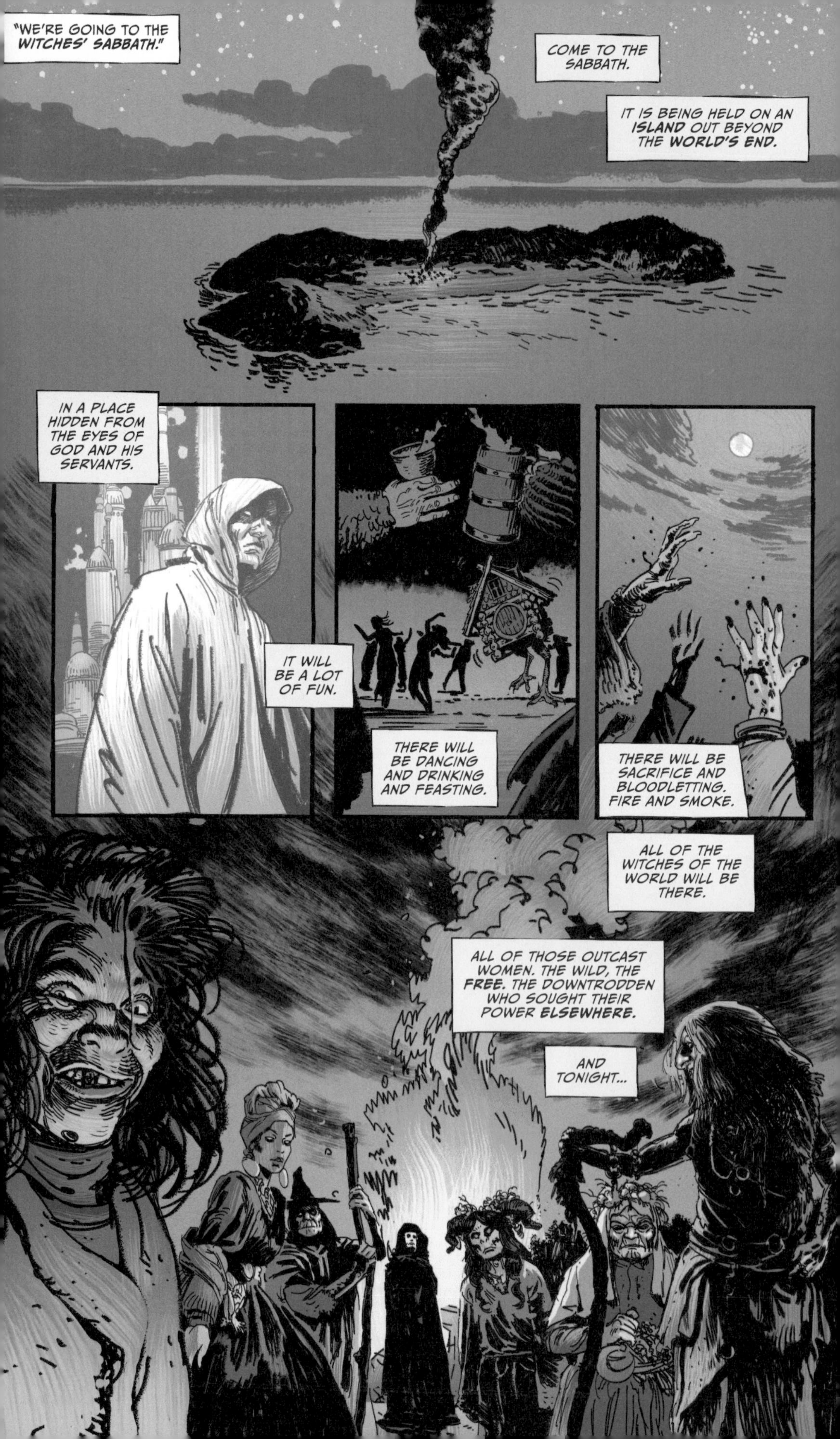
"WE'RE GOING TO THE WITCHES' SABBATH."
COME TO THE SABBATH.
IT IS BEING HELD ON AN ISLAND OUT BEYOND THE WORLD'S END.
IN A PLACE HIDDEN FROM THE EYES OF GOD AND HIS SERVANTS.
IT WILL BE A LOT OF FUN.
THERE WILL BE DANCING AND DRINKING AND FEASTING.
THERE WILL BE SACRIFICE AND BLOODLETTING. FIRE AND SMOKE.
ALL OF THE WITCHES OF THE WORLD WILL BE THERE.
ALL OF THOSE OUTCAST WOMEN. THE WILD, THE FREE. THE DOWNTRODDEN WHO SOUGHT THEIR POWER ELSEWHERE.
AND TONIGHT...

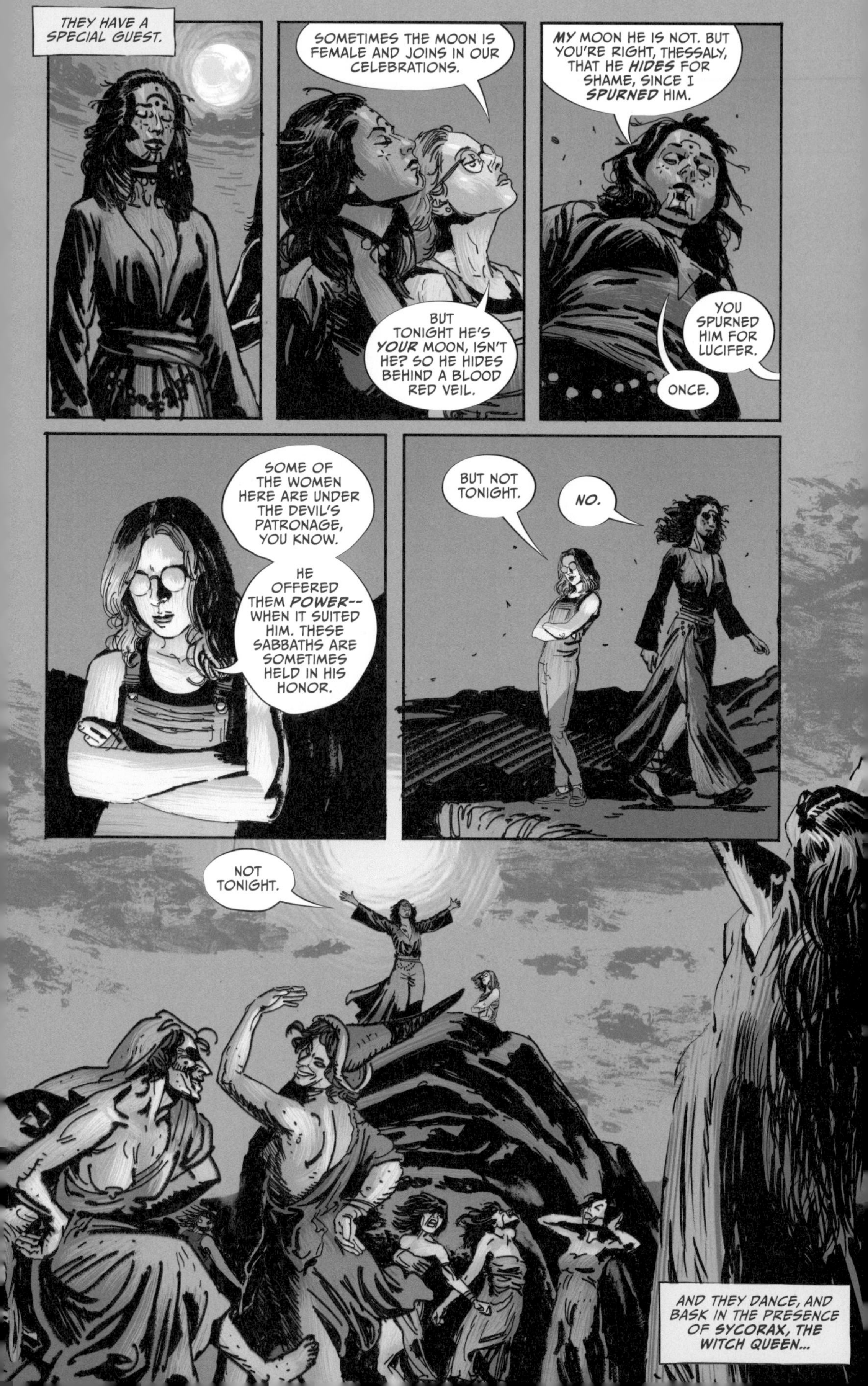
THEY HAVE A SPECIAL GUEST.
SOMETIMES THE MOON IS FEMALE AND JOINS IN OUR CELEBRATIONS.
BUT TONIGHT HE'S YOUR MOON, ISN'T HE? SO HE HIDES BEHIND A BLOOD RED VEIL.
MY MOON HE IS NOT. BUT YOU'RE RIGHT, THESSALY, THAT HE HIDES FOR SHAME, SINCE I SPURNED HIM.
YOU SPURNED HIM FOR LUCIFER.
ONCE.
SOME OF THE WOMEN HERE ARE UNDER THE DEVIL'S PATRONAGE, YOU KNOW.
HE OFFERED THEM POWER-- WHEN IT SUITED HIM. THESE SABBATHS ARE SOMETIMES HELD IN HIS HONOR.
BUT NOT TONIGHT.
NO.
NOT TONIGHT.
AND THEY DANCE, AND BASK IN THE PRESENCE OF SYCORAX, THE WITCH QUEEN...

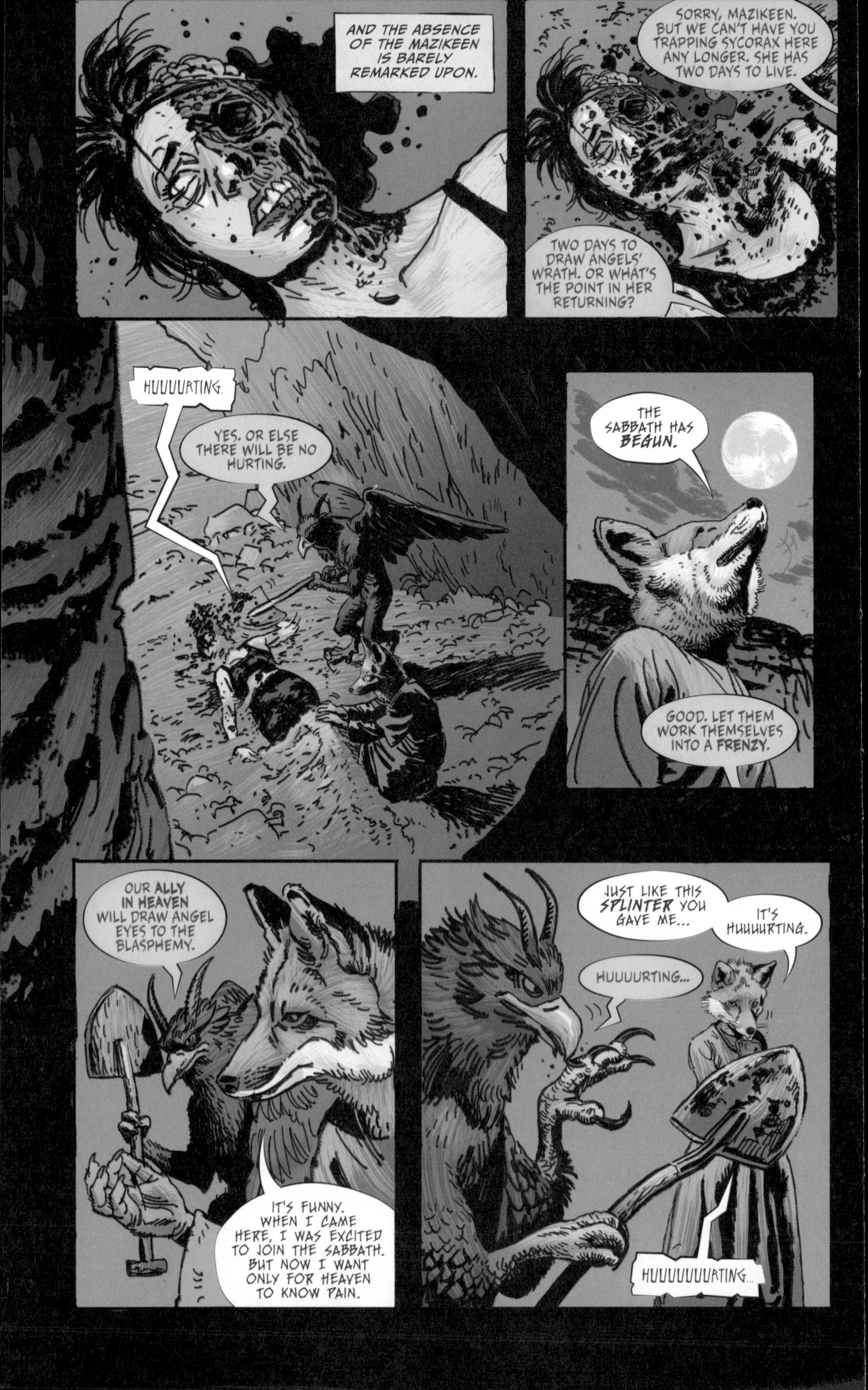
AND THE ABSENCE OF THE MAZIKEEN IS BARELY REMARKED UPON.
SORRY, MAZIKEEN. BUT WE CAN'T HAVE YOU TRAPPING SYCORAX HERE ANY LONGER. SHE HAS TWO DAYS TO LIVE.
TWO DAYS TO DRAW ANGELS' WRATH. OR WHAT'S THE POINT IN HER RETURNING?
HUUUURTING.
YES. OR ELSE THERE WILL BE NO HURTING.
THE SABBATH HAS BEGUN.
GOOD. LET THEM WORK THEMSELVES INTO A FRENZY.
OUR ALLY IN HEAVEN WILL DRAW ANGEL EYES TO THE BLASPHEMY.
IT'S FUNNY. WHEN I CAME HERE, I WAS EXCITED TO JOIN THE SABBATH. BUT NOW I WANT ONLY FOR HEAVEN TO KNOW PAIN.
JUST LIKE THIS SPLINTER YOU GAVE ME...
IT'S HUUUURTING.
HUUUURTING...
HUUUUUUURTING...

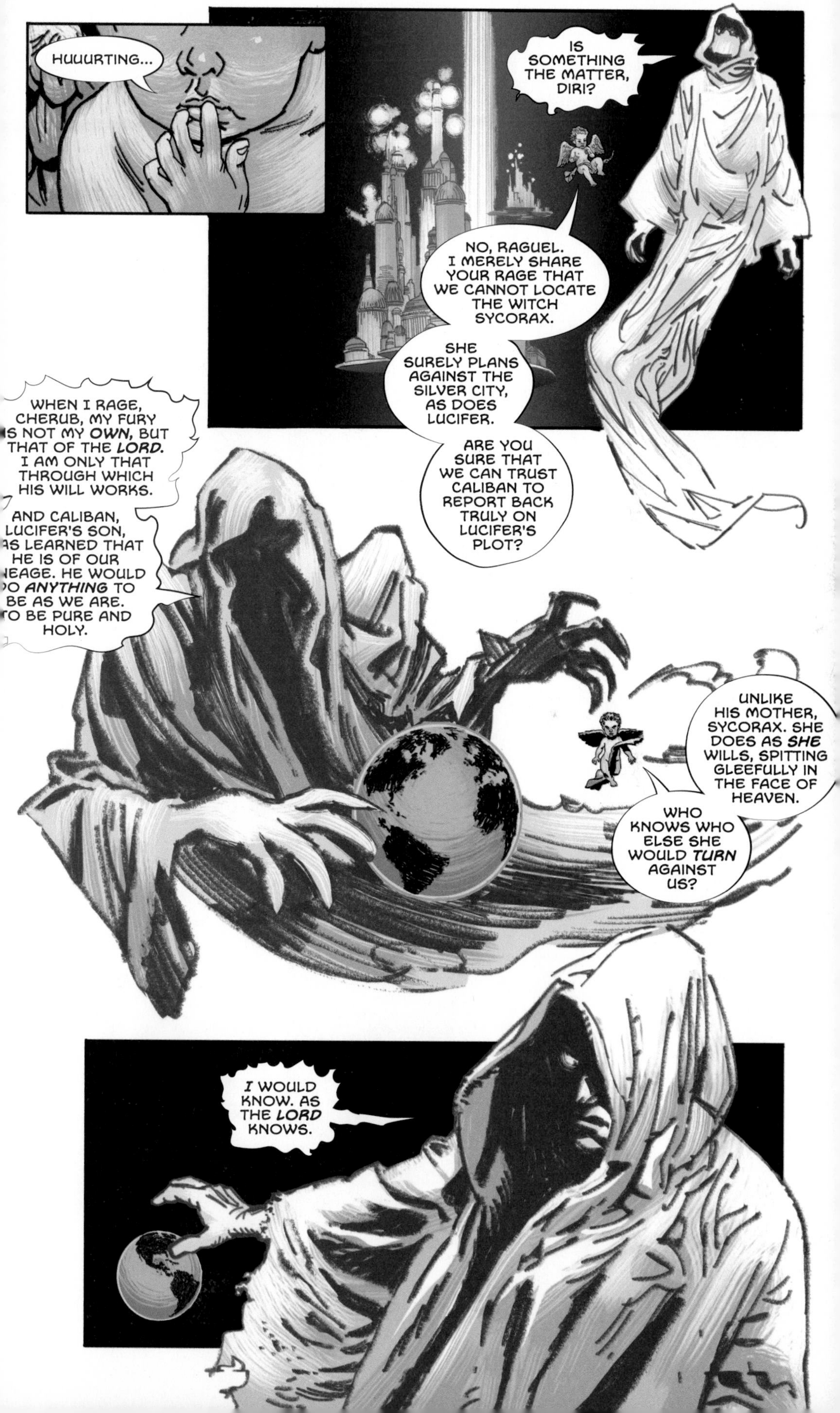
HUUURTING...
IS SOMETHING THE MATTER, DIRI?
NO, RAGUEL. I MERELY SHARE YOUR RAGE THAT WE CANNOT LOCATE THE WITCH SYCORAX.
SHE SURELY PLANS AGAINST THE SILVER CITY, AS DOES LUCIFER.
ARE YOU SURE THAT WE CAN TRUST CALIBAN TO REPORT BACK TRULY ON LUCIFER'S PLOT?
WHEN I RAGE, CHERUB, MY FURY IS NOT MY OWN, BUT THAT OF THE LORD. I AM ONLY THAT THROUGH WHICH HIS WILL WORKS.
AND CALIBAN, LUCIFER'S SON, HAS LEARNED THAT HE IS OF OUR LINEAGE. HE WOULD DO ANYTHING TO BE AS WE ARE. TO BE PURE AND HOLY.
UNLIKE HIS MOTHER, SYCORAX. SHE DOES AS SHE WILLS, SPITTING GLEEFULLY IN THE FACE OF HEAVEN.
WHO KNOWS WHO ELSE SHE WOULD TURN AGAINST US?
I WOULD KNOW. AS THE LORD KNOWS.

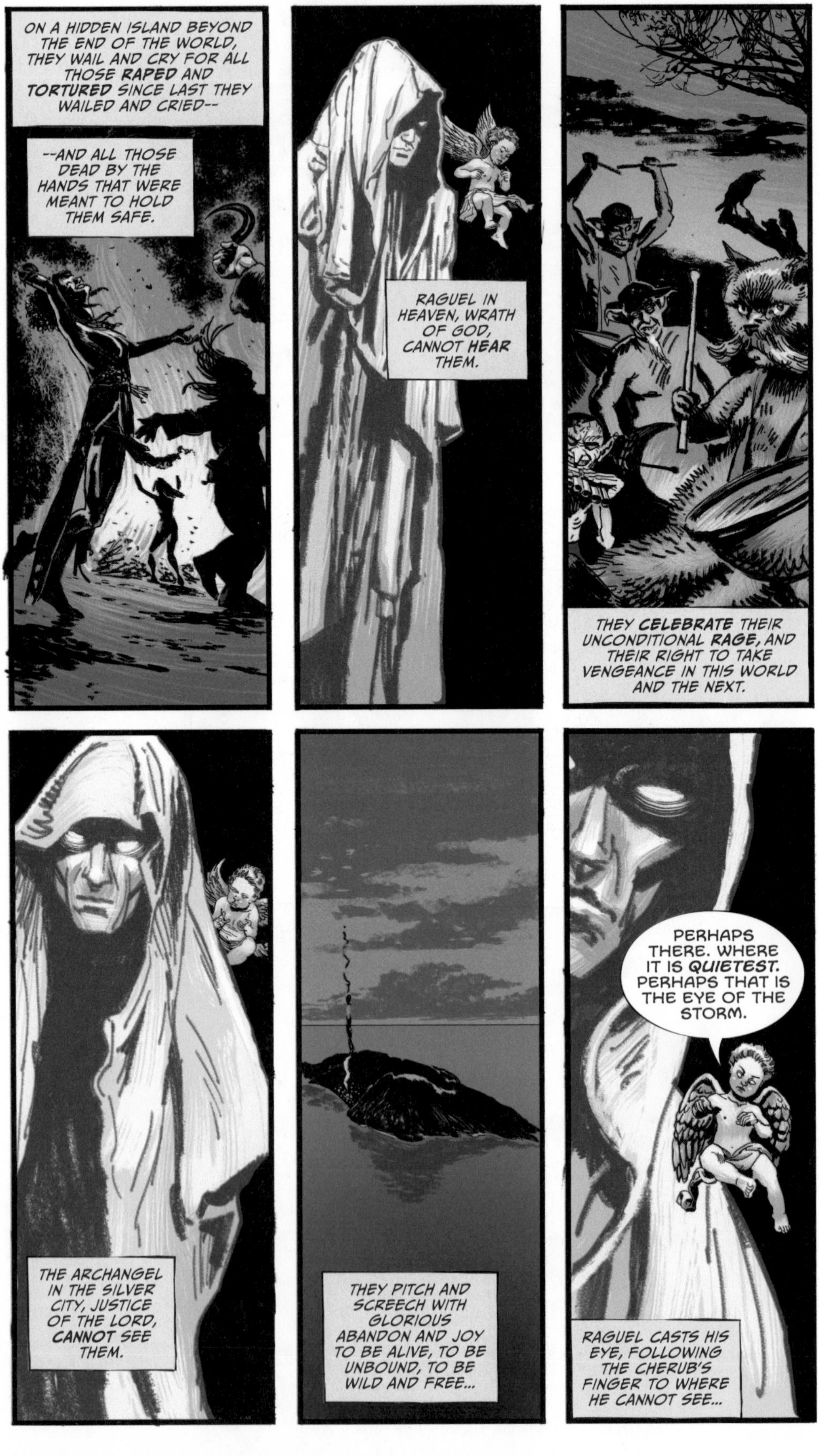
ON A HIDDEN ISLAND BEYOND THE END OF THE WORLD, THEY WAIL AND CRY FOR ALL THOSE RAPED AND TORTURED SINCE LAST THEY WAILED AND CRIED--
--AND ALL THOSE DEAD BY THE HANDS THAT WERE MEANT TO HOLD THEM SAFE.
RAGUEL IN HEAVEN, WRATH OF GOD, CANNOT HEAR THEM.
THEY CELEBRATE THEIR UNCONDITIONAL RAGE, AND THEIR RIGHT TO TAKE VENGEANCE IN THIS WORLD AND THE NEXT.
THE ARCHANGEL IN THE SILVER CITY, JUSTICE OF THE LORD, CANNOT SEE THEM.
THEY PITCH AND SCREECH WITH GLORIOUS ABANDON AND JOY TO BE ALIVE, TO BE UNBOUND, TO BE WILD AND FREE...
PERHAPS THERE. WHERE IT IS QUIETEST. PERHAPS THAT IS THE EYE OF THE STORM.
RAGUEL CASTS HIS EYE, FOLLOWING THE CHERUB'S FINGER TO WHERE HE CANNOT SEE...

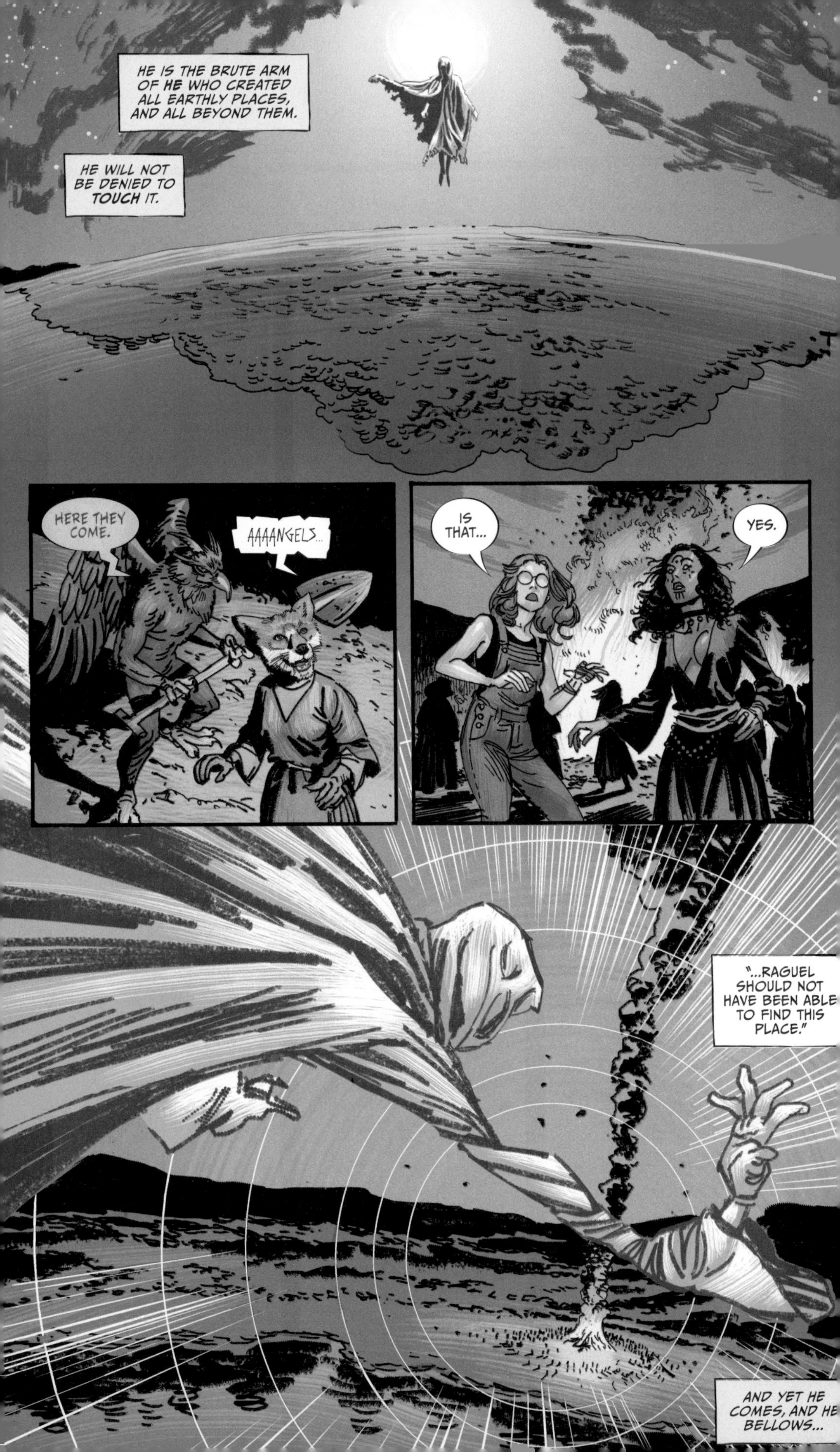
HE IS THE BRUTE ARM OF HE WHO CREATED ALL EARTHLY PLACES, AND ALL BEYOND THEM.
HE WILL NOT BE DENIED TO TOUCH IT.
HERE THEY COME.
AAAANGELS...
IS THAT...
YES.
"...RAGUEL SHOULD NOT HAVE BEEN ABLE TO FIND THIS PLACE."
AND YET HE COMES, AND HE BELLOWS...

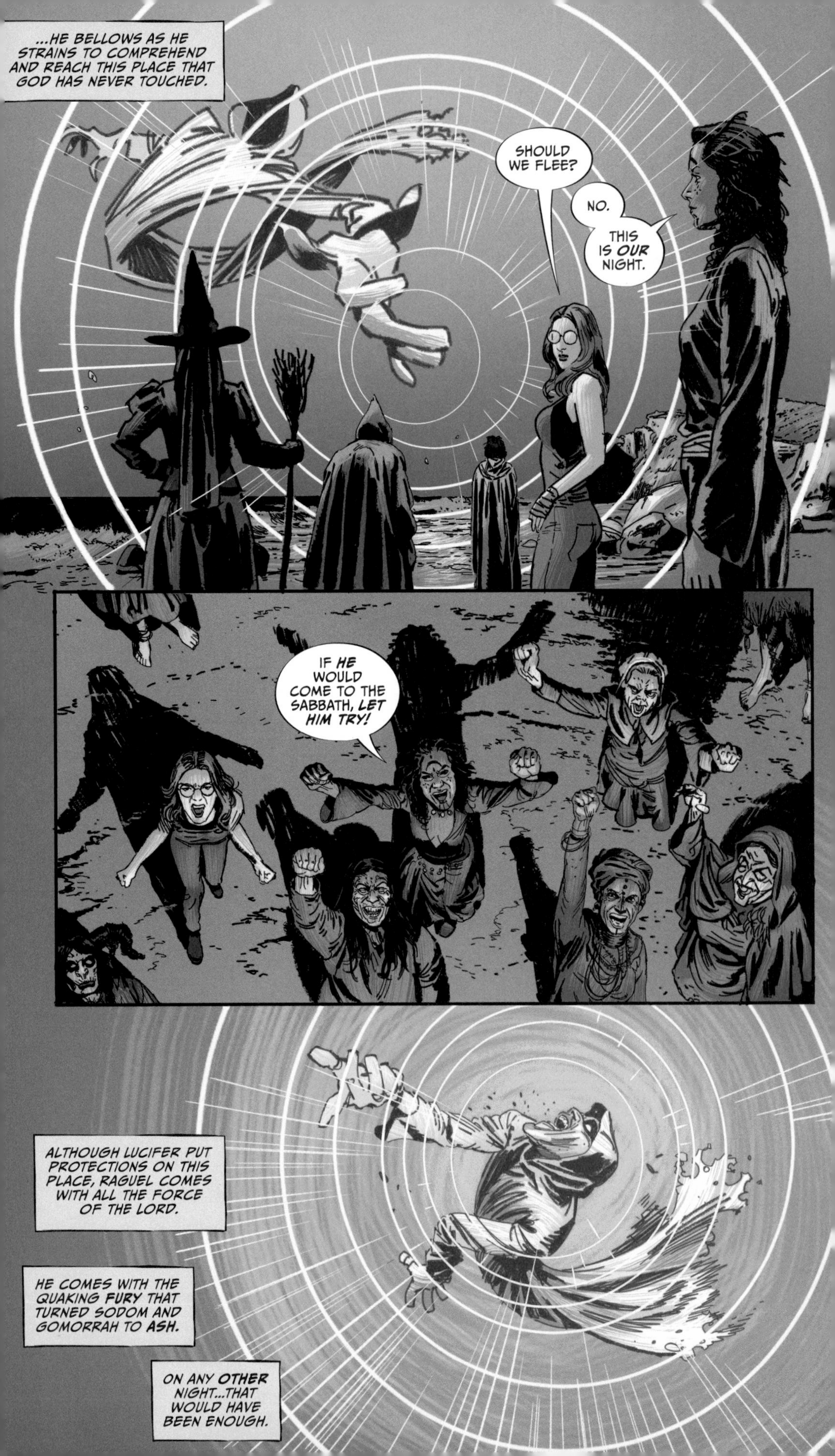

...HE BELLOWS AS HE STRAINS TO COMPREHEND AND REACH THIS PLACE THAT GOD HAS NEVER TOUCHED.
SHOULD WE FLEE?
NO.
THIS IS OUR NIGHT.
IF HE WOULD COME TO THE SABBATH, LET HIM TRY!
ALTHOUGH LUCIFER PUT PROTECTIONS ON THIS PLACE, RAGUEL COMES WITH ALL THE FORCE OF THE LORD.
HE COMES WITH THE QUAKING FURY THAT TURNED SODOM AND GOMORRAH TO ASH.
ON ANY OTHER NIGHT...THAT WOULD HAVE BEEN ENOUGH.

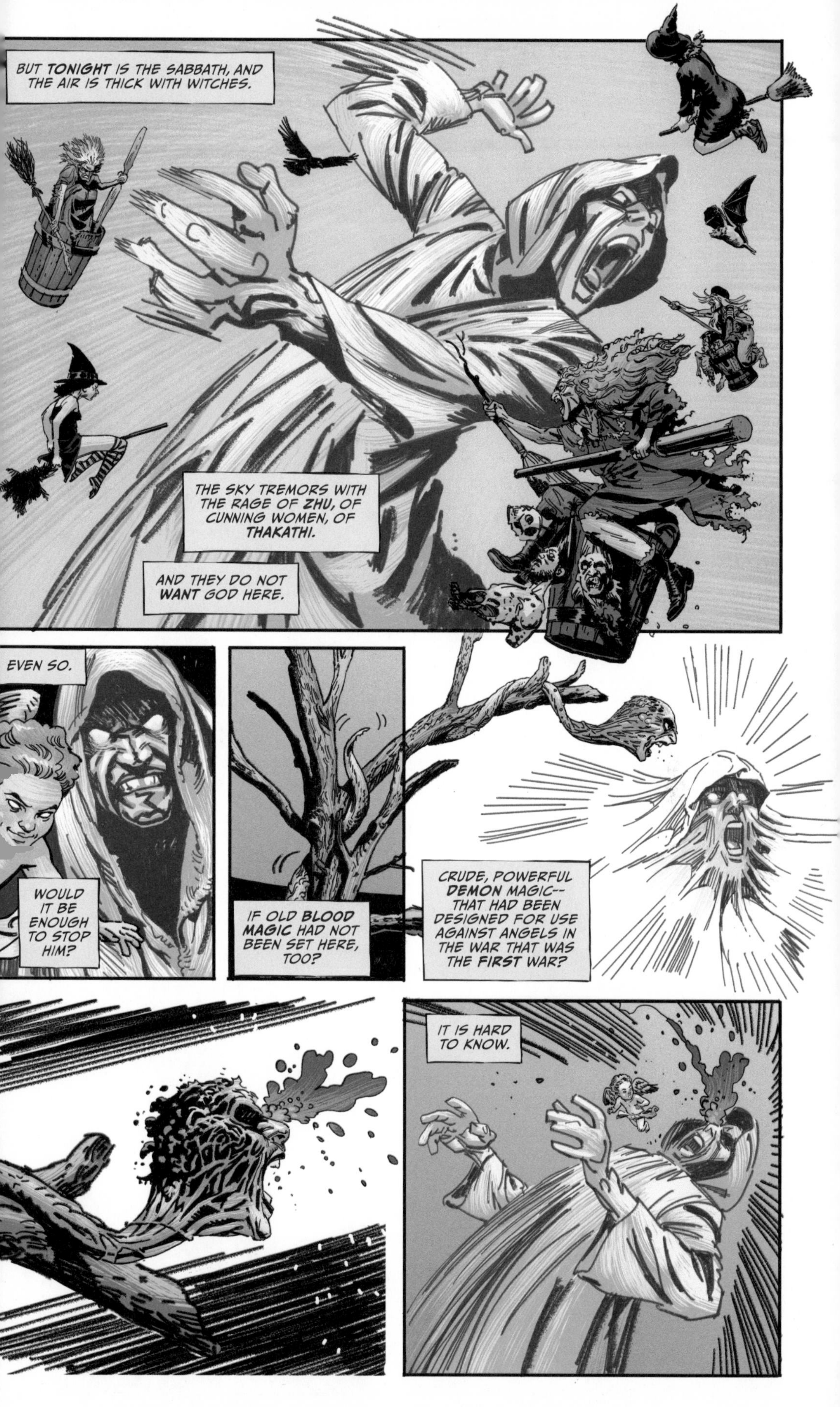
BUT TONIGHT IS THE SABBATH, AND THE AIR IS THICK WITH WITCHES.
THE SKY TREMORS WITH THE RAGE OF ZHU, OF CUNNING WOMEN, OF THAKATHI.
AND THEY DO NOT WANT GOD HERE.
EVEN SO.
WOULD IT BE ENOUGH TO STOP HIM?
IF OLD BLOOD MAGIC HAD NOT BEEN SET HERE, TOO?
CRUDE, POWERFUL DEMON MAGIC--THAT HAD BEEN DESIGNED FOR USE AGAINST ANGELS IN THE WAR THAT WAS THE FIRST WAR?
IT IS HARD TO KNOW.

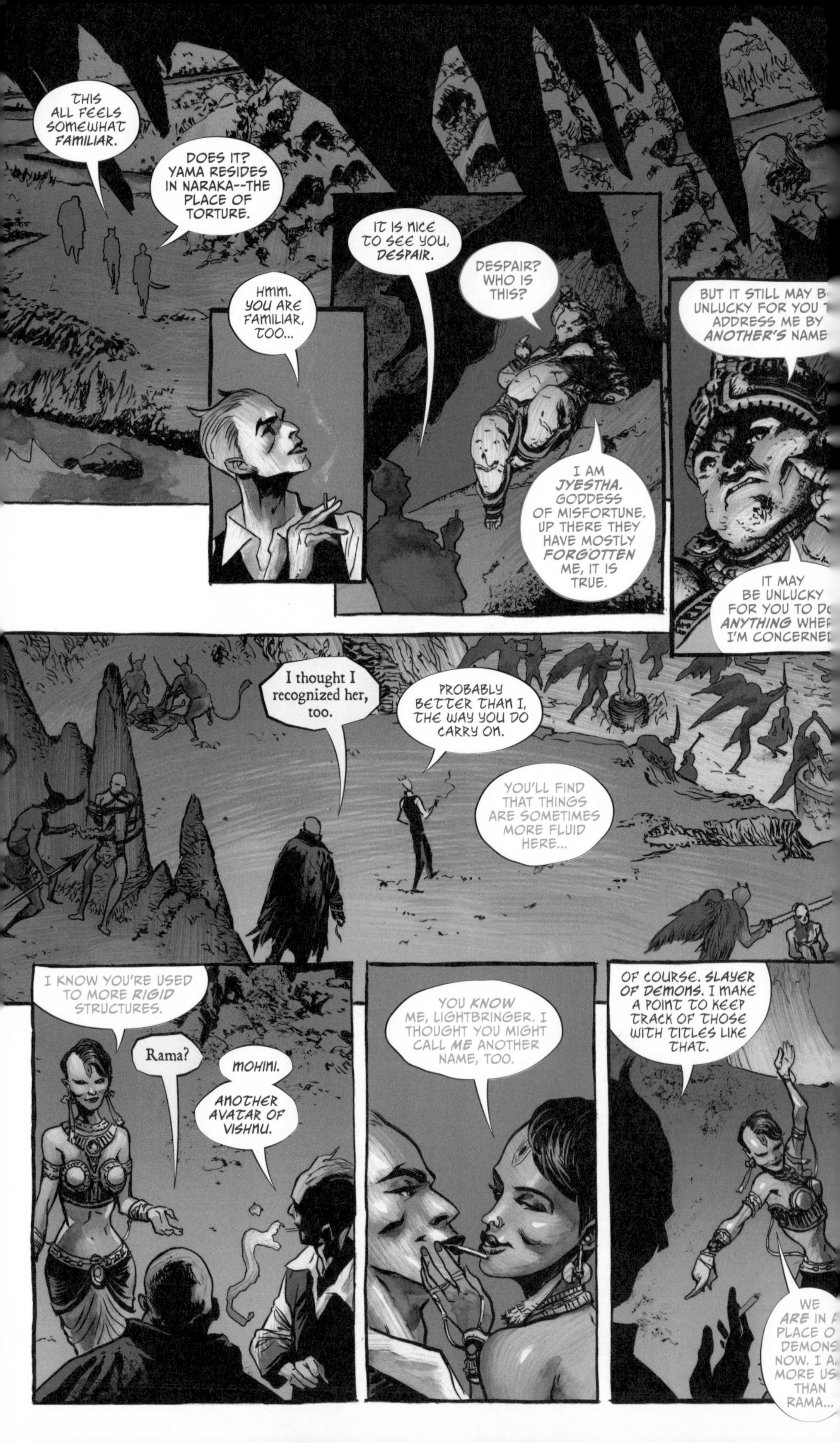
THIS ALL FEELS SOMEWHAT FAMILIAR.
DOES IT? YAMA RESIDES IN NARAKA--THE PLACE OF TORTURE.
HMM. YOU ARE FAMILIAR, TOO...
IT IS NICE TO SEE YOU, DESPAIR.
DESPAIR? WHO IS THIS?
I AM JYESTHA. GODDESS OF MISFORTUNE. UP THERE THEY HAVE MOSTLY FORGOTTEN ME, IT IS TRUE.
BUT IT STILL MAY B UNLUCKY FOR YOU ADDRESS ME BY ANOTHER'S NAME
IT MAY BE UNLUCKY FOR YOU TO D ANYTHING WHE I'M CONCERNE
I thought I recognized her, too.
PROBABLY BETTER THAN I, THE WAY YOU DO CARRY ON.
YOU'LL FIND THAT THINGS ARE SOMETIMES MORE FLUID HERE...
I KNOW YOU'RE USED TO MORE RIGID STRUCTURES.
Rama?
MOHINI.
ANOTHER AVATAR OF VISHNU.
YOU KNOW ME, LIGHTBRINGER. I THOUGHT YOU MIGHT CALL ME ANOTHER NAME, TOO.
OF COURSE. SLAYER OF DEMONS. I MAKE A POINT TO KEEP TRACK OF THOSE WITH TITLES LIKE THAT.
WE ARE IN PLACE O DEMONS NOW. I A MORE US THAN RAMA...

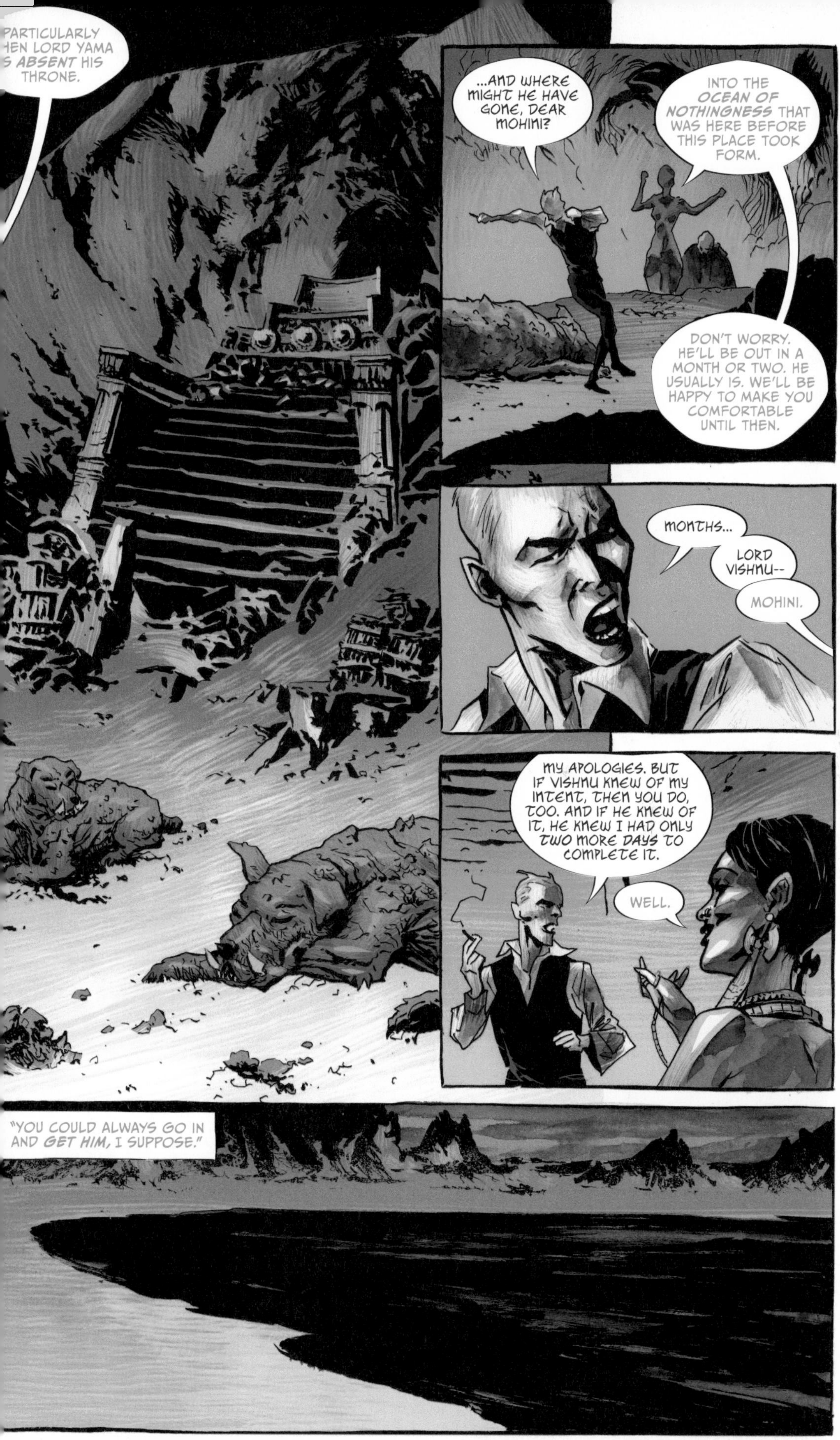
PARTICULARLY
HEN LORD YAMA
S ABSENT HIS
THRONE.
...AND WHERE
MIGHT HE HAVE
GONE, DEAR
MOHINI?
INTO THE
OCEAN OF
NOTHINGNESS THAT
WAS HERE BEFORE
THIS PLACE TOOK
FORM.
DON'T WORRY.
HE'LL BE OUT IN A
MONTH OR TWO. HE
USUALLY IS. WE'LL BE
HAPPY TO MAKE YOU
COMFORTABLE
UNTIL THEN.
MONTHS...
LORD
VISHNU--
MOHINI.
MY APOLOGIES. BUT
IF VISHNU KNEW OF MY
INTENT, THEN YOU DO,
TOO. AND IF HE KNEW OF
IT, HE KNEW I HAD ONLY
TWO MORE DAYS TO
COMPLETE IT.
WELL.
"YOU COULD ALWAYS GO IN
AND GET HIM, I SUPPOSE."

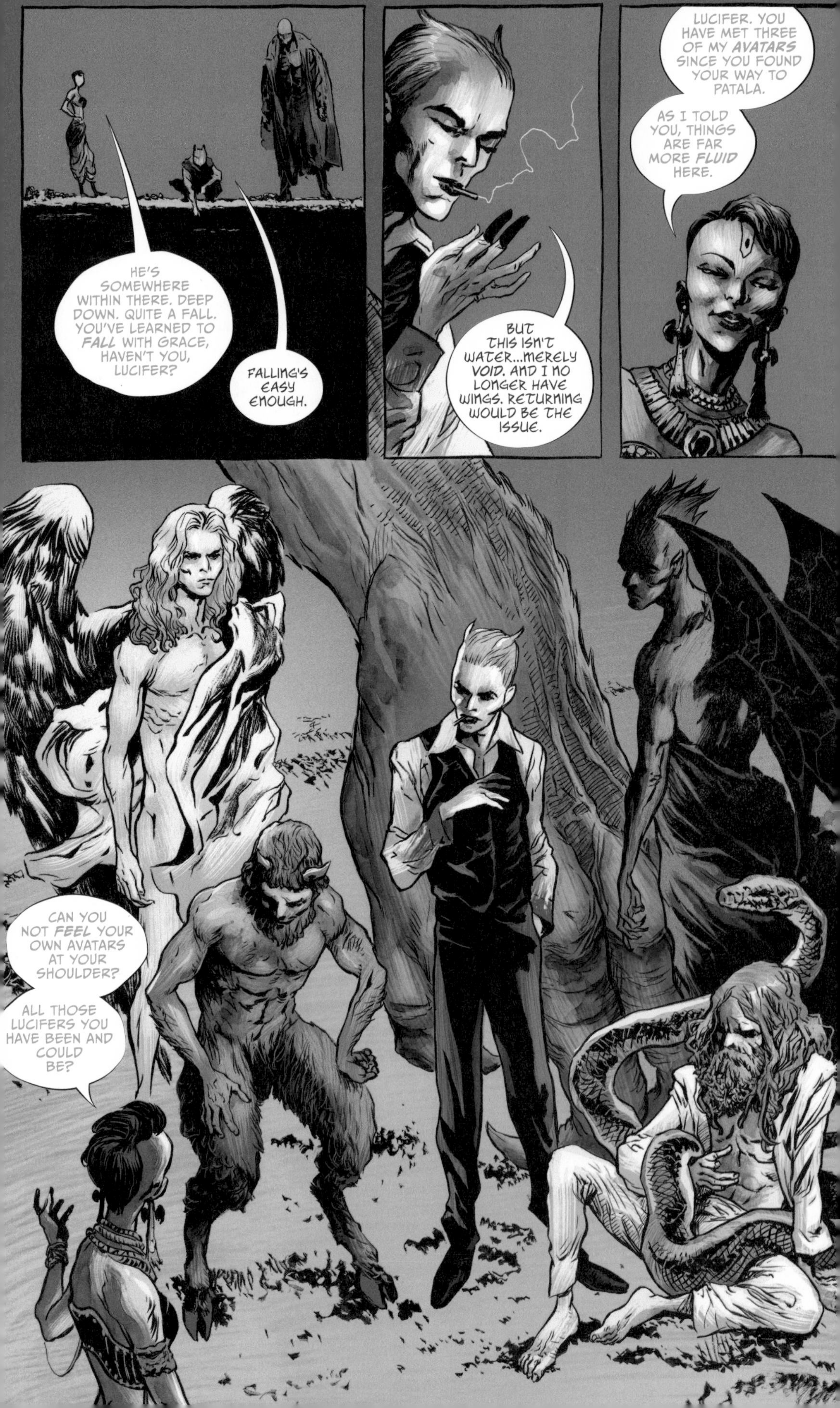
HE'S SOMEWHERE WITHIN THERE. DEEP DOWN. QUITE A FALL. YOU'VE LEARNED TO FALL WITH GRACE, HAVEN'T YOU, LUCIFER?
FALLING'S EASY ENOUGH.
BUT THIS ISN'T WATER...MERELY VOID. AND I NO LONGER HAVE WINGS. RETURNING WOULD BE THE ISSUE.
LUCIFER. YOU HAVE MET THREE OF MY AVATARS SINCE YOU FOUND YOUR WAY TO PATALA.
AS I TOLD YOU, THINGS ARE FAR MORE FLUID HERE.
CAN YOU NOT FEEL YOUR OWN AVATARS AT YOUR SHOULDER?
ALL THOSE LUCIFERS YOU HAVE BEEN AND COULD BE?

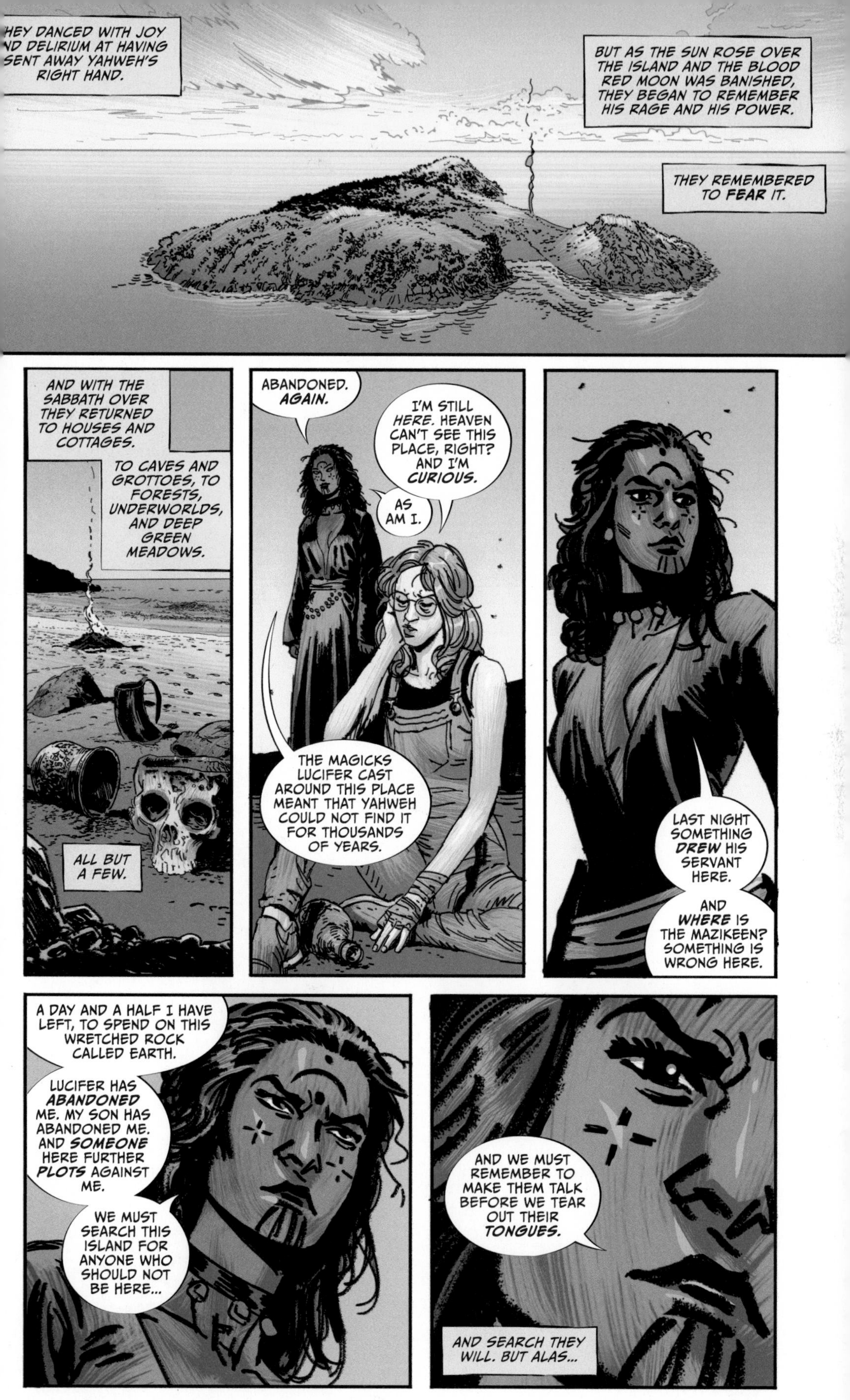

HEY DANCED WITH JOY
ND DELIRIUM AT HAVING
SENT AWAY YAHWEH'S
RIGHT HAND.
BUT AS THE SUN ROSE OVER THE ISLAND AND THE BLOOD RED MOON WAS BANISHED, THEY BEGAN TO REMEMBER HIS RAGE AND HIS POWER.
THEY REMEMBERED TO FEAR IT.
AND WITH THE SABBATH OVER THEY RETURNED TO HOUSES AND COTTAGES.
TO CAVES AND GROTTOES, TO FORESTS, UNDERWORLDS, AND DEEP GREEN MEADOWS.
ALL BUT A FEW.
ABANDONED. AGAIN.
I'M STILL HERE. HEAVEN CAN'T SEE THIS PLACE, RIGHT? AND I'M CURIOUS.
AS AM I.
THE MAGICKS LUCIFER CAST AROUND THIS PLACE MEANT THAT YAHWEH COULD NOT FIND IT FOR THOUSANDS OF YEARS.
LAST NIGHT SOMETHING DREW HIS SERVANT HERE.
AND WHERE IS THE MAZIKEEN? SOMETHING IS WRONG HERE.
A DAY AND A HALF I HAVE LEFT, TO SPEND ON THIS WRETCHED ROCK CALLED EARTH.
LUCIFER HAS ABANDONED ME. MY SON HAS ABANDONED ME. AND SOMEONE HERE FURTHER PLOTS AGAINST ME.
WE MUST SEARCH THIS ISLAND FOR ANYONE WHO SHOULD NOT BE HERE...
AND WE MUST REMEMBER TO MAKE THEM TALK BEFORE WE TEAR OUT THEIR TONGUES.
AND SEARCH THEY WILL. BUT ALAS...

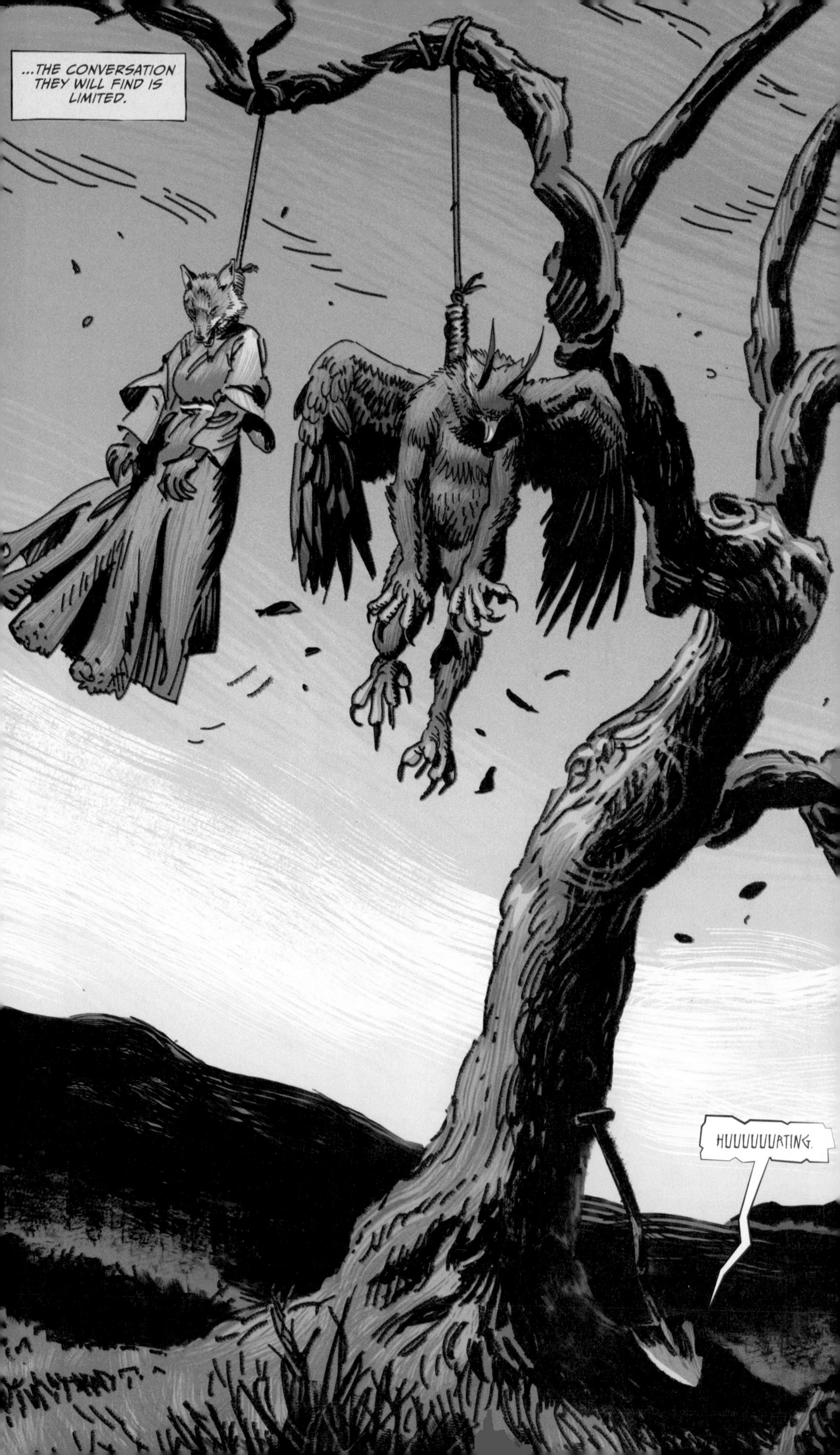
...THE CONVERSATION THEY WILL FIND IS LIMITED.
HUUUUUURTING.

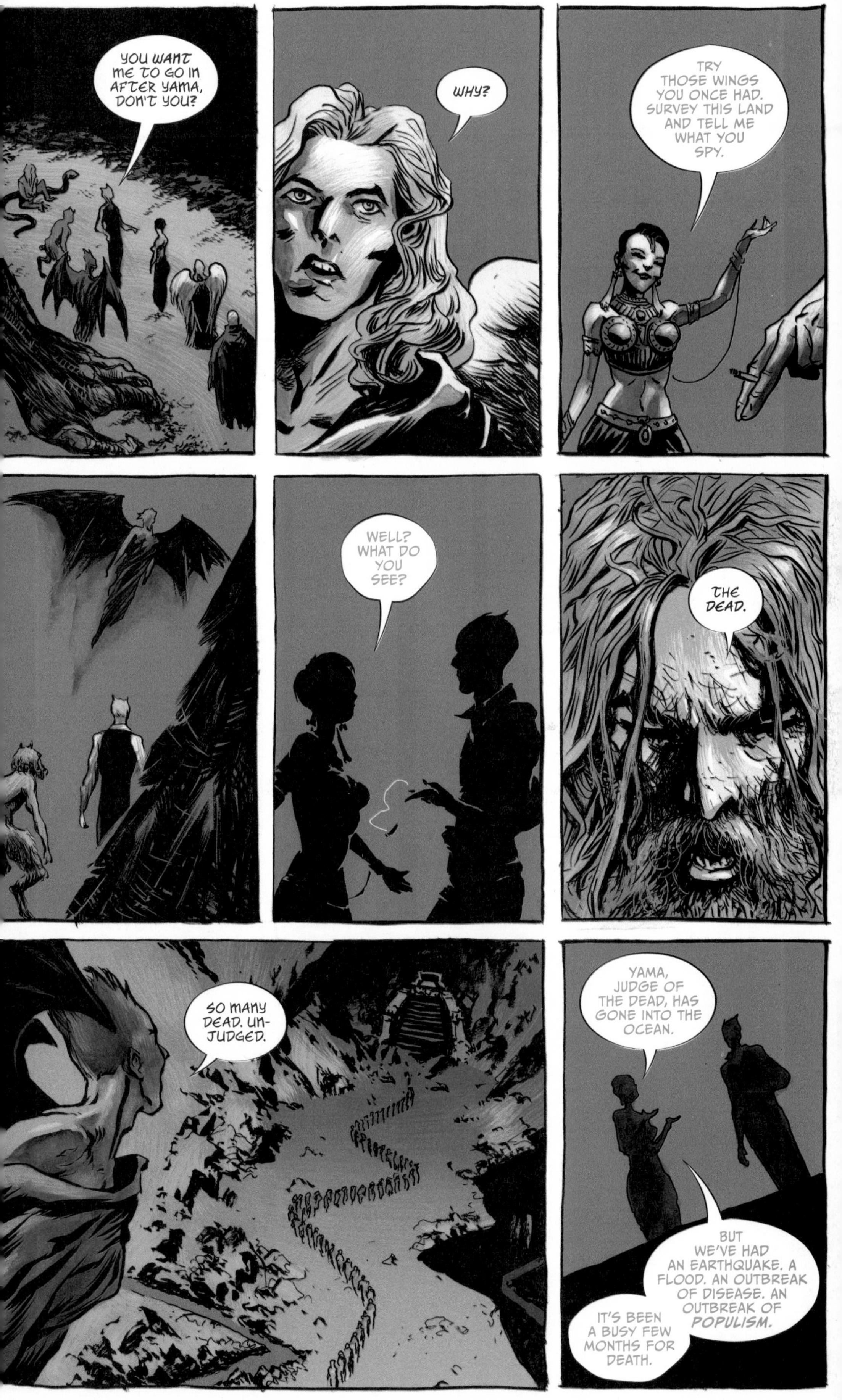
YOU WANT ME TO GO IN AFTER YAMA, DON'T YOU?
WHY?
TRY THOSE WINGS YOU ONCE HAD. SURVEY THIS LAND AND TELL ME WHAT YOU SPY.
WELL? WHAT DO YOU SEE?
THE DEAD.
SO MANY DEAD. UN-JUDGED.
YAMA, JUDGE OF THE DEAD, HAS GONE INTO THE OCEAN.
BUT WE'VE HAD AN EARTHQUAKE. A FLOOD. AN OUTBREAK OF DISEASE. AN OUTBREAK OF POPULISM.
IT'S BEEN A BUSY FEW MONTHS FOR DEATH.

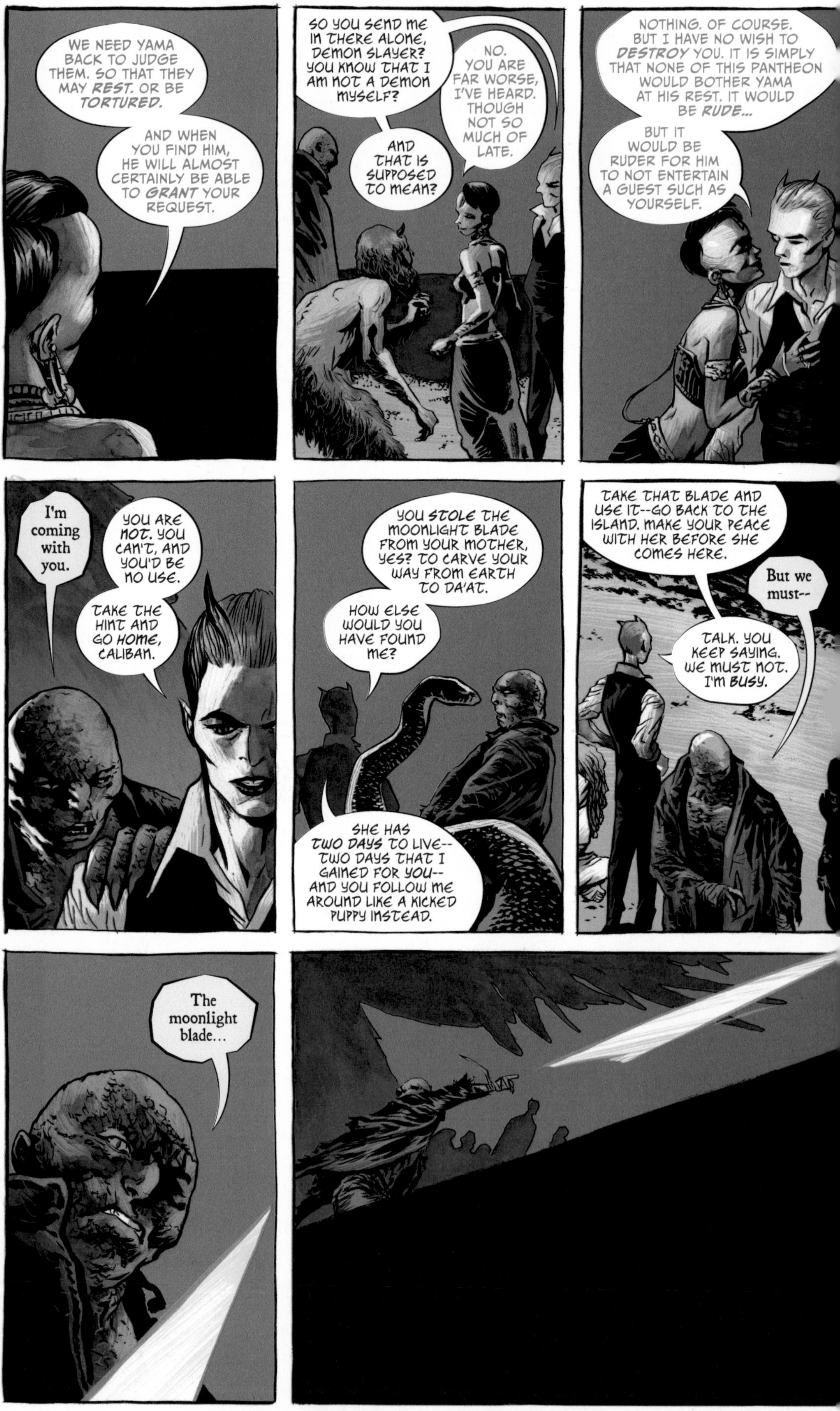
WE NEED YAMA BACK TO JUDGE THEM. SO THAT THEY MAY REST. OR BE TORTURED.
AND WHEN YOU FIND HIM, HE WILL ALMOST CERTAINLY BE ABLE TO GRANT YOUR REQUEST.
SO YOU SEND ME IN THERE ALONE, DEMON SLAYER? YOU KNOW THAT I AM NOT A DEMON MYSELF?
NO. YOU ARE FAR WORSE, I'VE HEARD. THOUGH NOT SO MUCH OF LATE.
AND THAT IS SUPPOSED TO MEAN?
NOTHING. OF COURSE. BUT I HAVE NO WISH TO DESTROY YOU. IT IS SIMPLY THAT NONE OF THIS PANTHEON WOULD BOTHER YAMA AT HIS REST. IT WOULD BE RUDE...
BUT IT WOULD BE RUDER FOR HIM TO NOT ENTERTAIN A GUEST SUCH AS YOURSELF.
I'm coming with you.
YOU ARE NOT. YOU CAN'T, AND YOU'D BE NO USE.
TAKE THE HINT AND GO HOME, CALIBAN.
YOU STOLE THE MOONLIGHT BLADE FROM YOUR MOTHER, YES? TO CARVE YOUR WAY FROM EARTH TO DA'AT.
HOW ELSE WOULD YOU HAVE FOUND ME?
SHE HAS TWO DAYS TO LIVE-- TWO DAYS THAT I GAINED FOR YOU-- AND YOU FOLLOW ME AROUND LIKE A KICKED PUPPY INSTEAD.
TAKE THAT BLADE AND USE IT--GO BACK TO THE ISLAND. MAKE YOUR PEACE WITH HER BEFORE SHE COMES HERE.
But we must--
TALK. YOU KEEP SAYING. WE MUST NOT. I'M BUSY.
The moonlight blade...

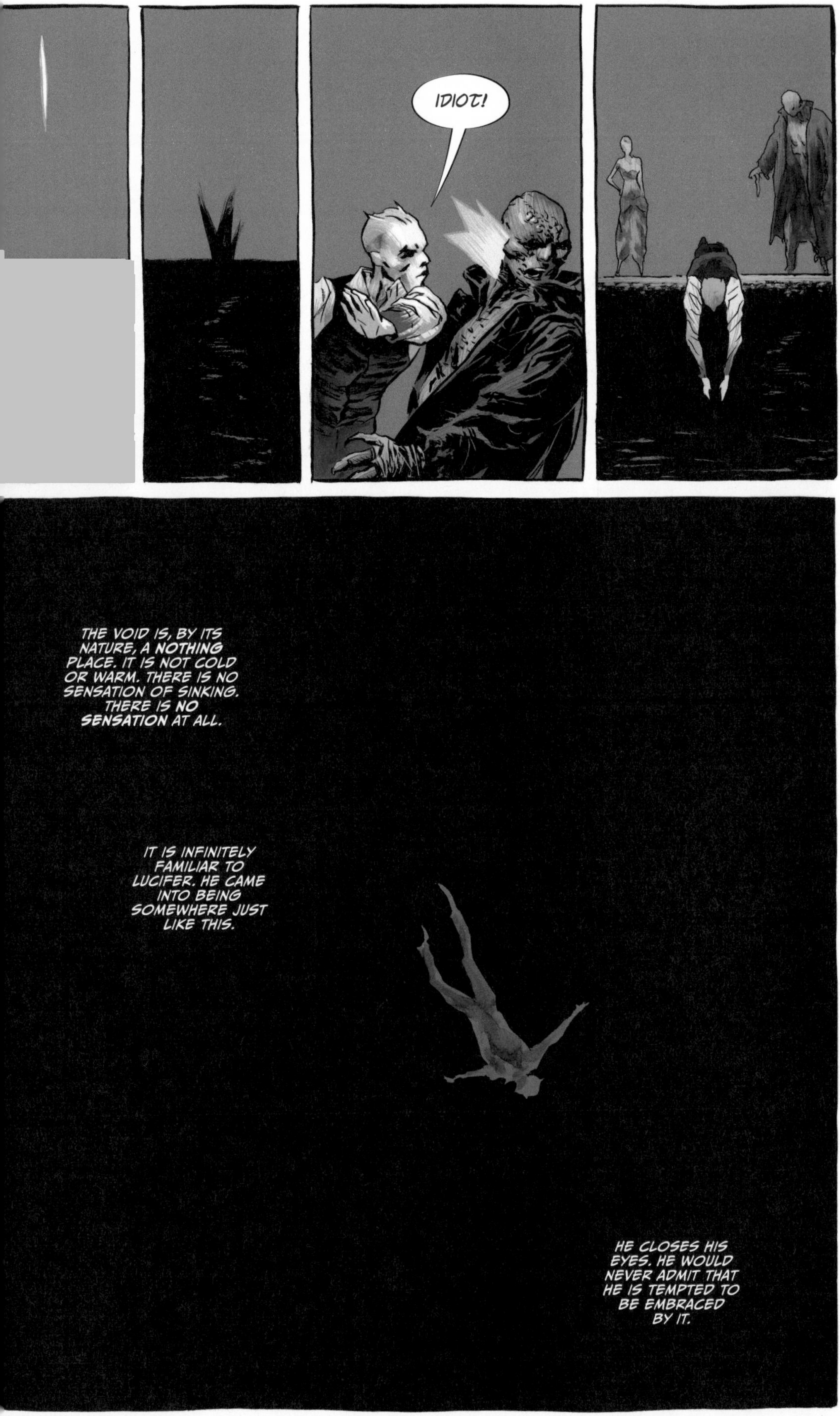
IDIOT!
THE VOID IS, BY ITS NATURE, A NOTHING PLACE. IT IS NOT COLD OR WARM. THERE IS NO SENSATION OF SINKING. THERE IS NO SENSATION AT ALL.
IT IS INFINITELY FAMILIAR TO LUCIFER. HE CAME INTO BEING SOMEWHERE JUST LIKE THIS.
HE CLOSES HIS EYES. HE WOULD NEVER ADMIT THAT HE IS TEMPTED TO BE EMBRACED BY IT.

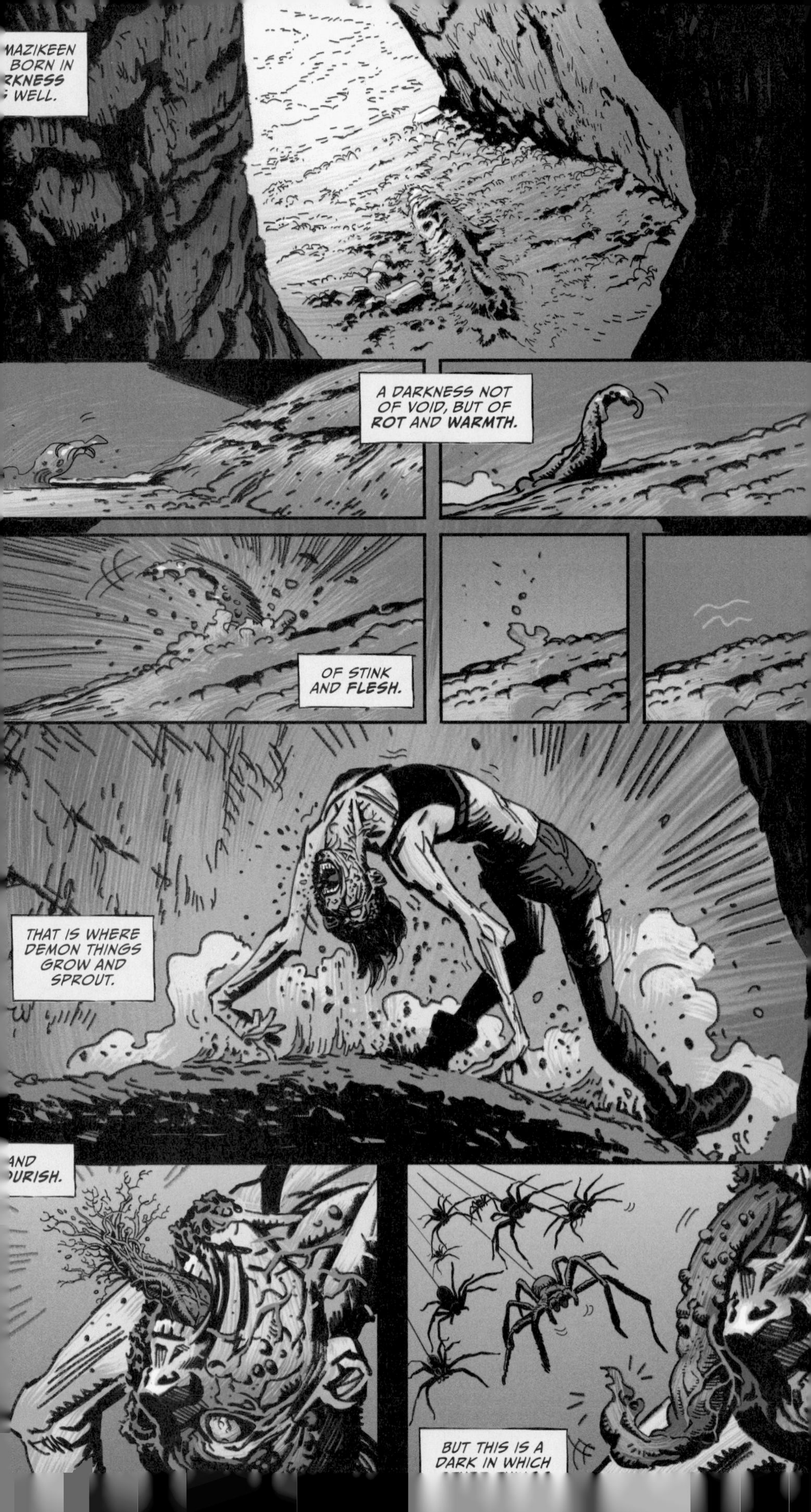
MAZIKEEN BORN IN RKNESS WELL.
A DARKNESS NOT OF VOID, BUT OF ROT AND WARMTH.
OF STINK AND FLESH.
THAT IS WHERE DEMON THINGS GROW AND SPROUT.
AND OURISH.
BUT THIS IS A DARK IN WHICH

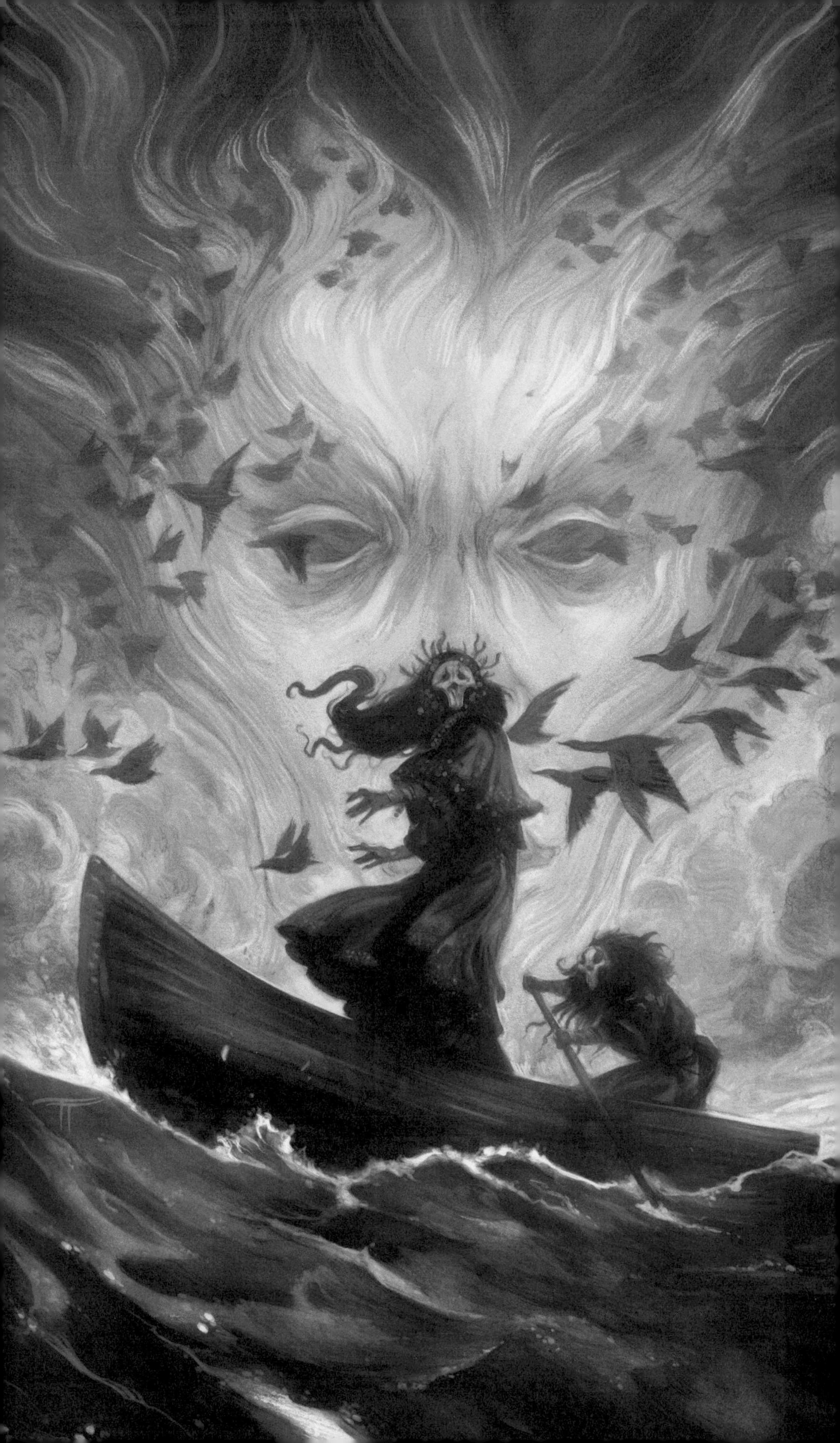

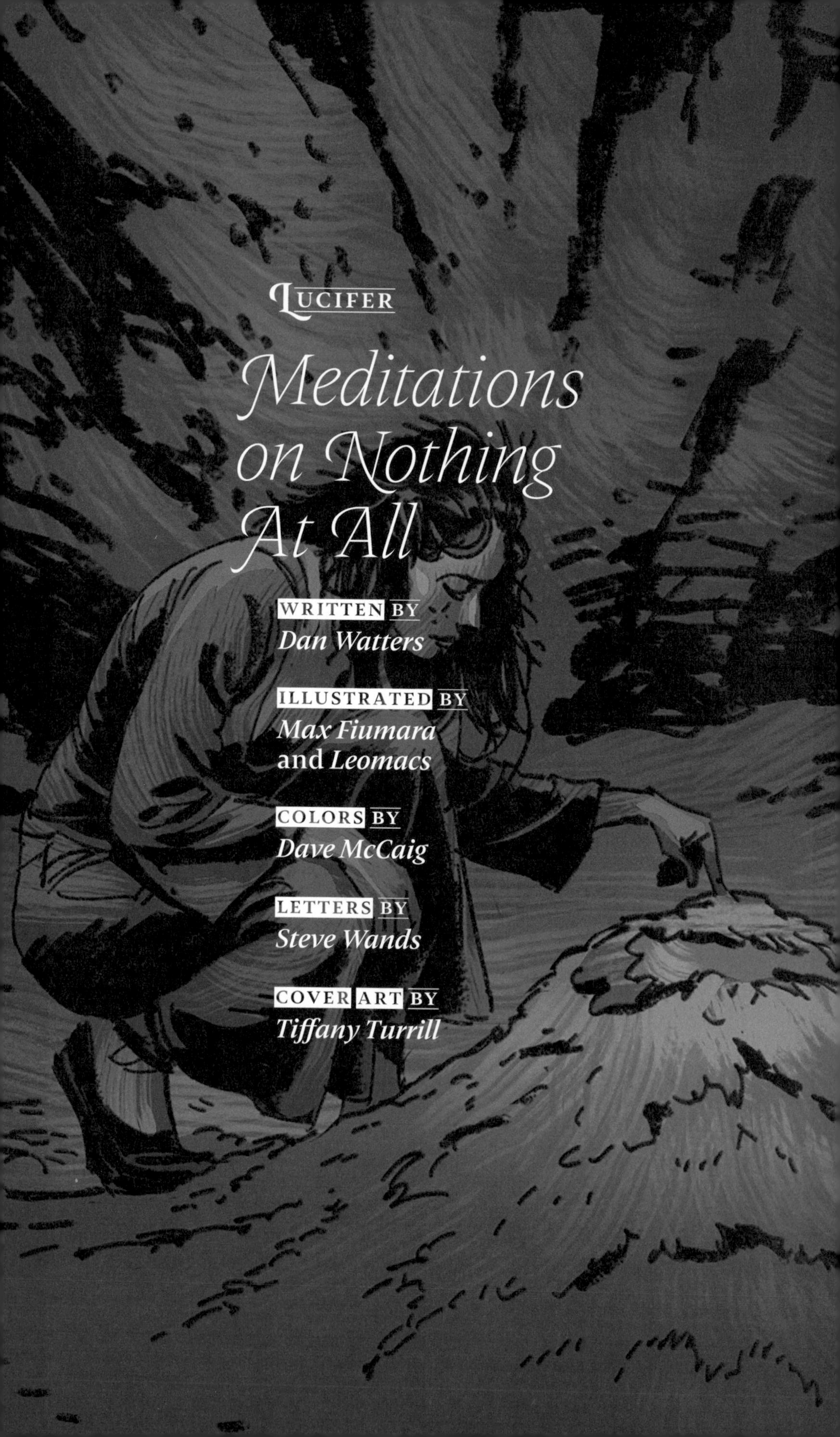

LUCIFER

Meditations on Nothing At All

WRITTEN BY
Dan Watters

ILLUSTRATED BY
Max Fiumara and *Leomacs*

COLORS BY
Dave McCaig

LETTERS BY
Steve Wands

COVER ART BY
Tiffany Turrill

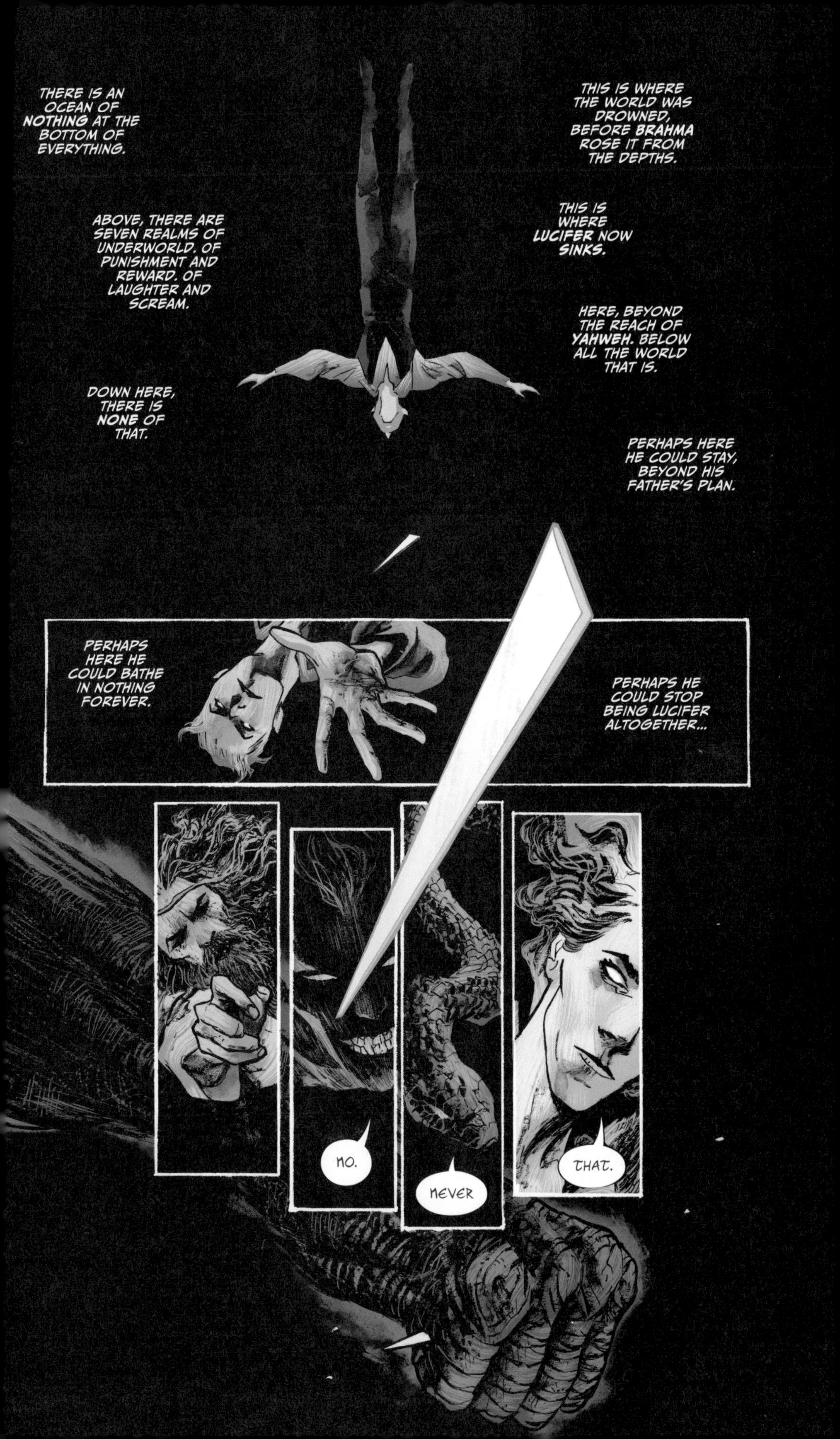
THERE IS AN OCEAN OF NOTHING AT THE BOTTOM OF EVERYTHING.
THIS IS WHERE THE WORLD WAS DROWNED, BEFORE BRAHMA ROSE IT FROM THE DEPTHS.
ABOVE, THERE ARE SEVEN REALMS OF UNDERWORLD. OF PUNISHMENT AND REWARD. OF LAUGHTER AND SCREAM.
THIS IS WHERE LUCIFER NOW SINKS.
HERE, BEYOND THE REACH OF YAHWEH. BELOW ALL THE WORLD THAT IS.
DOWN HERE, THERE IS NONE OF THAT.
PERHAPS HERE HE COULD STAY, BEYOND HIS FATHER'S PLAN.
PERHAPS HERE HE COULD BATHE IN NOTHING FOREVER.
PERHAPS HE COULD STOP BEING LUCIFER ALTOGETHER...
NO.
NEVER
THAT.

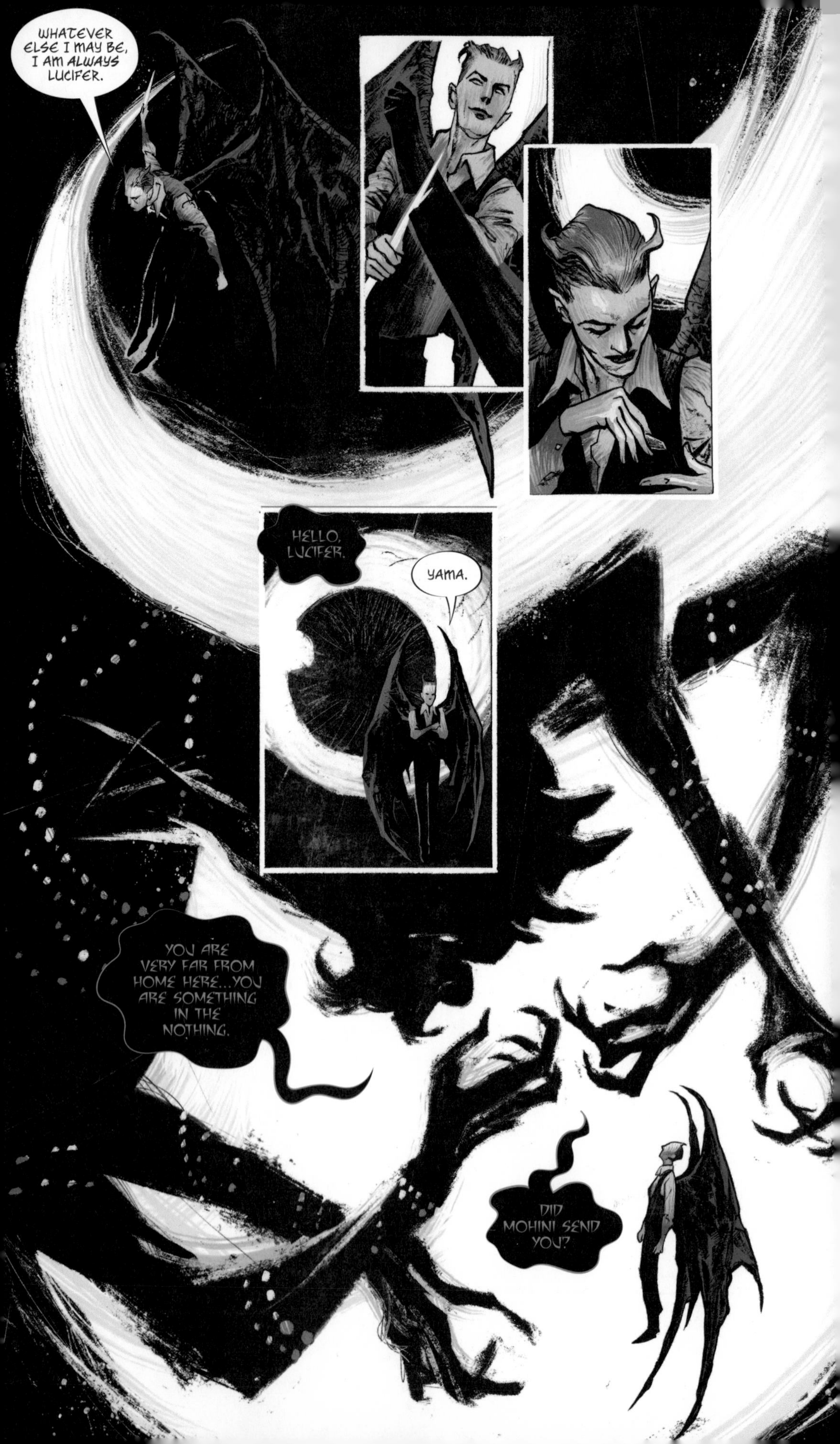
WHATEVER ELSE I MAY BE, I AM ALWAYS LUCIFER.
HELLO, LUCIFER.
YAMA.
YOU ARE VERY FAR FROM HOME HERE...YOU ARE SOMETHING IN THE NOTHING.
DID MOHINI SEND YOU?

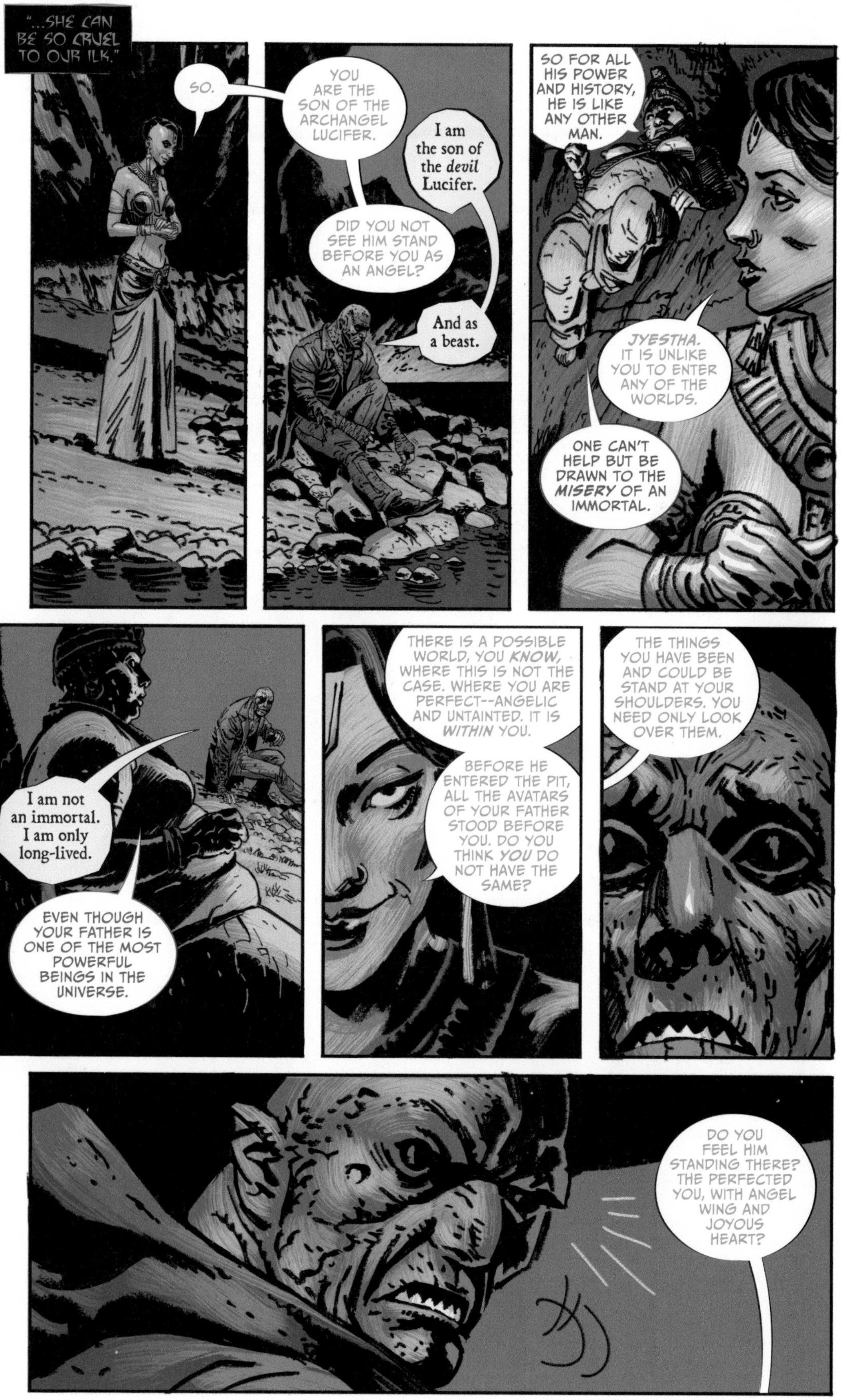
"...SHE CAN BE SO CRUEL TO OUR ILK."
SO.
YOU ARE THE SON OF THE ARCHANGEL LUCIFER.
I am the son of the *devil* Lucifer.
DID YOU NOT SEE HIM STAND BEFORE YOU AS AN ANGEL?
And as a beast.
SO FOR ALL HIS POWER AND HISTORY, HE IS LIKE ANY OTHER MAN.
JYESTHA. IT IS UNLIKE YOU TO ENTER ANY OF THE WORLDS.
ONE CAN'T HELP BUT BE DRAWN TO THE *MISERY* OF AN IMMORTAL.
I am not an immortal. I am only long-lived.
EVEN THOUGH YOUR FATHER IS ONE OF THE MOST POWERFUL BEINGS IN THE UNIVERSE.
THERE IS A POSSIBLE WORLD, YOU *KNOW,* WHERE THIS IS NOT THE CASE. WHERE YOU ARE PERFECT--ANGELIC AND UNTAINTED. IT IS *WITHIN* YOU.
BEFORE HE ENTERED THE PIT, ALL THE AVATARS OF YOUR FATHER STOOD BEFORE YOU. DO YOU THINK *YOU* DO NOT HAVE THE SAME?
THE THINGS YOU HAVE BEEN AND COULD BE STAND AT YOUR SHOULDERS. YOU NEED ONLY LOOK OVER THEM.
DO YOU FEEL HIM STANDING THERE? THE PERFECTED YOU, WITH ANGEL WING AND JOYOUS HEART?

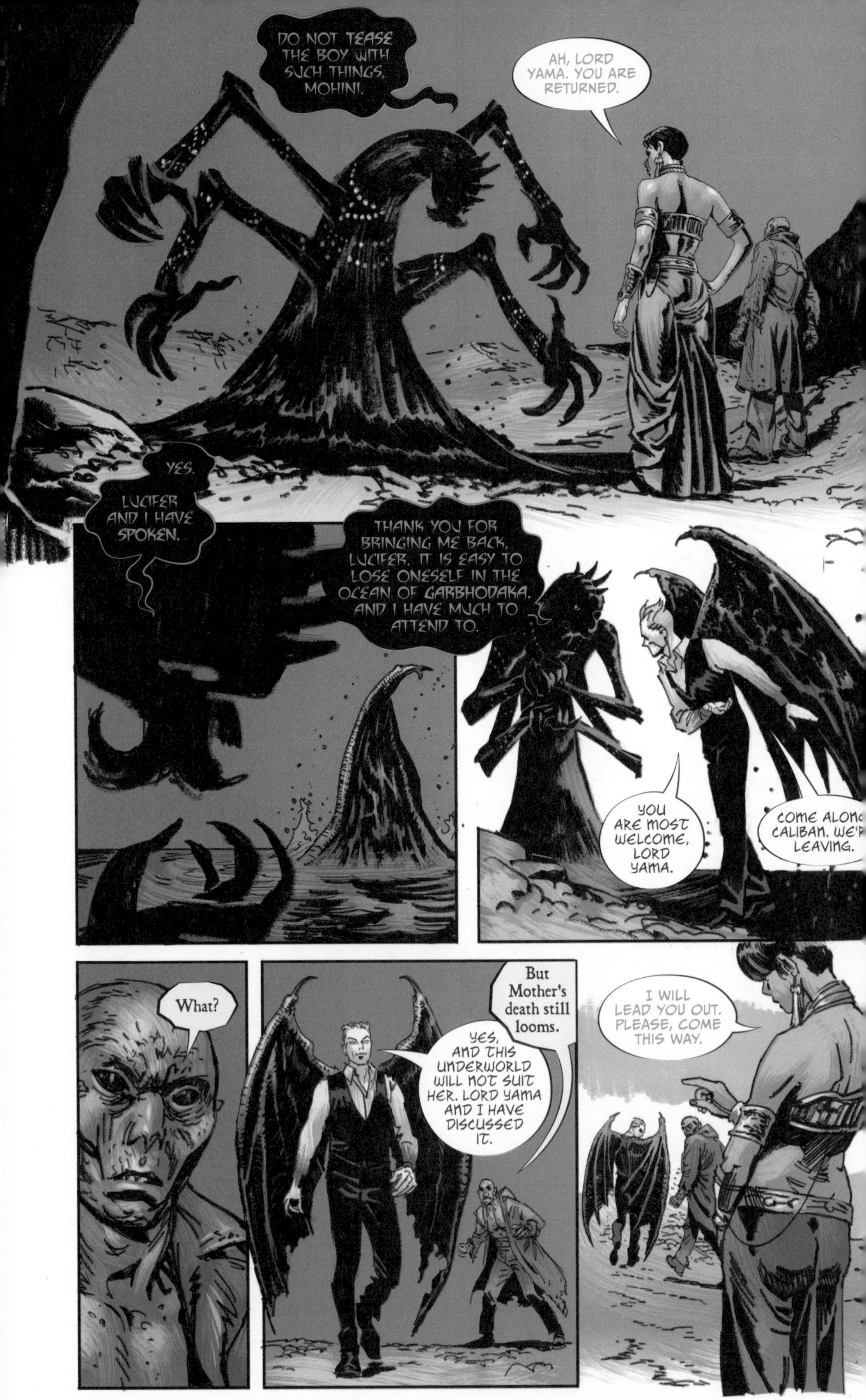
DO NOT TEASE THE BOY WITH SUCH THINGS, MOHINI.
AH, LORD YAMA. YOU ARE RETURNED.
YES.
LUCIFER AND I HAVE SPOKEN.
THANK YOU FOR BRINGING ME BACK, LUCIFER. IT IS EASY TO LOSE ONESELF IN THE OCEAN OF GARBHODAKA. AND I HAVE MUCH TO ATTEND TO.
YOU ARE MOST WELCOME, LORD YAMA.
COME ALON CALIBAN. WE' LEAVING.
What?
But Mother's death still looms.
YES, AND THIS UNDERWORLD WILL NOT SUIT HER. LORD YAMA AND I HAVE DISCUSSED IT.
I WILL LEAD YOU OUT. PLEASE, COME THIS WAY.

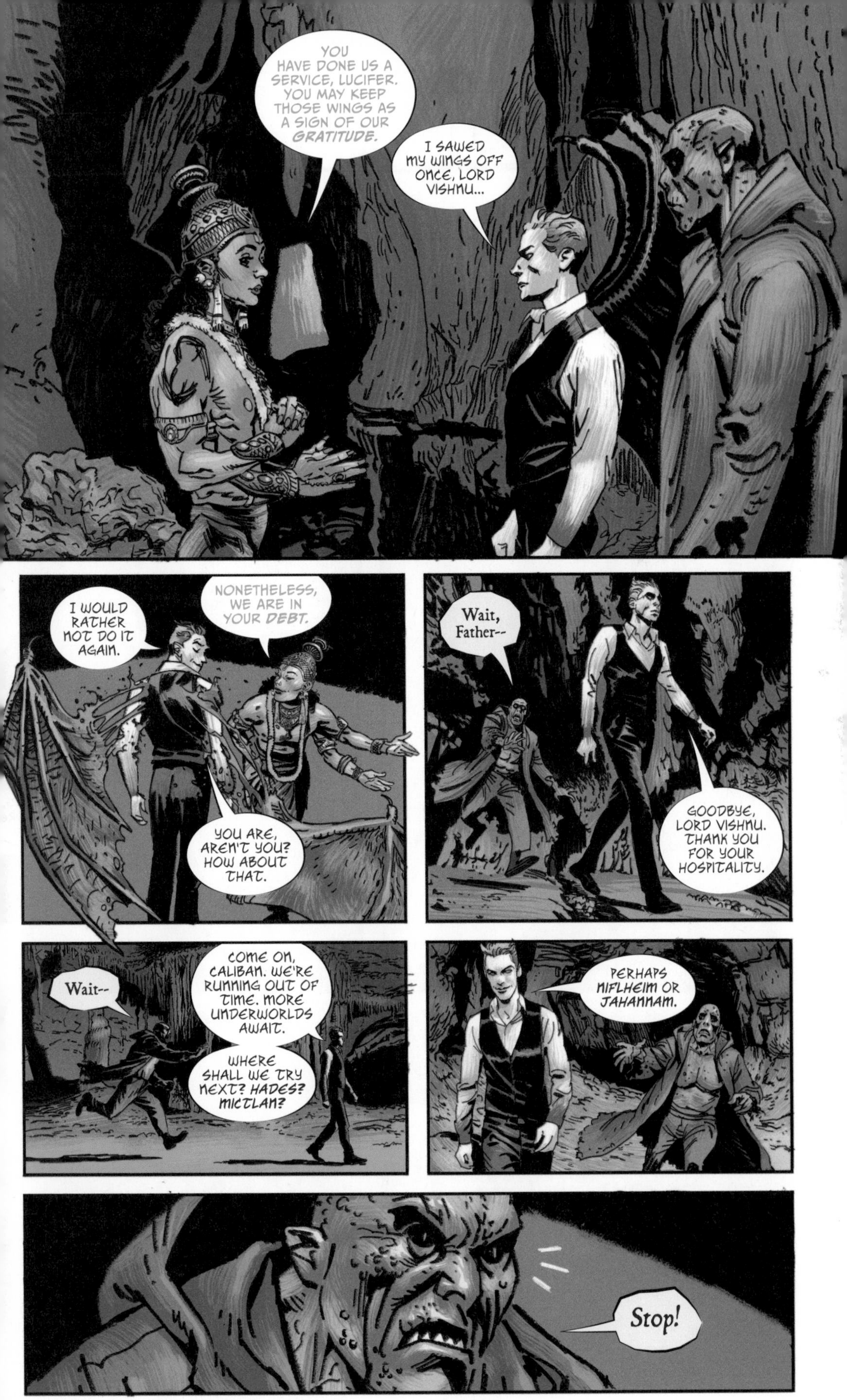
YOU HAVE DONE US A SERVICE, LUCIFER. YOU MAY KEEP THOSE WINGS AS A SIGN OF OUR GRATITUDE.
I SAWED MY WINGS OFF ONCE, LORD VISHNU...
I WOULD RATHER NOT DO IT AGAIN.
NONETHELESS, WE ARE IN YOUR DEBT.
YOU ARE, AREN'T YOU? HOW ABOUT THAT.
Wait, Father--
GOODBYE, LORD VISHNU. THANK YOU FOR YOUR HOSPITALITY.
Wait--
COME ON, CALIBAN. WE'RE RUNNING OUT OF TIME. MORE UNDERWORLDS AWAIT.
WHERE SHALL WE TRY NEXT? HADES? MICTLAN?
PERHAPS NIFLHEIM OR JAHANNAM.
Stop!

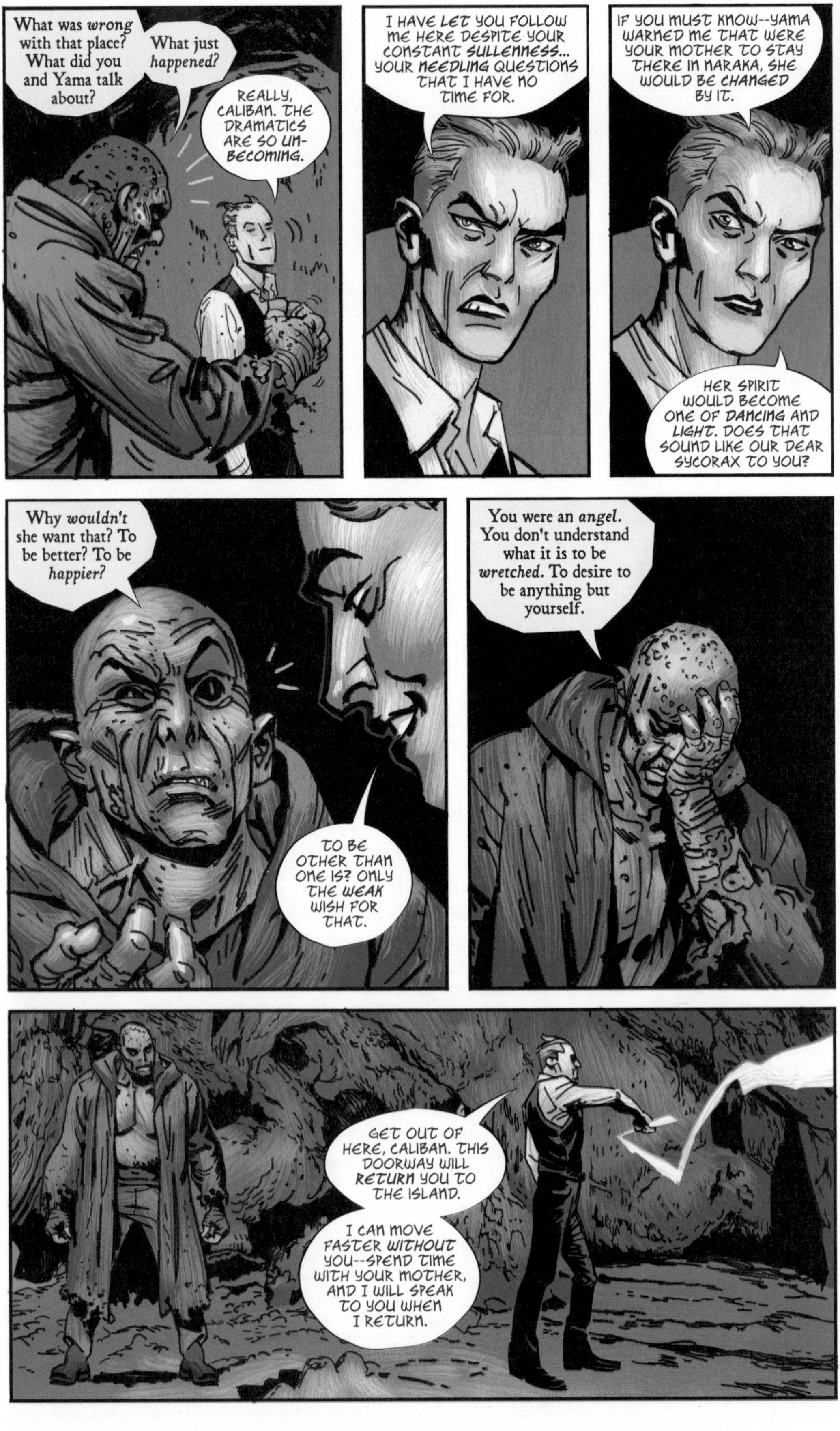

What was *wrong* with that place? What did you and Yama talk about?
What just *happened?*
REALLY, CALIBAN. THE DRAMATICS ARE SO UN-BECOMING.
I HAVE LET YOU FOLLOW ME HERE DESPITE YOUR CONSTANT SULLENNESS... YOUR NEEDLING QUESTIONS THAT I HAVE NO TIME FOR.
IF YOU MUST KNOW--YAMA WARNED ME THAT WERE YOUR MOTHER TO STAY THERE IN NARAKA, SHE WOULD BE CHANGED BY IT.
HER SPIRIT WOULD BECOME ONE OF DANCING AND LIGHT. DOES THAT SOUND LIKE OUR DEAR SYCORAX TO YOU?
Why *wouldn't* she want that? To be better? To be *happier?*
TO BE OTHER THAN ONE IS? ONLY THE WEAK WISH FOR THAT.
You were an *angel.* You don't understand what it is to be *wretched.* To desire to be anything but yourself.
GET OUT OF HERE, CALIBAN. THIS DOORWAY WILL RETURN YOU TO THE ISLAND.
I CAN MOVE FASTER WITHOUT YOU--SPEND TIME WITH YOUR MOTHER, AND I WILL SPEAK TO YOU WHEN I RETURN.

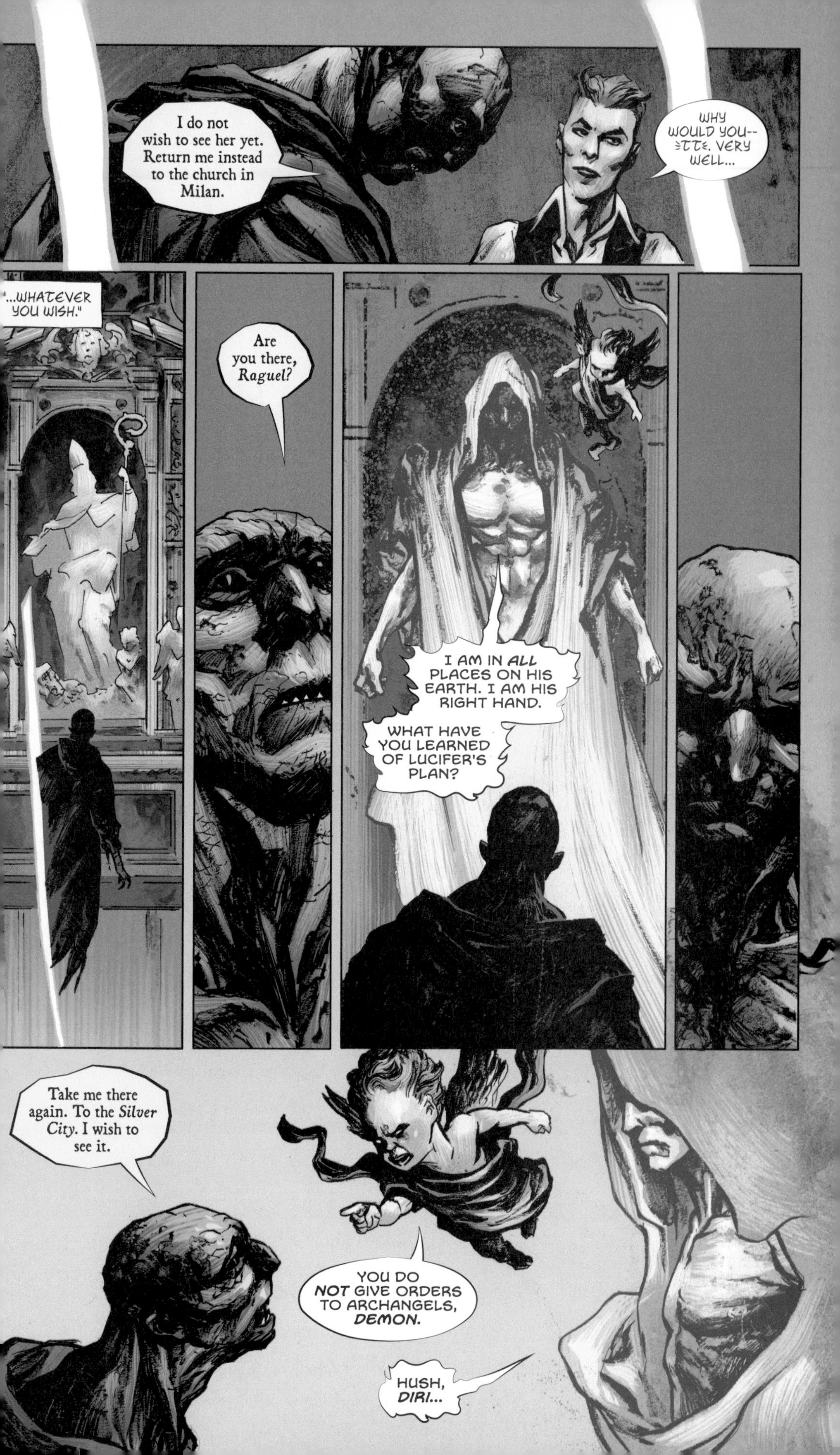
I do not wish to see her yet. Return me instead to the church in Milan.
WHY WOULD YOU-- TT. VERY WELL...
"...WHATEVER YOU WISH."
Are you there, *Raguel?*
I AM IN *ALL* PLACES ON HIS EARTH. I AM HIS RIGHT HAND.
WHAT HAVE YOU LEARNED OF LUCIFER'S PLAN?
Take me there again. To the *Silver City.* I wish to see it.
YOU DO **NOT** GIVE ORDERS TO ARCHANGELS, ***DEMON.***
HUSH, ***DIRI...***

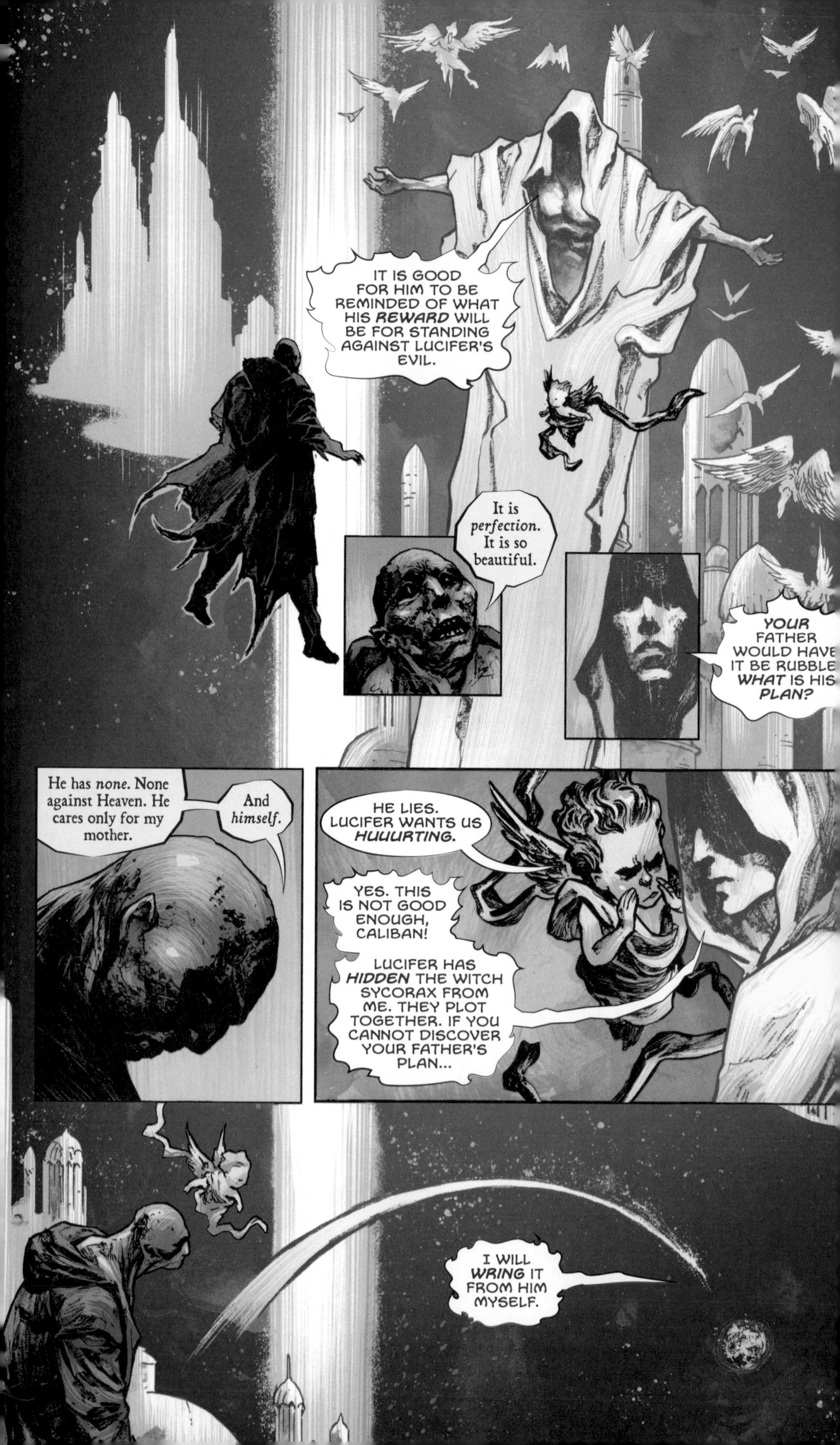
IT IS GOOD FOR HIM TO BE REMINDED OF WHAT HIS *REWARD* WILL BE FOR STANDING AGAINST LUCIFER'S EVIL.
It is *perfection.* It is so beautiful.
YOUR FATHER WOULD HAVE IT BE RUBBLE. *WHAT* IS HIS *PLAN?*
He has *none.* None against Heaven. He cares only for my mother.
And *himself.*
HE LIES. LUCIFER WANTS US *HUUURTING.*
YES. THIS IS NOT GOOD ENOUGH, CALIBAN!
LUCIFER HAS *HIDDEN* THE WITCH SYCORAX FROM ME. THEY PLOT TOGETHER. IF YOU CANNOT DISCOVER YOUR FATHER'S PLAN...
I WILL *WRING* IT FROM HIM MYSELF.

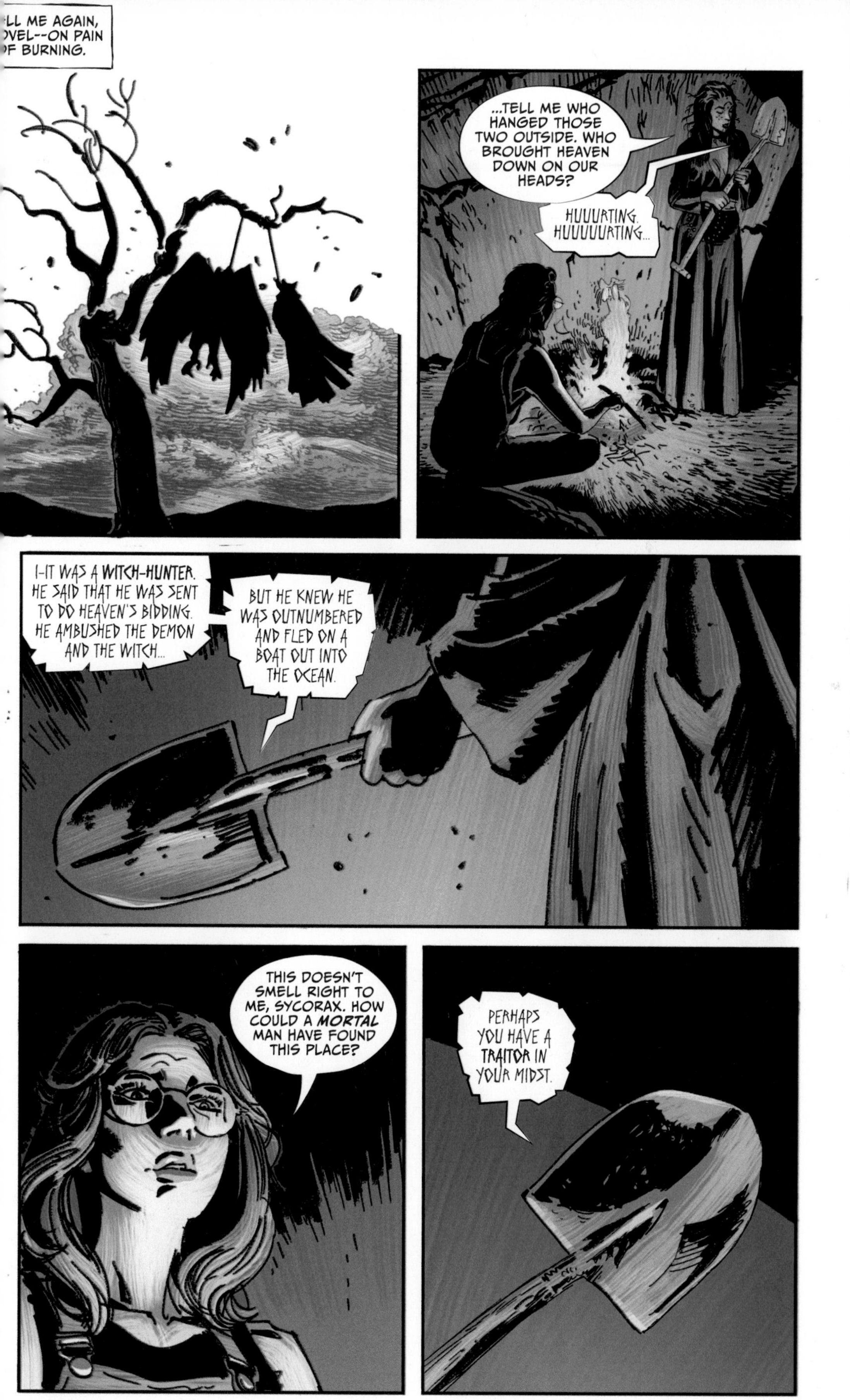
LL ME AGAIN,
OVEL--ON PAIN
OF BURNING.
...TELL ME WHO HANGED THOSE TWO OUTSIDE. WHO BROUGHT HEAVEN DOWN ON OUR HEADS?
HUUURTING. HUUUUURTING...
I-IT WAS A **WITCH-HUNTER**. HE SAID THAT HE WAS SENT TO DO HEAVEN'S BIDDING. HE AMBUSHED THE DEMON AND THE WITCH...
BUT HE KNEW HE WAS OUTNUMBERED AND FLED ON A BOAT OUT INTO THE OCEAN.
THIS DOESN'T SMELL RIGHT TO ME, SYCORAX. HOW COULD A ***MORTAL*** MAN HAVE FOUND THIS PLACE?
PERHAPS YOU HAVE A **TRAITOR** IN YOUR MIDST.

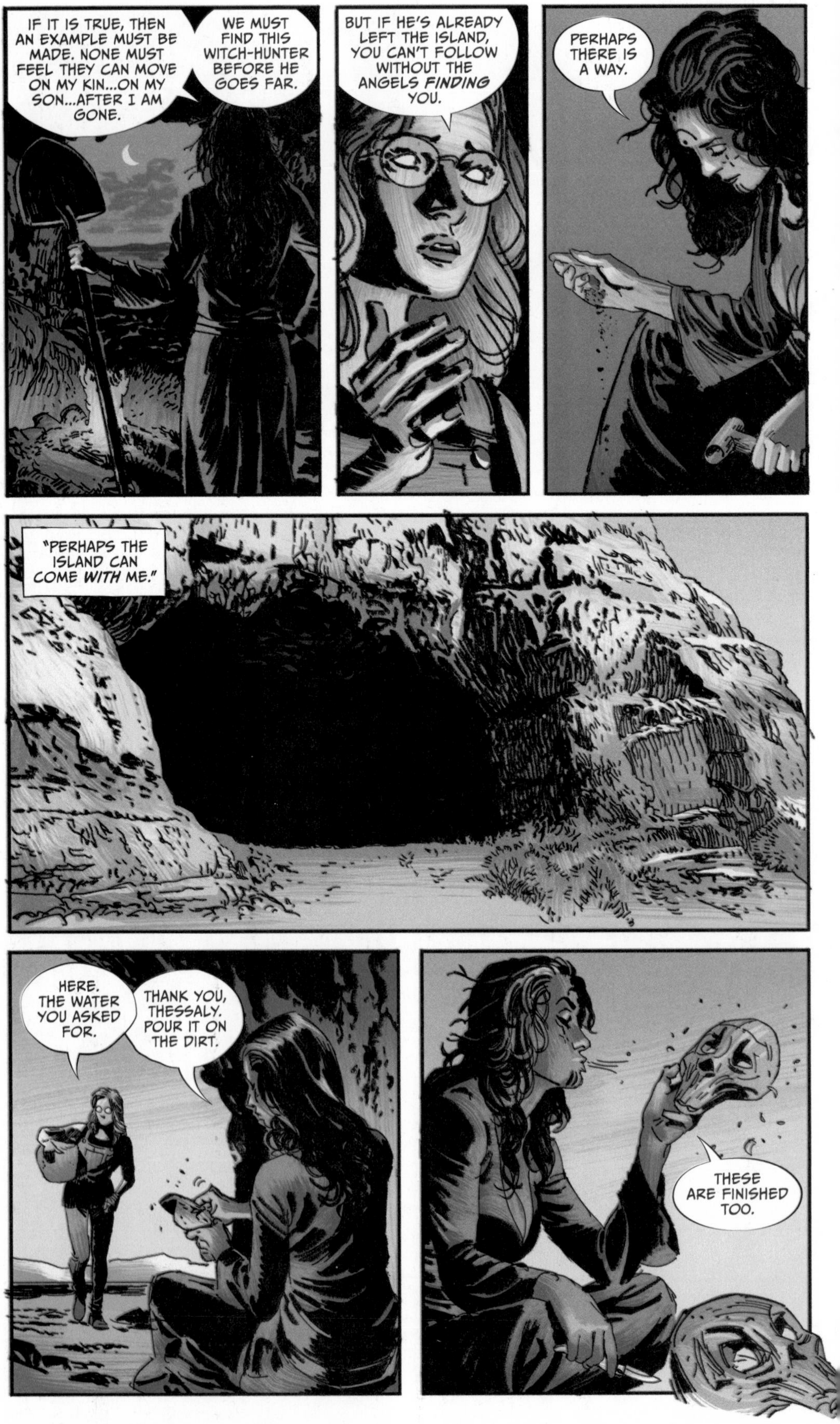
IF IT IS TRUE, THEN AN EXAMPLE MUST BE MADE. NONE MUST FEEL THEY CAN MOVE ON MY KIN...ON MY SON...AFTER I AM GONE.
WE MUST FIND THIS WITCH-HUNTER BEFORE HE GOES FAR.
BUT IF HE'S ALREADY LEFT THE ISLAND, YOU CAN'T FOLLOW WITHOUT THE ANGELS *FINDING* YOU.
PERHAPS THERE IS A WAY.
"PERHAPS THE ISLAND CAN COME *WITH* ME."
HERE. THE WATER YOU ASKED FOR.
THANK YOU, THESSALY. POUR IT ON THE DIRT.
THESE ARE FINISHED TOO.

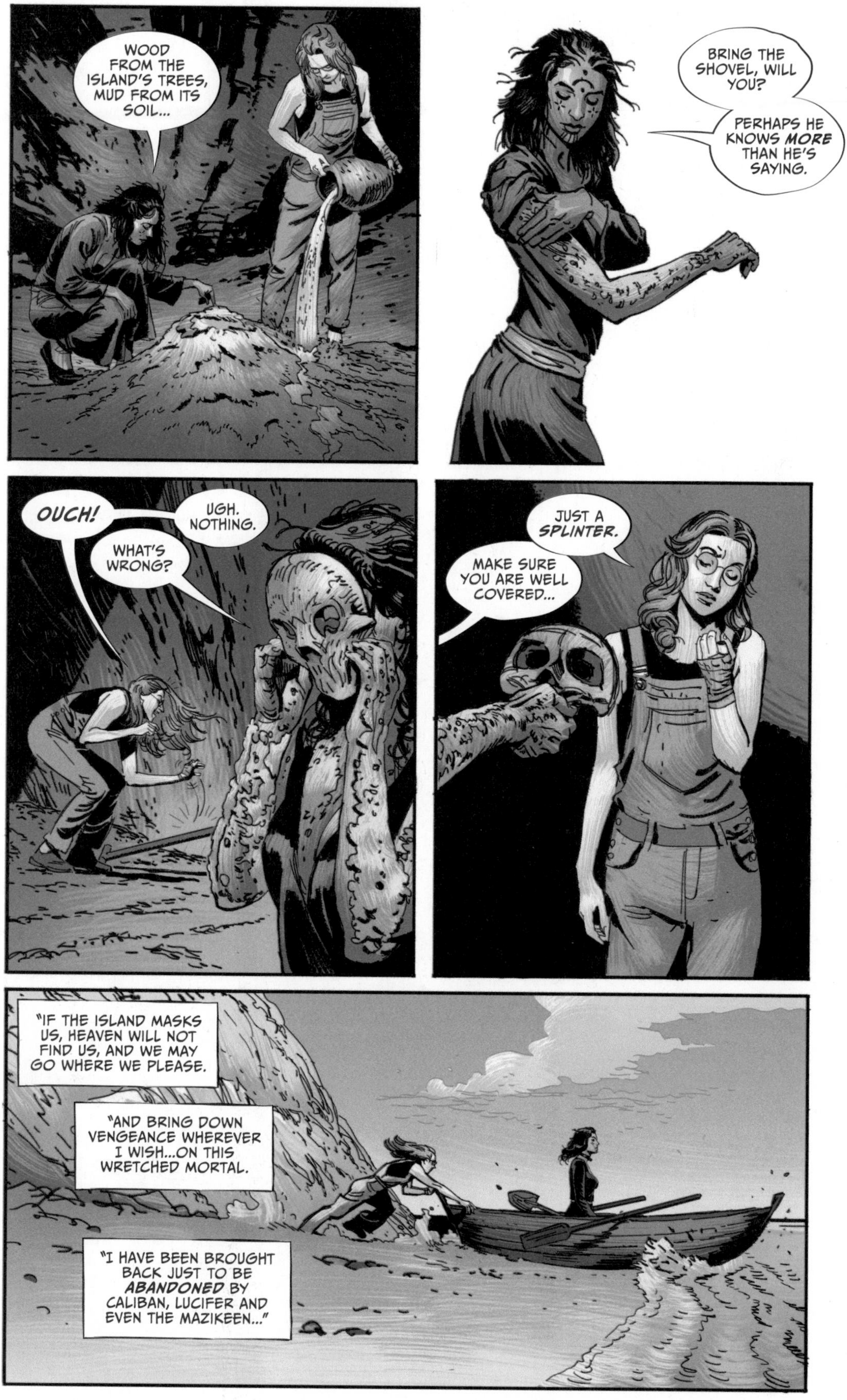
WOOD FROM THE ISLAND'S TREES, MUD FROM ITS SOIL...
BRING THE SHOVEL, WILL YOU?
PERHAPS HE KNOWS MORE THAN HE'S SAYING.
OUCH!
WHAT'S WRONG?
UGH. NOTHING.
JUST A SPLINTER.
MAKE SURE YOU ARE WELL COVERED...
"IF THE ISLAND MASKS US, HEAVEN WILL NOT FIND US, AND WE MAY GO WHERE WE PLEASE.
"AND BRING DOWN VENGEANCE WHEREVER I WISH...ON THIS WRETCHED MORTAL.
"I HAVE BEEN BROUGHT BACK JUST TO BE ABANDONED BY CALIBAN, LUCIFER AND EVEN THE MAZIKEEN..."

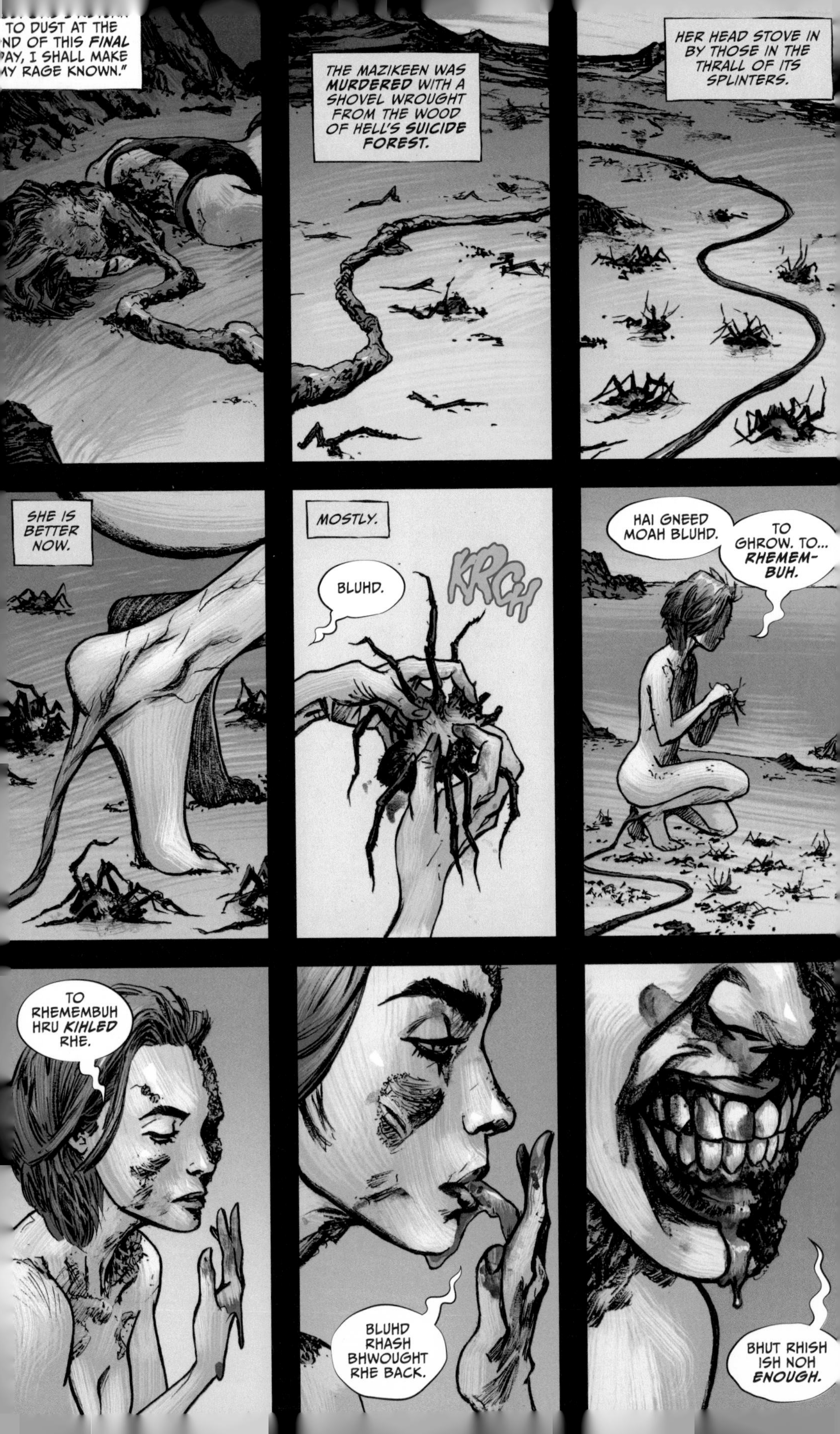

TO DUST AT THE END OF THIS FINAL DAY, I SHALL MAKE MY RAGE KNOWN."
THE MAZIKEEN WAS MURDERED WITH A SHOVEL WROUGHT FROM THE WOOD OF HELL'S SUICIDE FOREST.
HER HEAD STOVE IN BY THOSE IN THE THRALL OF ITS SPLINTERS.
SHE IS BETTER NOW.
MOSTLY.
BLUHD.
KRCH
HAI GNEED MOAH BLUHD.
TO GHROW. TO... RHEMEM-BUH.
TO RHEMEMBUH HRU KIHLED RHE.
BLUHD RHASH BHWOUGHT RHE BACK.
BHUT RHISH ISH NOH ENOUGH.

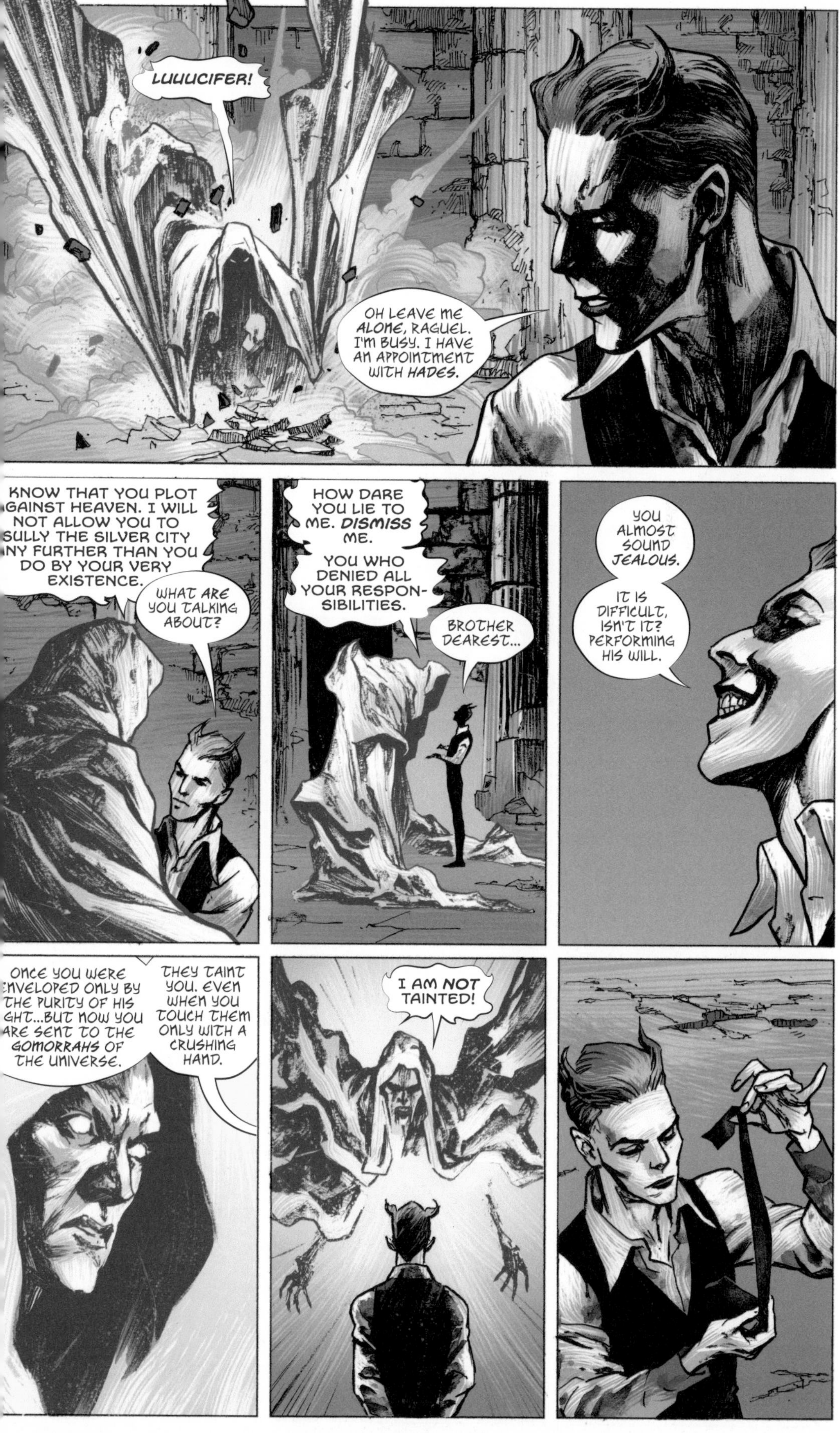
LUUUCIFER!
OH LEAVE ME ALONE, RAGUEL. I'M BUSY. I HAVE AN APPOINTMENT WITH HADES.
KNOW THAT YOU PLOT GAINST HEAVEN. I WILL NOT ALLOW YOU TO SULLY THE SILVER CITY NY FURTHER THAN YOU DO BY YOUR VERY EXISTENCE.
WHAT ARE YOU TALKING ABOUT?
HOW DARE YOU LIE TO ME. DISMISS ME.
YOU WHO DENIED ALL YOUR RESPONSIBILITIES.
BROTHER DEAREST...
YOU ALMOST SOUND JEALOUS.
IT IS DIFFICULT, ISN'T IT? PERFORMING HIS WILL.
ONCE YOU WERE ENVELOPED ONLY BY THE PURITY OF HIS GHT...BUT NOW YOU ARE SENT TO THE GOMORRAHS OF THE UNIVERSE.
THEY TAINT YOU. EVEN WHEN YOU TOUCH THEM ONLY WITH A CRUSHING HAND.
I AM NOT TAINTED!

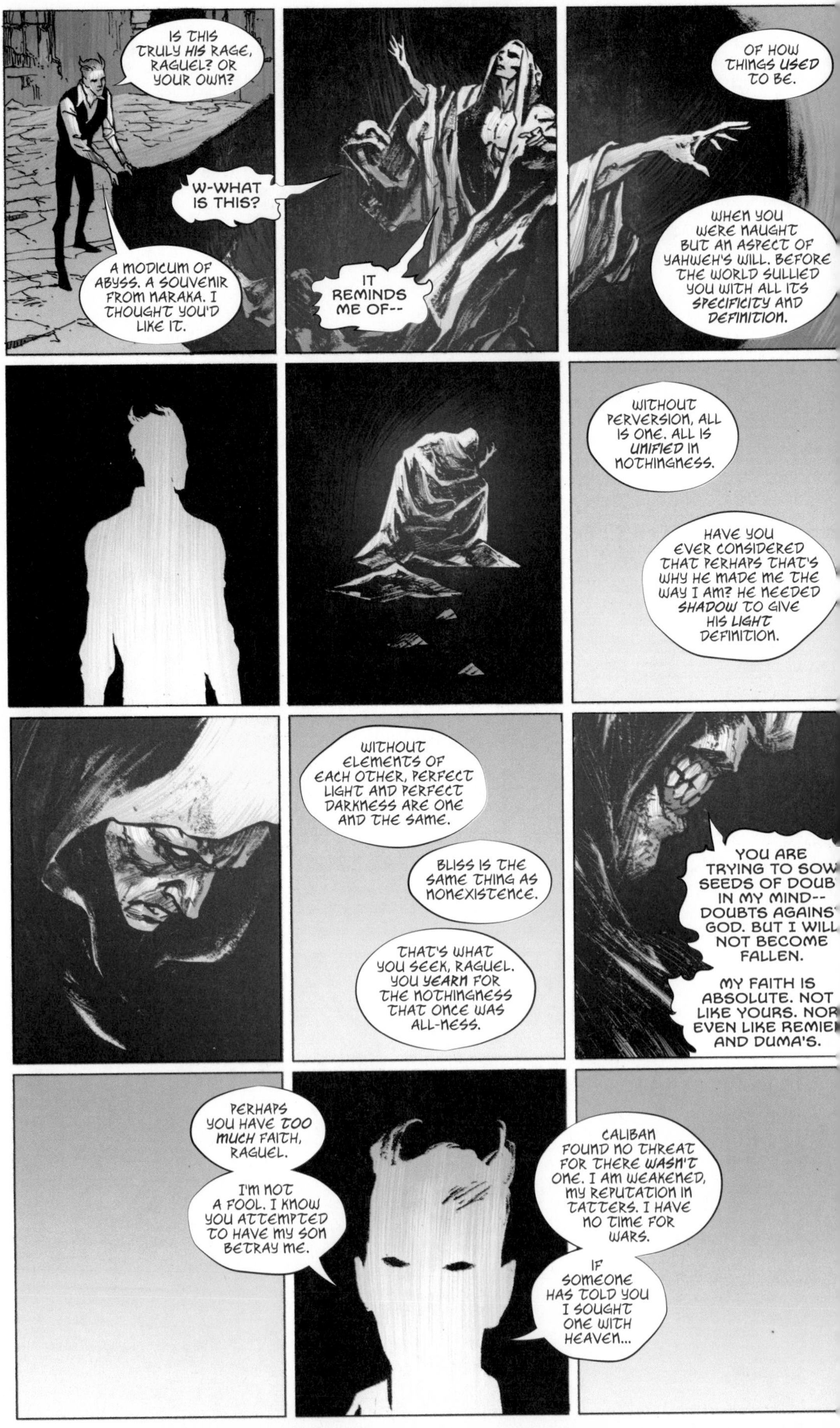
IS THIS TRULY HIS RAGE, RAGUEL? OR YOUR OWN?
W-WHAT IS THIS?
A MODICUM OF ABYSS. A SOUVENIR FROM NARAKA. I THOUGHT YOU'D LIKE IT.
IT REMINDS ME OF--
OF HOW THINGS USED TO BE.
WHEN YOU WERE NAUGHT BUT AN ASPECT OF YAHWEH'S WILL. BEFORE THE WORLD SULLIED YOU WITH ALL ITS SPECIFICITY AND DEFINITION.
WITHOUT PERVERSION, ALL IS ONE. ALL IS UNIFIED IN NOTHINGNESS.
HAVE YOU EVER CONSIDERED THAT PERHAPS THAT'S WHY HE MADE ME THE WAY I AM? HE NEEDED SHADOW TO GIVE HIS LIGHT DEFINITION.
WITHOUT ELEMENTS OF EACH OTHER, PERFECT LIGHT AND PERFECT DARKNESS ARE ONE AND THE SAME.
BLISS IS THE SAME THING AS NONEXISTENCE.
THAT'S WHAT YOU SEEK, RAGUEL. YOU YEARN FOR THE NOTHINGNESS THAT ONCE WAS ALL-NESS.
YOU ARE TRYING TO SOW SEEDS OF DOUB IN MY MIND-- DOUBTS AGAINS GOD. BUT I WILL NOT BECOME FALLEN.
MY FAITH IS ABSOLUTE. NOT LIKE YOURS. NOR EVEN LIKE REMIE AND DUMA'S.
PERHAPS YOU HAVE TOO MUCH FAITH, RAGUEL.
I'M NOT A FOOL. I KNOW YOU ATTEMPTED TO HAVE MY SON BETRAY ME.
CALIBAN FOUND NO THREAT FOR THERE WASN'T ONE. I AM WEAKENED, MY REPUTATION IN TATTERS. I HAVE NO TIME FOR WARS.
IF SOMEONE HAS TOLD YOU I SOUGHT ONE WITH HEAVEN...

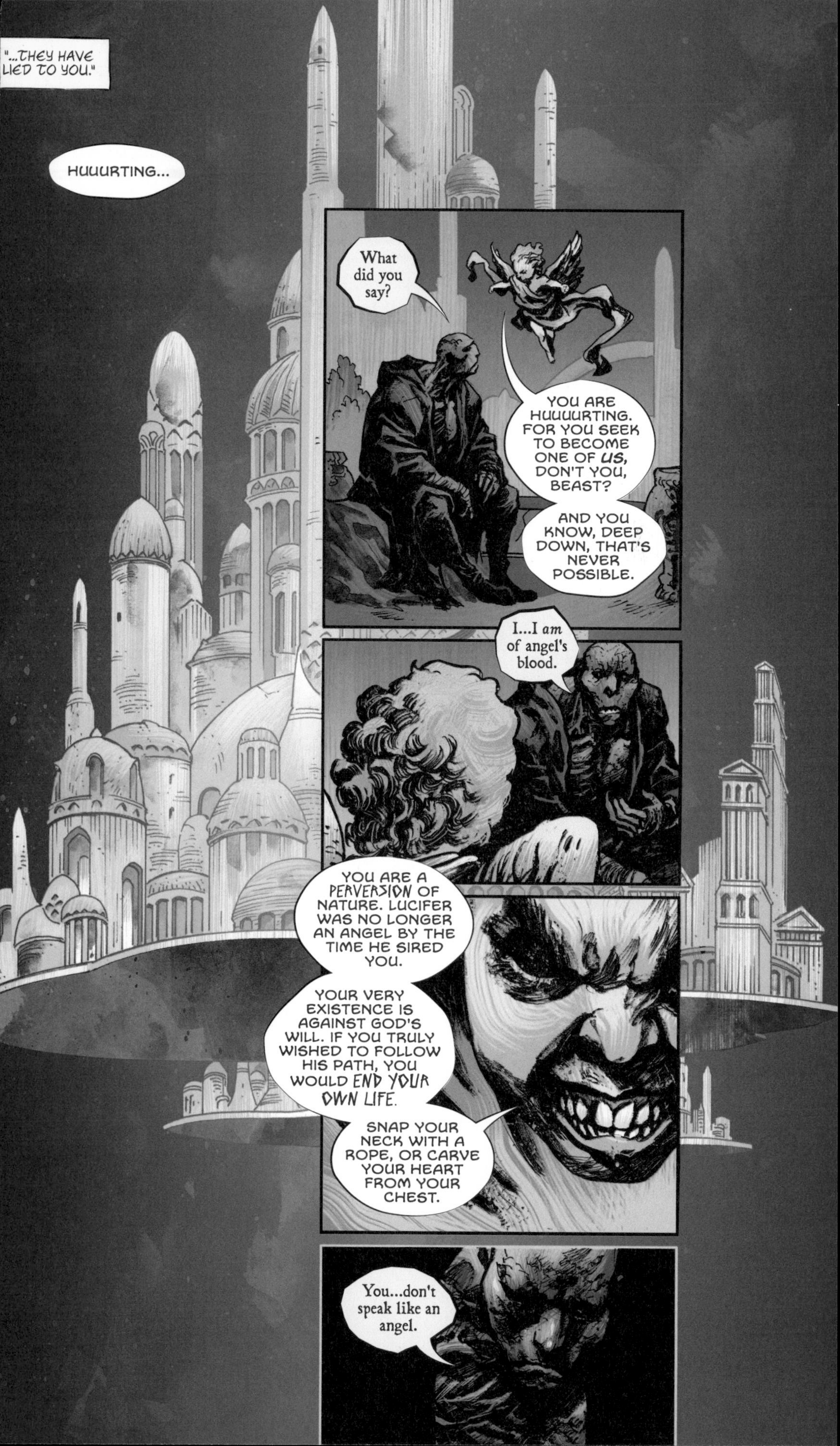
"...THEY HAVE LIED TO YOU."
HUUURTING...
What did you say?
YOU ARE HUUUURTING. FOR YOU SEEK TO BECOME ONE OF *US*, DON'T YOU, BEAST?
AND YOU KNOW, DEEP DOWN, THAT'S NEVER POSSIBLE.
I...I *am* of angel's blood.
YOU ARE A PERVERSION OF NATURE. LUCIFER WAS NO LONGER AN ANGEL BY THE TIME HE SIRED YOU.
YOUR VERY EXISTENCE IS AGAINST GOD'S WILL. IF YOU TRULY WISHED TO FOLLOW HIS PATH, YOU WOULD END YOUR OWN LIFE.
SNAP YOUR NECK WITH A ROPE, OR CARVE YOUR HEART FROM YOUR CHEST.
You...don't speak like an angel.

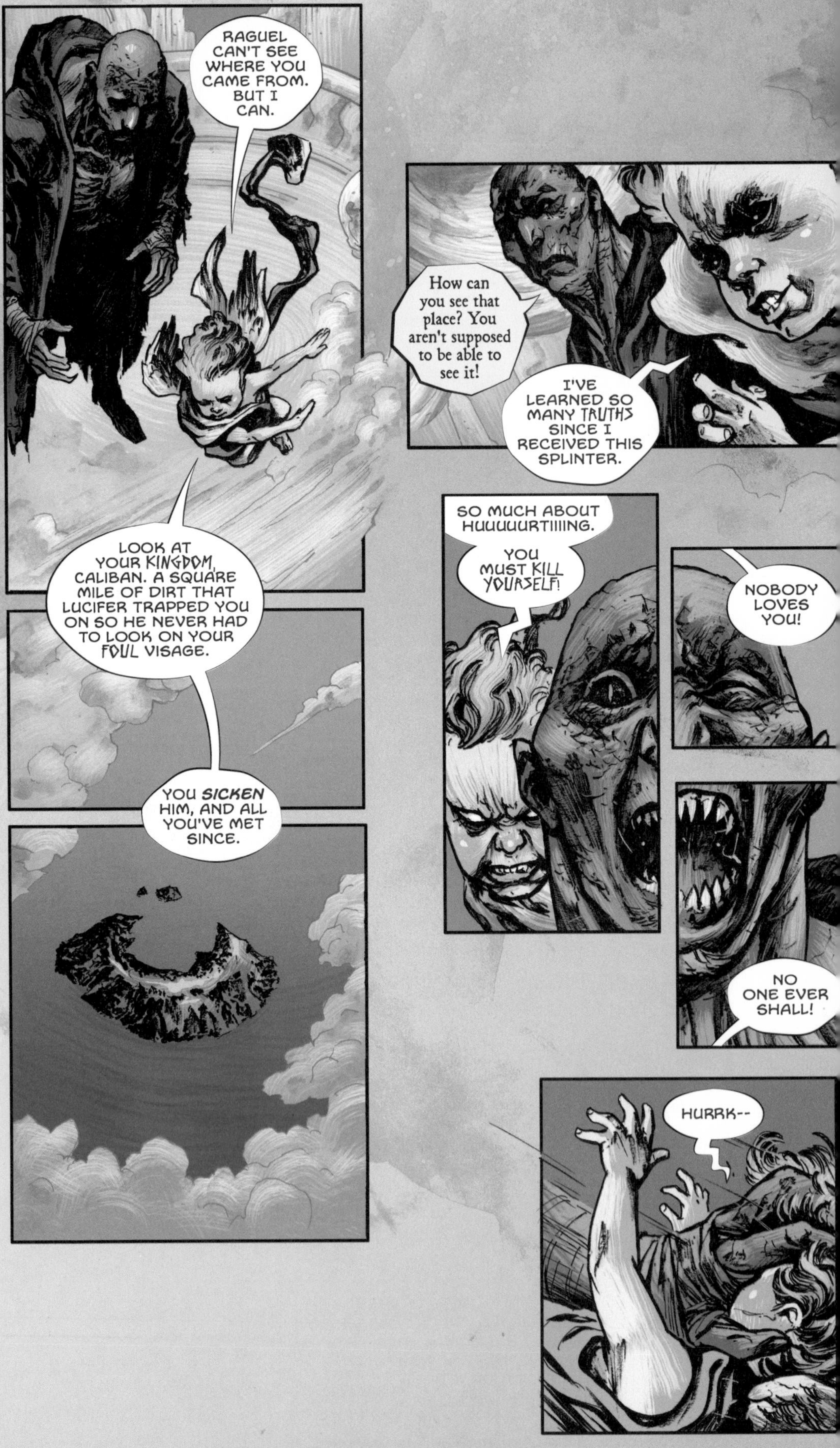
RAGUEL CAN'T SEE WHERE YOU CAME FROM. BUT I CAN.
LOOK AT YOUR KINGDOM, CALIBAN. A SQUARE MILE OF DIRT THAT LUCIFER TRAPPED YOU ON SO HE NEVER HAD TO LOOK ON YOUR FOUL VISAGE.
YOU SICKEN HIM, AND ALL YOU'VE MET SINCE.
How can you see that place? You aren't supposed to be able to see it!
I'VE LEARNED SO MANY TRUTHS SINCE I RECEIVED THIS SPLINTER.
SO MUCH ABOUT HUUUUURTIIIING.
YOU MUST KILL YOURSELF!
NOBODY LOVES YOU!
NO ONE EVER SHALL!
HURRK--

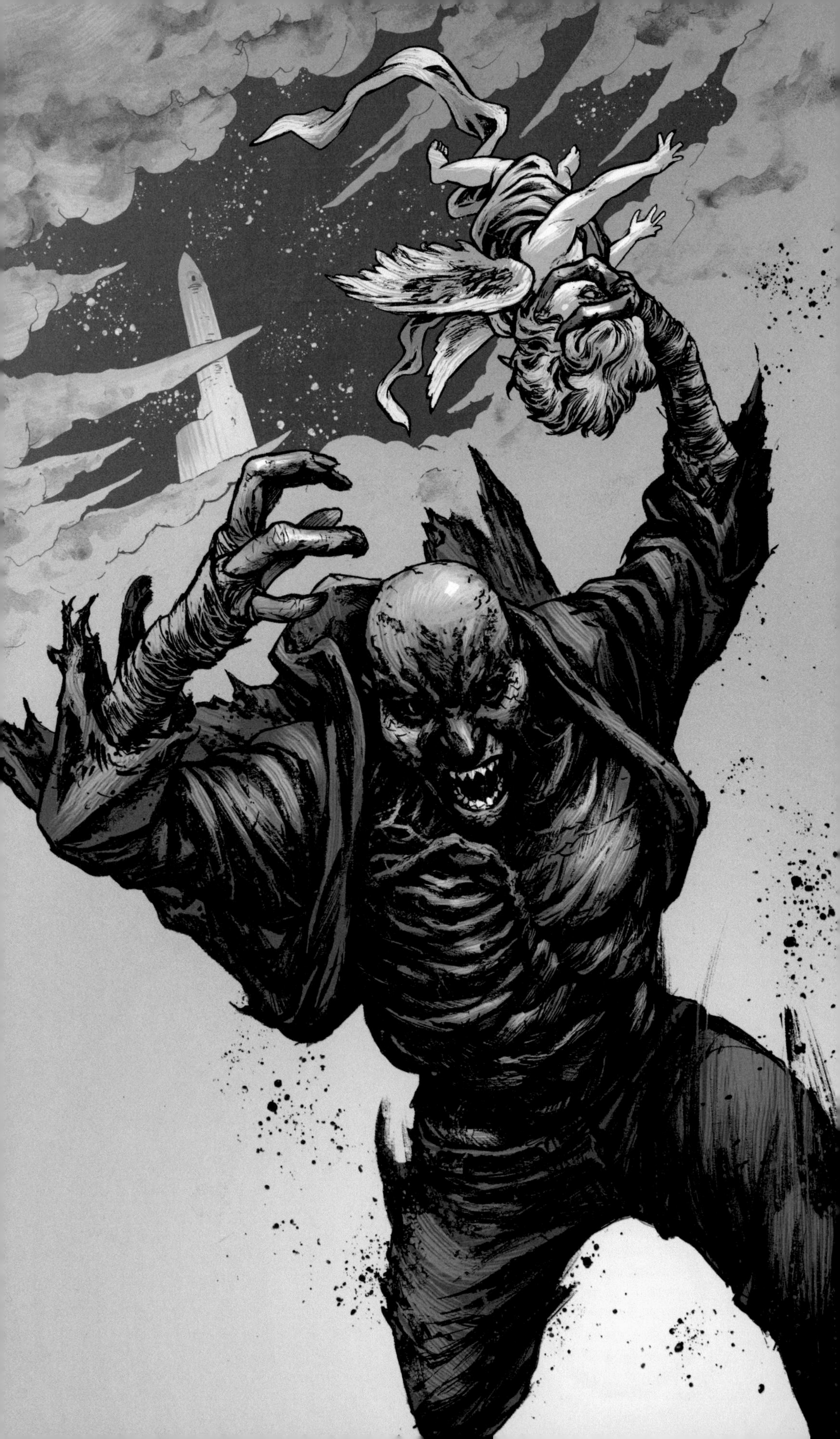

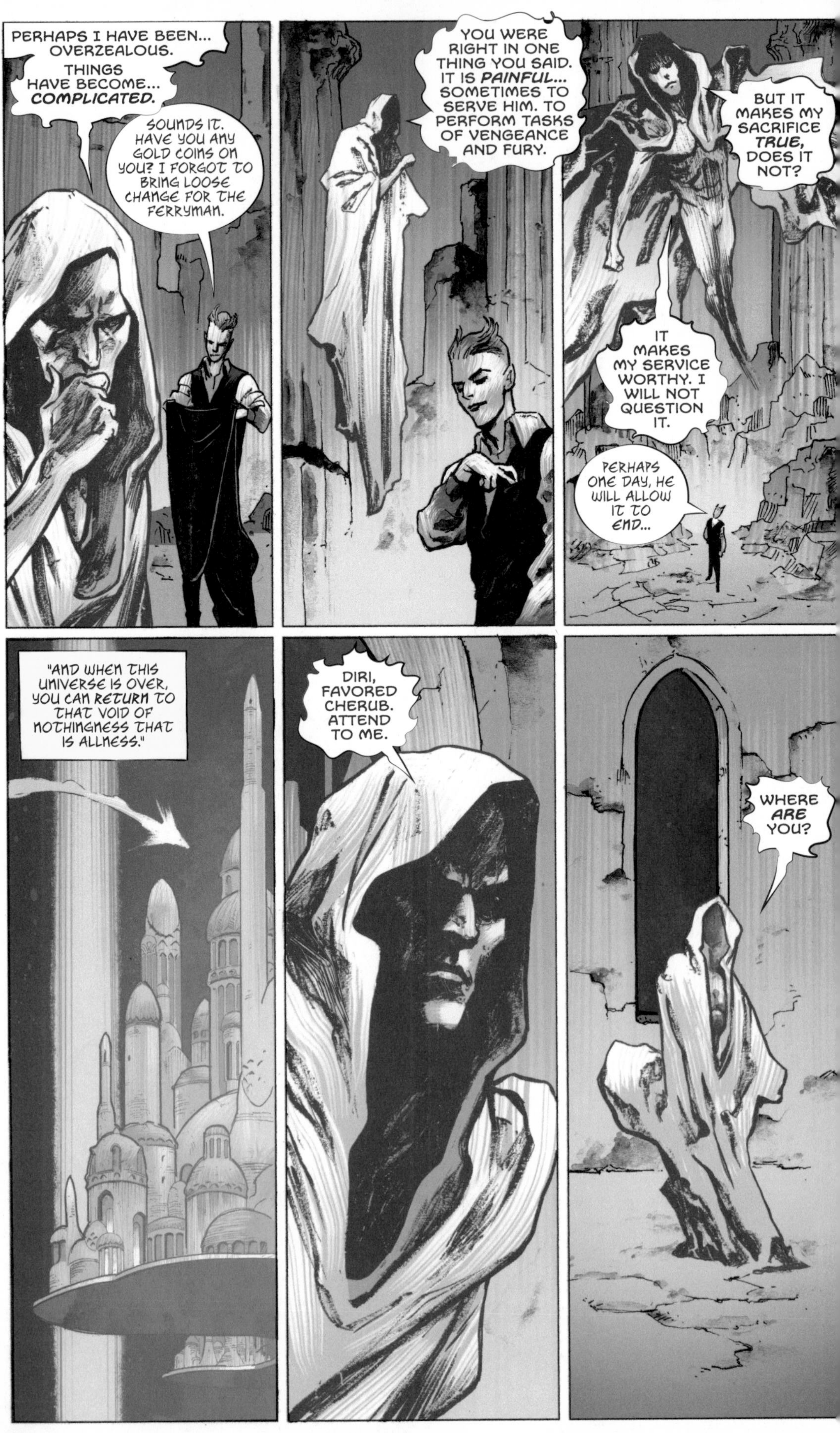
PERHAPS I HAVE BEEN... OVERZEALOUS.
THINGS HAVE BECOME... COMPLICATED.
SOUNDS IT. HAVE YOU ANY GOLD COINS ON YOU? I FORGOT TO BRING LOOSE CHANGE FOR THE FERRYMAN.
YOU WERE RIGHT IN ONE THING YOU SAID. IT IS PAINFUL... SOMETIMES TO SERVE HIM. TO PERFORM TASKS OF VENGEANCE AND FURY.
BUT IT MAKES MY SACRIFICE TRUE, DOES IT NOT?
IT MAKES MY SERVICE WORTHY. I WILL NOT QUESTION IT.
PERHAPS ONE DAY, HE WILL ALLOW IT TO END...
"AND WHEN THIS UNIVERSE IS OVER, YOU CAN RETURN TO THAT VOID OF NOTHINGNESS THAT IS ALLNESS."
DIRI, FAVORED CHERUB. ATTEND TO ME.
WHERE ARE YOU?

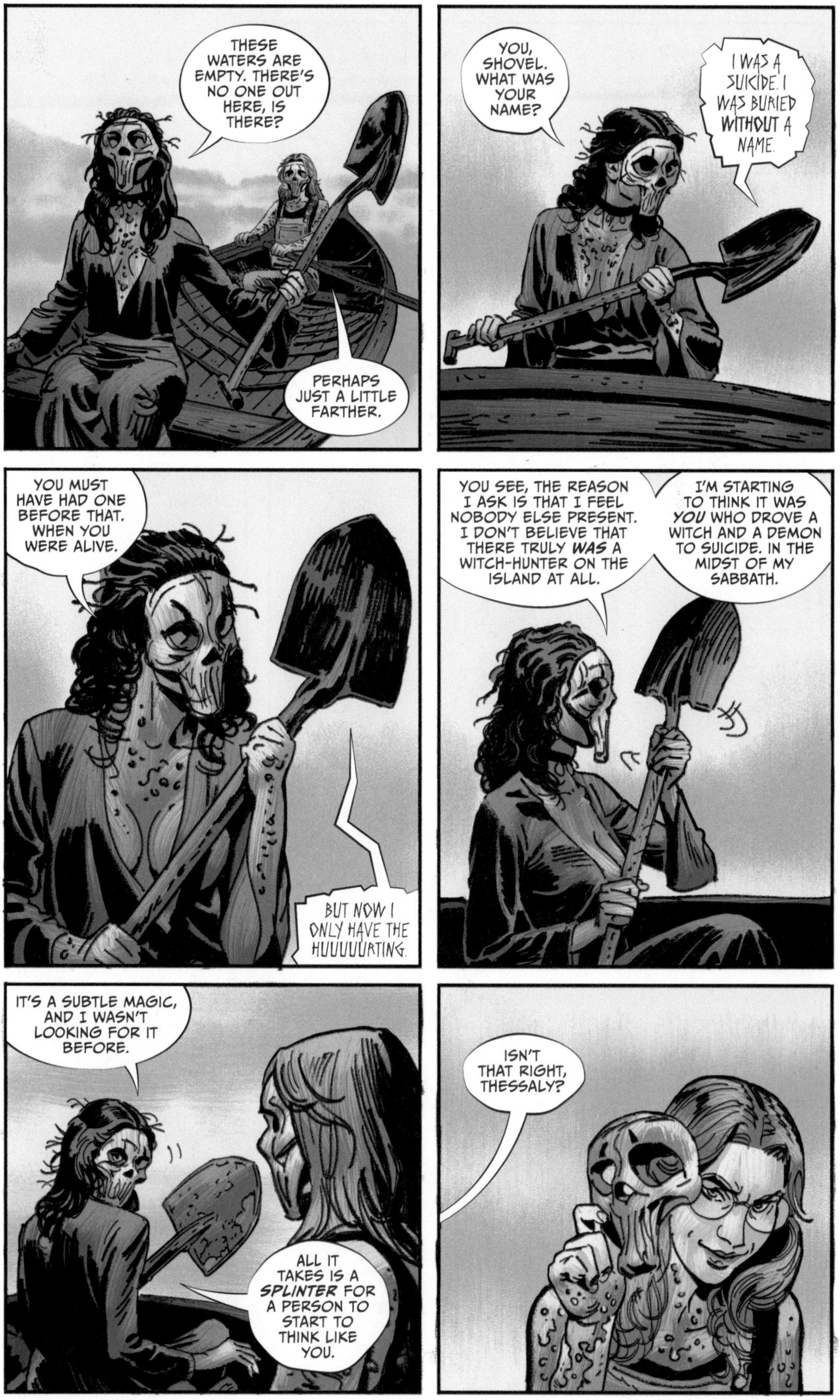
THESE WATERS ARE EMPTY. THERE'S NO ONE OUT HERE, IS THERE?
PERHAPS JUST A LITTLE FARTHER.
YOU, SHOVEL. WHAT WAS YOUR NAME?
I WAS A SUICIDE. I WAS BURIED WITHOUT A NAME.
YOU MUST HAVE HAD ONE BEFORE THAT. WHEN YOU WERE ALIVE.
BUT NOW I ONLY HAVE THE HUUUUURTING.
YOU SEE, THE REASON I ASK IS THAT I FEEL NOBODY ELSE PRESENT. I DON'T BELIEVE THAT THERE TRULY WAS A WITCH-HUNTER ON THE ISLAND AT ALL.
I'M STARTING TO THINK IT WAS YOU WHO DROVE A WITCH AND A DEMON TO SUICIDE. IN THE MIDST OF MY SABBATH.
IT'S A SUBTLE MAGIC, AND I WASN'T LOOKING FOR IT BEFORE.
ALL IT TAKES IS A SPLINTER FOR A PERSON TO START TO THINK LIKE YOU.
ISN'T THAT RIGHT, THESSALY?

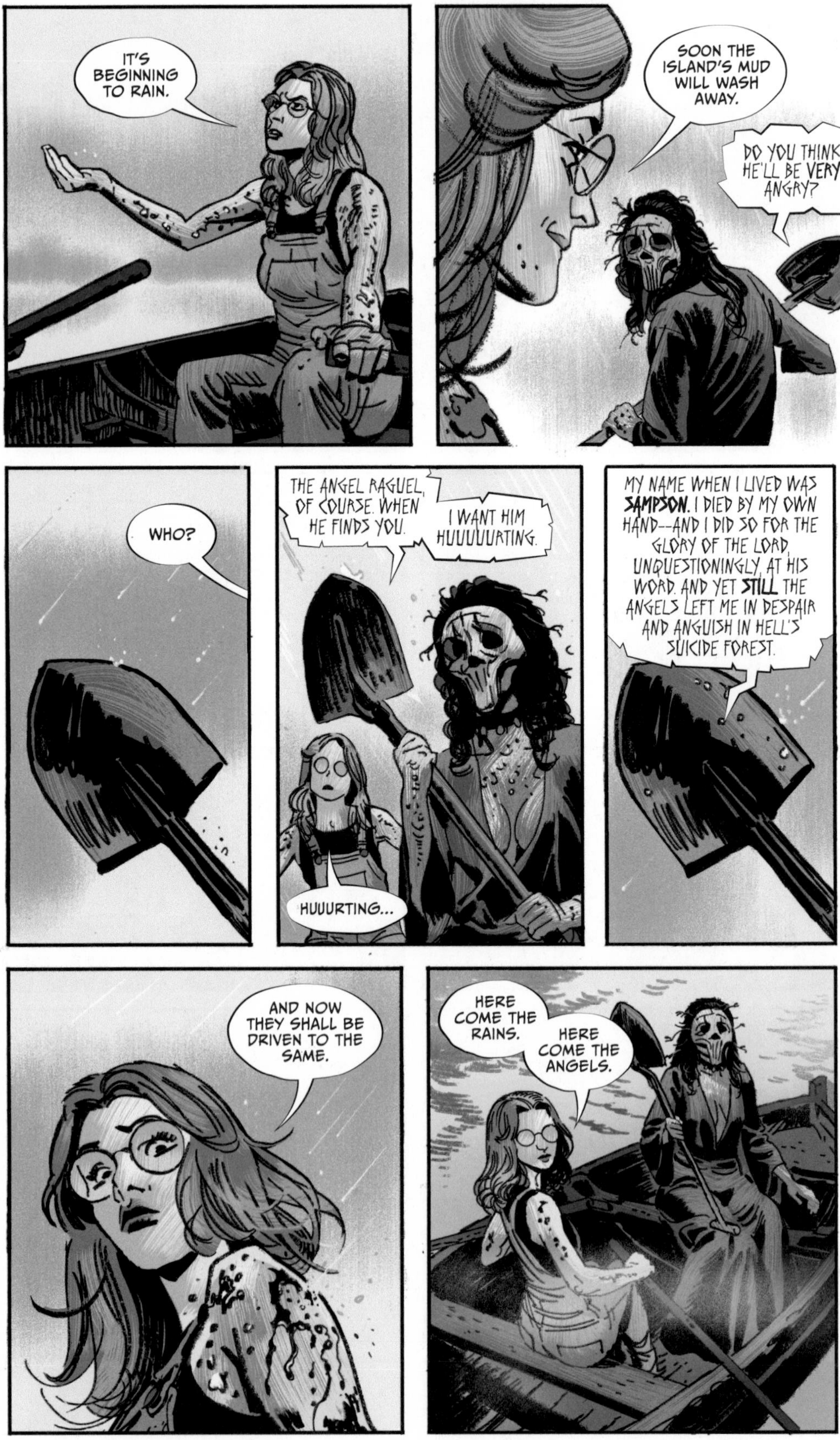
IT'S BEGINNING TO RAIN.
SOON THE ISLAND'S MUD WILL WASH AWAY.
DO YOU THINK HE'LL BE VERY ANGRY?
WHO?
THE ANGEL RAGUEL, OF COURSE. WHEN HE FINDS YOU.
I WANT HIM HUUUUURTING.
HUUURTING...
MY NAME WHEN I LIVED WAS SAMPSON. I DIED BY MY OWN HAND--AND I DID SO FOR THE GLORY OF THE LORD, UNQUESTIONINGLY, AT HIS WORD. AND YET STILL THE ANGELS LEFT ME IN DESPAIR AND ANGUISH IN HELL'S SUICIDE FOREST.
AND NOW THEY SHALL BE DRIVEN TO THE SAME.
HERE COME THE RAINS.
HERE COME THE ANGELS.

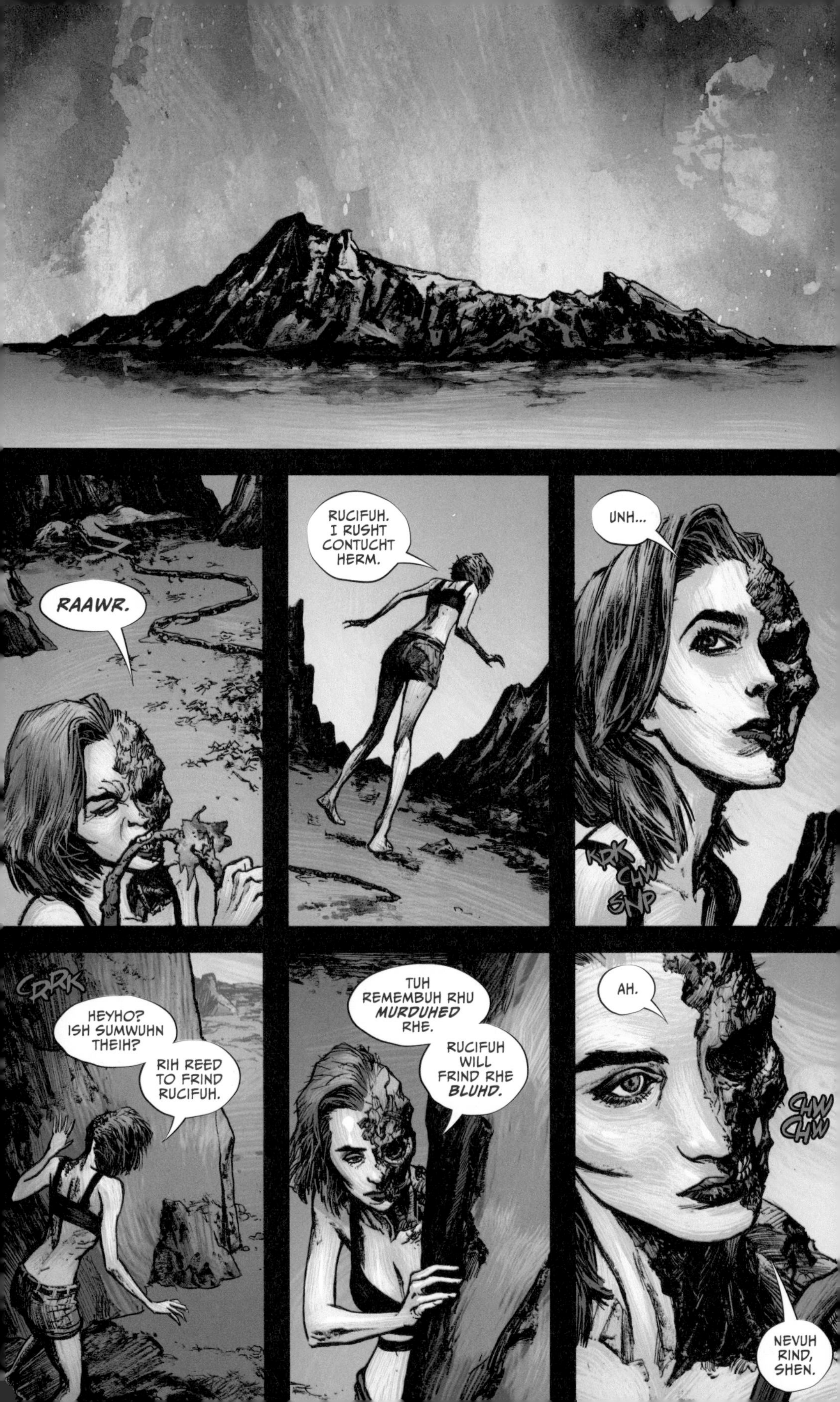
RAAWR.
RUCIFUH. I RUSHT CONTUCHT HERM.
UNH...
KRK CHW SNP
CRRK
HEYHO? ISH SUMWUHN THEIH?
RIH REED TO FRIND RUCIFUH.
TUH REMEMBUH RHU *MURDUHED* RHE.
RUCIFUH WILL FRIND RHE *BLUHD.*
AH.
CHW CHW
NEVUH RIND, SHEN.

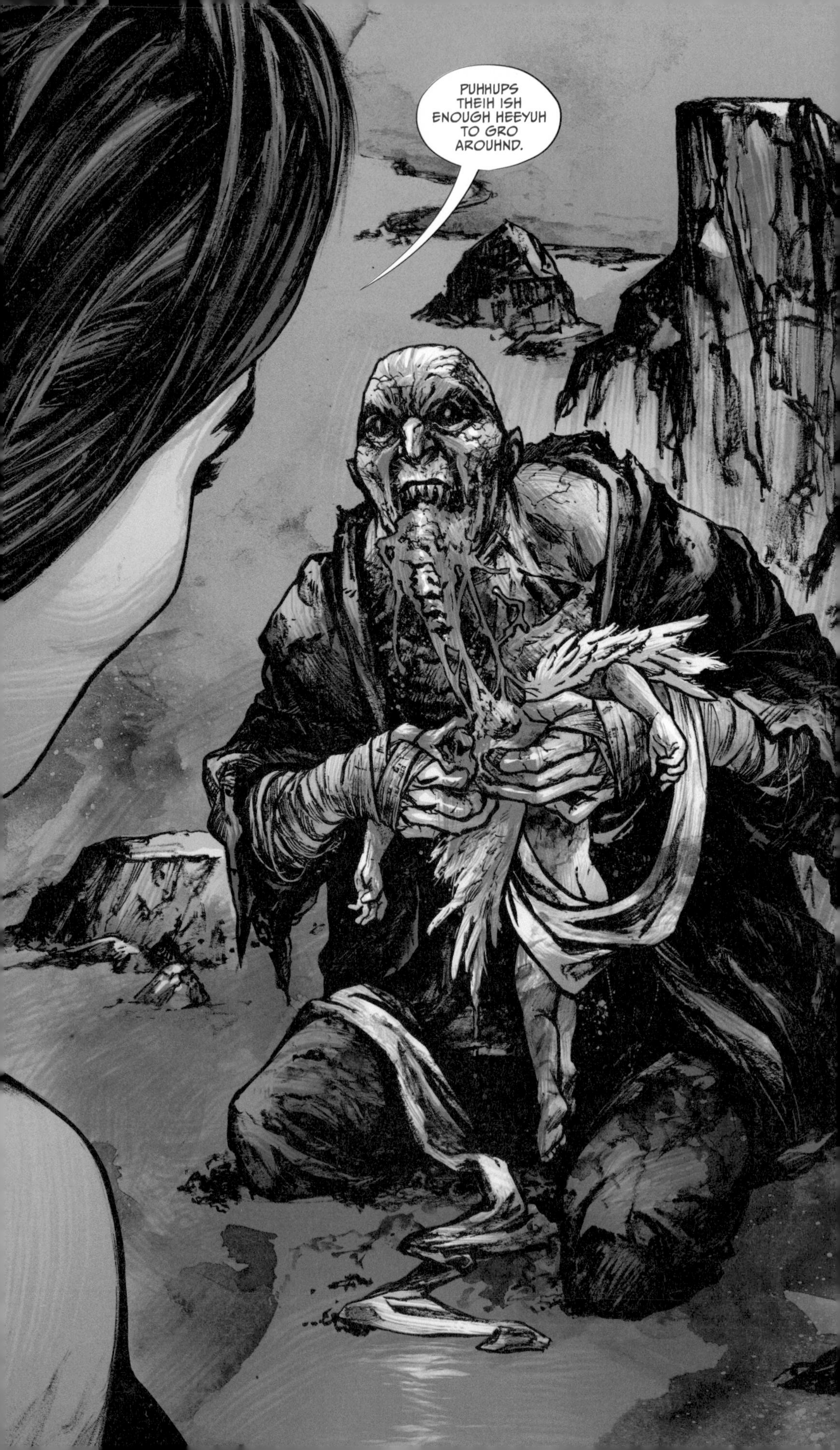
PUHHUPS THEIH ISH ENOUGH HEEYUH TO GRO AROUHND.

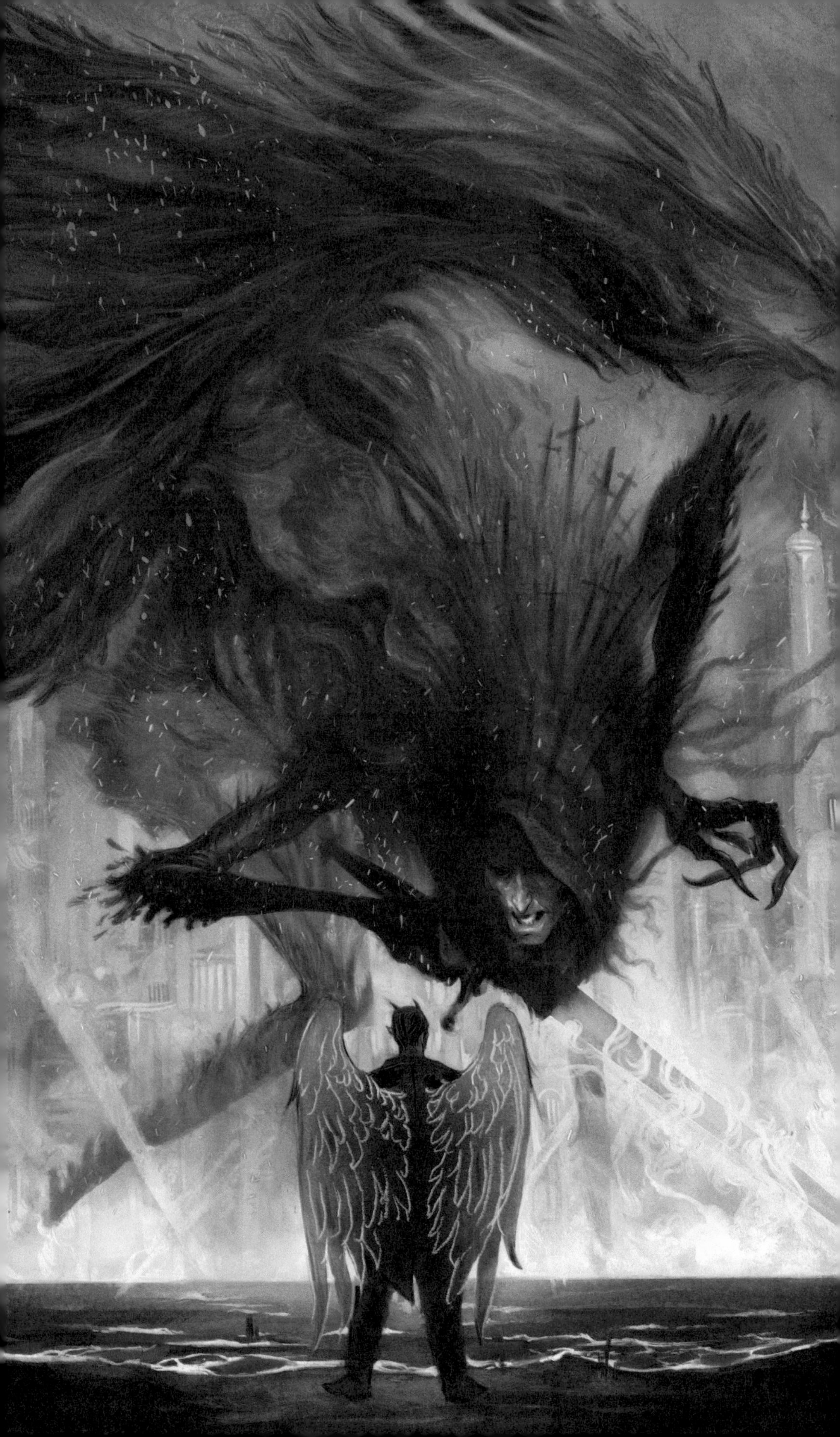

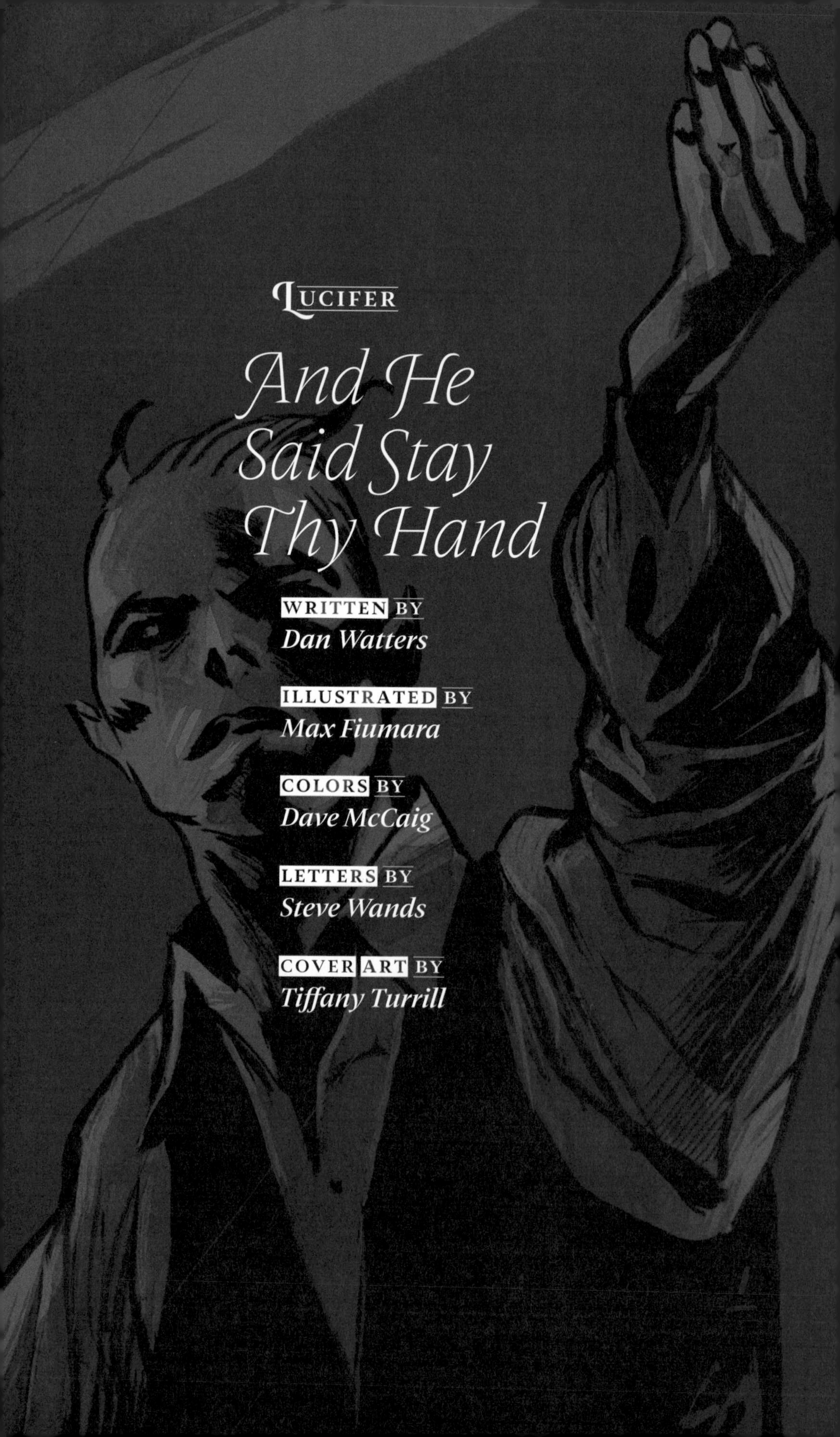

LUCIFER

And He Said Stay Thy Hand

WRITTEN BY
Dan Watters

ILLUSTRATED BY
Max Fiumara

COLORS BY
Dave McCaig

LETTERS BY
Steve Wands

COVER ART BY
Tiffany Turrill

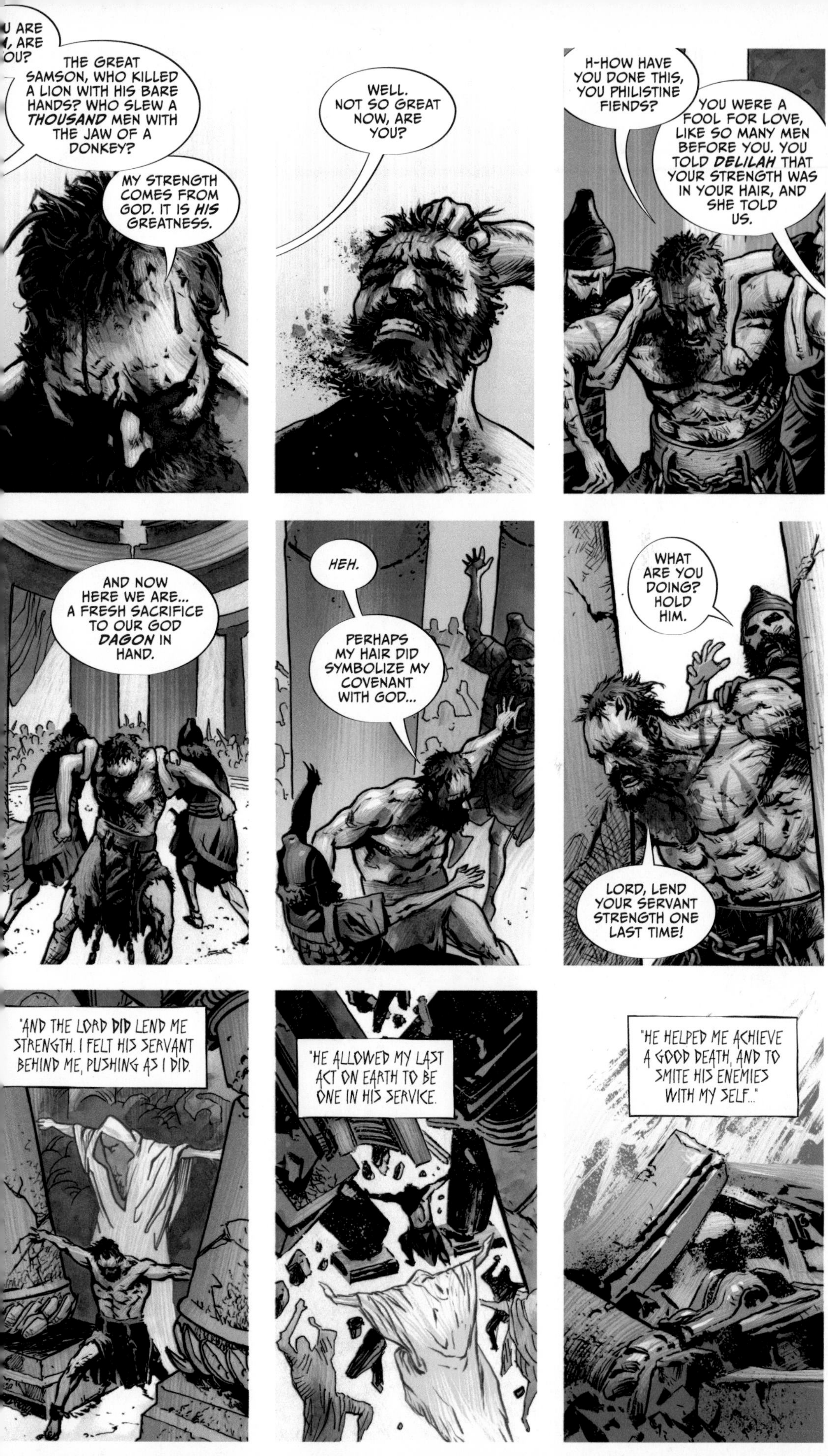
U ARE
, ARE
OU?
THE GREAT SAMSON, WHO KILLED A LION WITH HIS BARE HANDS? WHO SLEW A THOUSAND MEN WITH THE JAW OF A DONKEY?
MY STRENGTH COMES FROM GOD. IT IS HIS GREATNESS.
WELL. NOT SO GREAT NOW, ARE YOU?
H-HOW HAVE YOU DONE THIS, YOU PHILISTINE FIENDS?
YOU WERE A FOOL FOR LOVE, LIKE SO MANY MEN BEFORE YOU. YOU TOLD DELILAH THAT YOUR STRENGTH WAS IN YOUR HAIR, AND SHE TOLD US.
AND NOW HERE WE ARE... A FRESH SACRIFICE TO OUR GOD DAGON IN HAND.
HEH.
PERHAPS MY HAIR DID SYMBOLIZE MY COVENANT WITH GOD...
WHAT ARE YOU DOING? HOLD HIM.
LORD, LEND YOUR SERVANT STRENGTH ONE LAST TIME!
"AND THE LORD DID LEND ME STRENGTH. I FELT HIS SERVANT BEHIND ME, PUSHING AS I DID.
"HE ALLOWED MY LAST ACT ON EARTH TO BE ONE IN HIS SERVICE.
"HE HELPED ME ACHIEVE A GOOD DEATH, AND TO SMITE HIS ENEMIES WITH MY SELF..."

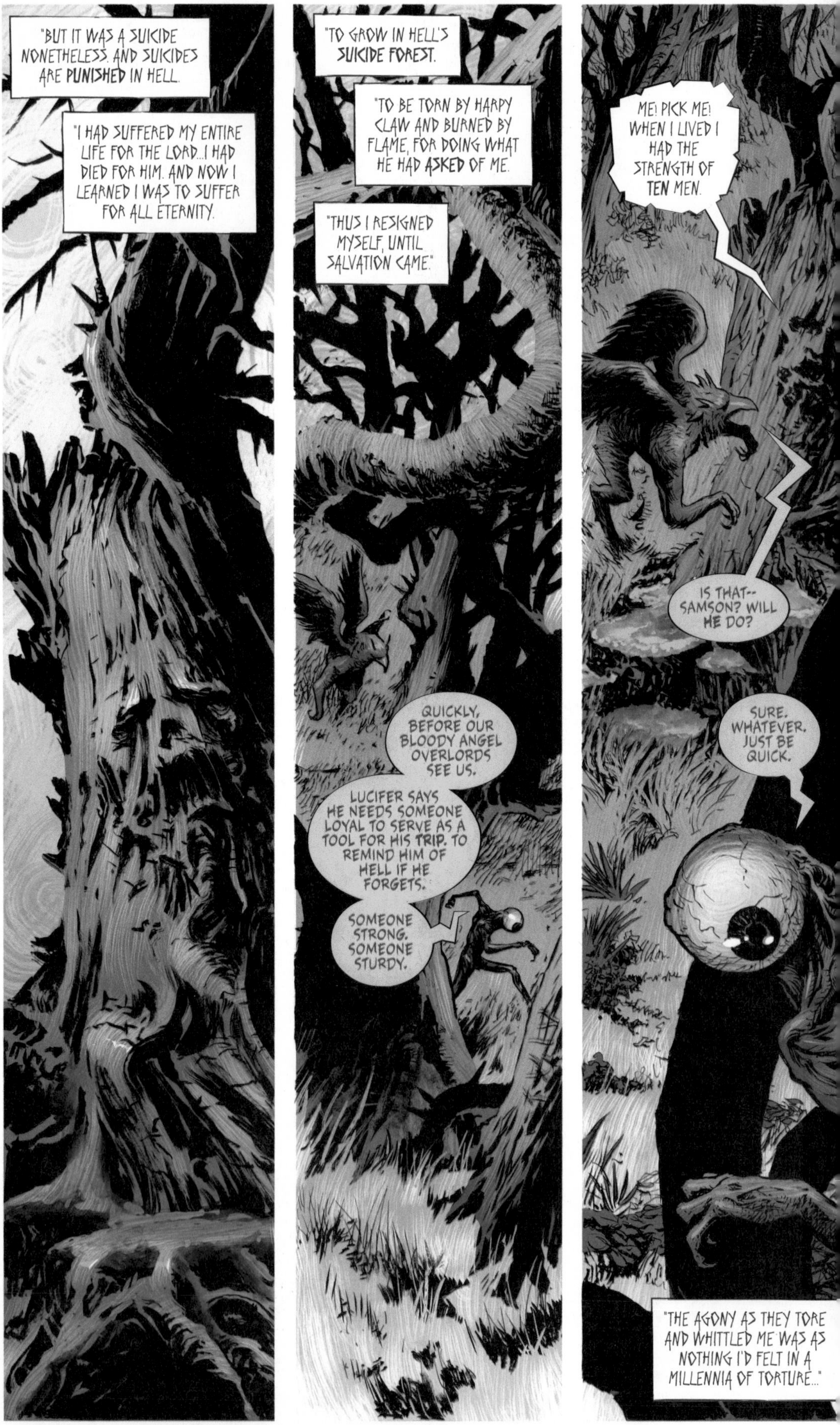
"BUT IT WAS A SUICIDE NONETHELESS. AND SUICIDES ARE PUNISHED IN HELL.
"I HAD SUFFERED MY ENTIRE LIFE FOR THE LORD...I HAD DIED FOR HIM. AND NOW I LEARNED I WAS TO SUFFER FOR ALL ETERNITY.
"TO GROW IN HELL'S SUICIDE FOREST.
"TO BE TORN BY HARPY CLAW AND BURNED BY FLAME, FOR DOING WHAT HE HAD ASKED OF ME.
"THUS I RESIGNED MYSELF, UNTIL SALVATION CAME."
QUICKLY, BEFORE OUR BLOODY ANGEL OVERLORDS SEE US.
LUCIFER SAYS HE NEEDS SOMEONE LOYAL TO SERVE AS A TOOL FOR HIS TRIP. TO REMIND HIM OF HELL IF HE FORGETS.
SOMEONE STRONG. SOMEONE STURDY.
ME! PICK ME! WHEN I LIVED I HAD THE STRENGTH OF TEN MEN.
IS THAT-- SAMSON? WILL HE DO?
SURE. WHATEVER. JUST BE QUICK.
"THE AGONY AS THEY TORE AND WHITTLED ME WAS AS NOTHING I'D FELT IN A MILLENNIA OF TORTURE..."

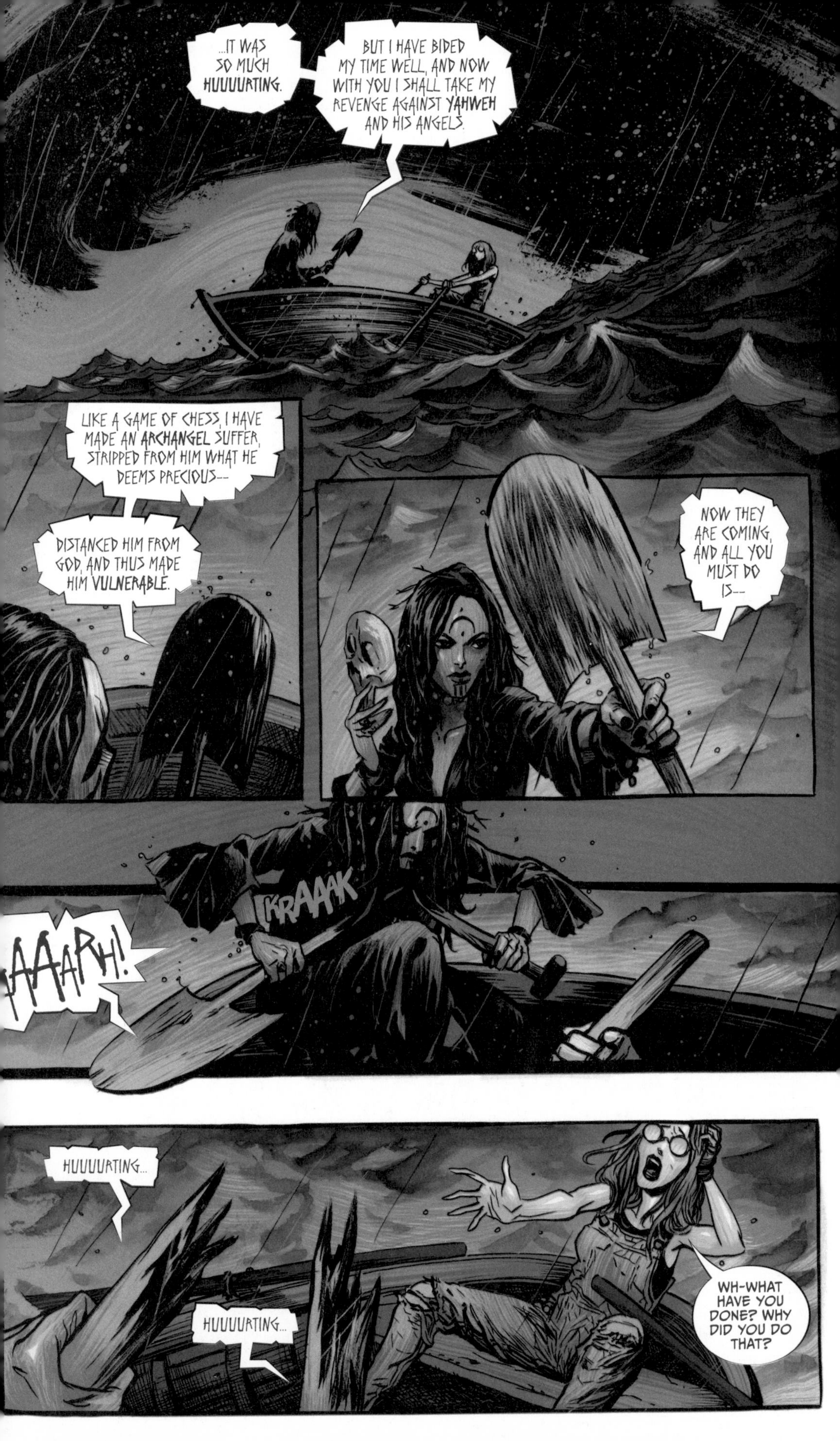
...IT WAS SO MUCH HUUUURTING.
BUT I HAVE BIDED MY TIME WELL, AND NOW WITH YOU I SHALL TAKE MY REVENGE AGAINST YAHWEH AND HIS ANGELS.
LIKE A GAME OF CHESS, I HAVE MADE AN ARCHANGEL SUFFER, STRIPPED FROM HIM WHAT HE DEEMS PRECIOUS--
DISTANCED HIM FROM GOD, AND THUS MADE HIM VULNERABLE.
NOW THEY ARE COMING, AND ALL YOU MUST DO IS--
KRAAAK
AAARH!
HUUUURTING...
HUUUURTING...
WH-WHAT HAVE YOU DONE? WHY DID YOU DO THAT?

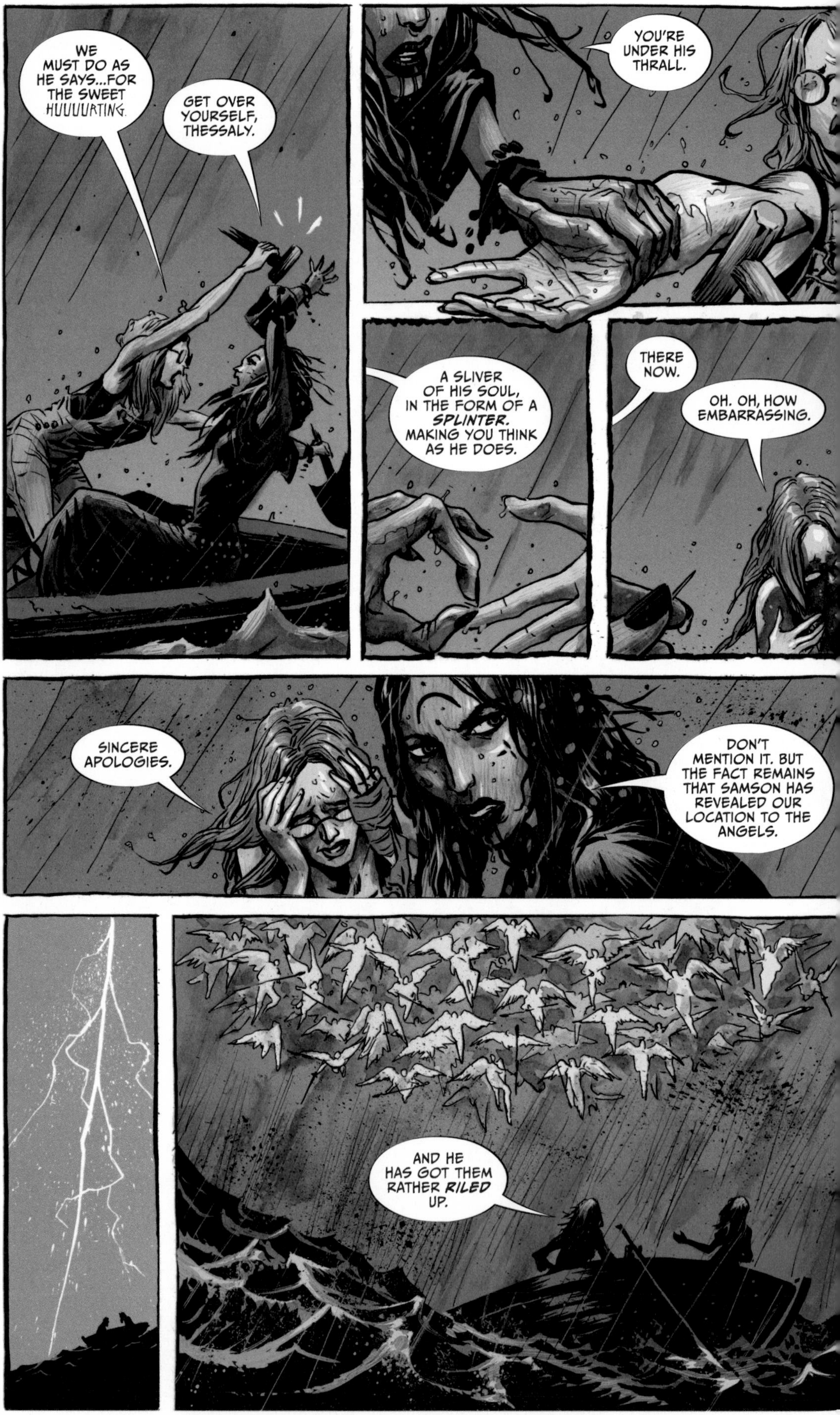
WE MUST DO AS HE SAYS...FOR THE SWEET HUUUURTING.
GET OVER YOURSELF, THESSALY.
YOU'RE UNDER HIS THRALL.
A SLIVER OF HIS SOUL, IN THE FORM OF A *SPLINTER.* MAKING YOU THINK AS HE DOES.
THERE NOW.
OH. OH, HOW EMBARRASSING.
SINCERE APOLOGIES.
DON'T MENTION IT. BUT THE FACT REMAINS THAT SAMSON HAS REVEALED OUR LOCATION TO THE ANGELS.
AND HE HAS GOT THEM RATHER *RILED* UP.

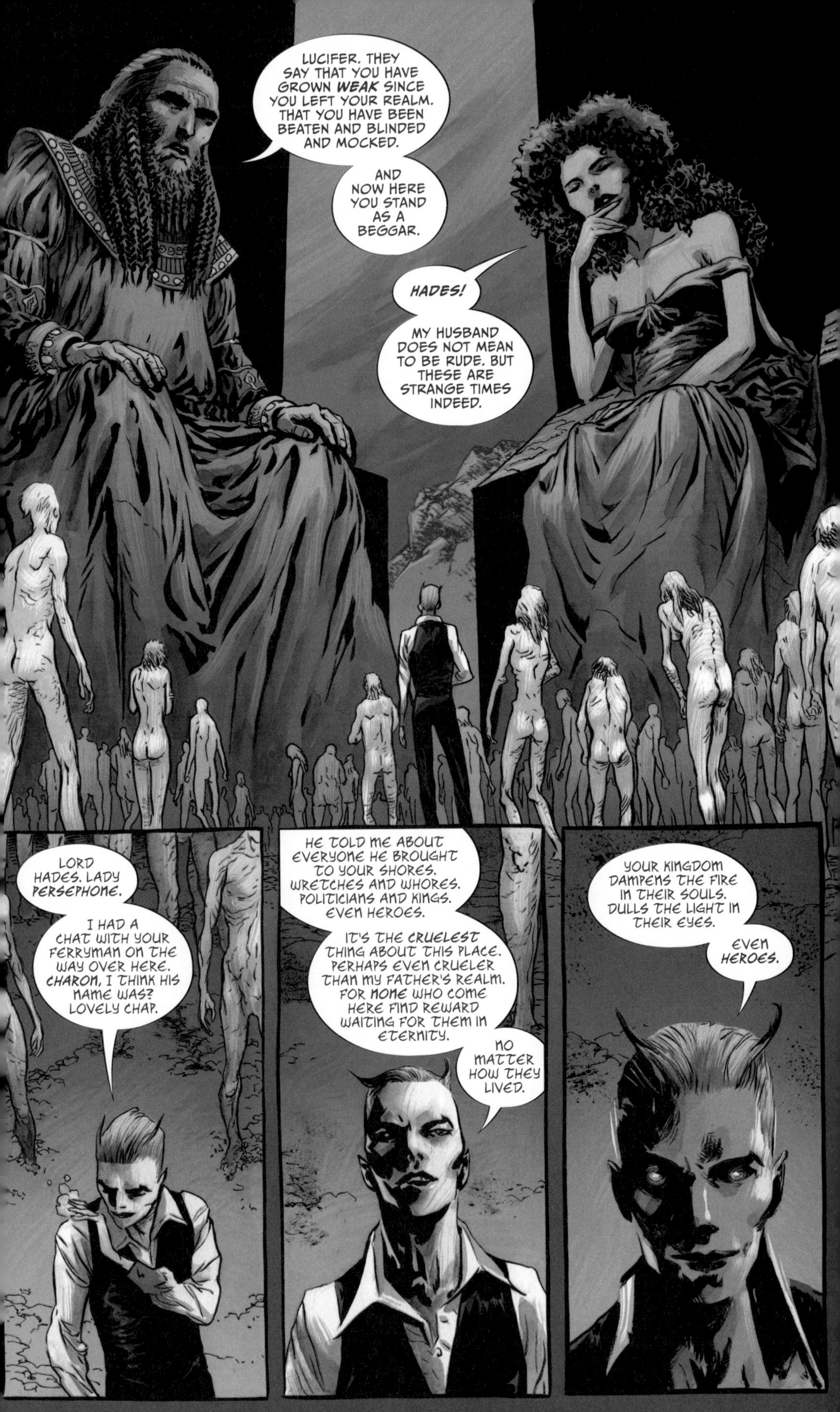

LUCIFER. THEY SAY THAT YOU HAVE GROWN WEAK SINCE YOU LEFT YOUR REALM. THAT YOU HAVE BEEN BEATEN AND BLINDED AND MOCKED.
AND NOW HERE YOU STAND AS A BEGGAR.
HADES!
MY HUSBAND DOES NOT MEAN TO BE RUDE. BUT THESE ARE STRANGE TIMES INDEED.
LORD HADES. LADY PERSEPHONE.
I HAD A CHAT WITH YOUR FERRYMAN ON THE WAY OVER HERE. CHARON, I THINK HIS NAME WAS? LOVELY CHAP.
HE TOLD ME ABOUT EVERYONE HE BROUGHT TO YOUR SHORES. WRETCHES AND WHORES. POLITICIANS AND KINGS. EVEN HEROES.
IT'S THE CRUELEST THING ABOUT THIS PLACE. PERHAPS EVEN CRUELER THAN MY FATHER'S REALM. FOR NONE WHO COME HERE FIND REWARD WAITING FOR THEM IN ETERNITY.
NO MATTER HOW THEY LIVED.
YOUR KINGDOM DAMPENS THE FIRE IN THEIR SOULS. DULLS THE LIGHT IN THEIR EYES.
EVEN HEROES.

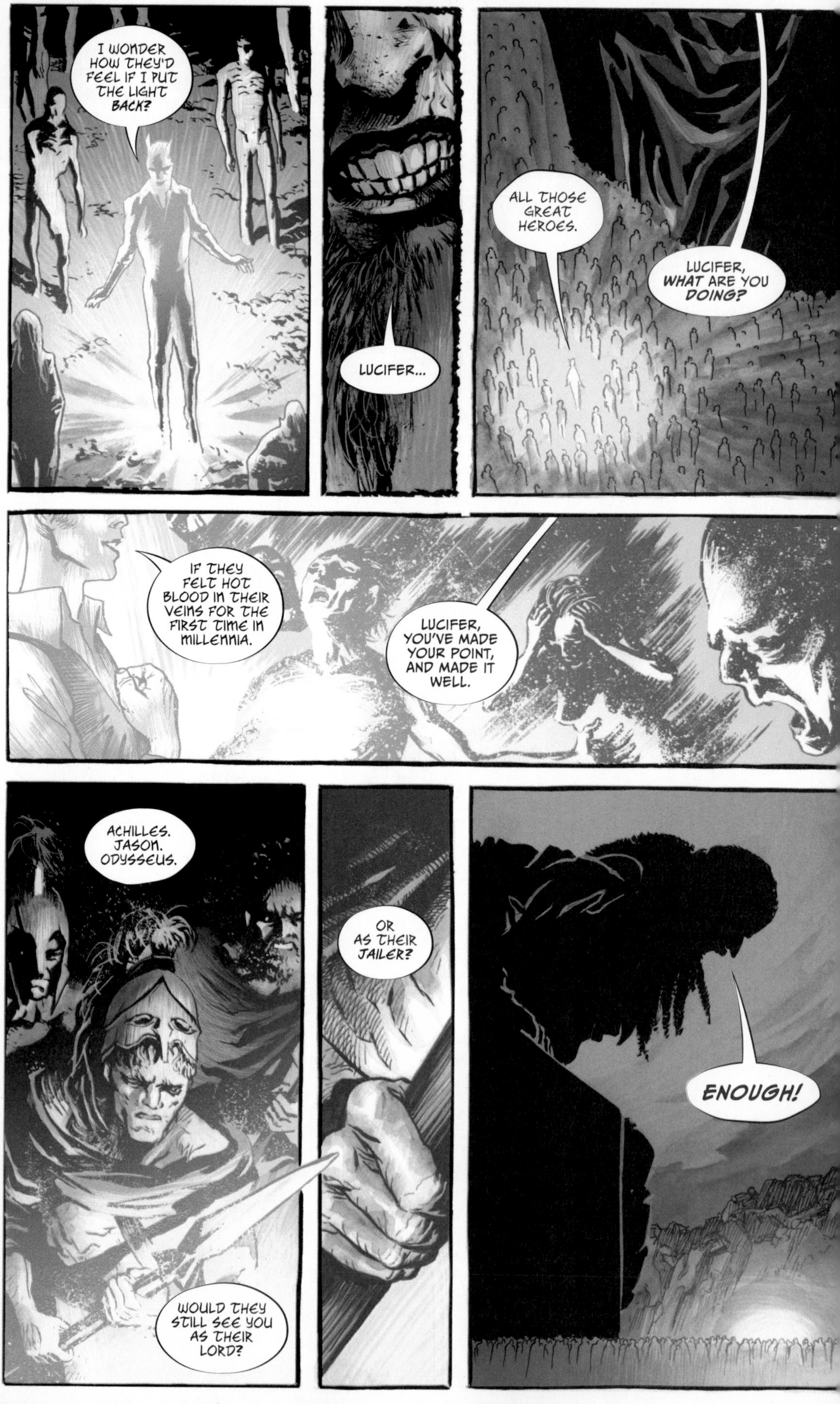
I WONDER HOW THEY'D FEEL IF I PUT THE LIGHT BACK?
LUCIFER...
ALL THOSE GREAT HEROES.
LUCIFER, WHAT ARE YOU DOING?
IF THEY FELT HOT BLOOD IN THEIR VEINS FOR THE FIRST TIME IN MILLENNIA.
LUCIFER, YOU'VE MADE YOUR POINT, AND MADE IT WELL.
ACHILLES. JASON. ODYSSEUS.
WOULD THEY STILL SEE YOU AS THEIR LORD?
OR AS THEIR JAILER?
ENOUGH!

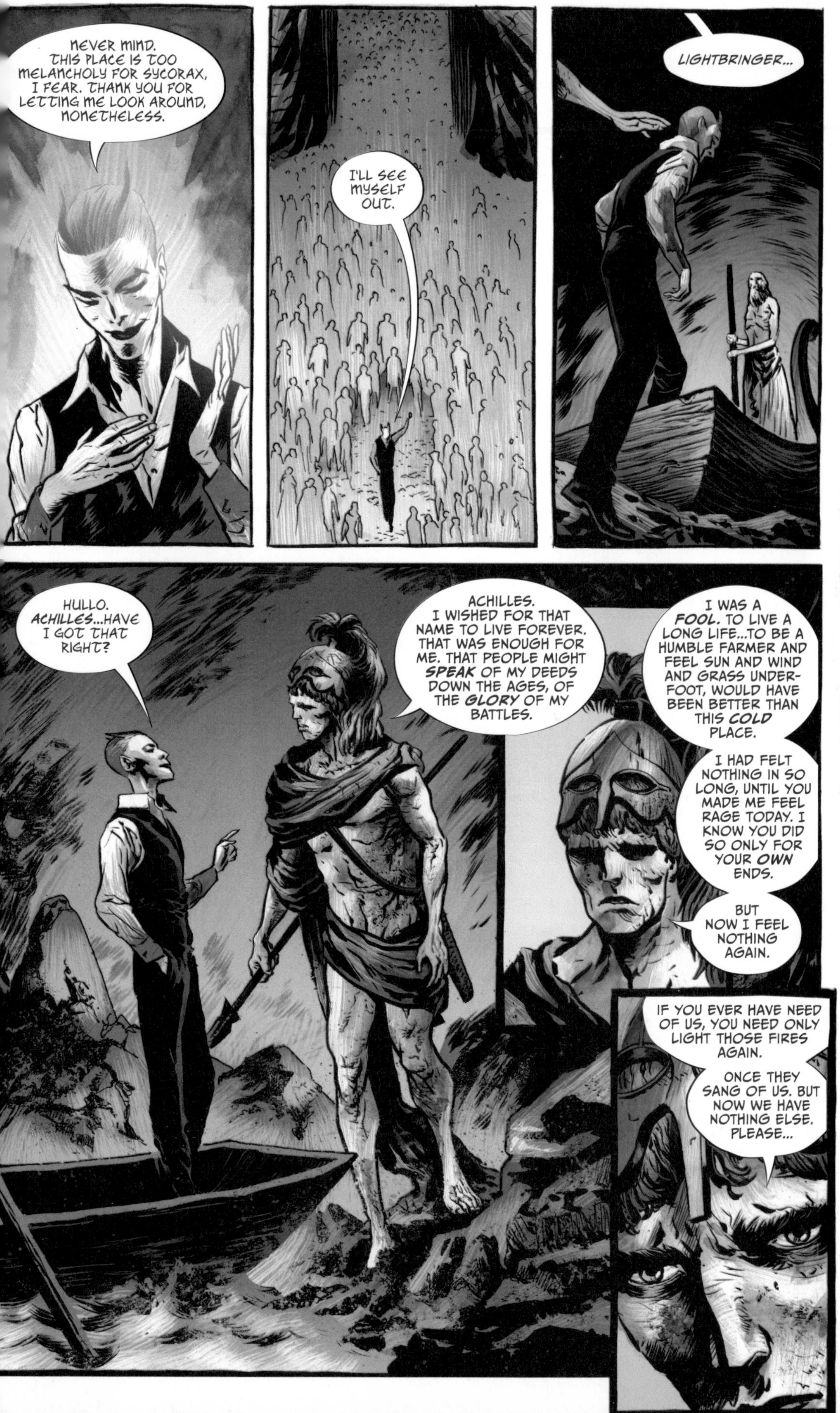
NEVER MIND. THIS PLACE IS TOO MELANCHOLY FOR SYCORAX, I FEAR. THANK YOU FOR LETTING ME LOOK AROUND, NONETHELESS.
I'LL SEE MYSELF OUT.
LIGHTBRINGER...
HULLO. ACHILLES...HAVE I GOT THAT RIGHT?
ACHILLES. I WISHED FOR THAT NAME TO LIVE FOREVER. THAT WAS ENOUGH FOR ME. THAT PEOPLE MIGHT SPEAK OF MY DEEDS DOWN THE AGES, OF THE GLORY OF MY BATTLES.
I WAS A FOOL. TO LIVE A LONG LIFE...TO BE A HUMBLE FARMER AND FEEL SUN AND WIND AND GRASS UNDER-FOOT, WOULD HAVE BEEN BETTER THAN THIS COLD PLACE.
I HAD FELT NOTHING IN SO LONG, UNTIL YOU MADE ME FEEL RAGE TODAY. I KNOW YOU DID SO ONLY FOR YOUR OWN ENDS.
BUT NOW I FEEL NOTHING AGAIN.
IF YOU EVER HAVE NEED OF US, YOU NEED ONLY LIGHT THOSE FIRES AGAIN.
ONCE THEY SANG OF US. BUT NOW WE HAVE NOTHING ELSE. PLEASE...

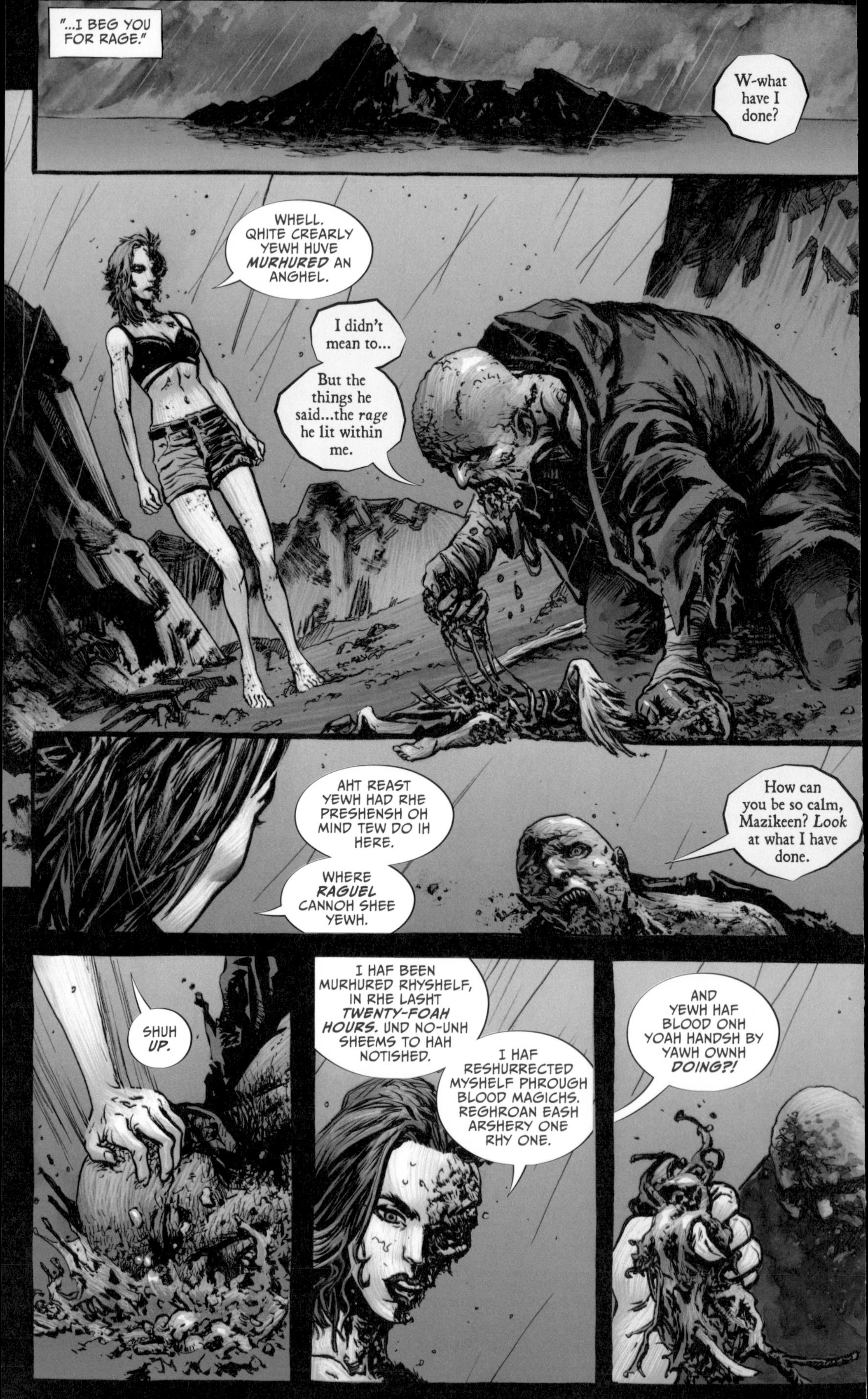
"...I BEG YOU FOR RAGE."
W-what have I done?
WHELL. QHITE CREARLY YEWH HUVE MURHURED AN ANGHEL.
I didn't mean to...
But the things he said...the rage he lit within me.
AHT REAST YEWH HAD RHE PRESHENSH OH MIND TEW DO IH HERE.
WHERE RAGUEL CANNOH SHEE YEWH.
How can you be so calm, Mazikeen? Look at what I have done.
SHUH UP.
I HAF BEEN MURHURED RHYSHELF, IN RHE LASHT TWENTY-FOAH HOURS. UND NO-UNH SHEEMS TO HAH NOTISHED.
I HAF RESHURRECTED MYSHELF PHROUGH BLOOD MAGICHS. REGHROAN EASH ARSHERY ONE RHY ONE.
AND YEWH HAF BLOOD ONH YOAH HANDSH BY YAWH OWNH DOING?!

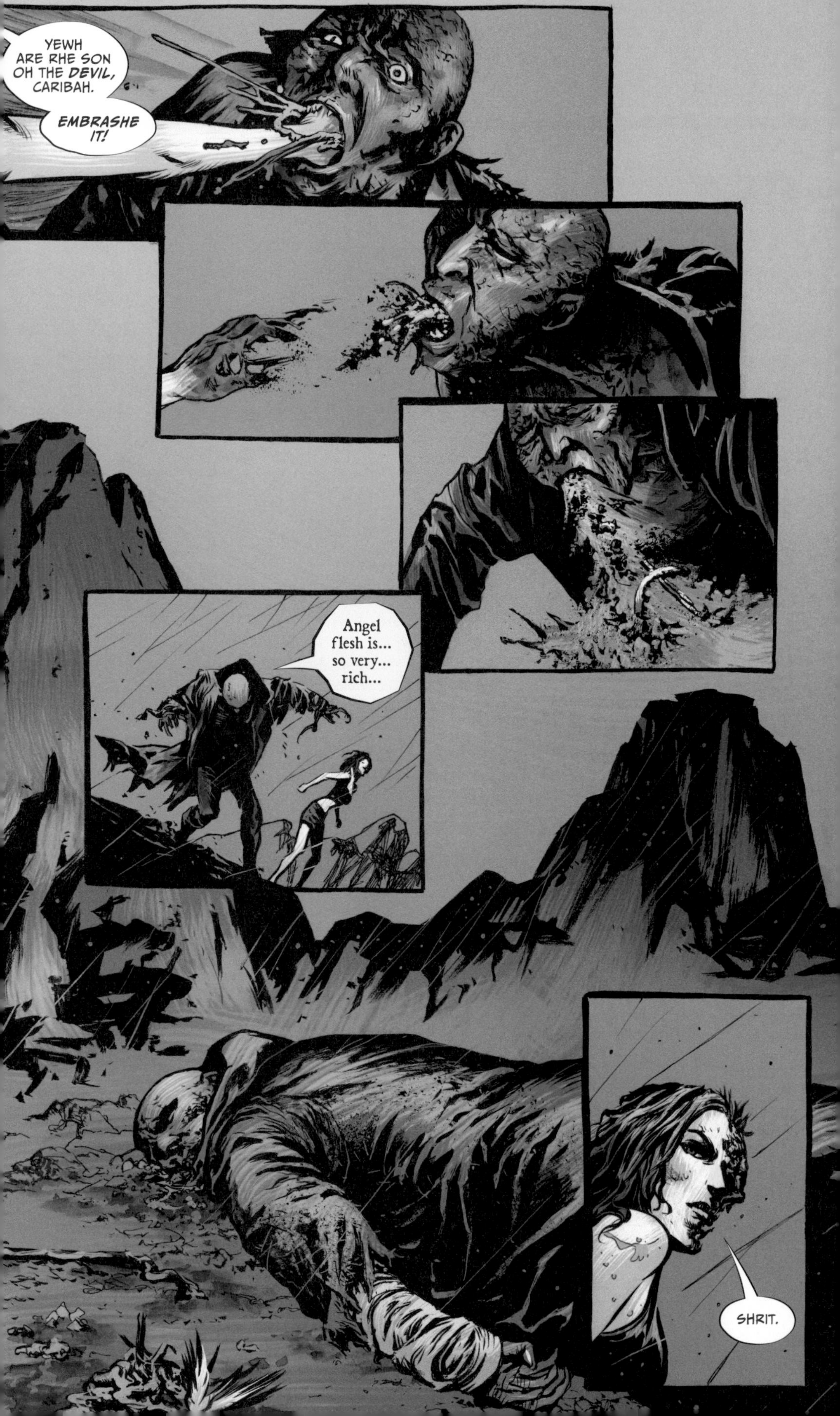
YEWH ARE RHE SON OH THE *DEVIL*, CARIBAH.
EMBRASHE IT!
Angel flesh is... so very... rich...
SHRIT.

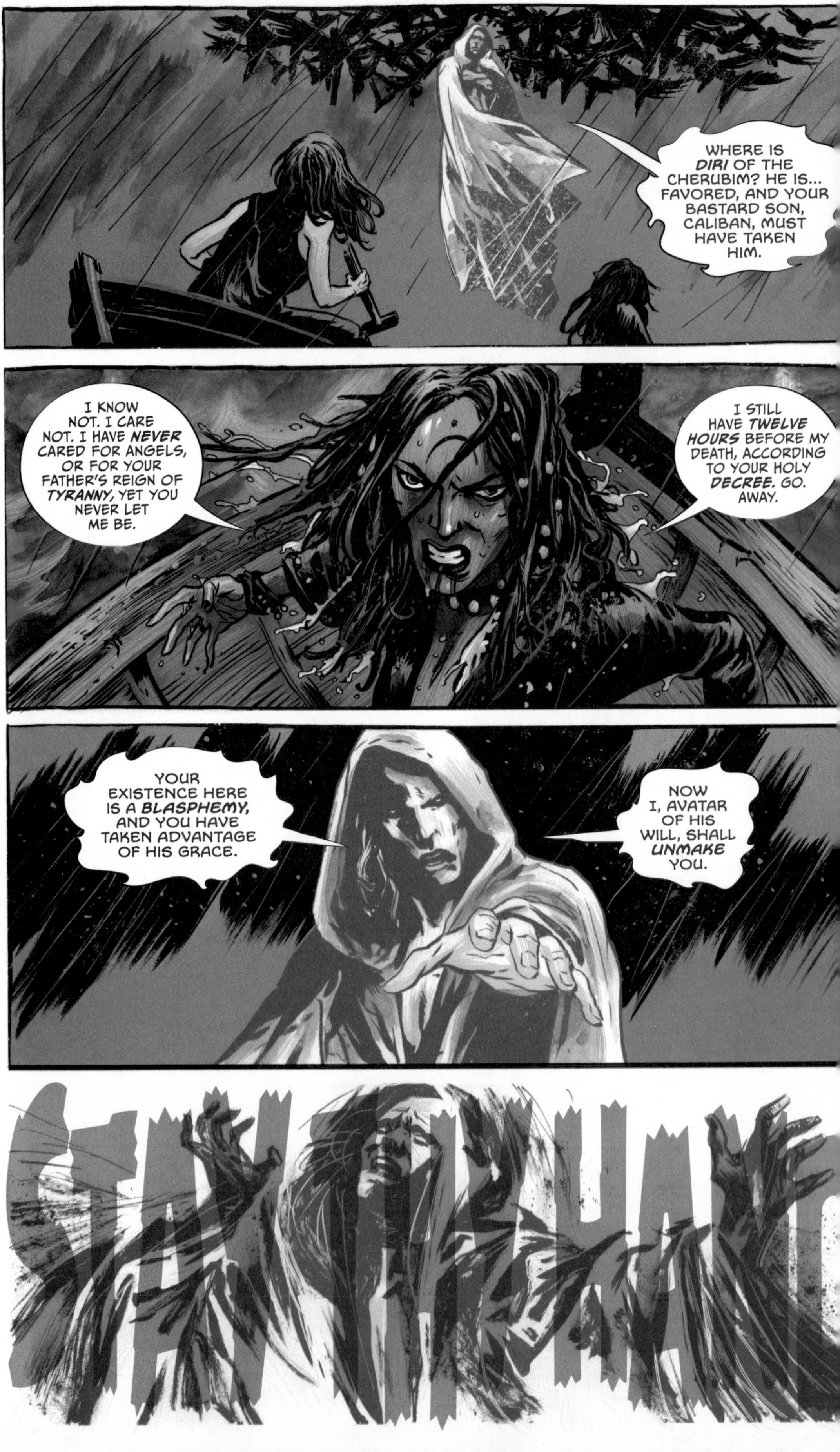
WHERE IS DIRI OF THE CHERUBIM? HE IS... FAVORED, AND YOUR BASTARD SON, CALIBAN, MUST HAVE TAKEN HIM.
I KNOW NOT. I CARE NOT. I HAVE NEVER CARED FOR ANGELS, OR FOR YOUR FATHER'S REIGN OF TYRANNY, YET YOU NEVER LET ME BE.
I STILL HAVE TWELVE HOURS BEFORE MY DEATH, ACCORDING TO YOUR HOLY DECREE. GO. AWAY.
YOUR EXISTENCE HERE IS A BLASPHEMY, AND YOU HAVE TAKEN ADVANTAGE OF HIS GRACE.
NOW I, AVATAR OF HIS WILL, SHALL UNMAKE YOU.

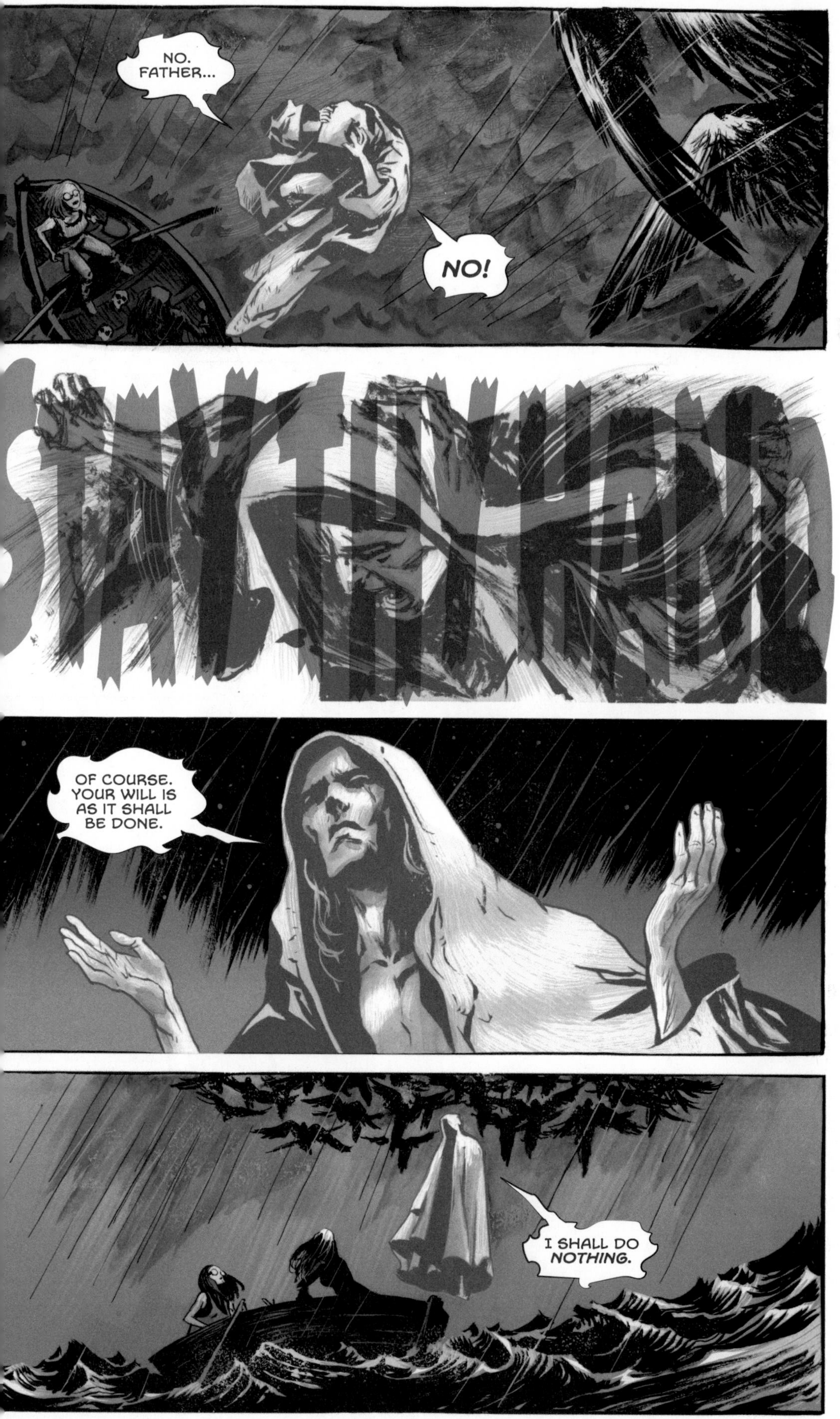
NO. FATHER...
NO!
STAY THY HAND
OF COURSE. YOUR WILL IS AS IT SHALL BE DONE.
I SHALL DO *NOTHING*.

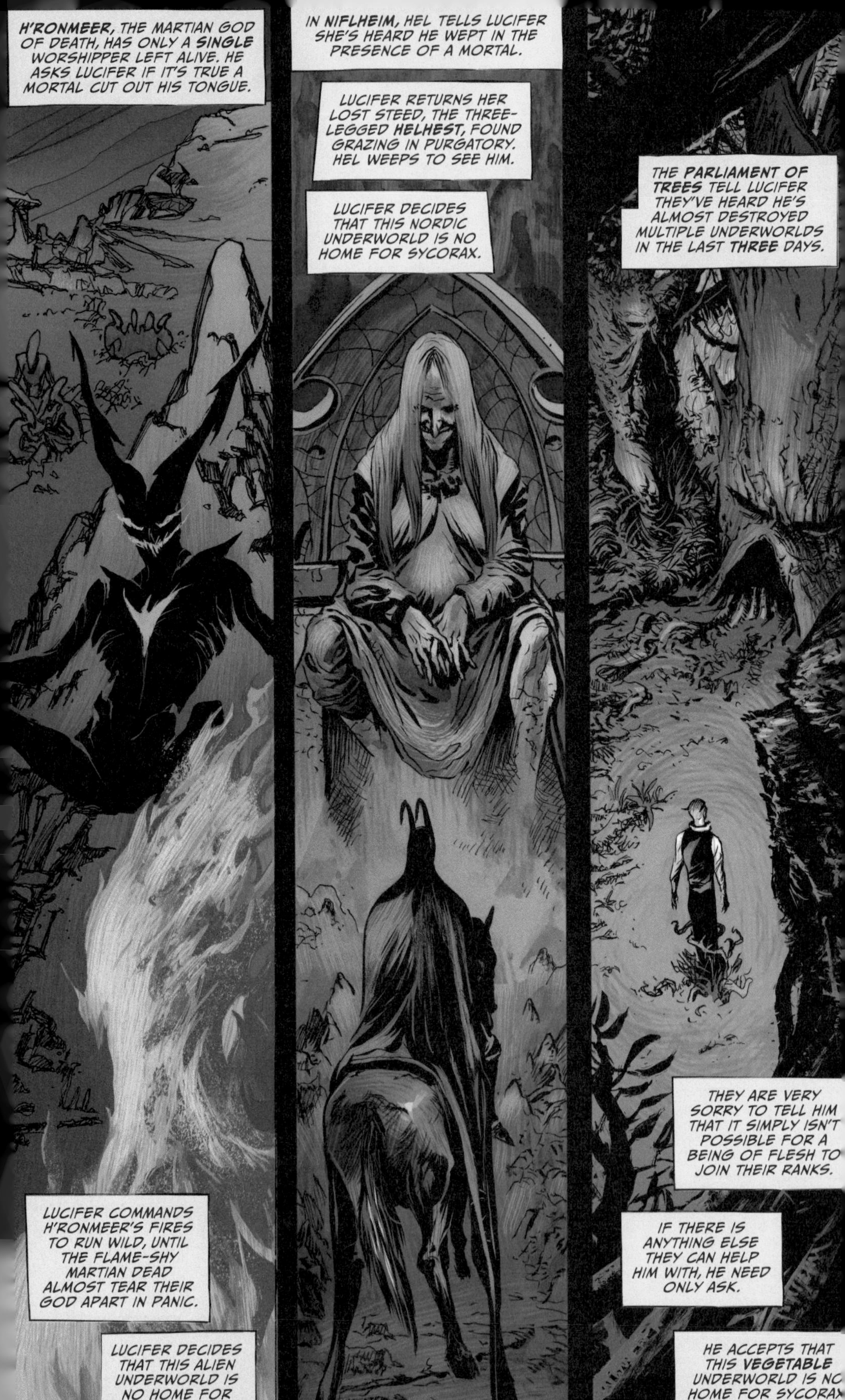
H'RONMEER, THE MARTIAN GOD OF DEATH, HAS ONLY A SINGLE WORSHIPPER LEFT ALIVE. HE ASKS LUCIFER IF IT'S TRUE A MORTAL CUT OUT HIS TONGUE.
LUCIFER COMMANDS H'RONMEER'S FIRES TO RUN WILD, UNTIL THE FLAME-SHY MARTIAN DEAD ALMOST TEAR THEIR GOD APART IN PANIC.
LUCIFER DECIDES THAT THIS ALIEN UNDERWORLD IS NO HOME FOR SYCORAX.
IN NIFLHEIM, HEL TELLS LUCIFER SHE'S HEARD HE WEPT IN THE PRESENCE OF A MORTAL.
LUCIFER RETURNS HER LOST STEED, THE THREE-LEGGED HELHEST, FOUND GRAZING IN PURGATORY. HEL WEEPS TO SEE HIM.
LUCIFER DECIDES THAT THIS NORDIC UNDERWORLD IS NO HOME FOR SYCORAX.
THE PARLIAMENT OF TREES TELL LUCIFER THEY'VE HEARD HE'S ALMOST DESTROYED MULTIPLE UNDERWORLDS IN THE LAST THREE DAYS.
THEY ARE VERY SORRY TO TELL HIM THAT IT SIMPLY ISN'T POSSIBLE FOR A BEING OF FLESH TO JOIN THEIR RANKS.
IF THERE IS ANYTHING ELSE THEY CAN HELP HIM WITH, HE NEED ONLY ASK.
HE ACCEPTS THAT THIS VEGETABLE UNDERWORLD IS NO HOME FOR SYCORAX

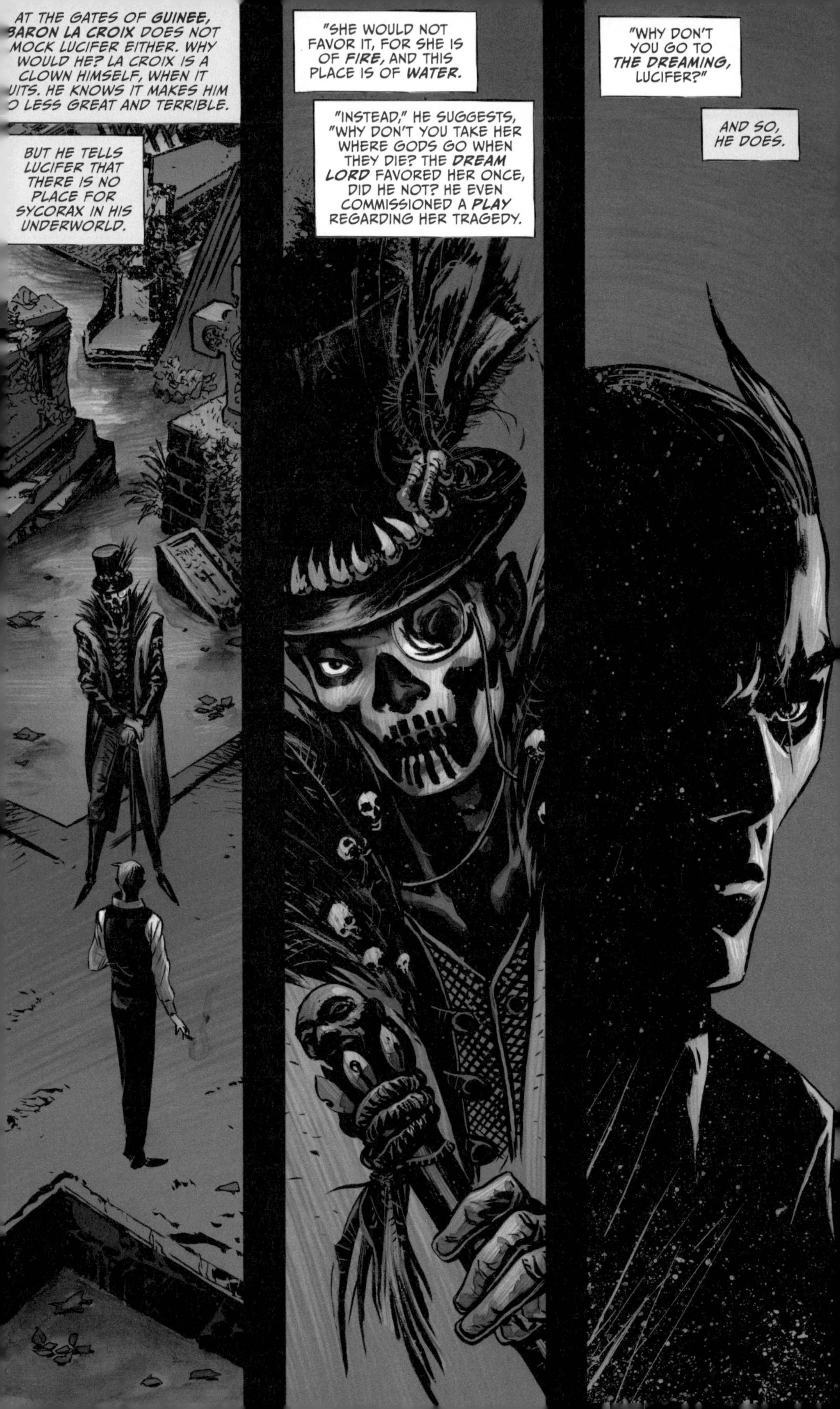

AT THE GATES OF GUINEE, BARON LA CROIX DOES NOT MOCK LUCIFER EITHER. WHY WOULD HE? LA CROIX IS A CLOWN HIMSELF, WHEN IT SUITS. HE KNOWS IT MAKES HIM NO LESS GREAT AND TERRIBLE.
BUT HE TELLS LUCIFER THAT THERE IS NO PLACE FOR SYCORAX IN HIS UNDERWORLD.
"SHE WOULD NOT FAVOR IT, FOR SHE IS OF FIRE, AND THIS PLACE IS OF WATER.
"INSTEAD," HE SUGGESTS, "WHY DON'T YOU TAKE HER WHERE GODS GO WHEN THEY DIE? THE DREAM LORD FAVORED HER ONCE, DID HE NOT? HE EVEN COMMISSIONED A PLAY REGARDING HER TRAGEDY.
"WHY DON'T YOU GO TO THE DREAMING, LUCIFER?"
AND SO, HE DOES.

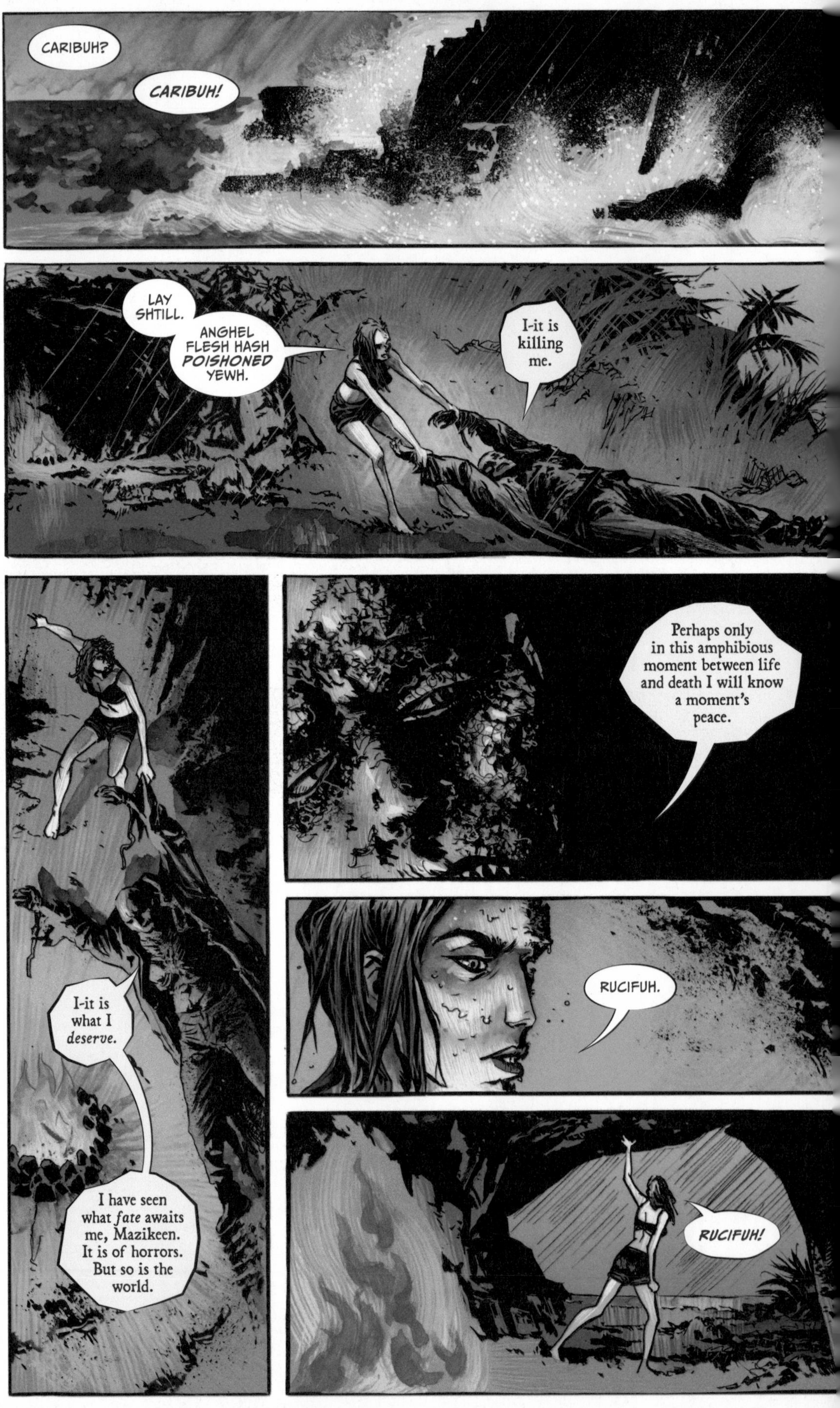
CARIBUH?
CARIBUH!
LAY SHTILL.
ANGHEL FLESH HASH *POISHONED* YEWH.
I-it is killing me.
I-it is what I *deserve.*
I have seen what *fate* awaits me, Mazikeen. It is of horrors. But so is the world.
Perhaps only in this amphibious moment between life and death I will know a moment's peace.
RUCIFUH.
RUCIFUH!

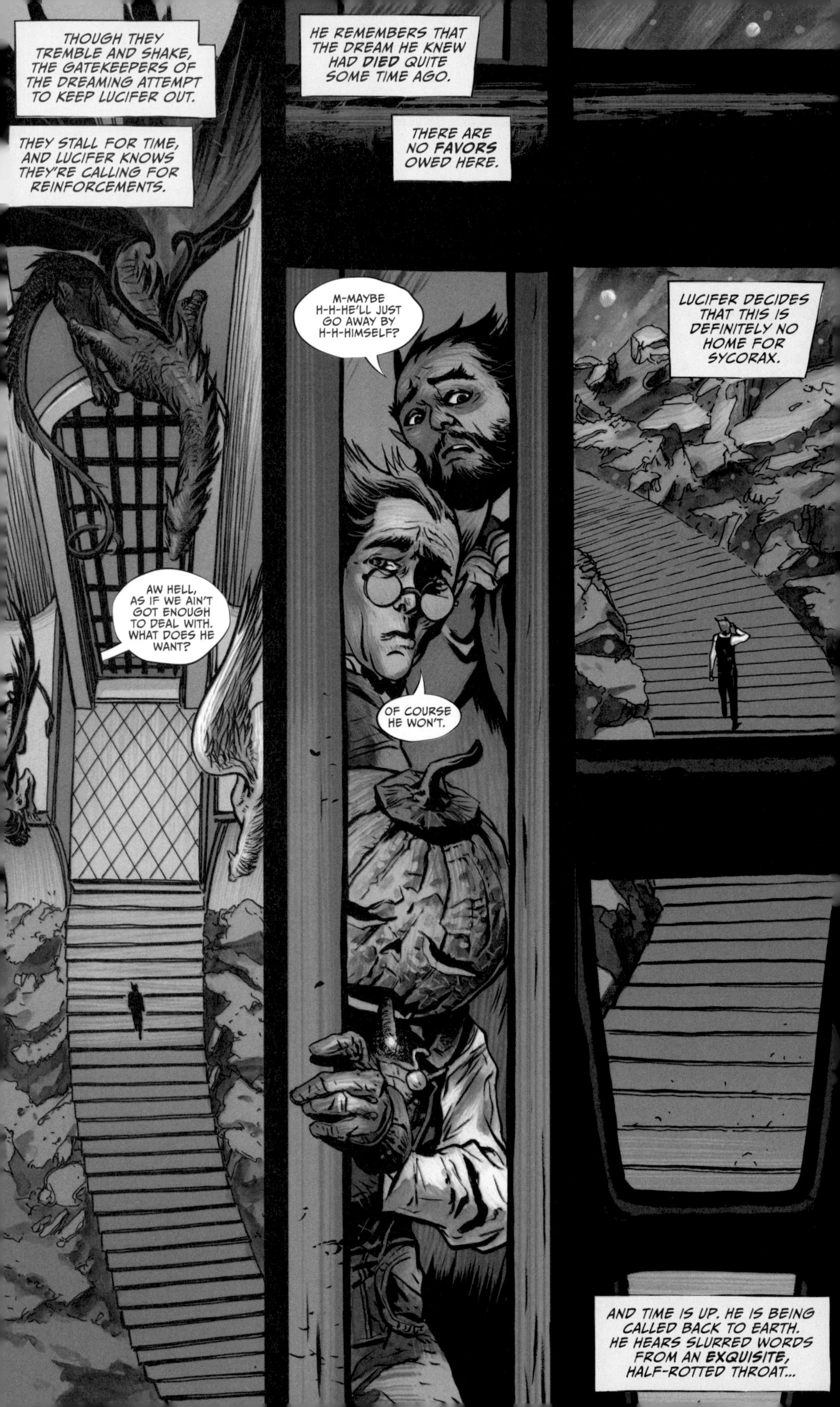
THOUGH THEY TREMBLE AND SHAKE, THE GATEKEEPERS OF THE DREAMING ATTEMPT TO KEEP LUCIFER OUT.
THEY STALL FOR TIME, AND LUCIFER KNOWS THEY'RE CALLING FOR REINFORCEMENTS.
AW HELL, AS IF WE AIN'T GOT ENOUGH TO DEAL WITH. WHAT DOES HE WANT?
HE REMEMBERS THAT THE DREAM HE KNEW HAD **DIED** QUITE SOME TIME AGO.
THERE ARE NO **FAVORS** OWED HERE.
M-MAYBE H-H-HE'LL JUST GO AWAY BY H-H-HIMSELF?
OF COURSE HE WON'T.
LUCIFER DECIDES THAT THIS IS DEFINITELY NO HOME FOR SYCORAX.
AND TIME IS UP. HE IS BEING CALLED BACK TO EARTH. HE HEARS SLURRED WORDS FROM AN **EXQUISITE**, HALF-ROTTED THROAT...

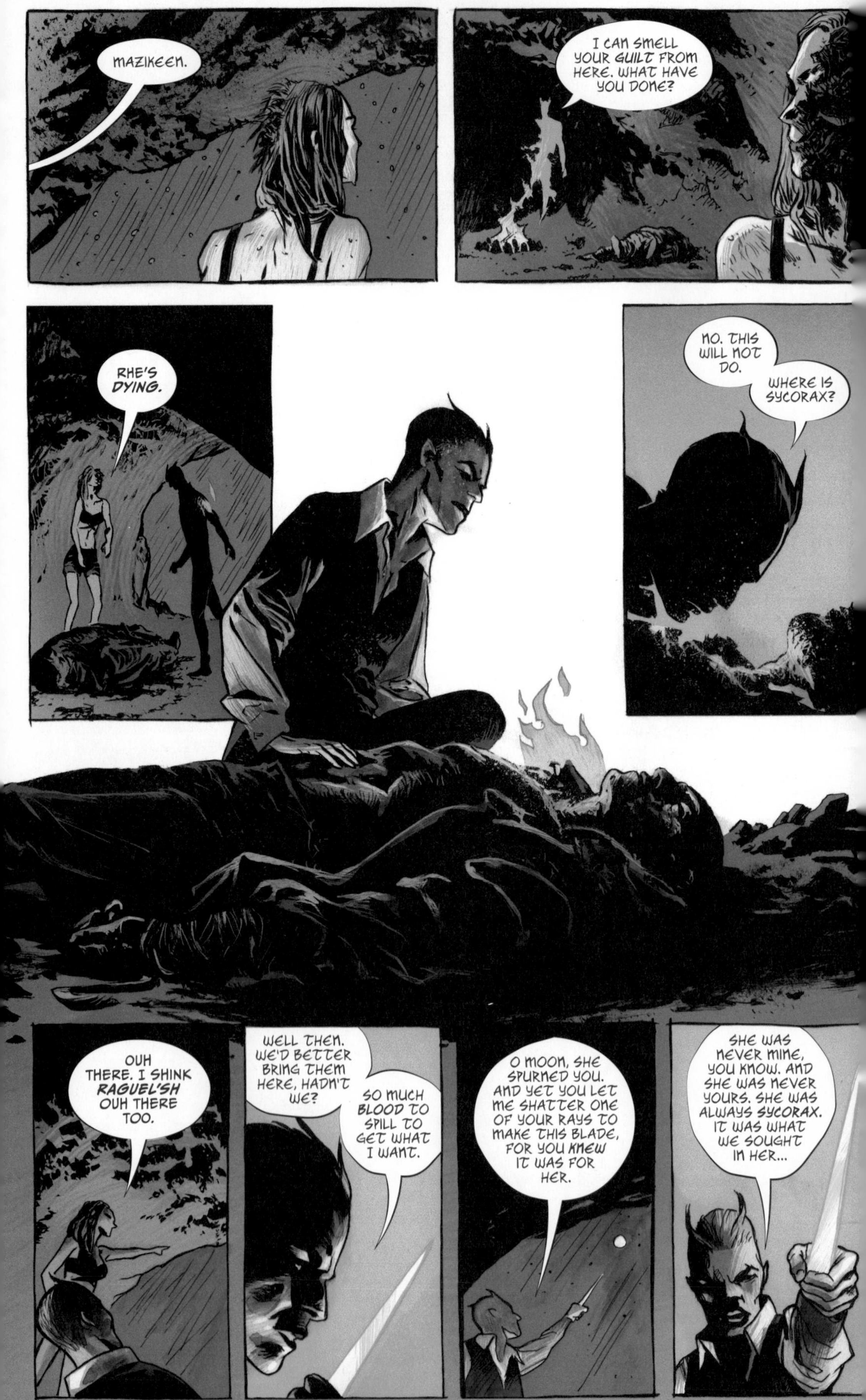
MAZIKEEN.
I CAN SMELL YOUR GUILT FROM HERE. WHAT HAVE YOU DONE?
RHE'S DYING.
NO. THIS WILL NOT DO.
WHERE IS SYCORAX?
OUH THERE. I SHINK RAGUEL'SH OUH THERE TOO.
WELL THEN. WE'D BETTER BRING THEM HERE, HADN'T WE?
SO MUCH BLOOD TO SPILL TO GET WHAT I WANT.
O MOON, SHE SPURNED YOU. AND YET YOU LET ME SHATTER ONE OF YOUR RAYS TO MAKE THIS BLADE, FOR YOU KNEW IT WAS FOR HER.
SHE WAS NEVER MINE, YOU KNOW. AND SHE WAS NEVER YOURS. SHE WAS ALWAYS SYCORAX. IT WAS WHAT WE SOUGHT IN HER...

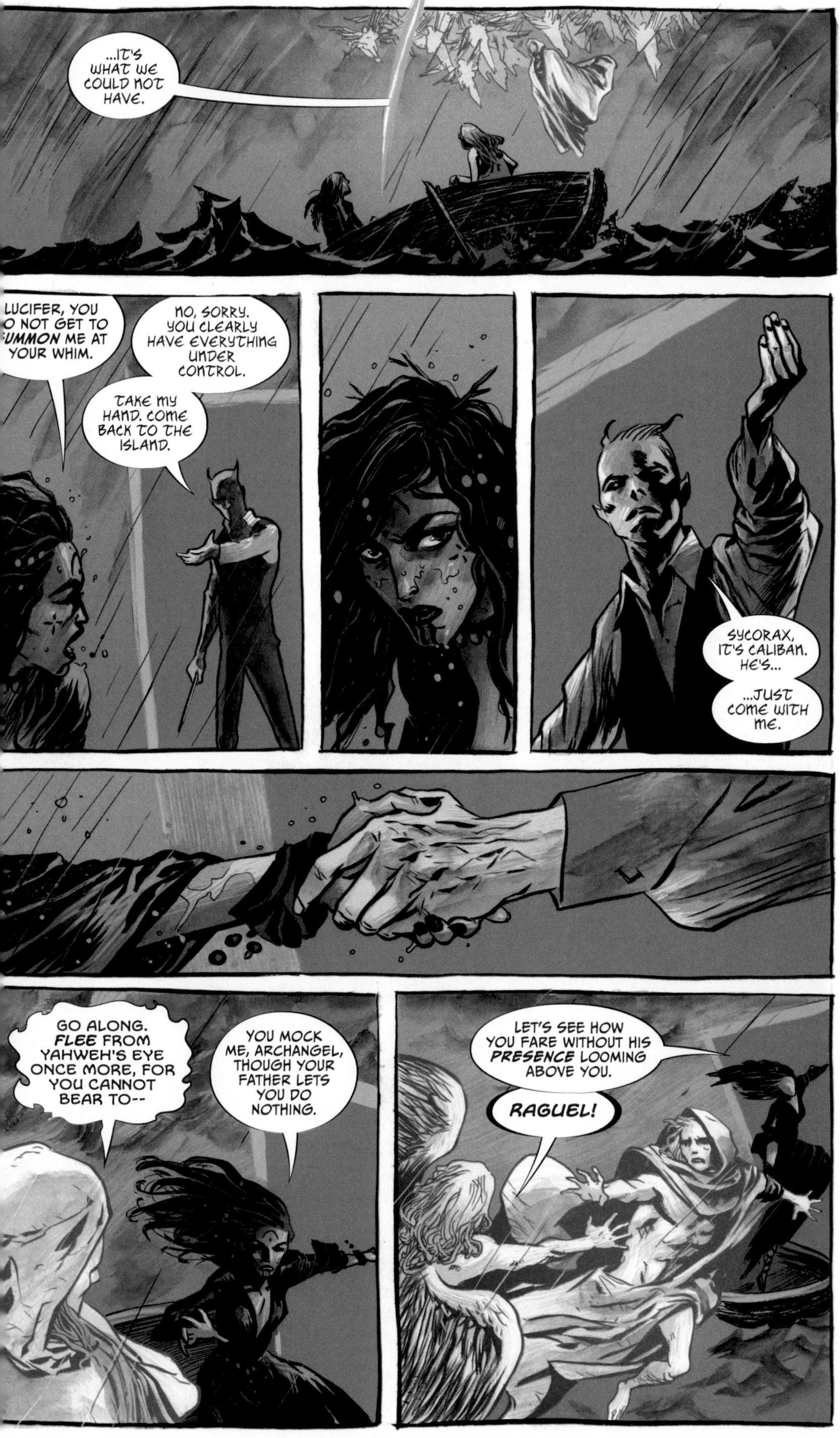

...IT'S WHAT WE COULD NOT HAVE.
LUCIFER, YOU DO NOT GET TO SUMMON ME AT YOUR WHIM.
NO, SORRY. YOU CLEARLY HAVE EVERYTHING UNDER CONTROL.
TAKE MY HAND. COME BACK TO THE ISLAND.
SYCORAX, IT'S CALIBAN. HE'S...
...JUST COME WITH ME.
GO ALONG. FLEE FROM YAHWEH'S EYE ONCE MORE, FOR YOU CANNOT BEAR TO--
YOU MOCK ME, ARCHANGEL, THOUGH YOUR FATHER LETS YOU DO NOTHING.
LET'S SEE HOW YOU FARE WITHOUT HIS PRESENCE LOOMING ABOVE YOU.
RAGUEL!

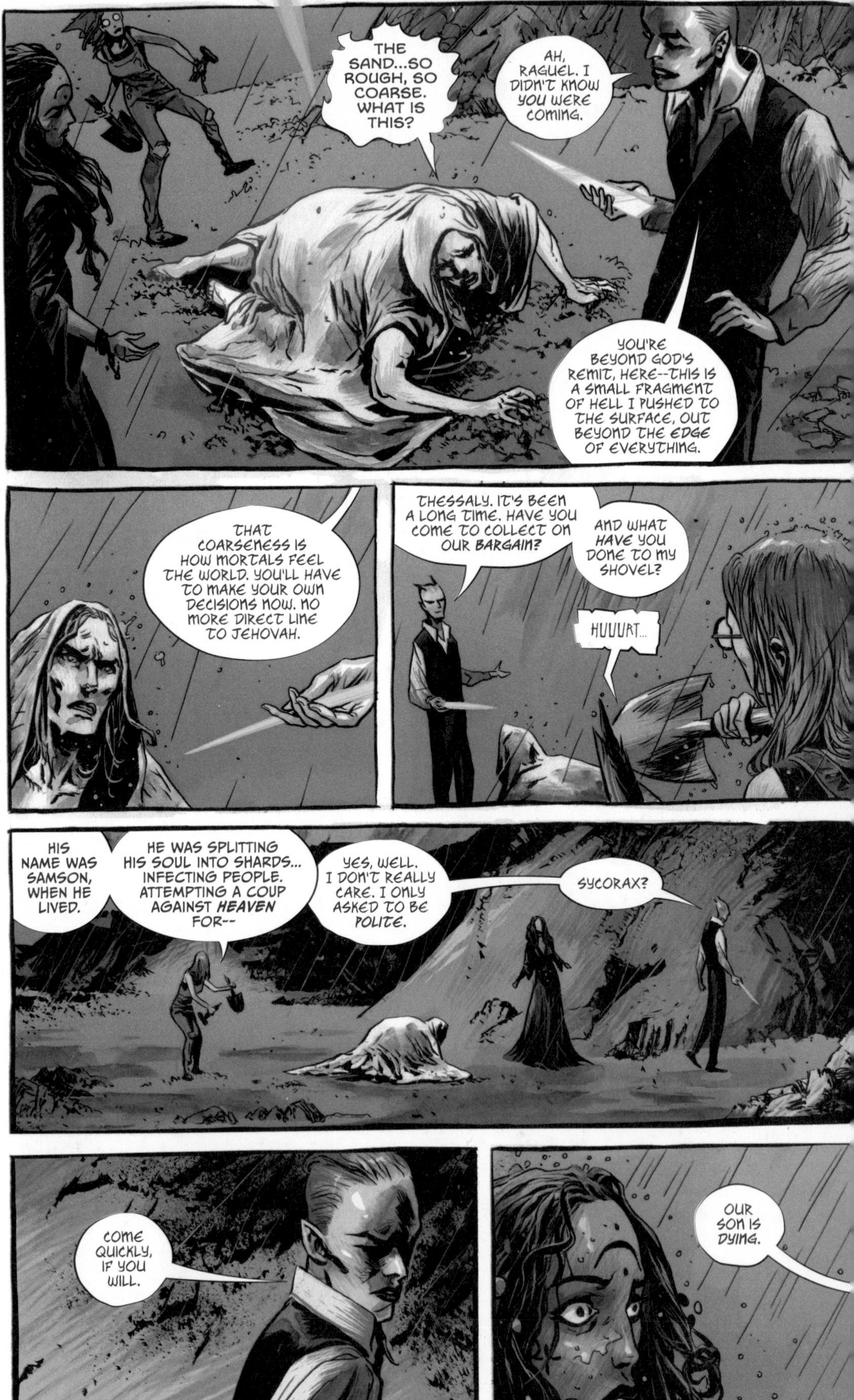
THE SAND...SO ROUGH, SO COARSE. WHAT IS THIS?
AH, RAGUEL. I DIDN'T KNOW YOU WERE COMING.
YOU'RE BEYOND GOD'S REMIT, HERE--THIS IS A SMALL FRAGMENT OF HELL I PUSHED TO THE SURFACE, OUT BEYOND THE EDGE OF EVERYTHING.
THAT COARSENESS IS HOW MORTALS FEEL THE WORLD. YOU'LL HAVE TO MAKE YOUR OWN DECISIONS NOW. NO MORE DIRECT LINE TO JEHOVAH.
THESSALY. IT'S BEEN A LONG TIME. HAVE YOU COME TO COLLECT ON OUR BARGAIN?
AND WHAT HAVE YOU DONE TO MY SHOVEL?
HUUURT...
HIS NAME WAS SAMSON, WHEN HE LIVED.
HE WAS SPLITTING HIS SOUL INTO SHARDS... INFECTING PEOPLE. ATTEMPTING A COUP AGAINST HEAVEN FOR--
YES, WELL. I DON'T REALLY CARE. I ONLY ASKED TO BE POLITE.
SYCORAX?
COME QUICKLY, IF YOU WILL.
OUR SON IS DYING.

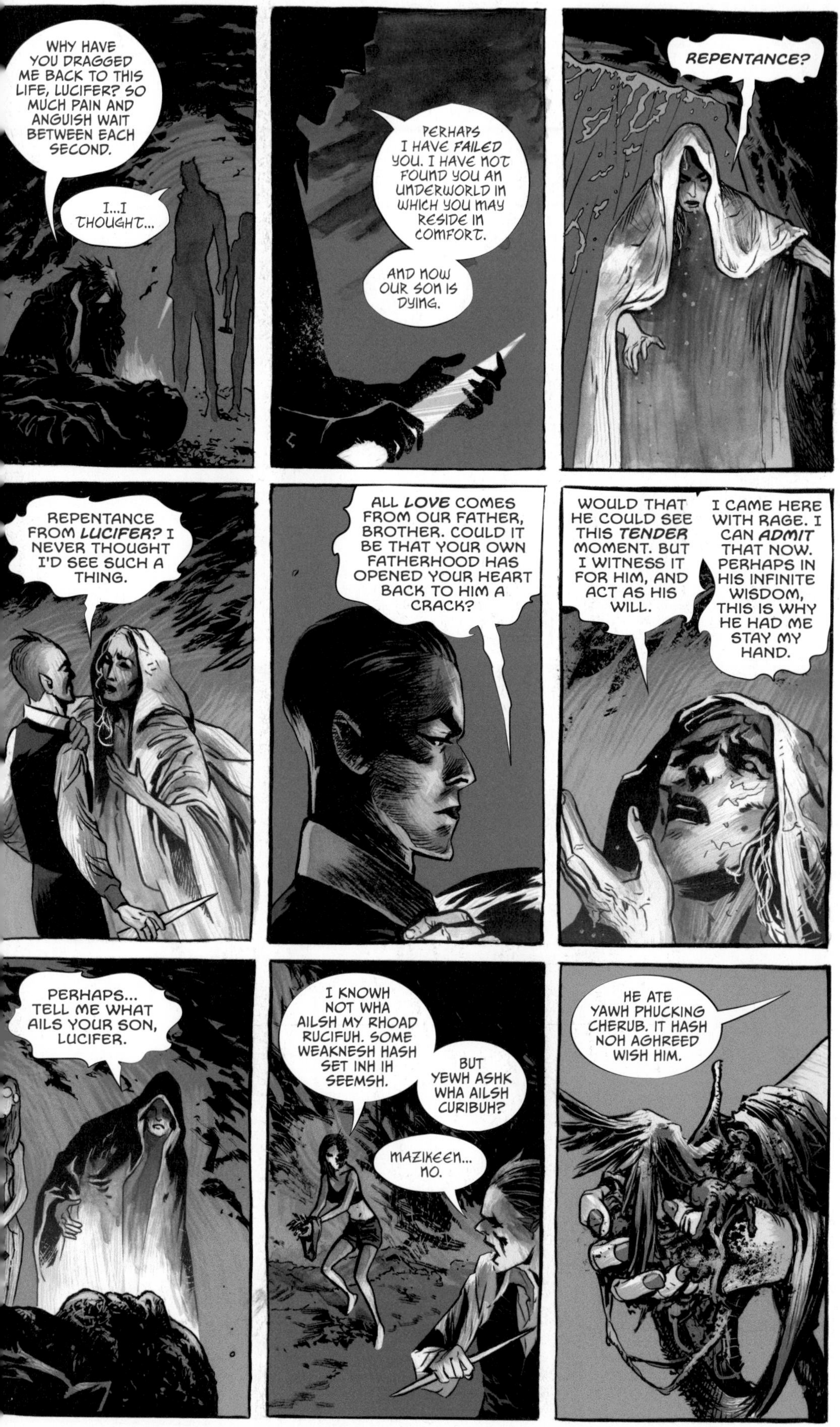

WHY HAVE YOU DRAGGED ME BACK TO THIS LIFE, LUCIFER? SO MUCH PAIN AND ANGUISH WAIT BETWEEN EACH SECOND.
I...I THOUGHT...
PERHAPS I HAVE FAILED YOU. I HAVE NOT FOUND YOU AN UNDERWORLD IN WHICH YOU MAY RESIDE IN COMFORT.
AND NOW OUR SON IS DYING.
REPENTANCE?
REPENTANCE FROM LUCIFER? I NEVER THOUGHT I'D SEE SUCH A THING.
ALL LOVE COMES FROM OUR FATHER, BROTHER. COULD IT BE THAT YOUR OWN FATHERHOOD HAS OPENED YOUR HEART BACK TO HIM A CRACK?
WOULD THAT HE COULD SEE THIS TENDER MOMENT. BUT I WITNESS IT FOR HIM, AND ACT AS HIS WILL.
I CAME HERE WITH RAGE. I CAN ADMIT THAT NOW. PERHAPS IN HIS INFINITE WISDOM, THIS IS WHY HE HAD ME STAY MY HAND.
PERHAPS... TELL ME WHAT AILS YOUR SON, LUCIFER.
I KNOWH NOT WHA AILSH MY RHOAD RUCIFUH. SOME WEAKNESH HASH SET INH IH SEEMSH.
BUT YEWH ASHK WHA AILSH CURIBUH?
MAZIKEEN... NO.
HE ATE YAWH PHUCKING CHERUB. IT HASH NOH AGHREED WISH HIM.

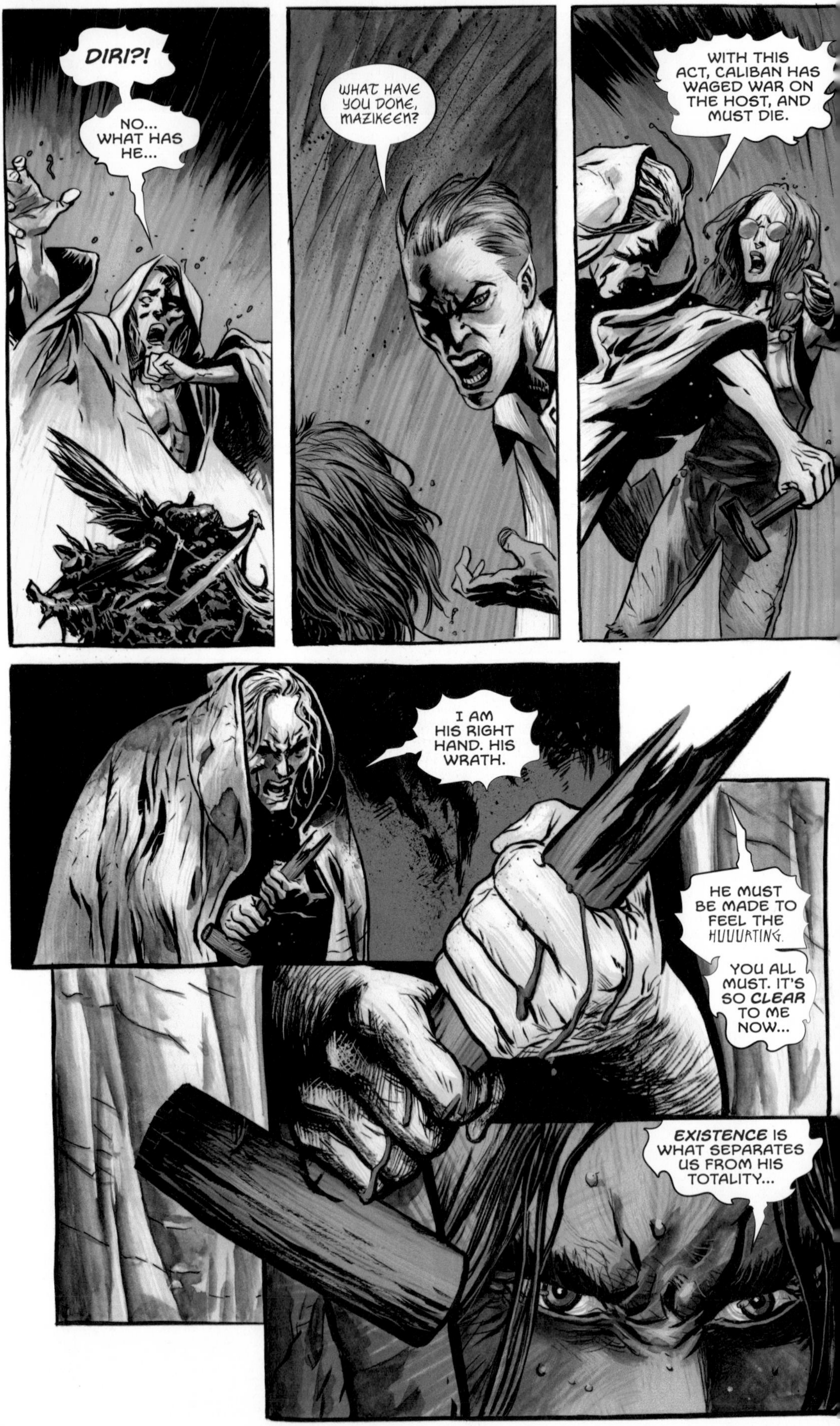
DIRI?!
NO... WHAT HAS HE...
WHAT HAVE YOU DONE, MAZIKEEN?
WITH THIS ACT, CALIBAN HAS WAGED WAR ON THE HOST, AND MUST DIE.
I AM HIS RIGHT HAND. HIS WRATH.
HE MUST BE MADE TO FEEL THE HUUURTING.
YOU ALL MUST. IT'S SO CLEAR TO ME NOW...
EXISTENCE IS WHAT SEPARATES US FROM HIS TOTALITY...

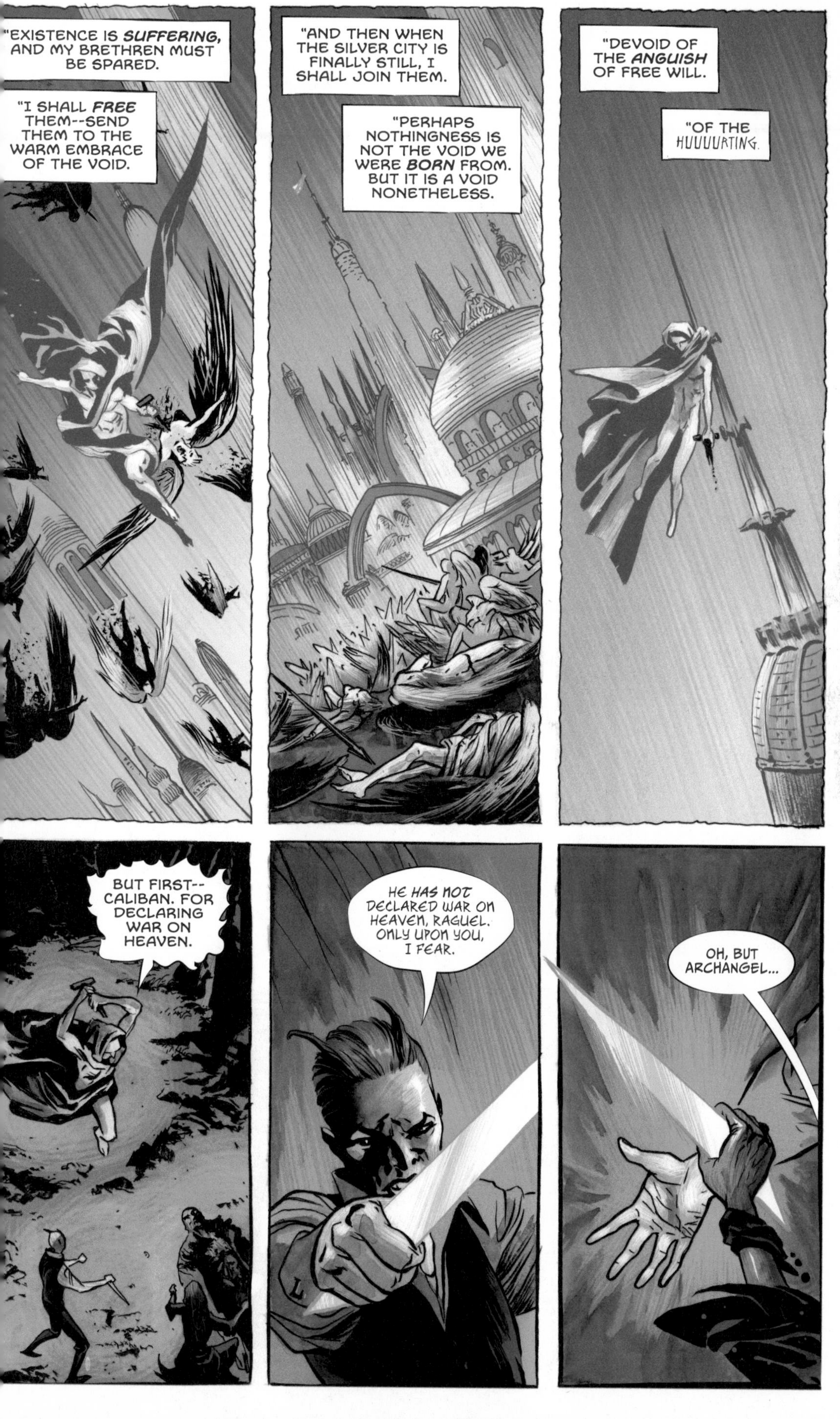
"EXISTENCE IS SUFFERING, AND MY BRETHREN MUST BE SPARED.
"I SHALL FREE THEM--SEND THEM TO THE WARM EMBRACE OF THE VOID.
"AND THEN WHEN THE SILVER CITY IS FINALLY STILL, I SHALL JOIN THEM.
"PERHAPS NOTHINGNESS IS NOT THE VOID WE WERE BORN FROM. BUT IT IS A VOID NONETHELESS.
"DEVOID OF THE ANGUISH OF FREE WILL.
"OF THE HUUUURTING.
BUT FIRST--CALIBAN. FOR DECLARING WAR ON HEAVEN.
HE HAS NOT DECLARED WAR ON HEAVEN, RAGUEL. ONLY UPON YOU, I FEAR.
OH, BUT ARCHANGEL...

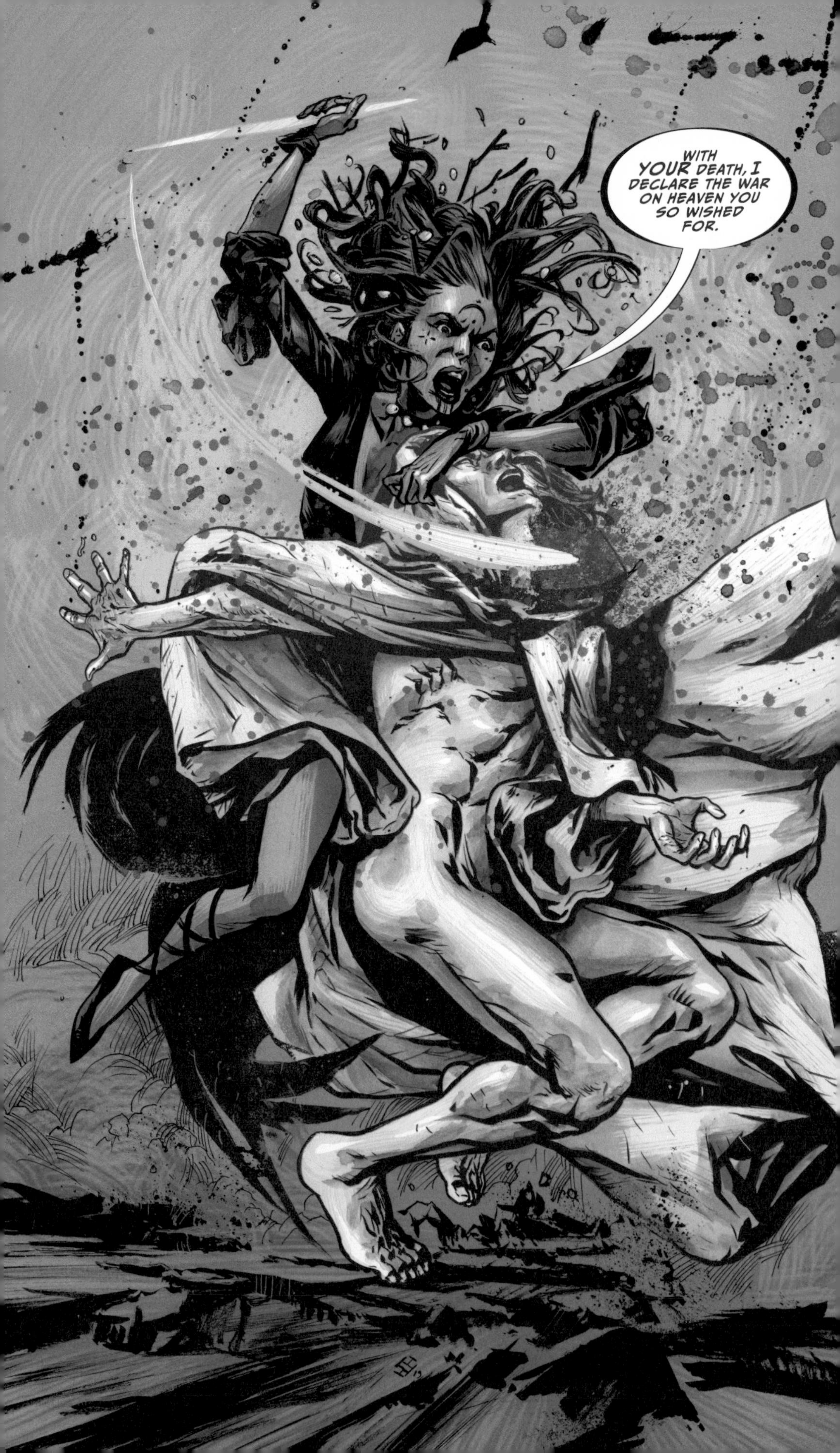
WITH YOUR DEATH, I DECLARE THE WAR ON HEAVEN YOU SO WISHED FOR.

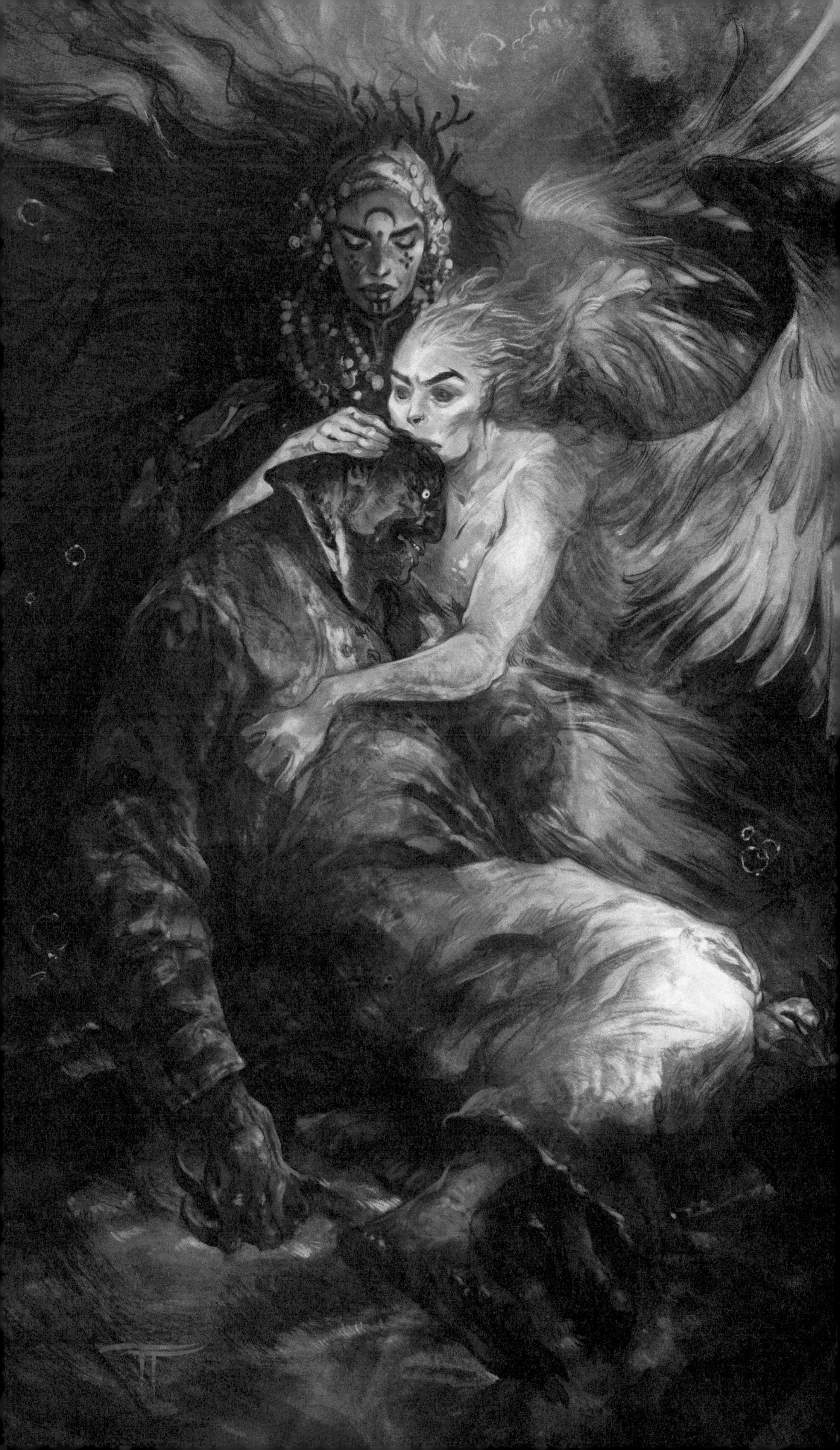

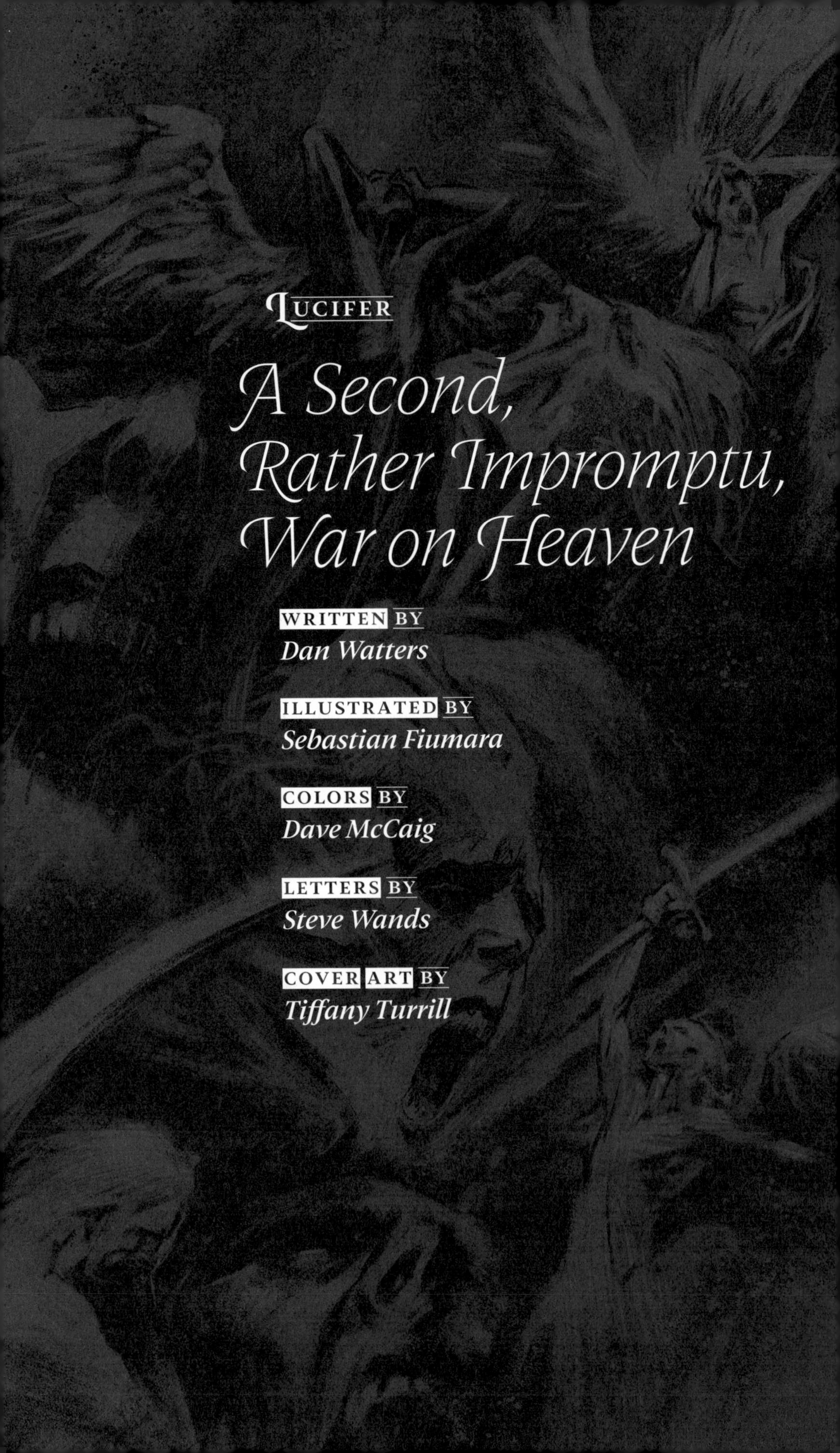

LUCIFER

A Second, Rather Impromptu, War on Heaven

WRITTEN BY
Dan Watters

ILLUSTRATED BY
Sebastian Fiumara

COLORS BY
Dave McCaig

LETTERS BY
Steve Wands

COVER ART BY
Tiffany Turrill

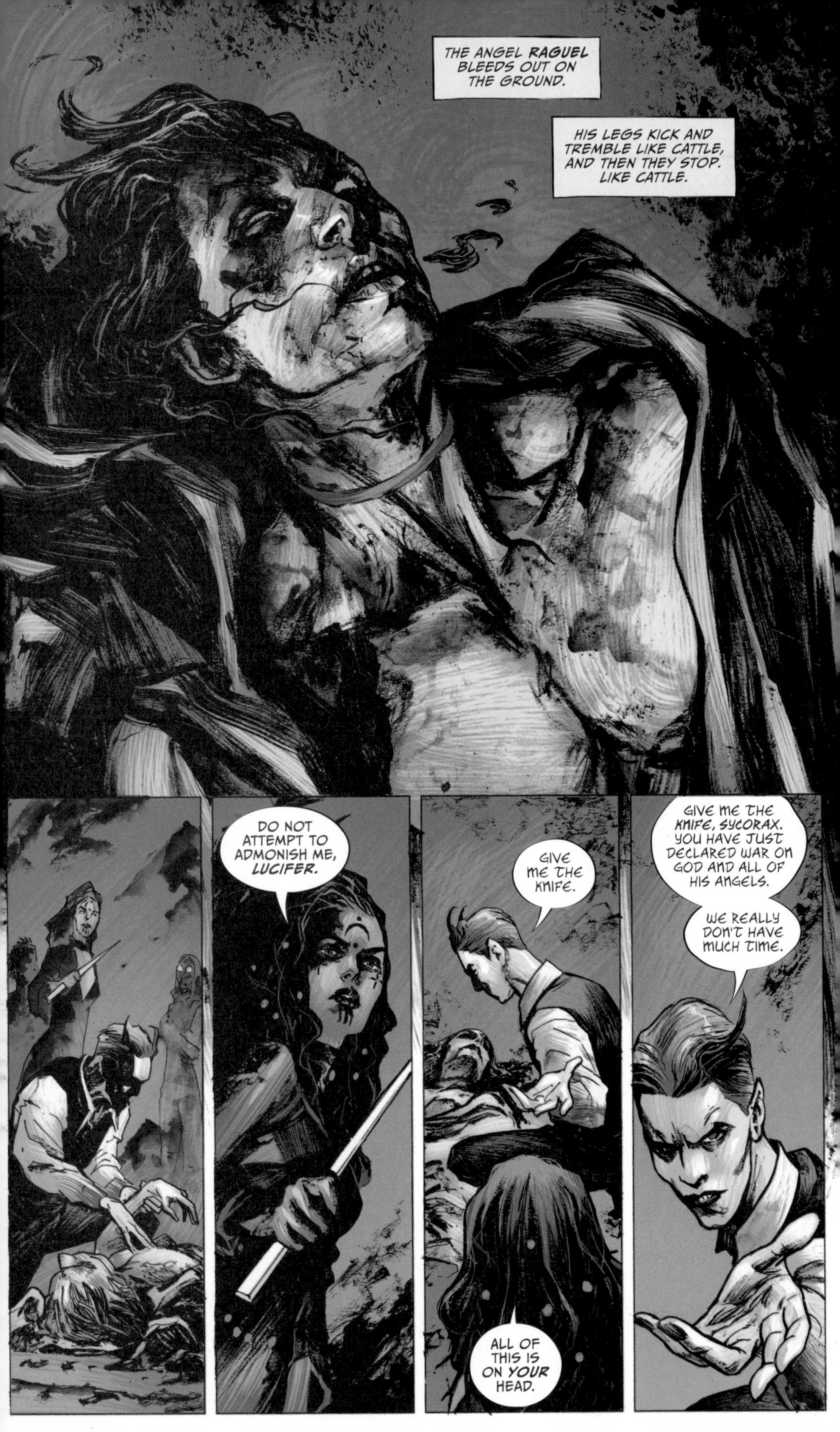
THE ANGEL RAGUEL BLEEDS OUT ON THE GROUND.
HIS LEGS KICK AND TREMBLE LIKE CATTLE, AND THEN THEY STOP. LIKE CATTLE.
DO NOT ATTEMPT TO ADMONISH ME, LUCIFER.
GIVE ME THE KNIFE.
ALL OF THIS IS ON YOUR HEAD.
GIVE ME THE KNIFE, SYCORAX. YOU HAVE JUST DECLARED WAR ON GOD AND ALL OF HIS ANGELS.
WE REALLY DON'T HAVE MUCH TIME.

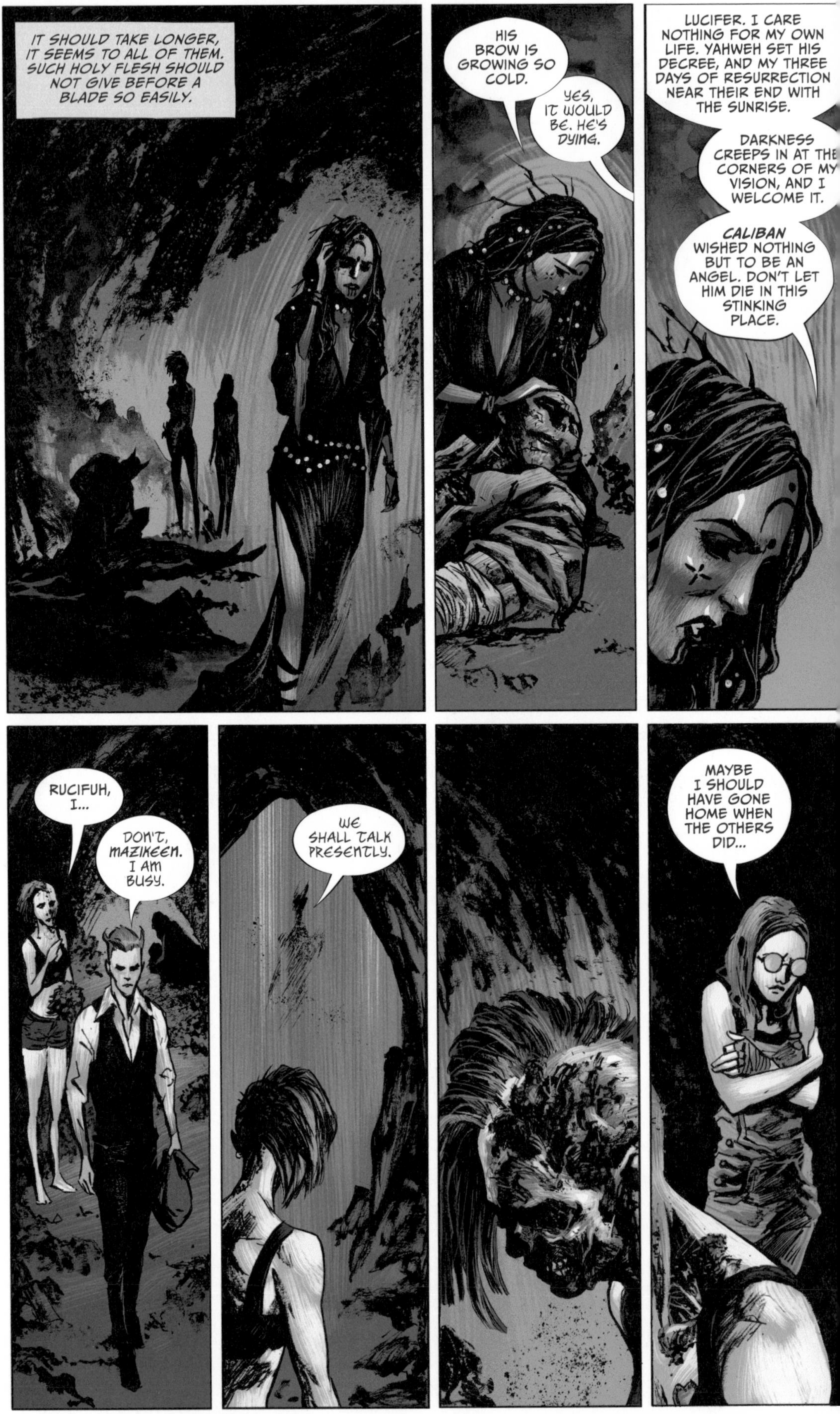
IT SHOULD TAKE LONGER, IT SEEMS TO ALL OF THEM. SUCH HOLY FLESH SHOULD NOT GIVE BEFORE A BLADE SO EASILY.
HIS BROW IS GROWING SO COLD.
YES, IT WOULD BE. HE'S DYING.
LUCIFER. I CARE NOTHING FOR MY OWN LIFE. YAHWEH SET HIS DECREE, AND MY THREE DAYS OF RESURRECTION NEAR THEIR END WITH THE SUNRISE.
DARKNESS CREEPS IN AT THE CORNERS OF MY VISION, AND I WELCOME IT.
CALIBAN WISHED NOTHING BUT TO BE AN ANGEL. DON'T LET HIM DIE IN THIS STINKING PLACE.
RUCIFUH, I...
DON'T, MAZIKEEN. I AM BUSY.
WE SHALL TALK PRESENTLY.
MAYBE I SHOULD HAVE GONE HOME WHEN THE OTHERS DID...

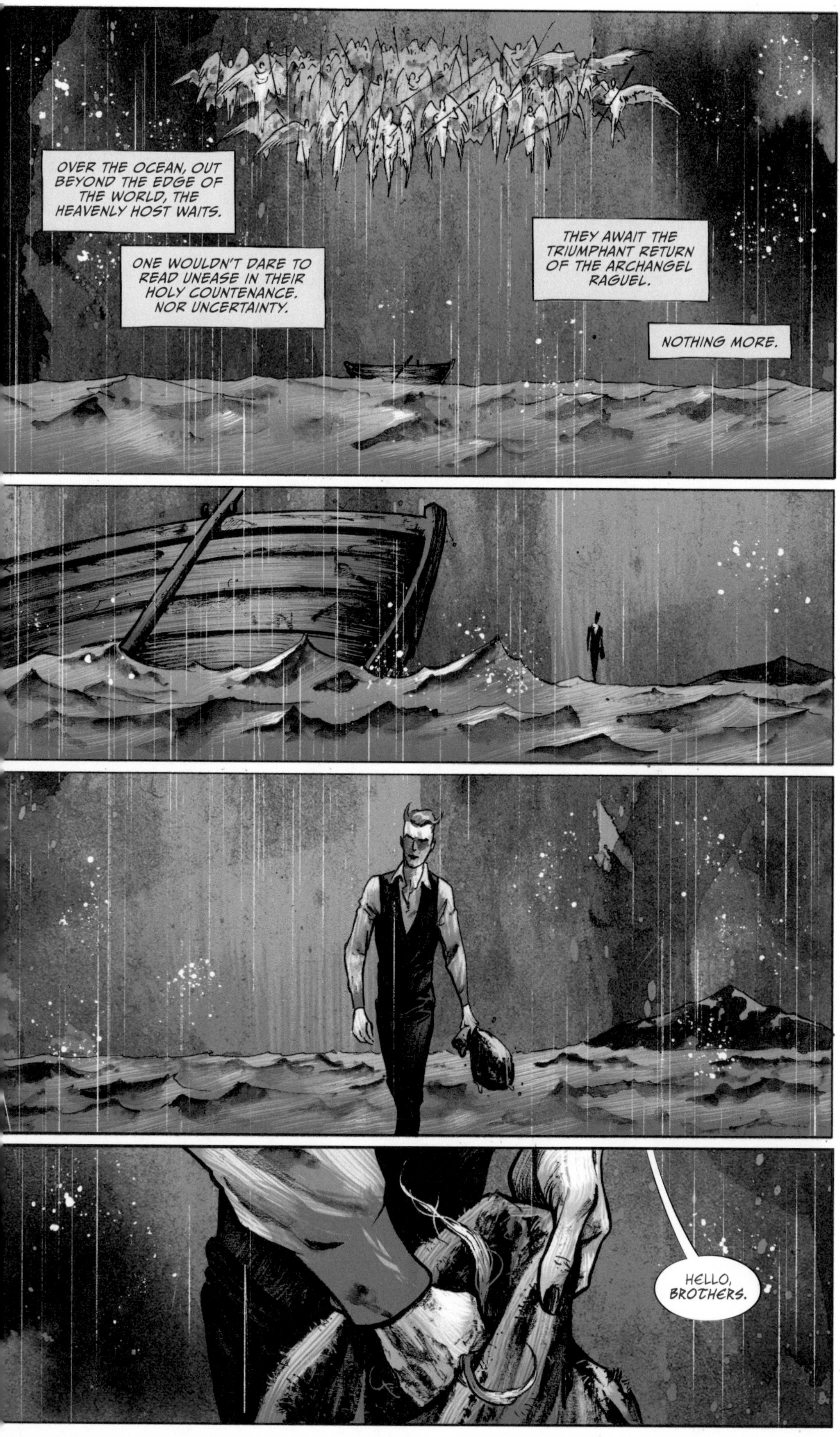
OVER THE OCEAN, OUT BEYOND THE EDGE OF THE WORLD, THE HEAVENLY HOST WAITS.
ONE WOULDN'T DARE TO READ UNEASE IN THEIR HOLY COUNTENANCE. NOR UNCERTAINTY.
THEY AWAIT THE TRIUMPHANT RETURN OF THE ARCHANGEL RAGUEL.
NOTHING MORE.
HELLO, BROTHERS.

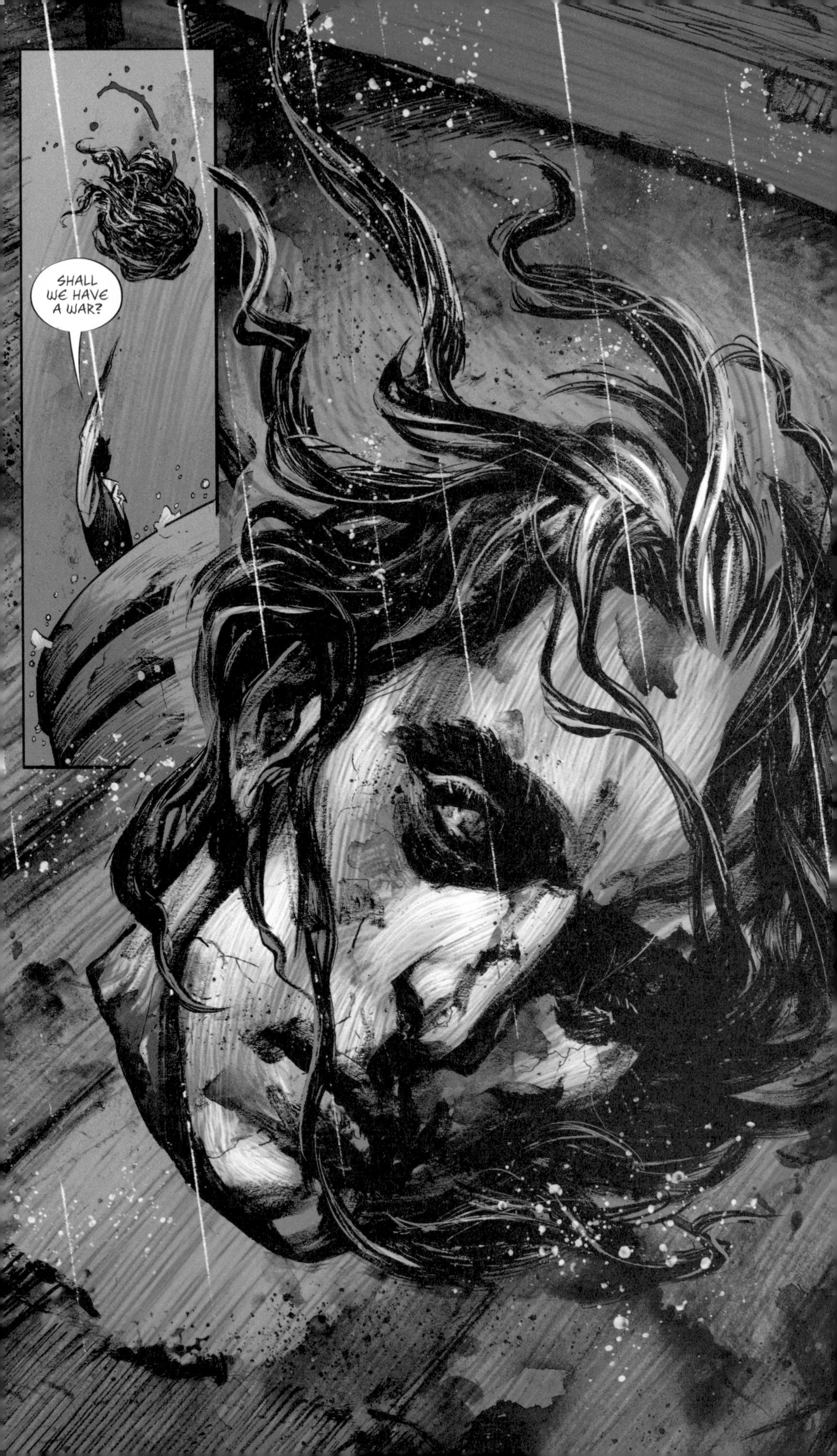
SHALL WE HAVE A WAR?

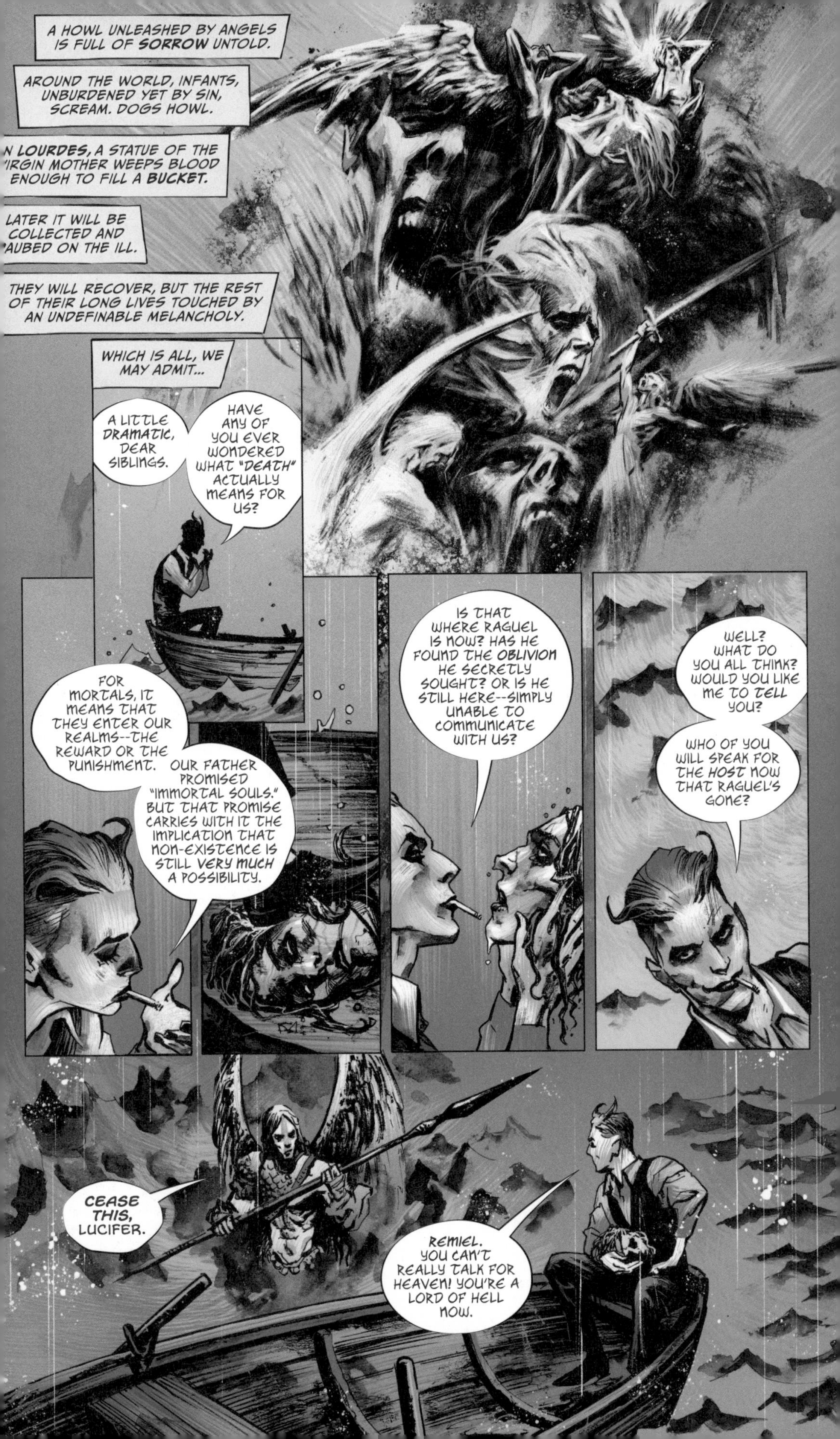
A HOWL UNLEASHED BY ANGELS IS FULL OF SORROW UNTOLD.
AROUND THE WORLD, INFANTS, UNBURDENED YET BY SIN, SCREAM. DOGS HOWL.
N LOURDES, A STATUE OF THE 'IRGIN MOTHER WEEPS BLOOD ENOUGH TO FILL A BUCKET.
LATER IT WILL BE COLLECTED AND 'AUBED ON THE ILL.
THEY WILL RECOVER, BUT THE REST OF THEIR LONG LIVES TOUCHED BY AN UNDEFINABLE MELANCHOLY.
WHICH IS ALL, WE MAY ADMIT...
A LITTLE DRAMATIC, DEAR SIBLINGS.
HAVE ANY OF YOU EVER WONDERED WHAT "DEATH" ACTUALLY MEANS FOR US?
FOR MORTALS, IT MEANS THAT THEY ENTER OUR REALMS--THE REWARD OR THE PUNISHMENT.
OUR FATHER PROMISED "IMMORTAL SOULS." BUT THAT PROMISE CARRIES WITH IT THE IMPLICATION THAT NON-EXISTENCE IS STILL VERY MUCH A POSSIBILITY.
IS THAT WHERE RAGUEL IS NOW? HAS HE FOUND THE OBLIVION HE SECRETLY SOUGHT? OR IS HE STILL HERE--SIMPLY UNABLE TO COMMUNICATE WITH US?
WELL? WHAT DO YOU ALL THINK? WOULD YOU LIKE ME TO TELL YOU?
WHO OF YOU WILL SPEAK FOR THE HOST NOW THAT RAGUEL'S GONE?
CEASE THIS, LUCIFER.
REMIEL. YOU CAN'T REALLY TALK FOR HEAVEN! YOU'RE A LORD OF HELL NOW.

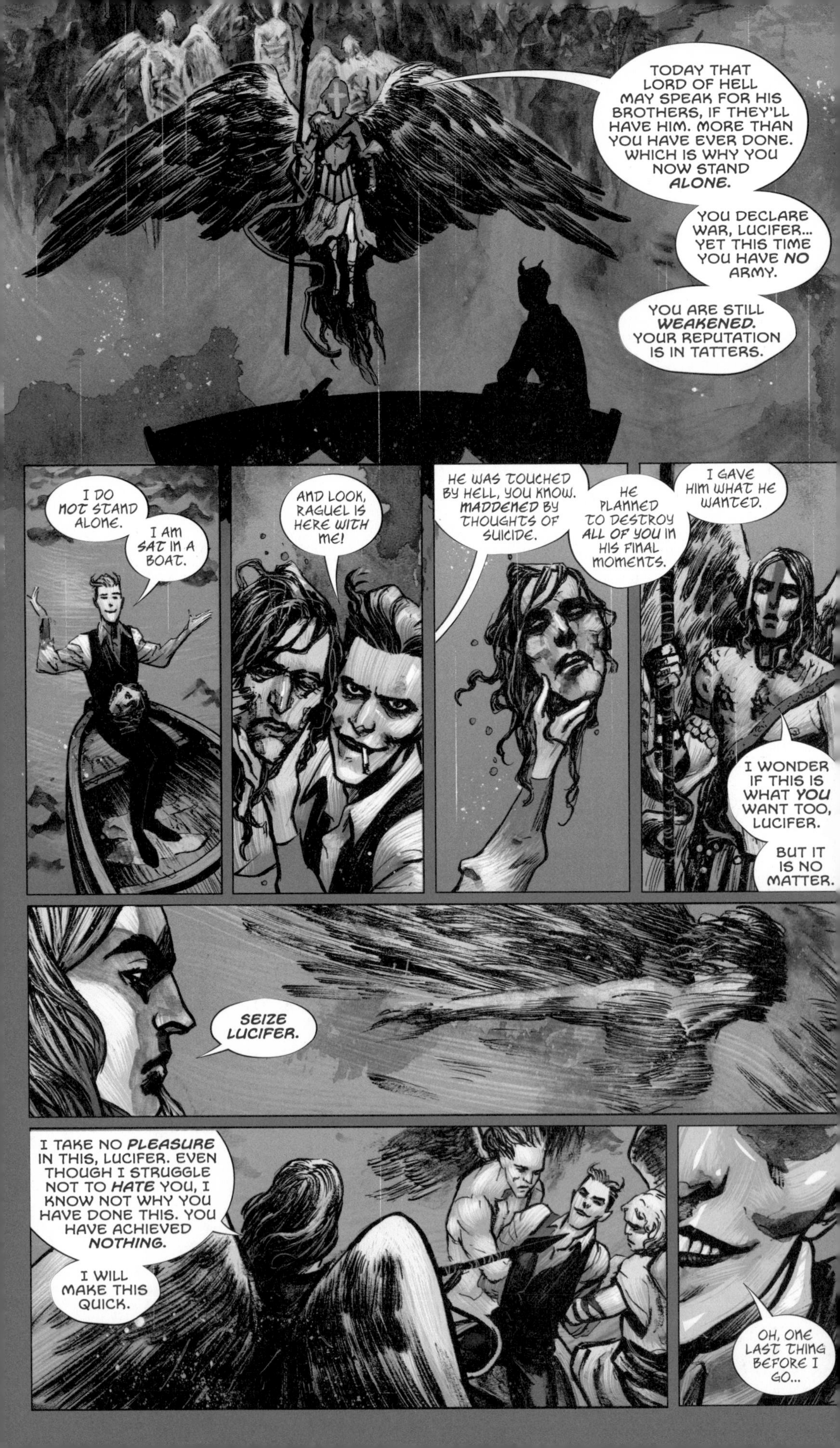
TODAY THAT LORD OF HELL MAY SPEAK FOR HIS BROTHERS, IF THEY'LL HAVE HIM. MORE THAN YOU HAVE EVER DONE. WHICH IS WHY YOU NOW STAND ALONE.
YOU DECLARE WAR, LUCIFER... YET THIS TIME YOU HAVE NO ARMY.
YOU ARE STILL WEAKENED. YOUR REPUTATION IS IN TATTERS.
I DO NOT STAND ALONE.
I AM SAT IN A BOAT.
AND LOOK, RAGUEL IS HERE WITH ME!
HE WAS TOUCHED BY HELL, YOU KNOW. MADDENED BY THOUGHTS OF SUICIDE.
HE PLANNED TO DESTROY ALL OF YOU IN HIS FINAL MOMENTS.
I GAVE HIM WHAT HE WANTED.
I WONDER IF THIS IS WHAT YOU WANT TOO, LUCIFER.
BUT IT IS NO MATTER.
SEIZE LUCIFER.
I TAKE NO PLEASURE IN THIS, LUCIFER. EVEN THOUGH I STRUGGLE NOT TO HATE YOU, I KNOW NOT WHY YOU HAVE DONE THIS. YOU HAVE ACHIEVED NOTHING.
I WILL MAKE THIS QUICK.
OH, ONE LAST THING BEFORE I GO...

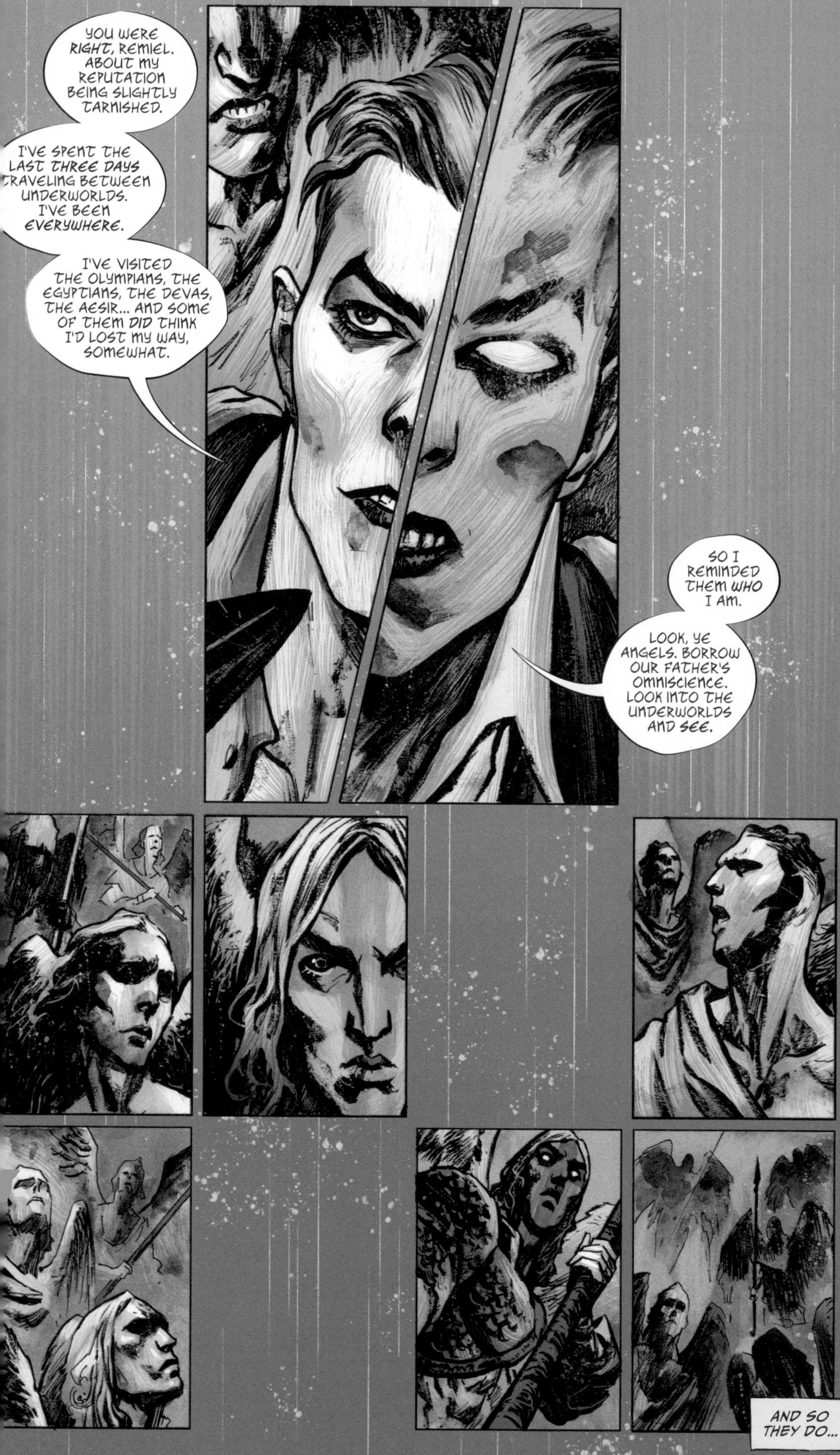
YOU WERE RIGHT, REMIEL. ABOUT MY REPUTATION BEING SLIGHTLY TARNISHED.
I'VE SPENT THE LAST THREE DAYS TRAVELING BETWEEN UNDERWORLDS. I'VE BEEN EVERYWHERE.
I'VE VISITED THE OLYMPIANS, THE EGYPTIANS, THE DEVAS, THE AESIR... AND SOME OF THEM DID THINK I'D LOST MY WAY, SOMEWHAT.
SO I REMINDED THEM WHO I AM.
LOOK, YE ANGELS. BORROW OUR FATHER'S OMNISCIENCE. LOOK INTO THE UNDERWORLDS AND SEE.
AND SO THEY DO...

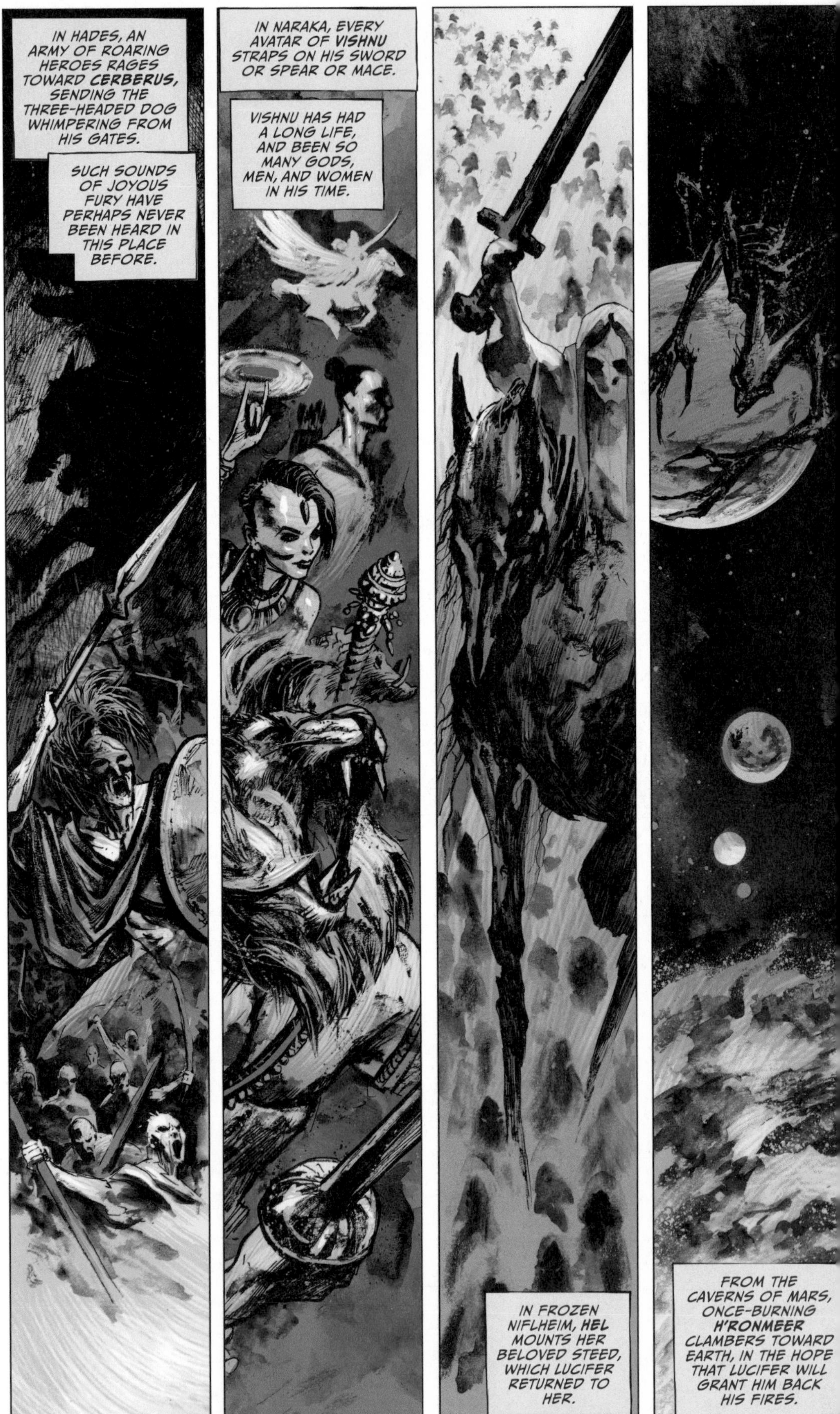
IN HADES, AN ARMY OF ROARING HEROES RAGES TOWARD **CERBERUS,** SENDING THE THREE-HEADED DOG WHIMPERING FROM HIS GATES.
SUCH SOUNDS OF JOYOUS FURY HAVE PERHAPS NEVER BEEN HEARD IN THIS PLACE BEFORE.
IN NARAKA, EVERY AVATAR OF **VISHNU** STRAPS ON HIS SWORD OR SPEAR OR MACE.
VISHNU HAS HAD A LONG LIFE, AND BEEN SO MANY GODS, MEN, AND WOMEN IN HIS TIME.
IN FROZEN NIFLHEIM, **HEL** MOUNTS HER BELOVED STEED, WHICH LUCIFER RETURNED TO HER.
FROM THE CAVERNS OF MARS, ONCE-BURNING **H'RONMEER** CLAMBERS TOWARD EARTH, IN THE HOPE THAT LUCIFER WILL GRANT HIM BACK HIS FIRES.

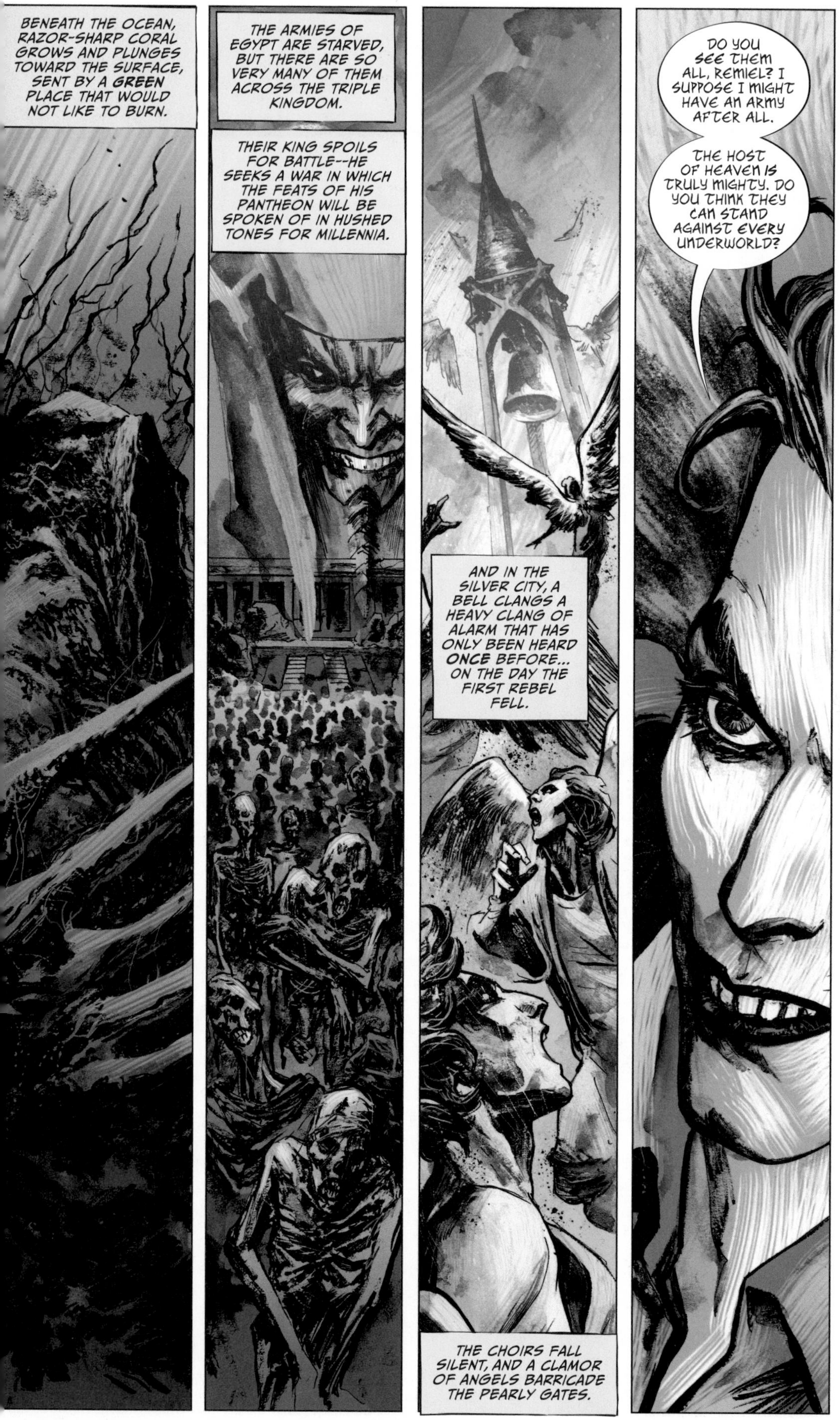
BENEATH THE OCEAN, RAZOR-SHARP CORAL GROWS AND PLUNGES TOWARD THE SURFACE, SENT BY A GREEN PLACE THAT WOULD NOT LIKE TO BURN.
THE ARMIES OF EGYPT ARE STARVED, BUT THERE ARE SO VERY MANY OF THEM ACROSS THE TRIPLE KINGDOM.
THEIR KING SPOILS FOR BATTLE--HE SEEKS A WAR IN WHICH THE FEATS OF HIS PANTHEON WILL BE SPOKEN OF IN HUSHED TONES FOR MILLENNIA.
AND IN THE SILVER CITY, A BELL CLANGS A HEAVY CLANG OF ALARM THAT HAS ONLY BEEN HEARD ONCE BEFORE... ON THE DAY THE FIRST REBEL FELL.
THE CHOIRS FALL SILENT, AND A CLAMOR OF ANGELS BARRICADE THE PEARLY GATES.
DO YOU SEE THEM ALL, REMIEL? I SUPPOSE I MIGHT HAVE AN ARMY AFTER ALL.
THE HOST OF HEAVEN IS TRULY MIGHTY. DO YOU THINK THEY CAN STAND AGAINST EVERY UNDERWORLD?

Y-YES. I DO. MY FAITH IS UNSHAKABLE.

AND IT ISN'T *EVERY* UNDERWORLD, LUCIFER.

YOU THINK NOT? THEN WHY DON'T YOU AND I RETURN TO HELL, REMIEL, AND ASK THEM ALL AGAIN...

...WILL THEY STAND WITH YOU, YAHWEH'S LACKEY, OR WITH HE WHO HAS SAWN THE HEAD FROM THE ARCHANGEL OF VENGEANCE?

...

YOU SAY THAT RAGUEL HAD TURNED UPON THE HOST.

IF THIS IS TRUE, THEN YOUR ACT MAY BE PARDONED.

YOU KNOW I DO NOT LIE, REMIEL...BUT WAR HAS ALREADY BEEN DECLARED. I DON'T KNOW IF I CAN CALL THEM OFF.

DON'T DO THIS, LUCIFER.

HERE THEY COME. SO MANY OF THEM...

BEST CALL MORE ANGELS.

I DON'T TRULY KNOW IF WE'LL WIN, BUT SO MUCH BLOOD WILL BE SPILLED. NEW GOSPELS WILL HAVE TO BE WRITTEN, I SUPPOSE...

LUCIFER!

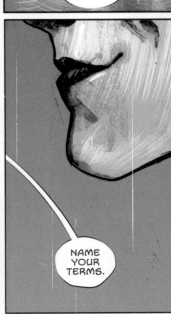

NAME YOUR TERMS.

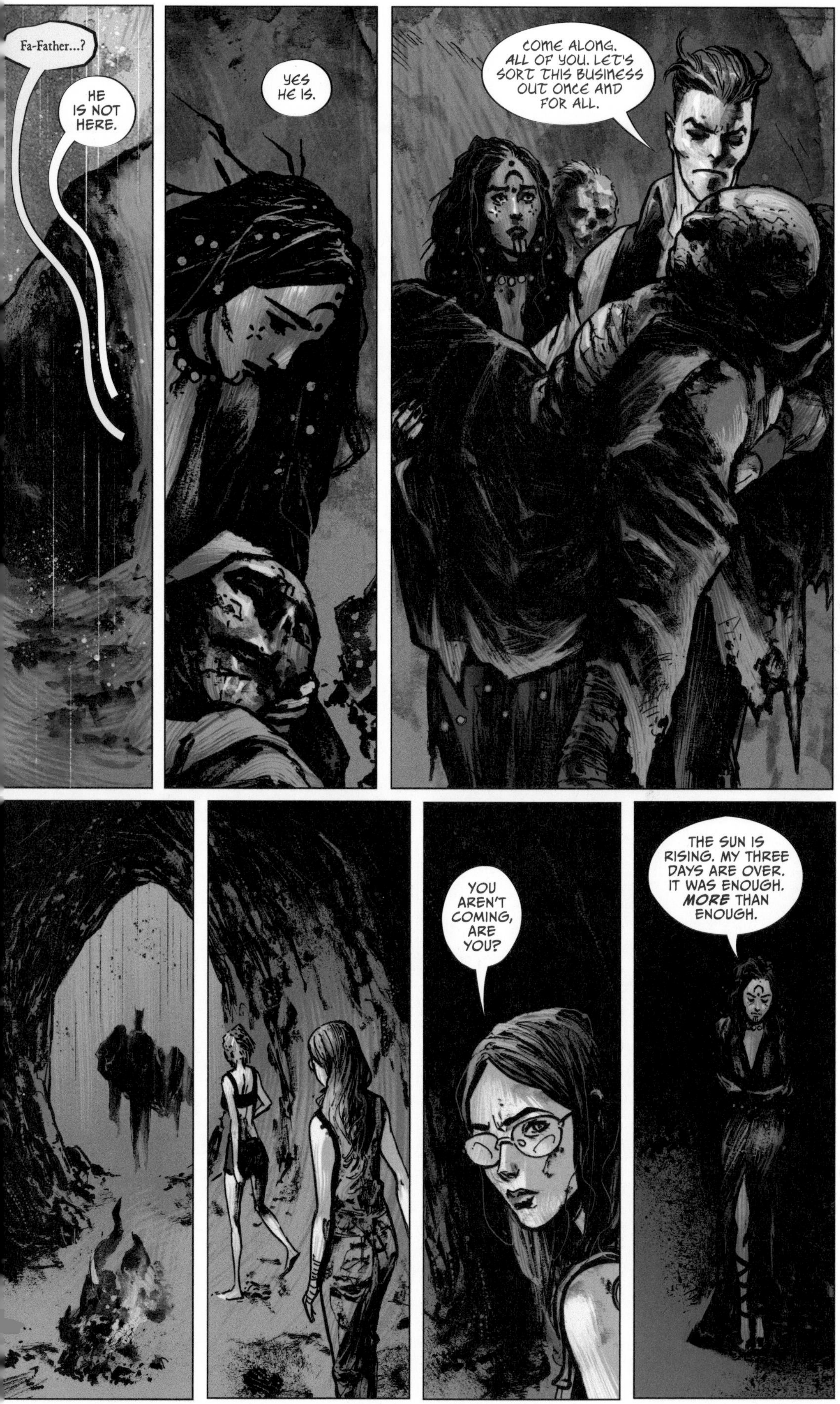
Fa-Father...?
HE IS NOT HERE.
YES HE IS.
COME ALONG. ALL OF YOU. LET'S SORT THIS BUSINESS OUT ONCE AND FOR ALL.
YOU AREN'T COMING, ARE YOU?
THE SUN IS RISING. MY THREE DAYS ARE OVER. IT WAS ENOUGH. MORE THAN ENOUGH.

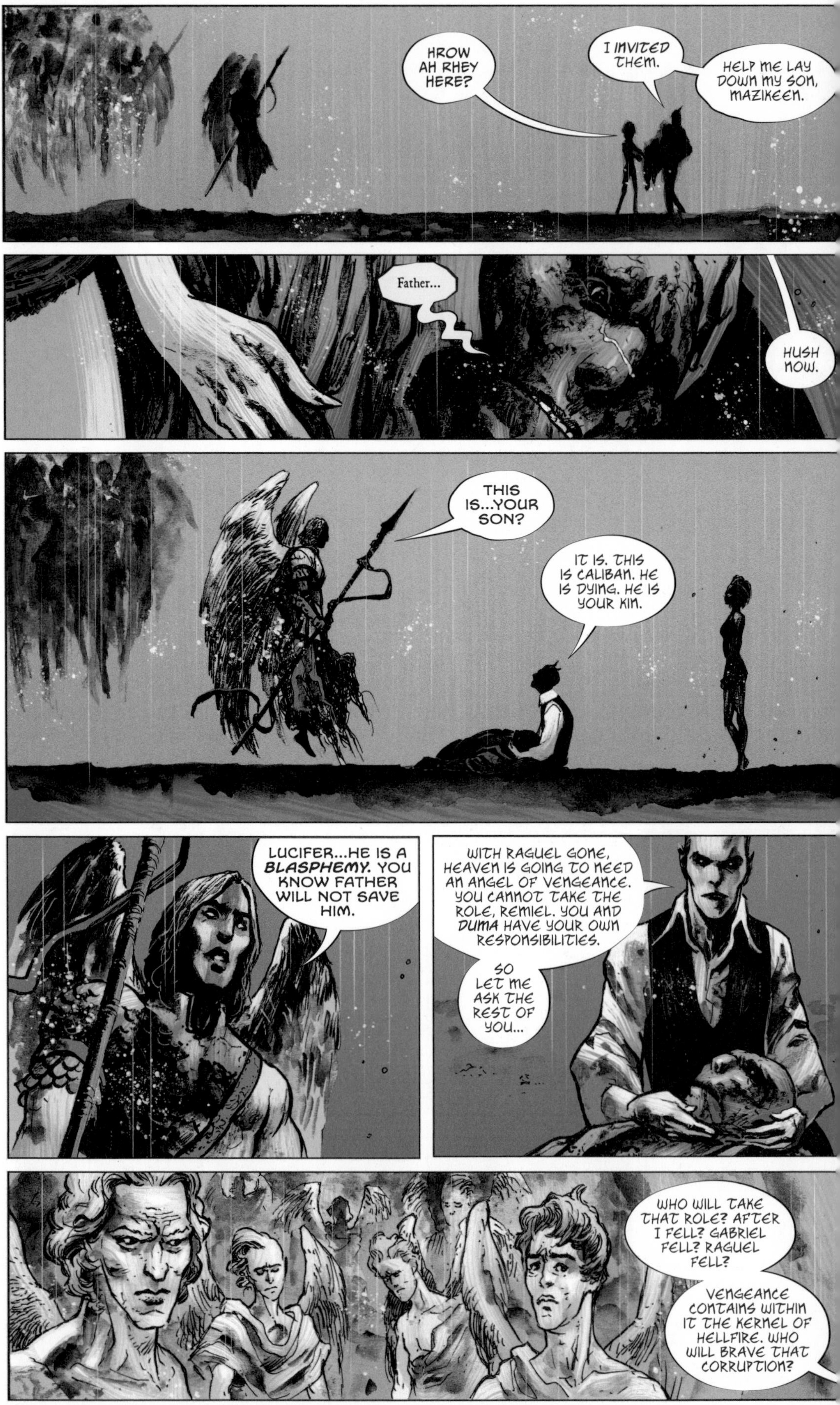
HROW AH RHEY HERE?
I INVITED THEM.
HELP ME LAY DOWN MY SON, MAZIKEEN.
Father...
HUSH NOW.
THIS IS...YOUR SON?
IT IS. THIS IS CALIBAN. HE IS DYING. HE IS YOUR KIN.
LUCIFER...HE IS A BLASPHEMY. YOU KNOW FATHER WILL NOT SAVE HIM.
WITH RAGUEL GONE, HEAVEN IS GOING TO NEED AN ANGEL OF VENGEANCE. YOU CANNOT TAKE THE ROLE, REMIEL. YOU AND DUMA HAVE YOUR OWN RESPONSIBILITIES.
SO LET ME ASK THE REST OF YOU...
WHO WILL TAKE THAT ROLE? AFTER I FELL? GABRIEL FELL? RAGUEL FELL?
VENGEANCE CONTAINS WITHIN IT THE KERNEL OF HELLFIRE. WHO WILL BRAVE THAT CORRUPTION?

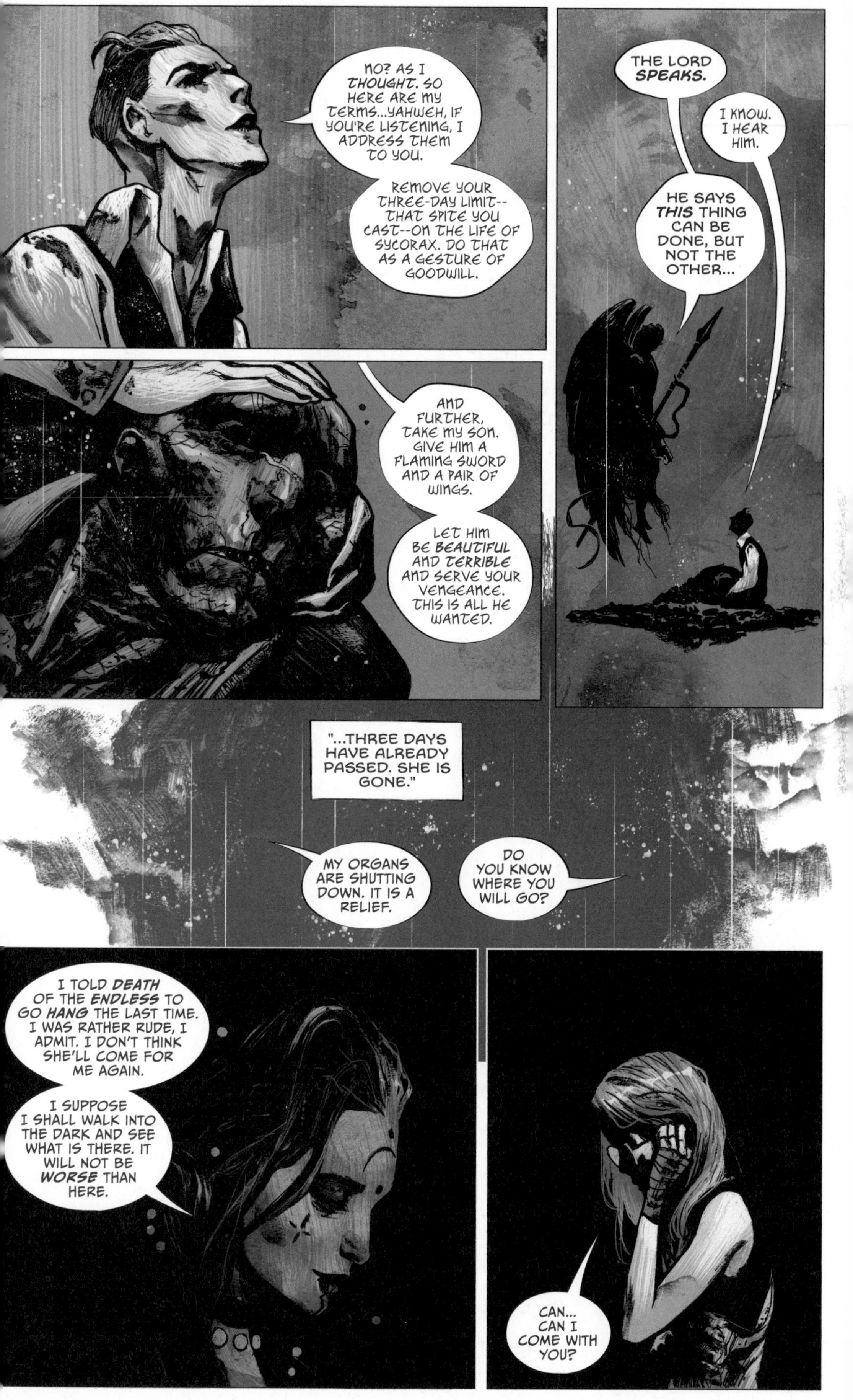

NO? AS I THOUGHT. SO HERE ARE MY TERMS...YAHWEH, IF YOU'RE LISTENING, I ADDRESS THEM TO YOU.
REMOVE YOUR THREE-DAY LIMIT--THAT SPITE YOU CAST--ON THE LIFE OF SYCORAX. DO THAT AS A GESTURE OF GOODWILL.
AND FURTHER, TAKE MY SON. GIVE HIM A FLAMING SWORD AND A PAIR OF WINGS.
LET HIM BE BEAUTIFUL AND TERRIBLE AND SERVE YOUR VENGEANCE. THIS IS ALL HE WANTED.
THE LORD SPEAKS.
I KNOW. I HEAR HIM.
HE SAYS THIS THING CAN BE DONE, BUT NOT THE OTHER...
"...THREE DAYS HAVE ALREADY PASSED. SHE IS GONE."
MY ORGANS ARE SHUTTING DOWN. IT IS A RELIEF.
DO YOU KNOW WHERE YOU WILL GO?
I TOLD DEATH OF THE ENDLESS TO GO HANG THE LAST TIME. I WAS RATHER RUDE, I ADMIT. I DON'T THINK SHE'LL COME FOR ME AGAIN.
I SUPPOSE I SHALL WALK INTO THE DARK AND SEE WHAT IS THERE. IT WILL NOT BE WORSE THAN HERE.
CAN... CAN I COME WITH YOU?

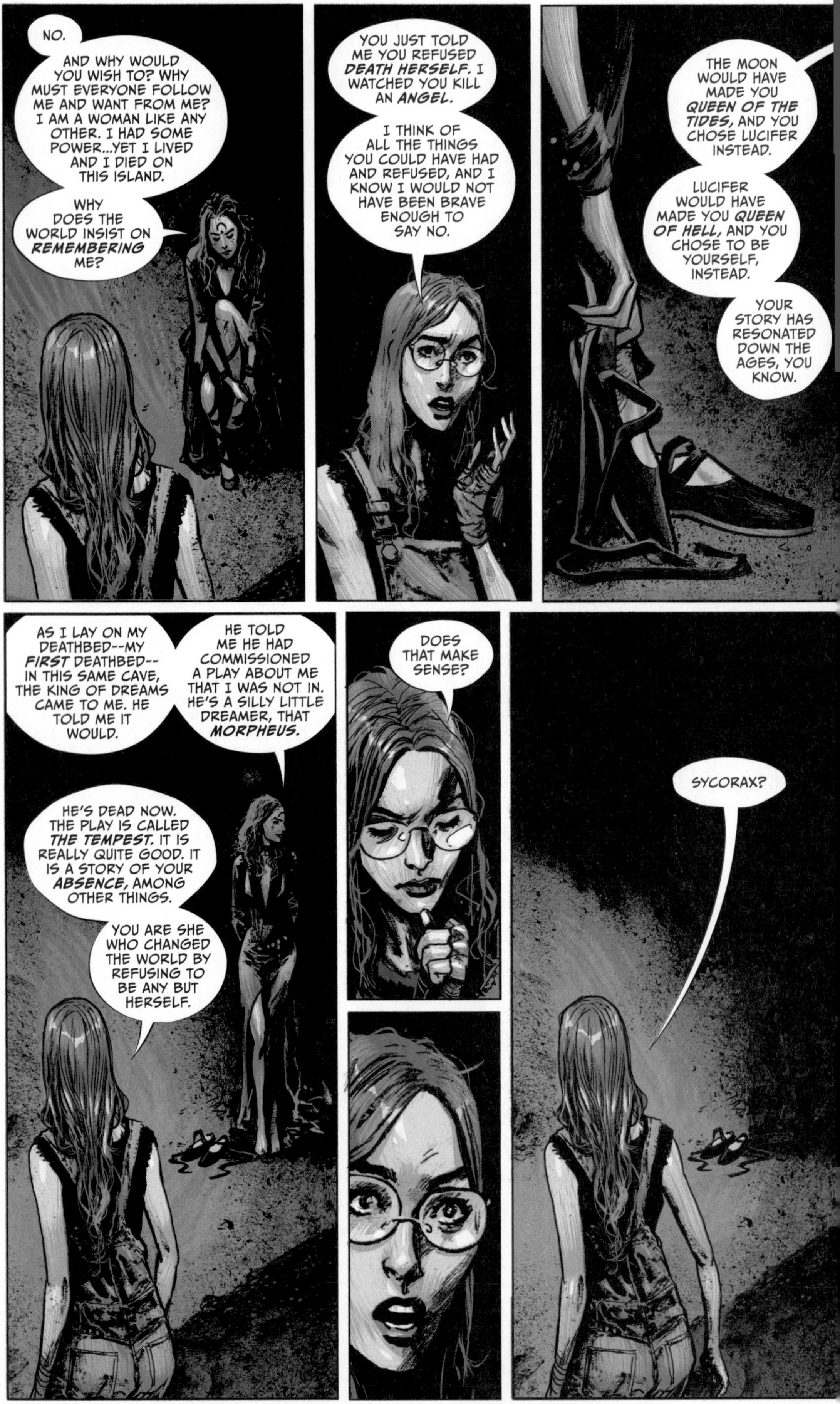
NO.
AND WHY WOULD YOU WISH TO? WHY MUST EVERYONE FOLLOW ME AND WANT FROM ME? I AM A WOMAN LIKE ANY OTHER. I HAD SOME POWER...YET I LIVED AND I DIED ON THIS ISLAND.
WHY DOES THE WORLD INSIST ON REMEMBERING ME?
YOU JUST TOLD ME YOU REFUSED DEATH HERSELF. I WATCHED YOU KILL AN ANGEL.
I THINK OF ALL THE THINGS YOU COULD HAVE HAD AND REFUSED, AND I KNOW I WOULD NOT HAVE BEEN BRAVE ENOUGH TO SAY NO.
THE MOON WOULD HAVE MADE YOU QUEEN OF THE TIDES, AND YOU CHOSE LUCIFER INSTEAD.
LUCIFER WOULD HAVE MADE YOU QUEEN OF HELL, AND YOU CHOSE TO BE YOURSELF, INSTEAD.
YOUR STORY HAS RESONATED DOWN THE AGES, YOU KNOW.
AS I LAY ON MY DEATHBED--MY FIRST DEATHBED--IN THIS SAME CAVE, THE KING OF DREAMS CAME TO ME. HE TOLD ME IT WOULD.
HE TOLD ME HE HAD COMMISSIONED A PLAY ABOUT ME THAT I WAS NOT IN. HE'S A SILLY LITTLE DREAMER, THAT MORPHEUS.
HE'S DEAD NOW. THE PLAY IS CALLED THE TEMPEST. IT IS REALLY QUITE GOOD. IT IS A STORY OF YOUR ABSENCE, AMONG OTHER THINGS.
YOU ARE SHE WHO CHANGED THE WORLD BY REFUSING TO BE ANY BUT HERSELF.
DOES THAT MAKE SENSE?
SYCORAX?

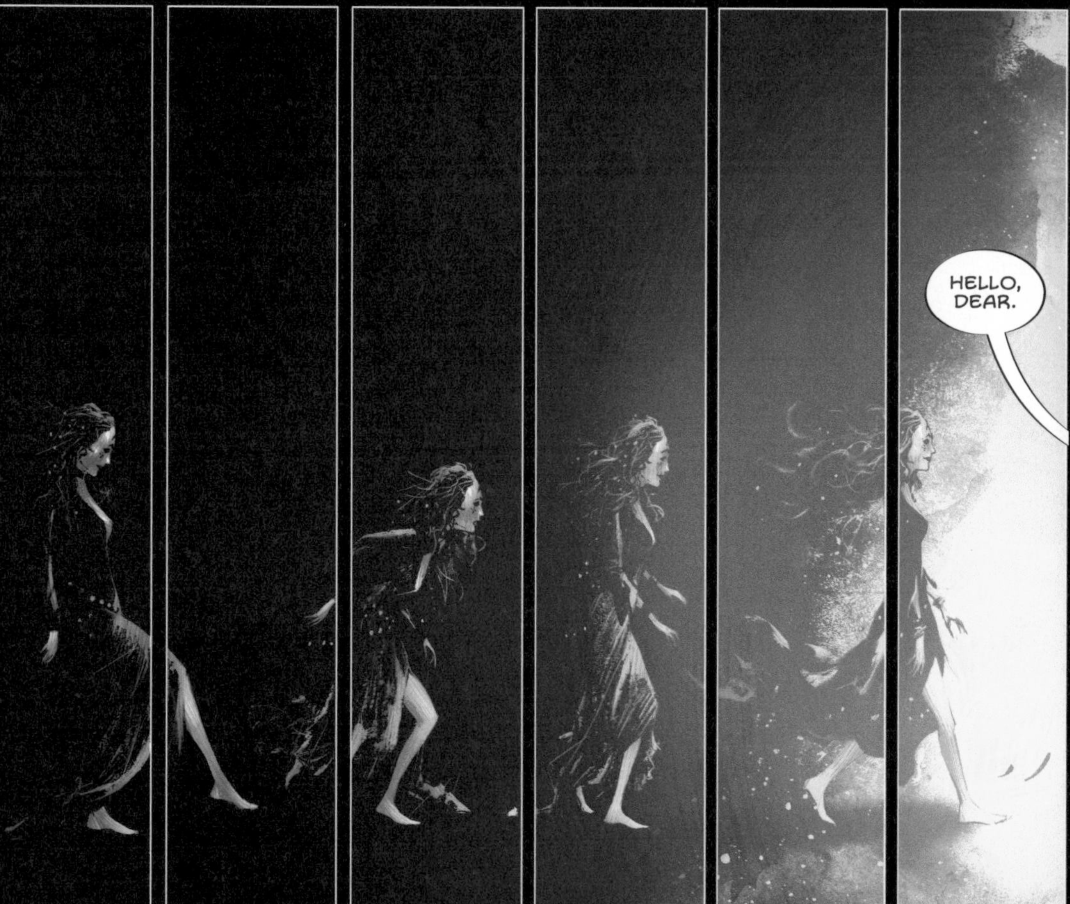
HELLO,
DEAR.

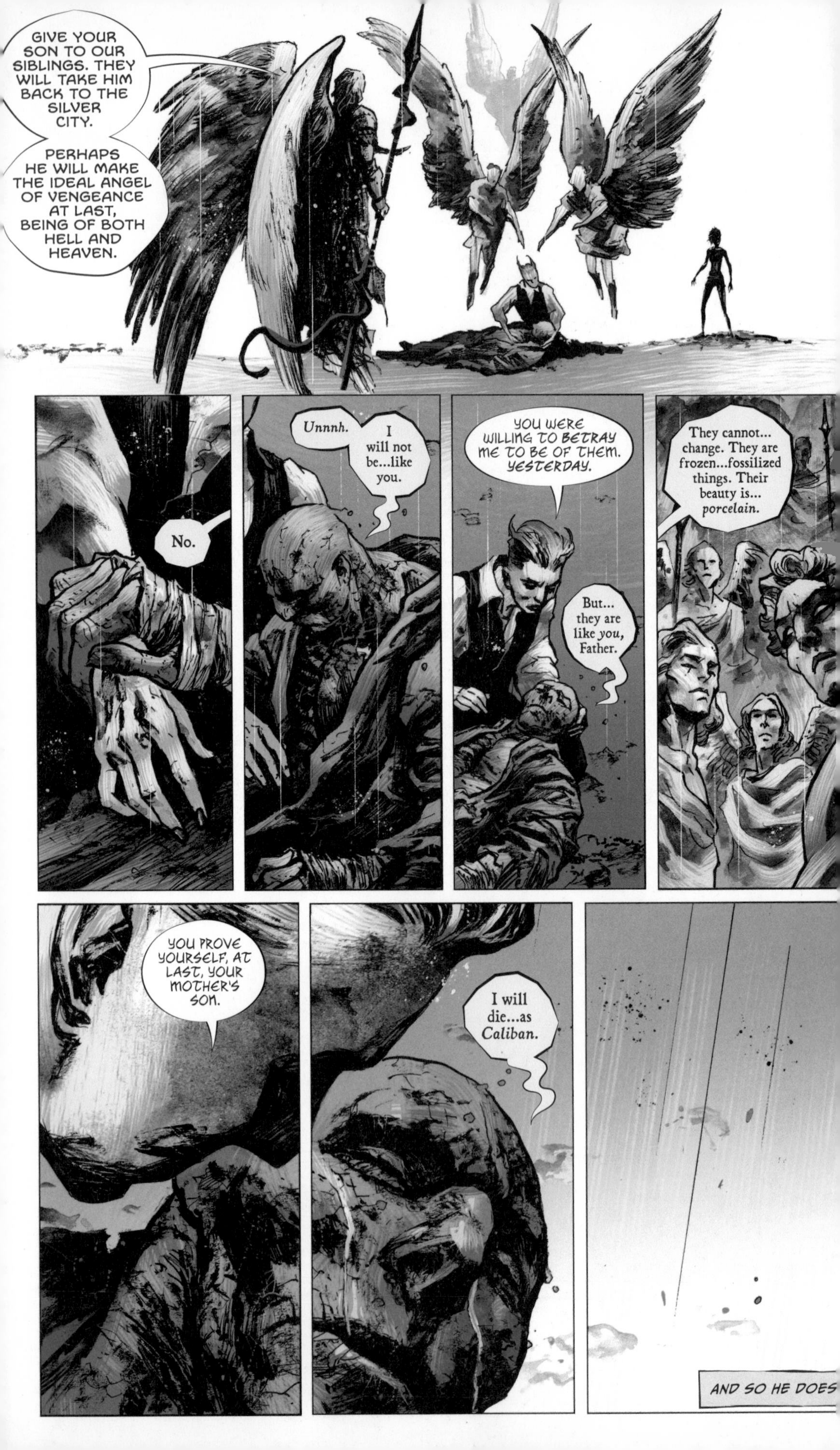
GIVE YOUR SON TO OUR SIBLINGS. THEY WILL TAKE HIM BACK TO THE SILVER CITY.
PERHAPS HE WILL MAKE THE IDEAL ANGEL OF VENGEANCE AT LAST, BEING OF BOTH HELL AND HEAVEN.
No.
Unnnh.
I will not be...like you.
YOU WERE WILLING TO BETRAY ME TO BE OF THEM. YESTERDAY.
But... they are like you, Father.
They cannot... change. They are frozen...fossilized things. Their beauty is... porcelain.
YOU PROVE YOURSELF, AT LAST, YOUR MOTHER'S SON.
I will die...as Caliban.
AND SO HE DOES

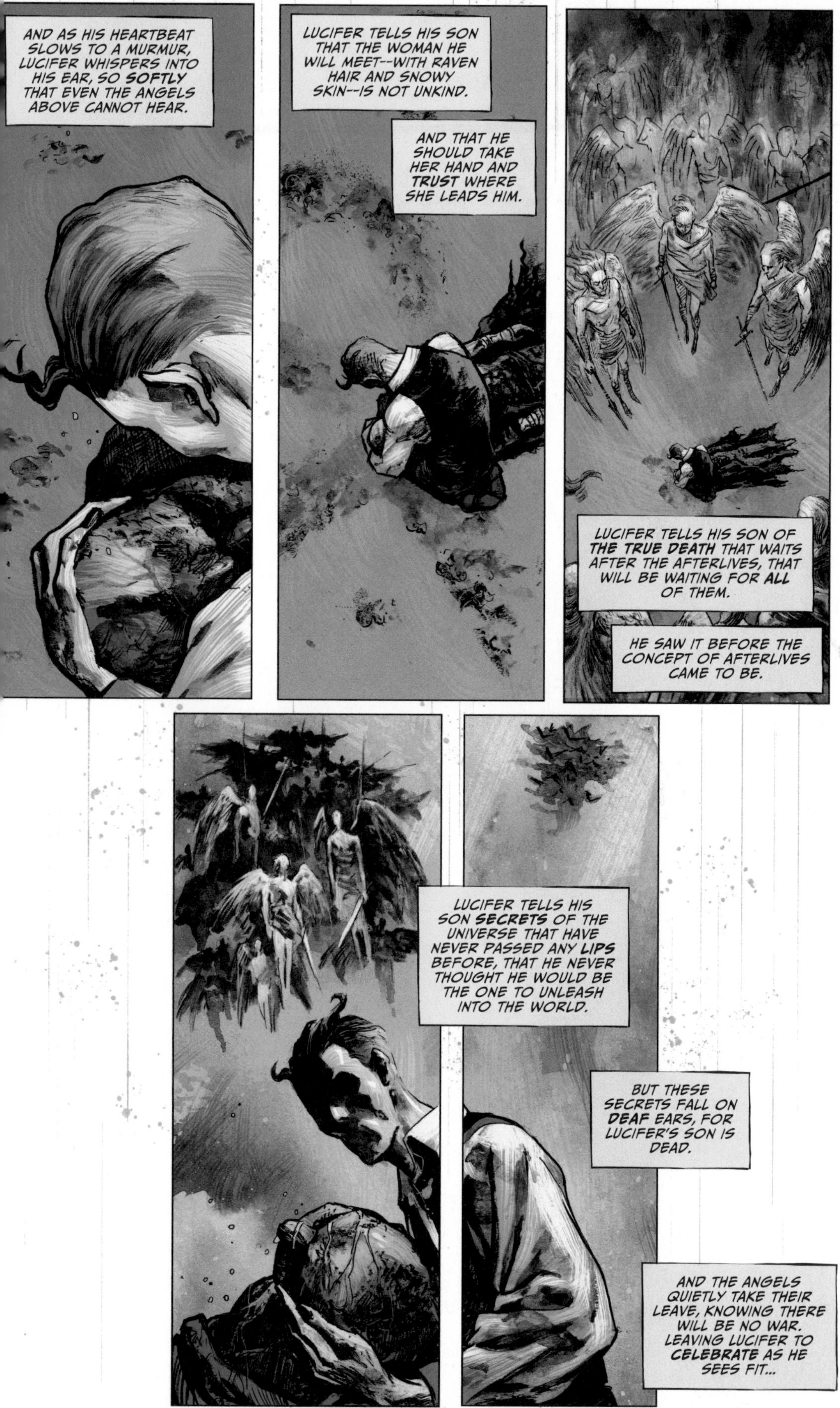
AND AS HIS HEARTBEAT SLOWS TO A MURMUR, LUCIFER WHISPERS INTO HIS EAR, SO SOFTLY THAT EVEN THE ANGELS ABOVE CANNOT HEAR.
LUCIFER TELLS HIS SON THAT THE WOMAN HE WILL MEET--WITH RAVEN HAIR AND SNOWY SKIN--IS NOT UNKIND.
AND THAT HE SHOULD TAKE HER HAND AND TRUST WHERE SHE LEADS HIM.
LUCIFER TELLS HIS SON OF THE TRUE DEATH THAT WAITS AFTER THE AFTERLIVES, THAT WILL BE WAITING FOR ALL OF THEM.
HE SAW IT BEFORE THE CONCEPT OF AFTERLIVES CAME TO BE.
LUCIFER TELLS HIS SON SECRETS OF THE UNIVERSE THAT HAVE NEVER PASSED ANY LIPS BEFORE, THAT HE NEVER THOUGHT HE WOULD BE THE ONE TO UNLEASH INTO THE WORLD.
BUT THESE SECRETS FALL ON DEAF EARS, FOR LUCIFER'S SON IS DEAD.
AND THE ANGELS QUIETLY TAKE THEIR LEAVE, KNOWING THERE WILL BE NO WAR. LEAVING LUCIFER TO CELEBRATE AS HE SEES FIT...

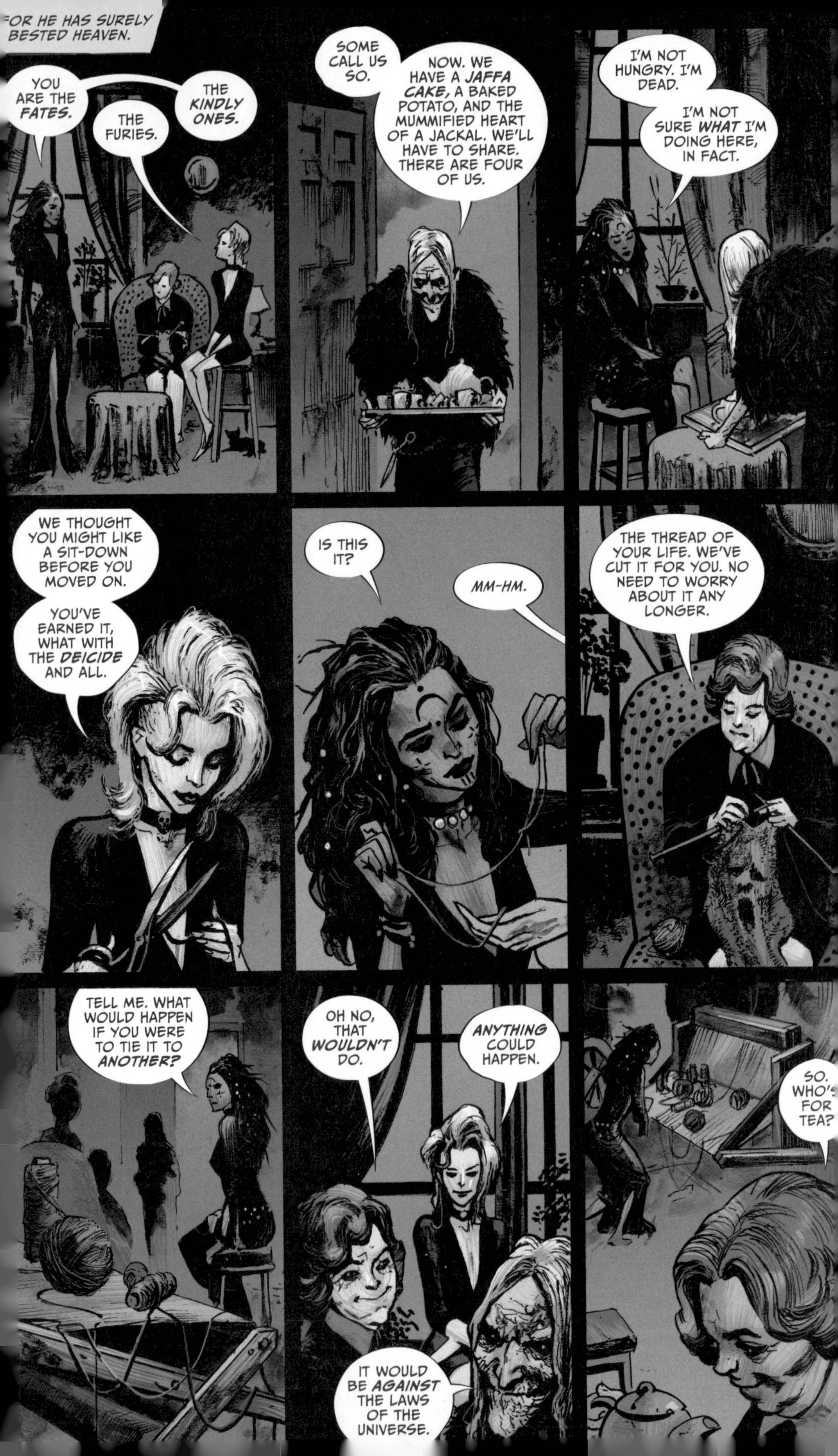
FOR HE HAS SURELY BESTED HEAVEN.
YOU ARE THE FATES.
THE FURIES.
THE KINDLY ONES.
SOME CALL US SO.
NOW. WE HAVE A JAFFA CAKE, A BAKED POTATO, AND THE MUMMIFIED HEART OF A JACKAL. WE'LL HAVE TO SHARE. THERE ARE FOUR OF US.
I'M NOT HUNGRY. I'M DEAD.
I'M NOT SURE WHAT I'M DOING HERE, IN FACT.
WE THOUGHT YOU MIGHT LIKE A SIT-DOWN BEFORE YOU MOVED ON.
YOU'VE EARNED IT, WHAT WITH THE DEICIDE AND ALL.
IS THIS IT?
MM-HM.
THE THREAD OF YOUR LIFE. WE'VE CUT IT FOR YOU. NO NEED TO WORRY ABOUT IT ANY LONGER.
TELL ME. WHAT WOULD HAPPEN IF YOU WERE TO TIE IT TO ANOTHER?
OH NO, THAT WOULDN'T DO.
ANYTHING COULD HAPPEN.
IT WOULD BE AGAINST THE LAWS OF THE UNIVERSE.
SO. WHO'S FOR TEA?

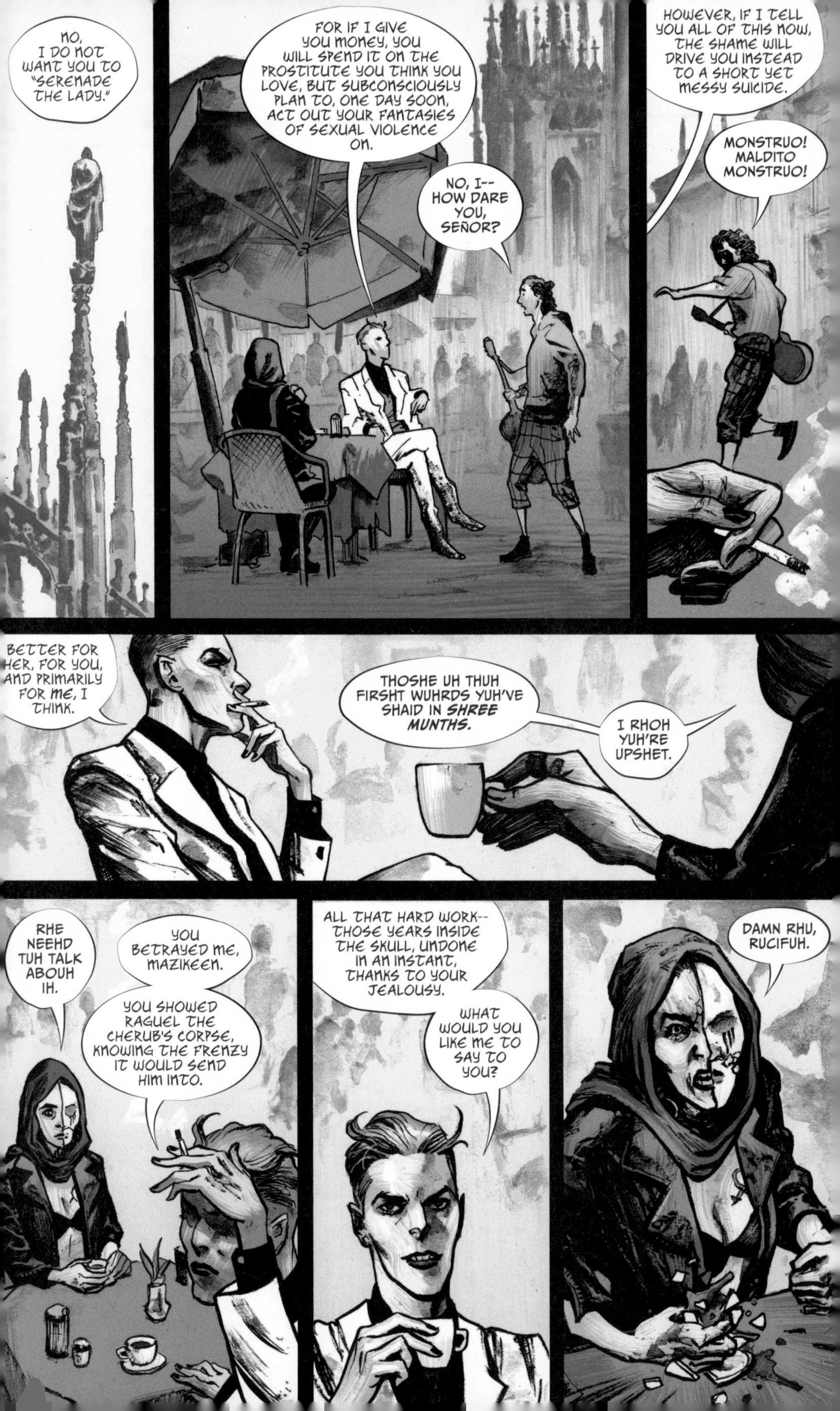
NO, I DO NOT WANT YOU TO "SERENADE THE LADY."
FOR IF I GIVE YOU MONEY, YOU WILL SPEND IT ON THE PROSTITUTE YOU THINK YOU LOVE, BUT SUBCONSCIOUSLY PLAN TO, ONE DAY SOON, ACT OUT YOUR FANTASIES OF SEXUAL VIOLENCE ON.
NO, I-- HOW DARE YOU, SEÑOR?
HOWEVER, IF I TELL YOU ALL OF THIS NOW, THE SHAME WILL DRIVE YOU INSTEAD TO A SHORT YET MESSY SUICIDE.
MONSTRUO! MALDITO MONSTRUO!
BETTER FOR HER, FOR YOU, AND PRIMARILY FOR *ME*, I THINK.
THOSHE UH THUH FIRSHT WUHRDS YUH'VE SHAID IN *SHREE MUNTHS.*
I RHOH YUH'RE UPSHET.
RHE NEEHD TUH TALK ABOUH IH.
YOU BETRAYED ME, MAZIKEEN.
YOU SHOWED RAGUEL THE CHERUB'S CORPSE, KNOWING THE FRENZY IT WOULD SEND HIM INTO.
ALL THAT HARD WORK-- THOSE YEARS INSIDE THE SKULL, UNDONE IN AN INSTANT, THANKS TO YOUR JEALOUSY.
WHAT WOULD YOU LIKE ME TO SAY TO YOU?
DAMN RHU, RUCIFUH.

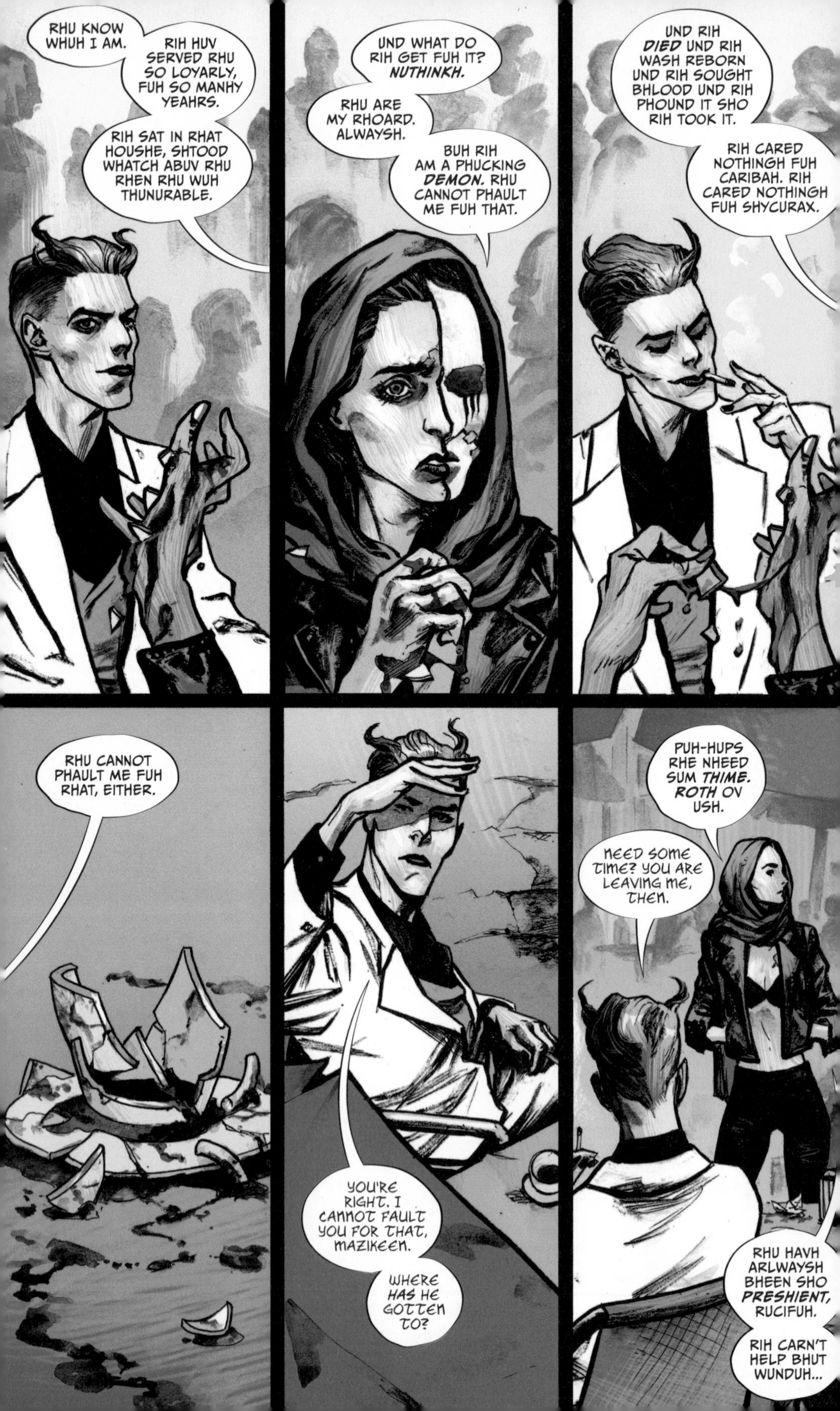
RHU KNOW WHUH I AM.
RIH HUV SERVED RHU SO LOYARLY, FUH SO MANHY YEAHRS.
RIH SAT IN RHAT HOUSHE, SHTOOD WHATCH ABUV RHU RHEN RHU WUH THUNURABLE.
UND WHAT DO RIH GET FUH IT? NUTHINKH.
RHU ARE MY RHOARD. ALWAYSH.
BUH RIH AM A PHUCKING DEMON. RHU CANNOT PHAULT ME FUH THAT.
UND RIH DIED UND RIH WASH REBORN UND RIH SOUGHT BHLOOD UND RIH PHOUND IT SHO RIH TOOK IT.
RIH CARED NOTHINGH FUH CARIBAH. RIH CARED NOTHINGH FUH SHYCURAX.
RHU CANNOT PHAULT ME FUH RHAT, EITHER.
YOU'RE RIGHT. I CANNOT FAULT YOU FOR THAT, MAZIKEEN.
WHERE HAS HE GOTTEN TO?
PUH-HUPS RHE NHEED SUM THIME. ROTH OV USH.
NEED SOME TIME? YOU ARE LEAVING ME, THEN.
RHU HAVH ARLWAYSH BHEEN SHO PRESHIENT, RUCIFUH.
RIH CARN'T HELP BHUT WUNDUH...

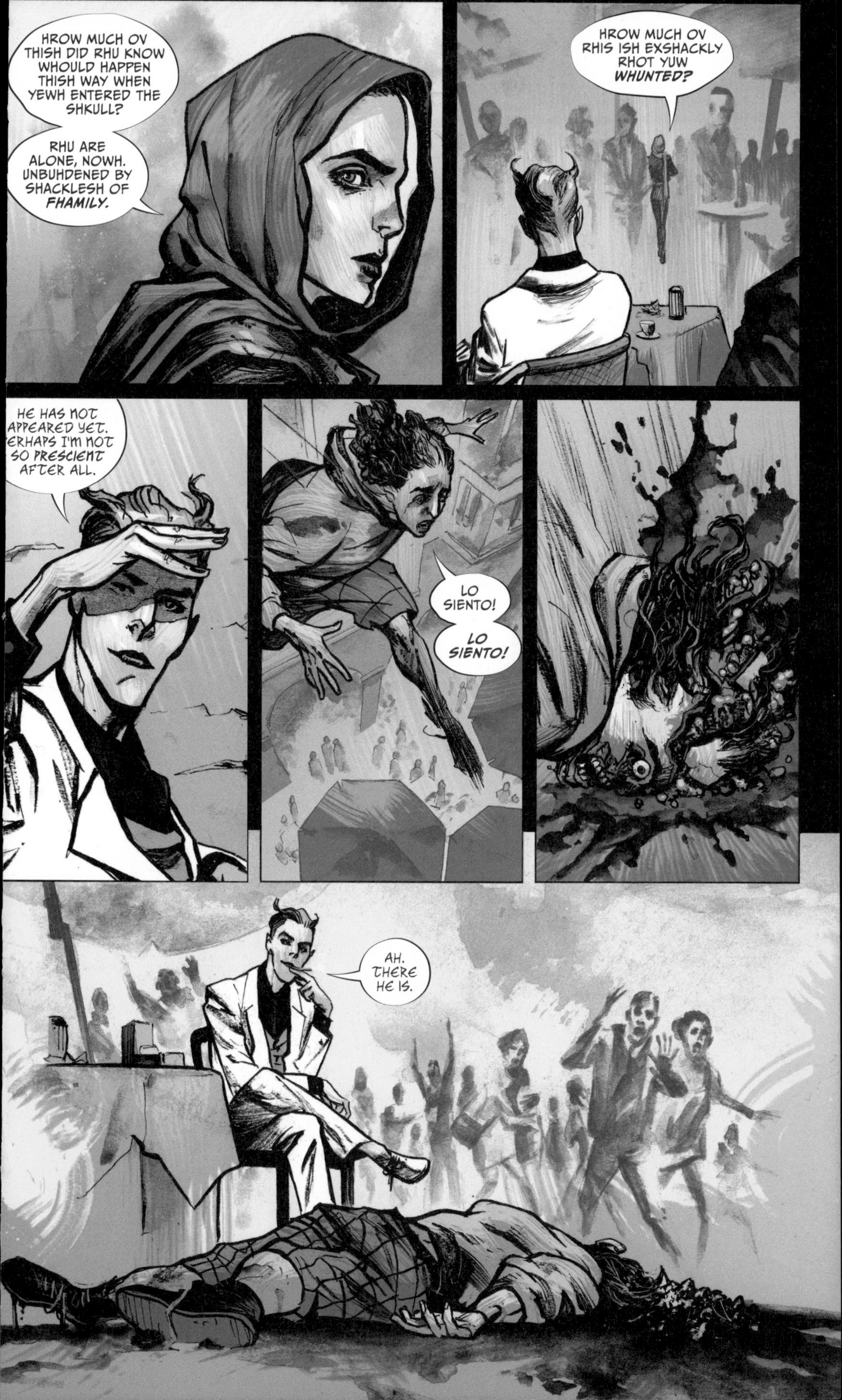
HROW MUCH OV THISH DID RHU KNOW WHOULD HAPPEN THISH WAY WHEN YEWH ENTERED THE SHKULL?
RHU ARE ALONE, NOWH. UNBUHDENED BY SHACKLESH OF *FHAMILY.*
HROW MUCH OV RHIS ISH EXSHACKLY RHOT YUW *WHUNTED?*
HE HAS NOT APPEARED YET. ERHAPS I'M NOT SO *PRESCIENT* AFTER ALL.
LO SIENTO!
LO SIENTO!
AH. THERE HE IS.

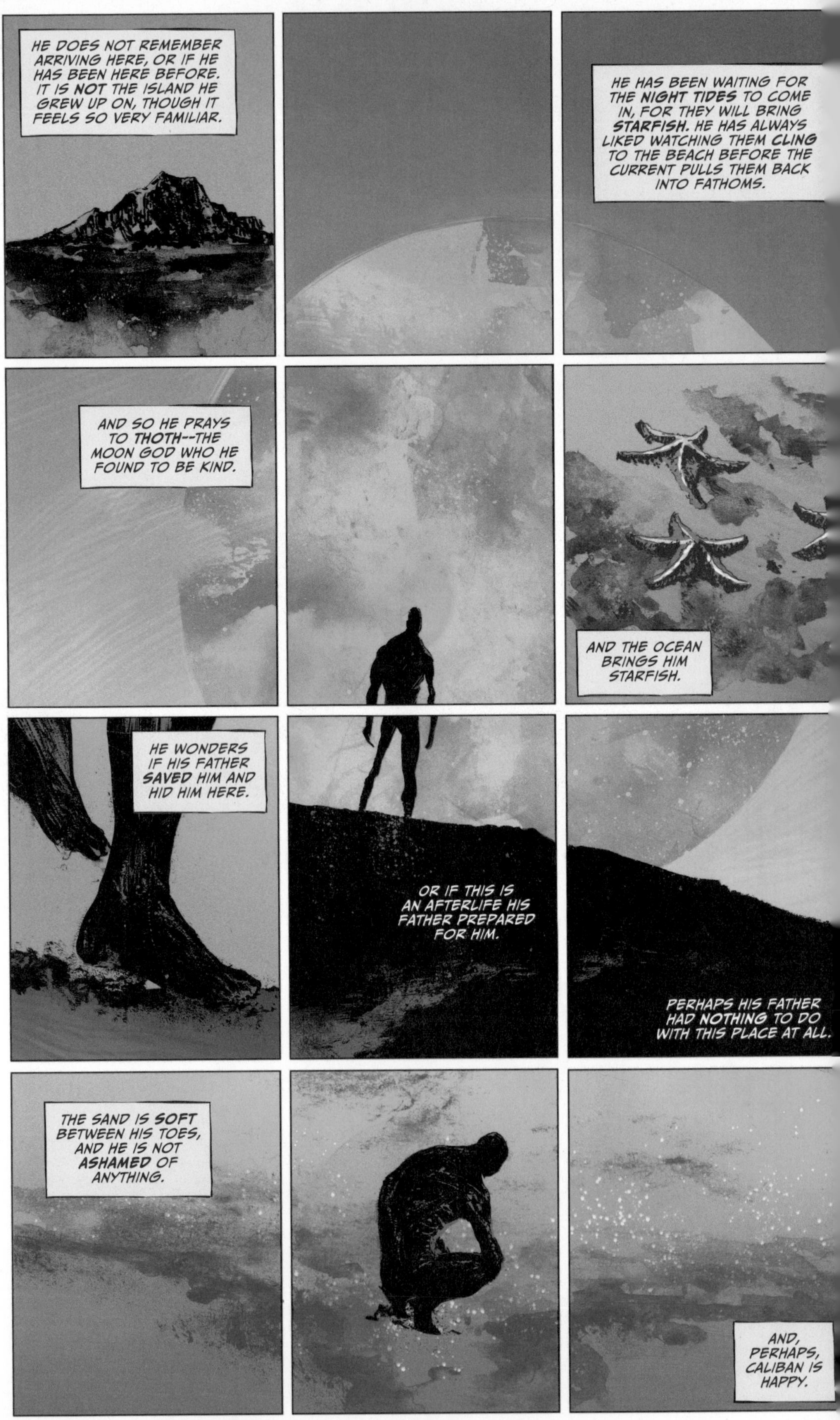
HE DOES NOT REMEMBER ARRIVING HERE, OR IF HE HAS BEEN HERE BEFORE. IT IS NOT THE ISLAND HE GREW UP ON, THOUGH IT FEELS SO VERY FAMILIAR.
HE HAS BEEN WAITING FOR THE NIGHT TIDES TO COME IN, FOR THEY WILL BRING STARFISH. HE HAS ALWAYS LIKED WATCHING THEM CLING TO THE BEACH BEFORE THE CURRENT PULLS THEM BACK INTO FATHOMS.
AND SO HE PRAYS TO THOTH--THE MOON GOD WHO HE FOUND TO BE KIND.
AND THE OCEAN BRINGS HIM STARFISH.
HE WONDERS IF HIS FATHER SAVED HIM AND HID HIM HERE.
OR IF THIS IS AN AFTERLIFE HIS FATHER PREPARED FOR HIM.
PERHAPS HIS FATHER HAD NOTHING TO DO WITH THIS PLACE AT ALL.
THE SAND IS SOFT BETWEEN HIS TOES, AND HE IS NOT ASHAMED OF ANYTHING.
AND, PERHAPS, CALIBAN IS HAPPY.

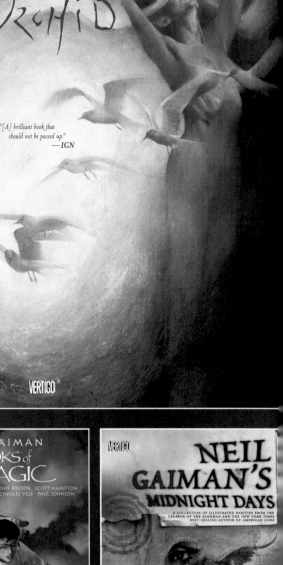
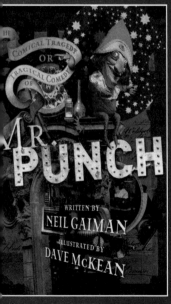

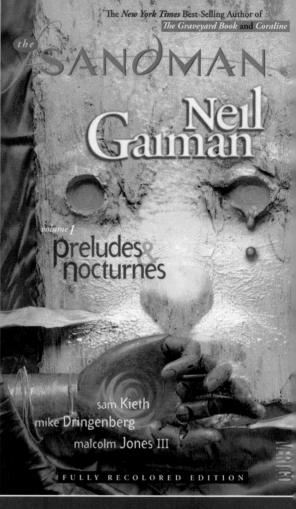

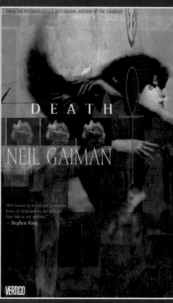